Long-Term Governance for Social– Ecological Change

IO028208

The book discusses how to tackle long-term social and ecological problems by using different environmental governance approaches to creating sustainable development. It explores opportunities and requirements for the governance of long-term problems, and examines how to achieve a lasting transformation.

Combining the perspectives on the different governance approaches and featuring cases studies on national, regional and global issues, *Long-Term Governance for Social–Ecological Change* will be of interest to policy makers, students and scholars of global environmental governance, development, sustainability, politics, economics, law and sociology.

Bernd Siebenhüner is Professor of Ecological Economics and Head of the GELENA-research group on social learning and sustainability located at Oldenburg University, Germany. He is also Deputy Leader of the Global Governance Project at the Potsdam Institute for Climate Impact Research (PIK) at the Global Change and Social Systems Department.

Marlen Arnold is a Senior Research Scientist and Project Manager at University of Oldenburg, Germany, and a Lecturer at various higher educational institutions, notably in Finland and Colombia.

Klaus Eisenack is Assistant Professor for Environment and Development Economics at the Carl von Ossietzky University Oldenburg, Germany, and heads the Chameleon Research Group.

Klaus Jacob is Research Director of the Environmental Policy Research Centre at the Freie Universitaet Berlin, Germany.

Environmental politics/Routledge research in environmental politics
Edited by Steve Vanderheiden
University of Colorado at Boulder

Over recent years environmental politics has moved from a peripheral interest to a central concern within the discipline of politics. This series aims to reinforce this trend through the publication of books that investigate the nature of contemporary environmental politics and show the centrality of environmental politics to the study of politics per se. The series understands politics in a broad sense and books will focus on mainstream issues such as the policy process and new social movements as well as emerging areas such as cultural politics and political economy. Books in the series will analyse contemporary political practices with regards to the environment and/or explore possible future directions for the 'greening' of contemporary politics. The series will be of interest not only to academics and students working in the environmental field, but will also demand to be read within the broader discipline.

The series consists of two strands:

Environmental Politics addresses the needs of students and teachers, and the titles will be published in paperback and hardback. Titles include:

Global Warming and Global Politics
Matthew Paterson

Politics and the Environment
James Connelly and Graham Smith

International Relations Theory and Ecological Thought
Towards Synthesis
Eric Laferrière and Peter Stoett

Planning Sustainability
Edited by Michael Kenny and James Meadowcroft

Deliberative Democracy and the Environment
Graham Smith

Routledge Research in Environmental Politics presents innovative new research intended for high-level specialist readership. These titles are published in hardback only and include:

Long-Term Governance for Social–Ecological Change

Edited by Bernd Siebenhüner,
Marlen Arnold, Klaus Eisenack
and Klaus Jacob

Routledge
Taylor & Francis Group

LONDON AND NEW YORK

First published 2013 by Routledge
2 Park Square, Milton Park, Abingdon, Oxon OX14 4RN

Simultaneously published in the USA and Canada
by Routledge
711 Third Avenue, New York, NY 10017, USA

First issued in paperback 2017

*Routledge is an imprint·of the Taylor & Francis Group, an informa
business.*

British Library Cataloguing in Publication Data
A catalogue record for this book is available from the British Library

Library ‎of Congress Cataloging in Publication Data
Long-term governance for social–ecological change/edited by Bernd
Siebenhuner, Marlen Arnold, Klaus Eisenack and Klaus Jacob.

    p. cm. – (Environmental politics/Routledge research in environmental
politics; v. 21)
    Includes bibliographical references and index.
    1. Environmental policy. 2. Sustainable development. I. Siebenhuner, [1]
Bernd. II. Arnold, Marlen. III. Eisenack, Klaus. IV. Jacob, Klaus. V.
Pregernig, Michael, 1968- Role of expertise in European environmenta
governance.
    GE170.L65 2013
    338.9'27–dc23
    2012038623

ISBN 13: 978-1-138-49627-9 (pbk)
ISBN 13: 978-0-415-63352-9 (hbk)

Typeset in Times New Roman
by OKS Prepress Services, Chennai, India

Contents

List of illustrations

Figures

Tables

Preface

Social–ecological change affects almost all areas of human life. Well-being, prosperity, health, food safety, social cohesion, energy supply, provision of drinking water, housing and alike are all characterised by the interaction of social and ecological dimensions and their services for humankind. They are closely connected with severe ecological problems such as climate change, loss of biodiversity, degrading ecosystem services, etc. What is more, all of these problems are long-term developments that require decades rather than months or years to be abated. Infrastructures as well as basic mechanisms of the earth system can only be altered over long time periods. This applies particularly to the energy supply system, food and crop systems, water supplies, patterns of mobility and others. The long-term dimension is a common characteristic of most of these problems of social–ecological change that pose particular challenges to decision-making processes in the political and economic realm. In particular, the short-term focus of democratic decision-making within four to five-year election periods and even shorter budget cycles and the focus on short-term profits in most businesses often hinder the effective combat and prevention of long-term problems of social–ecological change. This gap between the long-term dimension of the pressing problems and the short-termism of our current governance processes implies also a challenge for social science research that motivated us to work on this book.

This book emerged as a result of the Berlin Conference on the Human Dimensions of Global Environmental Change addressing the topic of 'Long-Term Policies: Governing Social–Ecological Change'. It was also the international conference of the Social–Ecological Research Programme of the German Federal Ministry of Education and Research (BMBF). Since 1999, this programme has addressed the challenges of social–ecological change in numerous research endeavours. Following an innovative inter- and transdisciplinary approach, this research has produced significant contributions to solve problems of long-term social–ecological change.

We would therefore like to thank the Federal Ministry of Education and Research (BMBF) as well as the conference hosts, namely the Oldenburg Centre for Sustainability Economics and Management (CENTOS) at Oldenburg University and the Environmental Policy Research Centre (FFU), Freie

Universität Berlin. We were particularly pleased about the endorsements of the Human Dimensions Programme on Global Environmental Change Programme (IHDP), the IHDP Earth System Governance Scientific Planning Committee and the German Association for Ecological Economic Research (VÖW)

This book came together as a selection of thematically best suited contributions to the conference. It was newly structured as we tried to develop some of the ideas and concepts further that were discussed at the conference. As a peer-reviewed product, it has benefited a lot from the comments by two reviewers. The editors and chapter authors express their gratitude for their efforts and helpful comments. We would also like to thank all contributors to this volume. In addition, we are most grateful to Nadja Carius, Lucienne Damm, Cecilia Homilius, Birgit Schelenz, Cornelia Wolter, Eike Zaumseil, and Ruben Zondervan for their organisational support and the formatting.

Marlen Arnold
Klaus Eisenack
Klaus Jacob
Bernd Siebenhüner

Contributors

Christian Albert, researcher at the Institute for Environmental Planning of the Leibniz University of Hannover, and at the Helmholtz Centre for Environmental Research (UFZ), Leipzig, Germany.

Marlen Arnold, sustainability researcher and project manager at Carl von Ossietzky University Oldenburg, Germany.

Michael Boecher, senior researcher in Environmental and Nature Conservation Policy at the Faculty of Forest Sciences and Forest Ecology of the University of Göttingen, Germany.

Lisa Bohunovsky, researcher at the Sustainable Europe Research Institute (SERI) in Vienna, Austria.

Klaus Eisenack, Head of the 'Chameleon Research Group' and Assistant Professor for Environment and Development Economics at Carl von Ossietzky University Oldenburg, Germany.

Stefan Hochrainer-Stigler, research scholar in the 'Risk and Vulnerability' Program at the International Institute for Applied Systems Analysis (IIASA) Laxenburg, Austria.

Diana Hummel, Head of the Research Unit 'Population and Supply Systems', and Coordinator for the cross-divisional area 'Academic Cooperation and Qualification of Young Scientists' at the Institute for Social–Ecological Research (ISOE) in Frankfurt, Germany.

Klaus Jacob, Research Director of the Environmental Policy Research Centre at the Freie Universität Berlin, Germany.

Jill Jäger, Senior Scientist at the Sustainable Europe Research Institute (SERI) in Vienna, Austria.

Martin Jänicke, Professor Emeritus of Political Science at the Freie Universität Berlin. He was Director of the Environmental Policy Research Centre from 1986 to 2007.

Cedric Janowicz, staff member at the German Federal Ministry of Education and Research, Germany.

Kristian Krieger, currently affiliated with the Department of War Studies of King's College London and the Institute for European Studies of the Free University of Brussels (VUB).

Louis Lebel, Director of the Unit for Social and Environmental Research at Chiang Mai University, Thailand.

Ho-Ching Lee, Professor at the Centre of General Education and Director of the Science Technology and Society (STS) Program, National Central University, Chung-Li, Taiwan.

Philip Leifeld, Post-doctoral researcher at the Swiss Federal Institute of Aquatic Science and Technology (Eawag) in Dübendorf, Switzerland.

Alexandra Lux, researcher in the research unit 'Water Infrastructure and Risk Analyses' at the Institute for Social–Ecological Research (ISOE) Frankfurt, Germany.

Thomas Malang, research fellow at the chair of International Relations and Conflict Management at the University of Konstanz, Germany.

Reinhard Mechler, leader of the research group on 'Disasters and Development' at the International Institute for Applied Systems Analysis (IIASA) and lecturer at the University for Economics and Business in Vienna, Austria.

Jan Nill, climate change and energy policy analyst at the Directorate General for Climate Action of the European Commission, unit Strategy and Economic Assessment, Brussels, Belgium.

Anél du Plessis, Professor of Local Government and Environmental Law at the North-West University (Potchefstroom Campus), South Africa.

Michael Pregernig, Professor of Environmental Governance at the Institute of Environmental Social Science and Geography at the Albert-Ludwigs-University Freiburg, Germany.

M. Brooke Rogers, Senior Lecturer in Risk and Terror in the Department of War Studies, and a co-director of the MA in Terrorism, Security and Society at King's College London, United Kingdom.

Katharina Schmitt, research fellow at the Oeko-Institut's Environmental Law and Governance Division, Berlin, Germany.

Volker Schneider, Professor of Political Science at the Chair of Empirical Theory of the State at the University of Konstanz, Germany.

Bernd Siebenhüner, Professor of Ecological Economics at Carl von Ossietzky University Oldenburg, Germany.

Hui-Yin Sung, post-doctoral fellow at the Center for General Education, National Central University, Taiwan.

Franziska Wolff, Deputy Head of the Environmental Law and Governance Division at the Oeko-Institut, Berlin, Germany.

1 Long-term governance for social– ecological change

Setting the scene

Bernd Siebenhüner, Marlen Arnold,
Klaus Eisenack and Klaus Jacob

Introduction

Long-term problems such as climate change or the over-exploitation of natural resources are characterized by the fact that the costs and benefits of addressing the problems are split up between different generations. Current and future climate change is caused by previous economic activities. Measures to mitigate CO_2 emissions will not have an immediate impact, but rather will only be effective in the long term. However, the costs of mitigation will be borne by the current generation. The loss of biodiversity, the overexploitation of ground water or land is subject to similar difficulties. The current institutional framework – largely based on principles of liberalism and pluralism – is not well equipped to overcome such difficulties; future generations are weakly represented – if at all – in decisions on the use of natural and economic resources. Hence, a central challenge to effective long-term policies is the development and establishment of conditions for appropriate political frameworks and institutions for long-term and sustainable action.

The basic relationship between humankind and nature within social–ecologic systems is marked by many such problems of intergenerational justice. The types of resources we extract and use, the infrastructure, the industrial structure, and the way cities are built and connected have a tremendous impact on the environment today, but policies to diminish these impacts will only affect future generations. Gains from our current investments will only be available for our children.

Similar incentive structures are visible in other cases as well: for politicians, costly policies with benefits beyond their electoral cycle are seen as problematic. Spending programs with goals and benefits beyond a budget cycle are equally critical. Companies are challenged with long-term problems when future profits are discounted or short-term profits for shareholders have to be earned that diminish the company's ability to provide additional financial capital for long-term profitable investments. These problems all suffer the same faulty logic: every generation has the primary incentive to lower their own costs and use existing resources to their own benefit.

Despite the governance apparatus that has evolved in the past two decades in the aftermath of the Rio Summit in 1992, most observers, both from a scientific perspective as well as policy practitioners, agree that no sufficient and effective responses exist to bring long-term problems into the core of the institutional framework (e.g. Sprinz 2009; Lafferty 2004; Jordan and Lenschow 2008). So far, long-term issues with few exceptions are not on an equal footing with other goals and principles of modern statehood. For example, sustainability issues are not as equally considered in constitutions as other goals of statehood or individual rights. Another case in point relates to government budgets – the negotiations about budgets are dominated by contemporary actors and their interests rather than future generations.

Consequently, this book draws on the debates on ecological research, which was extended conceptually in the direction of coupled socio-ecological systems and included infrastructures and governance mechanisms to master social and ecological challenges (e.g. Fischer-Kowalski and Haberl 2007; Ostrom 2009). A couple of authors have proposed governance mechanisms to deal with long-term change. For example, Voß *et al.* (2009) propose the concept of reflexive governance for sustainable development. This governance concept allows experimentation regarding various policy instruments and mechanisms focusing on steering long-term problems. Further, Voß *et al.* (2009) argue for effective policy integration regarding sustainable development and long-term environmental governance issues. The discussion of earth system governance looks into the long-term governance problems of interconnected ecosystems and environmental damages which are not limited to national borders. It gave rise to the debate about effective international (or global) environmental policy structures, mechanisms and instruments. Biermann *et al.* (2009) prominently argued for the institutionalization of global environmental governance. On the basis of a long-term study of a period of about 30 years, The Social Learning Group (2001) analysed the dynamics of environmental innovation policies and institutional learning in a long-term perspective. Other insights on integrated governance approaches to long-term sustainability can be drawn from research on transition management (Kemp *et al.* 2011, 2007; Geels and Schot 2007). They introduce transition management as a multilevel model of long-term governance shaping processes of co-evolution by using visions, transition experiments and cycles of learning and adaptation. In doing so, transition management is intended to help societies to transform themselves in a gradual, reflexive way through guided processes of variation and selection (Kemp *et al.* 2007). The concept of a far reaching transformation is also pursued by the German Advisory Council on Global Change (WBGU). To meet in particular the long-term challenges of climate change, they call for a new social contract allowing for a societal transformation similar to the industrial revolution (WBGU 2011). Following these lines of analysis, this book starts out more systematically from the nature and the specific governance challenges of long-term problems of sustainability.

What becomes clear from this stream of literature is the wide agreement on the need for transforming socio-ecological systems towards a pathway of sustainable development. Further, there is agreement, that institutions are core in achieving such transformation. However, the views on how this actually works and what kind of institutions would be suitable and required, vary considerably and depend on the underlying understanding and assumptions on governance and in particular how governments can become effective.

Against this background, the chapters of this book ask and seek to answer the question of what distinguishes long-term problems from other policy problems, what governance responses are available and used, and how could economic incentives, participation, as well as knowledge and learning help to address them. Consequently, this book represents a collection of inter- and trans-disciplinary work drawing on conceptual and empirical studies that study long-term sustainability problems and policies and resulting governance challenges from different scientific and methodological perspectives. It reflects an intellectual bridge between studies of coupled social–ecological systems (Young, Berkhout *et al.* 2006), social–ecological research (Becker, Jahn *et al.* 1997), evolutionary economics (Gowdy 1994; Dopfer 2001; Nill 2009) and institutionalism (Young *et al.* 2008, Biermann *et al.* 2009). Therefore, contributions to this volume present insights from transition research, integrated assessment, earth system governance, and sustainability science on how to analyse, transform, adapt, measure and how to solve long-term problems in an ecological and societal context. They apply an inter-disciplinary research toolbox and create an innovative approach to analysing long-term problems. It thus aims to assemble the actual scientific debate and relevant results of social-science research on long-term policies and enrich the scientific dialogue on long-term policies.

Defining long-term policies and problems

Voß *et al.* (2009: 276) characterise long-term policies as a response to social challenges by "[...] policy strategies that seek to change radically key societal structures. [...] The realization of long-term policy goals extends well beyond electoral cycles and management terms, even beyond a generation of civil servants." This is close to merely defining long-term policies as long-lasting processes, policy targets for the far future, or long-living institutions, by whatever reasons there might be in place. It leaves open the question of why there are (or should be) long-term policies. If we subscribe to the existence of objective problems, we might be interested in the features of such problems that make long-term policies adequate responses.

This is considered by Sprinz (2009), who defines long-term polices indirectly as responses to long-term policy challenges, that "[...] last at least one human generation, exhibit deep uncertainty exacerbated by the depth of time, and engender public good aspects both at the stage of problem generation as well as at the response stage". The need for long-term policies tends to be motivated by problems or trends that are slow and require substantial time to unfold completely. It is one underlying distinction that there are public issues that can be resolved quite quickly, while others need interventions over longer time frames.

What matters is not a definition of long-term policies by a precise time scale (years, decades, centuries), but by the properties that distinguish long-term policies from other policies pragmatically. Analysing the term "long-term problem" suggests the following properties:

1 problems which need a long time to unfold, e.g. due to long time lags between cause and effect, or due to slow or unnoticed change (creeping problems);
2 problems that involve issues of intergenerational equity and trade-offs, or where solutions involve issues of intergenerational equity and trade-offs. This type is clearly more general than just considering public-good problems. Even if we were living in an idealized world without intra- and inter-temporal market failures, issues of, e.g. intergenerational wealth distribution might be very pressing;
3 problems that cannot be resolved quickly, e.g. due to the dimension or complexity of the problem, or due to long time lags between implementation and effect.

Based on these considerations, long-term policies can be defined as institutions where current policy actions have effects in the (far) future, or that respond to problems resulting from current actions that have effects in the (far) future. These effects can take the form of bio-physical system changes, new or modified institutions becoming established, or of economic costs and benefits.

This suggests a short sketch of reasons that may render long-term policies desirable or necessary. If a problem in the far future can be anticipated, e.g. a large asteroid colliding with the Earth in 100 years, and there is much to do to solve that problem, e.g. evacuating an entire continent, this would be a case for starting a policy quite early and to design it in a way that makes it sustainable over that long period. However, if the problems lie far ahead, but solutions are simple to implement, there is no need to act immediately. The situation becomes more complicated when we consider uncertainty about the future – an unavoidable condition in most environmental problems. If, for instance, scientists foresee a problem in 50 years, e.g. strong changes in precipitation patterns due to climate change, but cannot predict anything about its properties, e.g. they cannot say where precipitation increases, and where it decreases, would this justify a long-term policy? It might be valuable to wait until uncertainties decrease, and act then. However, it might also be the case that there are means available that increase flexibility to be prepared for any change, in whatever direction that change might go. If this flexibility requires a long-term preparation, it would provide another case for long-term policy. These examples illustrate that the need for long-term policies depend on structural features of the perceived problems and the available repertoire of solutions. Depending on these, the need arises either for anticipatory long-term action or a reactive approach at a later stage after the problem has occurred or is more immediate.

Thus the central challenge of long-term policies lies in the connection between the properties of the specific long-term problem and the potential approaches for an effective solution. In this book, we will analyse four major venues for such long-term policies. This addresses first the formation of adequate regulation and formal institutions, e.g. to remind current political decision makers to include the interests of future generations into their present policies. These formal institutions build on legal instruments to address the challenge of long-term policies. By contrast and second, economic incentives can help to overcome some of the disincentives to care for future generations. The question is how to design these incentives and under which conditions such solutions would function. Third, there is a need to integrate relevant actors and stakeholders into the decision-making processes by means of participatory processes. Through this inclusion, a broader set of interests can be included into the decision-making considerations. Fourth, actors need sufficient knowledge and a capacity to learn and act accordingly. Thereby, they will be enabled to respond to long-term problems or be put in the position to prepare for future problems. Following this structure, the book is organized into four sections studying (i) governance and institutions, (ii) economics and tools, (iii) participation and (iv) knowledge and learning.

Part I: Institutions and governance mechanisms

Long-term problems are matters of distribution of income and living conditions between different generations: The generation that invests is not the same as the one that harvests the gains from this investment. Phrased negatively, the generation that causes damages to ecosystems and depletes natural resources is a different one than the one suffering from the consequences. The abstinence in exploiting resources to keep them for future generations is the other side of the coin, and of similar difficulty. In most countries, the current institutions have been set up to address distributional conflicts between different groups of society or between different regions. The very basic principles of statehood, the modern welfare state, democracy, civil rights or the rule of law are meant not only to protect individuals against arbitrary acts of the majority or the powerful. They have also been developed to balance decisions, to enforce compromises between different groups of society and their interests. In democratic political systems, legitimacy is based on the principle of majority within the jurisdiction and the lawfulness on the basis of constitutional principles.

How is sustainability in the sense of the long-term preservation of natural, economic and social capital integrated into this institutional landscape? The core of sustainability is to fulfil the needs of the present generation without limiting the options of future generations (WCED 1987). Modern western statehood appears to be well developed to meet the needs of the present generation, but at the expense of other regions of the world and on future generations. Future generations are hardly represented in the present institutions, they have no veto power, and they are hardly protected by judicial review. There are almost no interest groups or political parties which form their basis by representing the future at the expense of the present. In distributional conflicts, the present generation is by far better represented than the future ones.

While this diagnosis is widely accepted among academics as well as policy makers in the field of sustainability, there are some exemptions in which states either provide the investments necessary for the long term (e.g. for infrastructures or education) or they provide the regulatory framework for private actors with a focus on long-term problems (e.g. regulations on the use of resources or land use planning). It is obviously the state that is particularly challenged to solve these kinds of problems while individuals or companies in most cases do not have the necessary resources and incentives to contribute or to preserve resources. It is thus worth studying these existing examples and exploring how governance approaches and their institutional framework can be applied to other long-term problems of environmental degradation or resource extraction.

Still, during the past 20 years, many efforts have been undertaken to overcome this situation and to integrate the long-term perspective of sustainability into the institutional framework of governments. The Agenda 21 as agreed upon at the 1992 Rio Summit is the most important cornerstone in this respect. Several discourses and related policy processes have spun off from this document. First, there is a management approach to strengthen and to integrate the concerns of sustainability into governmental decisions. Sustainable development is being implemented by means of determining goals, action plans for their achievements and indicators to measure success or failure. Evaluations and progress reports are meant to correct or to reinforce actions taken in safeguarding sustainability. Decision making in government, civil society and enterprises can thus be rationalized e.g. by procedures for evidence-based decision making. Second, participatory processes become increasingly accepted as part of long-term policy making representing more societal stakes than in conventional policy making contexts (see below). Third, an organizational approach can be observed that is, however, much less applied than in other policy domains, where institutions have been established to represent actors and their interests in decision making concerning sustainability. For example, only few countries have established ministries for sustainable development. There are few civil society organizations under the flag of sustainability. Sustainability is considered to be a subject matter that needs integration rather than specialization and therefore, it has to be addressed and integrated in the existing landscape of actors and organizations.

Rather than aiming at super-institutions such as a veto-right for future generations, it could be more realistic and appropriate to develop institutions that are able to learn, and to adapt to changing demands and conditions. Thus, more incremental approaches seem more likely to be implemented in today's political systems. However, adaptiveness and learning to encounter long-term challenges of societies need direction (Biermann *et al.* 2009). Therefore, a discourse on the values of common goods, transparency in decision making, equal opportunities to participate, a stronger call for evidence-based decision making would unfold stronger impacts and might increase openness to change.

The literature on adapting institutions to the long-term challenges demonstrates that there are no simple and straightforward governance solutions (Newig *et al.*

2008; Jänicke and Jörgens 2000). Despite many overlaps and complementarities, there are quite different approaches on how to prepare institutions for the future: By means of rendering decision making more rational? By means of knowledge and learning or participation? By means of strengthening actors and interests representing the future? By integrating sustainability into the core set of institutions? Or by extending adaptiveness and learning in general?

The chapters in Part I address these questions. They highlight that successful long-term policies need governance processes and mechanisms on all institutional decision-making levels – from the international to the local level. It is not yet clear which governance approaches will be more successful, but their applicability depends on the specific properties of the long-term problems they are intended to solve. Adaptive and reflexive governance approaches are at the centre of the chapters in this section as well as decentralized approaches. Furthermore, the contributions to this section deal with different institutions. They evaluate the possibilities and limitations of systems to react to long-term problems. This includes an analysis and discussion of factors for successful long-term governance approaches. These chapters focus mainly on normative problems, such as the limited legitimacy of institutions which are withdrawn from democratic processes and mechanisms such as the German Bundesbank. They find that the identification of and public discourse about long-term environmental problems will increase pressures within society and its relevant actors to address these issues. Studies on the diffusion of innovative policy instruments and institutions such as national sustainability strategies or impact assessments show that innovative mechanisms have the capacity to influence national decisions and politics. It also becomes clear that innovation does not only mean new policy instruments and institutions but that one also has to acknowledge the importance of technological innovations for effective environmental policy.

The chapter by Michael Pregernig and Michael Böcher focuses on the role of scientific knowledge in European environmental governance. In their contribution, they study the role of scientific experts in environmental decision-making contexts in 16 European cases of forest governance. Viewed in the light of three conceptual approaches, they conclude that neither a pure instrumental understanding of scientific expertise is sufficient to describe the science-policy interface nor a more strategic conceptualization of the role of scientists in political decision making. It is rather more a co-production of knowledge which can be found in most cases.

Martin Jänicke and Klaus Jacob analyse possible economic and social impacts of a comprehensive industrial transformation as well as the challenges for the steering capacities of societies. They compare the anticipated transformation to a low carbon, resource-efficient economy with the previous industrial revolutions. Similar to previous transitions, a shift in the energy basis of economies is in the core of the development. The first industrial revolution was not possible without the technologies, the societal and the organizational innovations which enabled the exploitation of coal as the energy basis for the emerging industries. The second industrial revolution which paved the way for mass consumption was based on the use of oil. A third industrial revolution based on renewable energies is on the horizon. As in previous transformations, the change will not be limited to a replacement of energy, but it will also affect many other economic, societal and governmental aspects. The requirements for governance in these societies are enormous, but there are indications that societies are better prepared to meet these challenges and to overcome possible social disruptions than in previous transformations. There is, however, a competition emerging between the large economic regions in Europe, North America and Asia. The newly emerging economies play a crucial role in setting the pace for the transformation. The authors expect those regions to be successful that have the capacities to innovate, the resources to introduce new technologies in the market, opportunities to compensate disadvantaged regions and sectors, as well as an ambitious framework for environmental policies.

A large number of countries have introduced rules and principles in their constitutional laws to protect the environment. Similarly, international law provides such directions for the governance of socio-ecological change. But what does this mean in practice for governance? In his analysis of the constitutional provisions protecting the environment, Anél du Plessis identifies seven different activities to comply with the duties generated by constitutional environmental law. These include: public participation, development and implementation of environmental policies, law and programs, the enforcement of compliance with environmental law, the provision of environmental infrastructures, the establishment of environmental partnerships, environmental education and environmental information. Du Plessis demonstrates that the governance of long-term socio-ecological change demands a reflection and an assessment of different activities of governments. The analysis of constitutional law, international law and planning could open up directions which are so far not sufficiently explored.

Part II: Economics

What is the role of markets and economic institutions in causing and tackling long-term problems? Targets for income distribution that might be motivated by equity considerations (see last sections) require policy instruments such as taxes, subsidies or tariffs. From an economic point of view, these public policy measures can also be justified through other arguments. First, market failures cause inefficient allocation of resources and policies to remove market distortions (or to introduce institutions that provide the right incentives, such as the internalization of externalities), result in social gains. Second, governments are called upon to enforce at least basic institutions or "formal rules of the game" (Williamson 2000), e.g. secure property rights or contract law (e.g. North 1991).

When it comes to long-term policies, at least further considerations become relevant, namely inter-temporal trade-offs and the long-term stability or permanence of institutions. Some kinds of market failure only occur when time is considered. Prime examples are common property stock resources or, more precisely, open access resources such as marine fish. Overuse today is motivated by not properly accounting for the consequent losses in the future (Hardin 1968). Distributional policies become a long-term problem when future and current government revenues and expenditures are interlinked, e.g. by public debt or a public pensions system. To sustain the permanence of basic institutions, such as financial capabilities of nation states, a long-term oriented monetary policy will be necessary.

In economic terms, efficient long-term policies are determined by comparing present and future net benefits by means of a discount rate. If the policy can be described by the path of a variable in time, e.g. a tax rate for each year, optimal control methods are available for deriving an efficient path. Additional policy objectives, such as avoiding consumption to decrease over time, can be complemented by formal constraints to the optimization problem. An alternative to this approach is a Rawlsian maximin criterion: maximizing the benefits of the generation that is worst off (see Solow 1974, for an example). In this approach, however, it is by no means evident that all long-term policy goals can be achieved at all. Hartwick (1977) investigates weak sustainability in the sense that aggregate consumption can be permanently prevented from decreasing when production needs a limited natural resource as input. This is only possible if certain properties of the production technology are satisfied. But when a long-term policy is achievable in principle, the question for an appropriate institutional design becomes apparent. We briefly focus on two aspects of the permanence of long-term policy design in the following: establishing/sustaining permanence and dealing with change.

Long-term policies may become obsolete if time consistency is not given (Kydland and Prescott 1977). When there are incentives for deviating from a drafted government plan later, it is not credible that this plan will be actually exercised. Thus, economic actors may not consider the policy in their long-term planning. An example for time-inconsistency is the proposal to limit global warming by sealing fossil resources to prevent the carbon being emitted to the atmosphere (see Eisenack *et al.* 2012). If such a proposal can be agreed upon, the permitted fossil resources would first be extracted for agreed-upon purposes such as research and development – most likely at a higher price, since the resource has become more scarce. Then, however, resource owners would have an incentive to break the agreement and extract the remainder. Public policy would not achieve its goal. A variant of this consideration is the property of coalitions being proof against re-negotiation (Farrell and Maskin 1989) that has been applied to international agreements for climate protection (e.g. Asheim and Holtsmark 2009).

In the presence of time inconsistency, reputation or other more formal institutions can restore credibility. Kydland and Prescott (1977) propose to devise fixed rules that "compute" the policy variables in the future depending on the condition at each time. This is the underlying idea of monetary policy institutions such as the European Central Bank. It is set up as a body that has to follow legal rules, but the decisions are (officially) independent from European governments that otherwise might feel tempted to deviate from long-term objectives to solve, e.g. budget problems.

A less conventional way to establish permanence can be the creation of path dependencies (David 1985; Arthur 1989). In general, path dependencies can occur due to economies of scale and network externalities in sustainable and less sustainable directions. Small differences in parameters or initial conditions of an economic process can then lead to profound differences in equilibria or long-term outcomes. This lock-in of conditions can only be changed at high cost or is stabilized by incentives. Further path-dependencies can be introduced through partially irreversible investments, e.g. long-lasting infrastructures (see Hummel, Chapter 6 in this volume). The mere existence of large projects such as extended solar power plants in the Sahara or the Panama Canal set landmarks for further policy processes. As physical objects they cannot simply be modified by changing power constellations or due to time-inconsistent incentives. Thus, with the right timing, relatively small decisions may kick-off irreversible policy plans and establish permanence. A thorough assessment of the long-term consequences of such investments becomes inevitable to avoid high-regret solutions.

When the institutional system allows for setting long-term policies that become permanent the political economy of drafting policies points at further problems. One crucial difference between market interaction and government policies is that the former are only made, at least in theory, voluntarily when there are gains of trade for all partners, while the latter is coercive (Moe 1990). Thus, lobbying for public policies to promote private interests is a good way to obtain rents or to avoid diminishing rents, but it leads to regulatory capture (Stigler 1971). For a more pronounced expected permanence of the policy, the incentives for regulatory capture are higher. However, if there is the possibility to re-adjust the policy at least from time to time, e.g. after an election period, Moe (1990) warns that there will be a trade-off between policy efficiency and policy stability. To avoid institutions being changed by subsequent governments, complex bureaucratic procedures or path dependencies are built in. That comes at the price that these institutions do not achieve their objectives in the best way. Decision makers will tend to take that price to reduce the uncertainty that the permanence of the institution may be destroyed.

Uncertainty is one example of the problems of dealing with change when establishing or sustaining long-term governance approaches. When making investments in a project with longer life-time but with future benefits depending on a stochastic process, i.e. uncertainty, it is known that there is a premium to wait with investment (Pindyck 1991). By waiting, more information about the uncertain future will be revealed. In analogy to long-term policies this leads to postponing implementation. This effect is similar to the older argument by Arrow and Fisher (1974) that irreversible decisions with uncertain payoffs should err on the side of precaution (see Stecker *et al.* 2011, for a similar argument with respect to adaptation to climate change).

However, when an institution is established in an uncertain or changing environment, change in the environment that was considered as being very unlikely at the beginning might jeopardize the institution. This is even more pressing when there is completely unexpected change. In a game theoretic setting analysing environmental agreements, the payoff functions of actors might change due to new preferences. A technological breakthrough can utterly change the problem that is addressed by the policy or can render the policy unnecessary. When long-term governance solutions are supported by infrastructure with long life-times, efficiency requires anticipatory consideration of (uncertain) effects from global environmental change (Stecker *et al.* 2011). Errors are difficult to correct. There might be misuse from powerful actors (e.g. of facilities for geo-engineering), and there might be inflexibilities being introduced which cause further long-term problems. In short, when a policy was successfully designed to solve an original problem with the permanence necessary to achieve an effective solution, unexpected change in the environment might favor a change of the policy over its permanence. In the ideal case, even permanent institutions are sufficiently flexible to adjust to change. Since the latter is more or less a contradiction, it is likely that there is a similar trade-off as discussed by Moe (1990), i.e. more flexibility may come at the price of less effectiveness.

Long-term environmental challenges such as climate change or the loss of biodiversity require an adjustment in existing political, economic, technological, and social systems. But how should the required adaptation processes look like? Part II: Economics will go into what different adaptive capabilities natural and social systems have. What are the necessary investments and subsequent costs of this process? What are the social and political implications of the different instruments and processes? Additionally, the section will address investments which are necessary today but mainly have effects or benefits in the future.

In their contribution, Stefan Hochrainer-Stigler and Reinhard Mechler investigate the long-term trends in fiscal stress and other sectoral costs from natural disasters in Europe. They focus on the time scale by contrasting immediate and long-term costs and considering sectorally different planning horizons of up to several years in the future. By using a quantitative model, they are able to assess both the direct and the indirect economic burden of disasters. For adapting to climate change, primarily risk financing instruments are considered. These are basically short- or medium-term in nature, since e.g. an insurance premium can be easily adjusted to new conditions. The risk, however, also depends on long-term adaptation, e.g. with respect to land use of high risk areas. As example applications, the authors calculate national flood loss distributions and the expected long-term viability of the European Solidarity Fund for disaster relief in the EU.

The contribution by Diana Hummel, Cedric Janowicz, and Alexandra Lux puts long-living supply systems into the centre of their analysis, with water systems as the main example. Supply systems are considered as boundary objects that require a social–ecological perspective, e.g. by considering the institutional arrangements of users, the technological infrastructure and the natural resource base.

Such systems cannot be easily changed on the short time-scale when conditions change. They interact with other long-term trends such as demographic change. Against this background, the authors identify a set of properties that contribute to the adaptive capacity and sustainability of supply systems. This includes "functionality" referring to the basic ability of service quality, while "adaptivity" is the flexibility to revise past decisions. More fundamentally, "transformation openness" is required to reform or to develop the structure of the supply system. This requires the integration of interested stakeholders.

In his contribution Jan Nill analyses opportunities for the transition of technological regimes from the viewpoint of evolutionary economics. There are critical moments in time during which technological pathways can change in a non-incremental way. In such transitions, path dependencies and technological lock-ins can be overcome. However, even if environmental problems are recognized they are not easily taken into account in economic development. Regulatory interventions are needed to stimulate transitions to environmentally friendlier regimes. Nill distinguishes three different strategic approaches to support such transitions: policies to support the search for new techno-economic guideposts, policies to prepare transition windows and policies to utilize transition windows. He focuses on the preparation of transition windows and suggests different implementation strategies for their accomplishment. Addressing the case of sustainable housing in Germany, he analyses the relevance and the impacts of the strategies to prepare a transition window. In his conclusion, he suggests that an appropriate phase-specific policy mix is desirable which combines framework instruments with appropriately timed impulses. Thereby, state policies can play an important role in shaping niche dynamics and preparing transition windows. Policies have to be, however, adaptive to changing circumstances and will have to remain experimental. Nill calls for further research on the co-evolution of policies and techno-economic regimes to respond to environmental problems. Some first steps are taken, utilizing the multiple streams approach of Kingdon (1995) to understand this co-evolution. However, this is yet rather a heuristic starting point than a full-fledged analytical approach. The joint analysis of techno-economic dynamics and political and social systems has the potential as a bridging concept to enable interdisciplinary research.

Part III: Participation

Another strategy in tackling long-term problems is the inclusion of participatory approaches into governance processes. The particular characteristics of long-term problems such as uncertainty about longer term consequences and future events and the need to decide about the timing of particular policy measures require a broad knowledge base. The inclusion of various societal groups and their knowledge backgrounds could thus be helpful in a reflexive and anticipatory governance mode. Voß et al. (2009) highlight the bottom-up elements of long-term governance, e.g. to organize processes of interactive learning between societal actors and policy actors by a mix of instruments. Including young people and representatives of future generations into societal decision-making processes can help to strengthen the long-term perspectives in the deliberation phase. A number of actors, such as companies, retailers, consumers, governmental and non-governmental organizations also need to be involved in participatory long-term governance processes.

Long-term governance solutions need cooperation between various market actors and a higher involvement of stakeholders in the production and consumption processes on the one side and in policy-making processes on the other side. However, there is always the problem of either too much participation or too little participation causing ineffective or imbalanced outcomes. Well-organized and economically potent groups usually are able to participate continuously and with a stronger role in governance processes than less well-organized groups such as many local non-governmental groups or individual citizens (Fung 2006; Bulkeley and Mol 2003; Pellizzoni 2003). A French student once summarised this imbalance by a slogan on a banner: "I participate, you participate, he participates, we participate, you all participate [. . .] they profit" (cited from Arnstein 1969: 218). In addition, there is almost always the challenge of how to communicate with and understand each other in participatory processes (Connor 2007).

What is more, not all forms of participation are equally effective. According to Arnstein (1969), one of the participation pioneers, citizen participation and citizen power depend on the level of participation. Therefore, a proper classification of participation is called for by, e.g. asking who is able and allowed to participate, how communication or decision making is structured and how much power is related to participation (Fung 2006). Reisch (2004) argues that specific participatory approaches have had hardly any political influence so far. She refers to examples such as climate change advisory commissions (see also Maggioni *et al.* 2009), open innovation processes to design new products, consumer advisory boards in retail companies, ethics councils and stakeholder dialogues of large companies. Over recent years, participatory elements became more common, e.g. in the development of comprehensive sustainability strategies or when initiating multi-stakeholder processes by both politics and companies (Yates 2008). Processes of stakeholder involvement in governance processes are also becoming more pervasive in the field of long-term problems (Lubell *et al.* 2008; Sabatier and Weible 2007; Zafonte and Sabatier 2004). In addition, the scope of actors involved in these governance processes has been extended. Local communities and civil society organizations have become accepted as legitimate actors in local governance processes. In many countries, commissions and councils have been set up representing a broad range of societal actors. This consultation and the participation of a wide spectrum of societal actors provide a different source of legitimacy to decisions as compared to the rationalization of policy making.

In the social science literature, governance processes including stakeholder participation are widely discussed as a pragmatic reaction to the crisis of administrative rationalism (Dryzek 2005). Other arguments are based on the decline of public confidence in national governments and the conventional deliberative processes (Renn *et al.* 1995; Rowe and Frewer 2004; Hajer and Wagenaar 2003). Participation is a broadly accepted element of local sustainability in the context of the Local Agenda 21, where it is a crucial condition for developing and accomplishing long-term policy goals. As numerous empirical studies could show, stakeholder involvement enhances ownership of the outcomes of the participatory process by the stakeholders (Fiorino 1990; Joss and Durant 1995; Siebenhüner 2004). Nevertheless, from a long-term governance perspective the question arises to what extent stakeholder integration supports long-term problem solving efficiently. Moreover, it has to be asked whether participation processes are effective in terms of improving the policy output, reducing conflicts and fostering smoother implementation in the long run.

According to Smith and Stirling (2007), each of the actors involved in governance processes has only a limited view of the entire complexity of problems, and a constructive view on elements of the problems. As each of them has restricted capacities to influence outcomes and participating actors need a certain quality (Avelino 2009), it has to be asked how useful participation is and what consequences an increase in the diversity of stakeholders concerning long-term problems has. In addition, there is always the risk that any kind of participation can be misused for reputational purposes and as a tool for retarding decisions. Therefore, the role of participation processes within formal decision-making structures needs to be clarified.

However, a great advantage of participation processes is the possibility of expanding the knowledge base and opening the perspectives on *ad hoc* or continuous communication with citizens (Hart 2007). This can open up sustainability-oriented learning as well as behavioural change with many actors.

Having been hailed as one paradigm of the twenty-first century, the notion of "power of consumer citizenship" highlights the active role of citizen participation in governance as well as in consumption and production processes (OECD 2009). Therefore, the education of diverse stakeholders and citizens as well as training general skills and sustainability are necessary preconditions. Nonetheless, as important as participation and learning processes with respect to long-term policy are, as important is their effectiveness in terms of improving the policy output, reducing conflicts and strengthening implementation (Maggioni *et al.* 2009).

In Part III, interactive elements for strengthening and fostering sustainability-oriented long-term governance will be analysed. Questions in this section focus on how different actors from private and civil society backgrounds could effectively integrate long-term policies and what the potential consequences are, particularly regarding legitimacy, accountability and democratic transparency within political processes. Thus, a critical reflection of the possibility of "too much" participation is the focal point of this section. How effective is the increasing participation of various actors in long-term governance approaches? What positive and negative consequences might an increase in the diversity of stakeholders have on effectiveness, transparency, and legitimacy?

Hui-Yin Sung and Ho-Ching Lee tackle these questions. Their chapter focuses on participation problems in the European Union's environmental governance efforts. Facing the critics of democratic deficit and the growing distrust of scientific knowledge, they argue, the enlargement of participation in policy formulation at the EU level is unavoidable. Their findings clearly demonstrate that the enlargement of participation towards processes of risk assessment is necessary but not sufficient to improve EU environmental governance.

In their chapter, Franziska Wolff and Katharina Schmitt focus on the integration of CSR into long-term political approaches by European fish producers. The authors discuss the effectiveness as well as the consequences on transparency and legitimacy of an integration of private sector participants in long-term governance processes. One of their major conclusions is that the benefits of including the business sector are balanced by systematic limits, and that CSR can only contribute to mitigating long-term challenges where these limits are accounted for. They further argue that when designing the involvement of non-governmental actors in the development and implementation of public strategies, a balanced participation of different stakeholders is necessary.

The chapter by Kristian Krieger and M Brooke Rogers strives to explain variation between individual NGOs and their partnership potential by examining organizational factors. They aim to discover limitations and benefits of partnerships and participatory schemes. Both authors view partnerships as part of the increasingly important theme of participation in environmental governance. Changing business behaviour permanently can be brought about by so called "soft rules" and advisory services in partnerships; however, the authors also stress the importance of "transformative" partnerships to establish partnerships that generate environmental benefits. Krieger and Rogers stress that participation does not ensure effective and democratic environmental governance *per se*, it is always a question of how much participation, what kind of participation with whom, and to which purpose.

The last contribution to this section by Christian Albert considers an overview of the characteristics of participatory scenarios. He discusses the ways in which they can contribute to long-term governance and identifies criteria for participatory scenarios to be influential in public discussions and decisions. His study concludes that the effectiveness of participatory scenarios in that regard depends on the function, subject, vantage point, inclusion of values, inputs, the level and frequency of involvement, characteristics of meetings and resource availability.

Part IV: Knowledge and learning

In long-term governance, knowledge and learning play a particular role. Since most long-term problems can only be experienced in the future, knowledge about these problems and their potential consequences becomes essential, in particular when it comes to problems with time lags between causation and impacts. Climate change is a prime example for this class of problems. The consequences of rising greenhouse gas concentrations in the atmosphere observable today such as changing migration patterns of species, melting of polar ice and glaciers or increasing numbers and intensity of extreme weather events, result also from 10- to 20-year-old emissions. Today's emissions will generate additional and most likely more severe consequences in the future. This gap between causation and impacts requires a solid knowledge base in governance processes. As argued for in the last section of this book, involving various societal groups can often lead to better accepted results and to those forms of knowledge that are relevant for societal problems rather than being restricted to scientific debates (Luks and Siebenhüner 2007; Hirsch Hadorn, Hoffmann-Riem *et al.* 2008).

A second indication for the particular role of foresight knowledge is the character of creeping problems as described by Schneider *et al.* (Chapter 12 in this volume). Long-term problems such as climate change or biodiversity loss are in most parts marked by slow and incremental changes rather than abrupt and very severe catastrophes that immediately catch high media and public attention. By contrast, creeping problems can only be detected by longer term monitoring and well-prepared modelling and forecasting studies.

This applies in particular to the societal reaction to these types of long-term developments. Natural phenomena in essence call for scientific research and long-term projections where much of the burden to provide adequate knowledge is put on scientific institutions. By contrast, societal phenomena including the causation, mitigation and adaptation of many global environmental change problems require knowledge about societies which, in principle, are able to adapt and react to this knowledge. This knowledge could be rendered irrelevant due to the different character of self-reflexive societies vis-à-vis natural phenomena. This capacity of reflection, however, remains one of the most important means to effectively address these challenges requiring adequate institutions and infrastructures as well as processes to connect knowledge to decision making.

What is meant by "knowledge" in this context? The term is multi-faceted and difficult to define. Broadly speaking, knowledge refers to a mental representation of the world and its components. It is more than mere data or information and includes "all types of understanding gained through experience or study" (Hess and Ostrom 2007: 8). Knowledge can thus be used in one form or another by humans, be it for mastering their daily lives, developing technologies and new practices or for intellectual debate or spiritual exchange.

Long-term problems, however, relate to the temporal dimension of knowledge. They imply a challenge to the presence-bound concept of knowledge since knowledge in the context of long-term problems in most cases cannot be exact and in multiple ways verified knowledge, but is in large parts uncertain (Faucheux and Froger 1995; Jänicke and Jörgens 2000; Newig, Voß *et al.* 2008). It often includes projections, scenarios and extrapolations which help to limit the number of possible future conditions and developments (see Albert and Lebel, Chapters 11 and 13 respectively in this volume). At the same time, this knowledge is also highly relevant for human activities and has to be so. It needs to be related to today's behaviour and its consequences for the future. This implies an enormous governance challenge for societies, individuals, governments or organizations and groups to take decisions in the face of uncertainty and to include long-term consequences into present decision making in general. Thus, one guiding question for the contributions to this book is what forms and substances of knowledge do actors need to act in the field of largely uncertain long-term problems?

Knowledge has to be developed, discovered, experienced, tested, processed, communicated and diffused, which relates to the notion of learning and social learning in particular. In parallel to knowledge, learning is a complex issue with multiple perspectives and conceptualizations (The Social Learning Group 2001; Zollo and Winter 2002; Haas 2004; Siebenhüner 2008). Given the focus on usability of knowledge, the term learning can be broadly defined as any form of changes in practices, processes and strategies of an individual, collective actor or a society caused by a change in knowledge. On the basis of this definition, learning can be studied through its outcomes, namely the changes in practices and behaviour. At the same time learning can be understood as a test of the applicability and usability of knowledge in practice. Nevertheless, uncertain knowledge on long-term problems can hardly be proven right or wrong in short time frames. The long-term consequences often remain inexperienced for decades. This poses another challenge for learning in the context of long-term problems: How to learn in situations of long-term uncertainty and the absence of regulating knowledge feedbacks?

The governance of learning and knowledge vis-à-vis long-term problems thus has to address the grand challenges of finding knowledge about uncertain futures and to learn how to deal with them in advance. Current institutions of knowledge generation and learning are oftentimes ill-prepared for this challenge since they focus on certain and presence-related knowledge, like most scientific institutions. The question for governance therefore is how institutions could or should be designed to help societies and their actors to develop relevant knowledge and to render it usable for their current and future behaviour. This requires the effective integration of science, politics and society to facilitate the relevance and the usability of knowledge.

In this perspective, the section on "Knowledge and Learning" in this book focusses on the interplay between science, politics, and society. It thus addresses the question how best to generate trans-disciplinary knowledge. For example, the Intergovernmental Panel on Climate Change (IPCC) and its accepted assessments and political approval mechanism play a central role in producing and distributing the known long-term consequences of climate change. Through leaders such as the IPCC and other international assessment processes, e.g. within the United Nations, the benefits of producing trans-disciplinary knowledge are becoming increasingly evident. Managing sustainability through long-term policies is not just a problem for governmental actors. All affected groups, governmental and non-governmental, public and private alike, need to be involved in decision-making processes and the implementation of long-term policies.

In their chapter, Volker Schneider, Philip Leifeld and Thomas Malang focus on the problem of creeping catastrophes as a challenge for the political system. These catastrophes are often long-term, difficult to detect, result in large, but uncertain, damages in the future, which often come slowly and not as a major catastrophe at one point in time. Thereby, they evade conventional patterns of public and political attention and are difficult to tackle in formal political processes given their largely reactive setup. These problems thus require adequate knowledge and communication to enable societies and political systems to react adequately and timely. However, as Schneider *et al.* analyse in greater detail, political systems worldwide are able to address this challenge to different degrees. In general, democratic systems seem to be better equipped for this purpose since they require the development of knowledge and public understanding of the problems at hand.

Louis Lebel reflects on scenario analyses as a tool for long-term planning of water resources and services in a case study on the Mekong region. Although scenario processes bear promise in bringing together different stakeholders and to reach legitimate decisions with a long time range, a critical assessment of that promise is in order. He thoroughly compares several water management scenario studies from the Mekong region as example. The focus is both on the properties of the scenarios as "products", and the process of the scenario development itself, where he distinguishes initiation, construction and exploration. Long-term planning with scenarios requires addressing the actors involved in the process, the nature of the products of the process, and the influence of the scenarios on decision making. Analysing the examples in this framework, Lebel shows that scenario exercises are often only expert driven and results are often only communicated to a narrow audience.

Stakeholder integration and social learning in a case of integrated sustainability assessment is the topic of the chapter by Lisa Bohunovsky and Jill Jäger. They portray integrated sustainability assessments as a means of knowledge generation and decision support on specific solutions to long-term problems. In the context of an EU research project, these assessment processes followed specific process steps and were applied in different cases such as water management, agriculture and forestry, sustainable mobility or sustainable housing. What is shown in the chapter is the evidence of learning by the stakeholders involved. The participatory and inclusive design of these assessments through the integration of stakeholders contributed significantly to the development of a broader knowledge base for each respective decision-making situation. It could thus be shown that the involvement of stakeholders is a helpful means to further knowledge generation and learning vis-à-vis particular long-term sustainability problems.

Conclusions

Meeting the challenges of long-term problems and overcoming the dilemmas which societies face in providing public goods and limiting the use of resources to sustainable levels has no easy and straightforward solution. The main challenges of long-term governance originate in rather complex and dynamic problems combined with uncertainties in knowledge and regarding the diverse actors involved. In addition, the characteristics of social–ecological systems and behavioural patterns of actors are deeply embedded in culture, society and technology. In facing international challenges, many different cultural systems and business patterns have to be addressed. Governments are bound to their constitutions, constituencies and to international law which limits their possibilities to restrict citizens and enterprises in using resources in favor of the future. It is also tempting for governments to exploit resources in the present as this guarantees employment and income, hence also taxes. However, as contributions to this book and other sources show, there are a number of solutions to these dilemmas.

Do markets provide a solution? Industrialism has changed our societies and the whole world. Humans have gathered an enormous wealth by pursuing their individual interests and by exchanging goods. While this has caused social disruptions, environmental degradation and overuse in resources, markets have in parts also been able to create the resources that were needed to overcome these problems. Are markets hence also able to meet the challenges of long-term sustainability? In essence, markets fail in this regard exactly because of their foundations in the self-interest of individuals and not in future generations. How can the power of markets be redirected to meet the needs of the future? There are numerous on-going activities to increase the transparency, effectiveness and credibility of markets in order to facilitate better and more legitimate decisions about long-term problems. However, it is open to investigation if these are effective and sufficient framework conditions to overcome the related market failures.

Given the limitations of governments and markets, is it civil society that can solve the problems? Many hopes are connected to broadening participation of various actor groups in decision making. But is it realistic to rely on civil society organizations to preserve the common good by bringing in their expertise and their commitment? An optimistic view would claim that there are opportunities of collective knowledge production, a fairer distribution and access to resources, even a more balanced negotiation of resource allocation and use of resources and a holistic risk assessment while dealing with ambiguity. However, it would be naïve to ignore the fact that more inclusive decision making also means opening it up to all conflicting and also particulate interests. There is always the risk of wrong, too much or too little participation or the formation of an exclusive "cartel of elites". It is costly in the sense that decision making takes longer or even entails the risks of stalemates. Participatory approaches may also entail greater risks for decisions that follow the NIMBY (Not-in-my-backyard) pattern (Coenen 2008). Still, there are many examples of good practice, such as Unilever's Fish Sustainability Initiative (FSI), UNCED's Agenda 21, the United Nation's Global Compact, the Auto-Oil program, the European Climate Change Program (ECCP), and the Clean Air for Europe Programme (CAFE).

In consequence, are an improved and extended knowledge base and learning processes the last resort? It is only through foresight activities and scientific research that long-term problems became noticeable allowing societal decision makers to address them. Therefore, multi-stakeholder dialogues, partnerships, scenario development and assessment and public policy alliance play a crucial role. More and more governments are seeking scientific expertise and a solid knowledge base for their decision making, e.g. by means of Policy Impact Assessment (Jacob *et al.* 2011). However, most governance decisions are related to values and can hardly be founded on objective scientific evidence. In addition, most knowledge is being generated in a political context and can hardly be separated from politics. What is more, long-term problems are difficult to predict in detail and no certain scientific knowledge is available for future time spans of several decades. This knowledge requires interpretation and will not set current decision makers free of value-related choices.

While all four avenues alone thus have severe deficiencies, a thoughtful combination can be expected to deliver better outcomes in a long-term perspective (see also Brousseau *et al.* 2012). As several examples, including those documented in this book, demonstrate, the smart combination of modes of governance delivers promising answers to the question of how long-term problems of sustainability can be adequately addressed.

However, combining different modes is not a trivial effort, which can be implemented by simply choosing approaches from textbooks or from toolboxes. In fact, the different modes of governance which have been identified in the literature and further analysed in this book, bear the risk of mutual deterioration.

Using economic instruments is not always complementary to conventional governmental regulation. There is a broad literature on potential conflicts between economic incentives and intrinsic motivations of actors to consider environmental problems in their current behaviour (e.g. Frey 1992). Nevertheless, many modern governance instruments seek to combine economic incentives with regulatory elements which allow for different and often smarter ways of redirecting societal trends towards long-term problems (Thaler and Sunstein 2008).

Also, traditional hierarchical decision making by governments is increasingly being challenged by the demand for public participation. What does it mean for governments and parliaments if citizens oppose investments which are meant to serve the needs of future generations? There is no warranty that participation will automatically promote the long-term common good. In fact, the "NIMBY" phenomenon is a frequent problem of public participation. Thus, combining hierarchy and participatory approaches is not straightforward since it bears the potential of frustrating or de-legitimising the one or the other mode of decision making.

Similar, there are tensions between modes of governance on the basis of evidence, foresight and knowledge on the one hand and hierarchy on the other hand. Governments and parliaments tend to seek compromise between different interest groups, regions and ideologies. Evidence is just one among many sources of legitimacy in this context. Here again, there is the risk of mutual de-legitimisation: Scientific knowledge oftentimes challenges political decisions and becomes political through a stronger role in decision making (Jasanoff 2004).

Further trade-offs between governmental policy and knowledge are also well investigated. In addition to the trade-offs raised in this book, Ziesemer and

Michaelis (2011) stressed that governments and societal decision makers often do not have access to new or specific long-term related knowledge. Therefore, policy decisions often need to be based on rough estimates of assumed consequences. This is connected to an underestimation of the benefits from learning. In addition, it is highlighted in the book that new long-term related knowledge often cannot be easily integrated into policy measures due to given structures or missing holistic mechanisms.

A third potential trade-off between the different modes of governance has attracted less attention so far. How does decision making based on scientific knowledge and evidence relate to decision making based on participation? How do citizens react if scientific evidence challenges their positions, and vice versa, how are scientists able to take up the considerations and demands of scientists? The NIMBY phenomenon stresses the need for a better understanding of the dynamics of participatory approaches. Unfortunately, a linear approach, like the more comprehensive the knowledge the better participatory decisions, does not work. The personal concern and involvement might cloud the objectivity of knowledge. Hisschemöller *et al.* (2001) argue that especially environmental risks are mostly non-negotiable for many people. This might be explained by the quality of emotional conflicts that hinder mitigation or compensation as means of finding compromise. Vulnerable conflicts need government mechanisms and protection and cannot be part of a trade-off. The potential trade-offs and synergies between these elements of knowledge-based and participatory governance and the potentials for smart and mutually beneficial combinations towards more reflexive and at the same time inclusive governance have not been explored in sufficient detail.

To sum up, long-term problems need clear and balanced mechanisms for ruling conflicts and mitigating risks. Long-term governance requires a mix of governance approaches that employs a variety of tools in order to be able to foster social–ecological change. There are strong interrelations between knowledge and learning, participation, markets and governance that need to be better understood. Some of these interrelations and possible strategies in handling trade-offs are discussed in this book. It analyses some of these elementary trade-offs and provides some new insights into how to govern long-term problems.

References

Arnstein, S. R. 1969. "A Ladder of Citizen Participation". *Journal of the American Planning Association* 35(4): 216–24.

Arrow, K. J. and Fisher, A. C. 1974. "Environmental Preservation, Uncertainty and Irreversibility". *Quarterly Journal of Economics*, 88: 312–19.

Arthur, W. B. 1989. "Competing Technologies Increasing Returns and Lock-in by Historical Events". *The Economic Journal*, 99: 116–31.

Asheim, G. B. and Holtsmark, B. 2009. "Renegotiation-Proof Climate Agreements with Full Participation: Conditions for Pareto-Efficiency". *Environmental Resource Economics*, 43: 519–33.

Avelino, F. 2009. "Empowerment and the Challenge of Applying Transition Management to Ongoing Projects". *Policy Science*, 42: 369–90.

Becker, E., Jahn, T., Tiess, I. and Wehling, P. 1997. *Sustainability: A Cross- Disciplinary Concept for Social Transformations*. Paris, Unesco.

Biermann, F., Betsill, M. M., Gupta, J., Kanie, N., Lebel, L., Liverman, D., Schroeder, H., Siebenhüner, B., Conca, K., de Costa Ferreira, L., Desai, B., Tay, S. and Zondervan, R. 2009. *Earth System Governance: People, Places and the Planet. Science and Implementation Plan of the Earth System Governance Project*. Bonn, IHDP: The Earth System Governance Project.

Brousseau, E., Dedeurwaerdere, T. and Siebenhüner, B. (eds.). 2012. *Reflexive Governance and Global Public Goods*. Cambridge: MIT Press.

Bulkeley, H. and Mol, A. P. J. 2003. "Participation and Environmental Governance: Consensus, Ambivalence and Debate". *Environmental Values*, 12: 143–54.

Coenen, F. H. J. M. (ed.) 2008. *Public Participation and Better Environmental Decisions*. Springer.

Connor, D. M. 2007. "A New Ladder of Citizen Participation". *National Civic Review*, 77(3): 249–57.

David, P. A. 1985. "Clio and the Economics of QWERTY". *AEA Papers and Proceedings*, 75: 332–7.

Dopfer, K. (ed.) 2001. *Evolutionary Economics. Program and Scope*. Boston: Kluwer.

Dryzek, J. S. 2005. *The Politics of the Earth*. Oxford, UK: Oxford University Press.

Eisenack, K., Edenhofer, O. and Kalkuhl, M. 2012. "Resource Rents: The Effects of Energy Taxes and Quantity Instruments for Climate Protection", *Energy Policy*, 48: 159–66.

Farrell, J. and Maskin, E. 1989. "Renegotiations in Repeated Games". *Games and Economic Behaviour*, 1: 327–60.

Faucheux, S. and Froger, G. 1995. "Decision-making under Environmental Uncertainty: Methodological and Ideological Options". *Ecological Economics* 15(1): 29–42.

Fiorino, D. J. 1990. "Citizen Participation and Environmental Risk: A Survey of Institutional Mechanisms". *Science, Technology & Human Values* 15(2): 226–43.

Fischer-Kowalski, M. and Haberl, H. (eds) 2007. *Socioecological Transitions and Global Change: Trajectories of Social Metabolism and Land Use*. Cheltenham: Edward Elgar.

Frey, B. S. 1992. "Tertium Datur: Pricing, Regulating and Intrinsic Motivation". *Kyklos* 45(2): 161–84.

Fung, A. 2006. "Varieties of Participation in Complex Governance". *Public Administration Review*, 66: 66–75.

Geels, F. W. and Schot, J. 2007. "Typology of Sociotechnical Transition Pathways". *Research Policy*, 36: 399–417.

Gowdy, J. 1994. *Coevolutionary Economics: The Economy, Society and the Environment*. Boston: Kluwer.

Haas, P. M. 2004. "When does Power Listen to Truth? A Constructivist Approach to the Policy Process". *Journal of European Public Policy* 11(4): 569–92.

Hajer, M. A. and Wagenaar, H. 2003. *Deliberative Policy Analysis, Understanding Governance in the Network Society*. Cambridge, UK: Cambridge University Press.

Hardin, G. 1968. "The Tragedy of the Commons". *Science* 162(3859): 1243–8.

Hart, A. 2007. *Foundations of a Customer-Oriented Strategy: Integration and Involvement*. Saarbrücken: VDM Verlag Dr. Müller.

Hartwick, J. 1977. "Intergenerational Equity and the Investing of Rents from Exhaustible Resources". *American Economic Review* 67(5): 972–4.

Hess, C. and Ostrom, E. (eds) 2007. *Understanding Knowledge as a Commons: From Theory to Practice.* Cambridge, MA: MIT Press.

Hirsch Hadorn, G., Hoffmann-Riem, H., Biber-Klemm, S., Grossenbacher-Mansuy, W., Joye, D., Pohl, C., Wiesmann, U. and Zemp, E. (eds) 2008. *Handbook of Transdisciplinary Research.* Heidelberg, Berlin, Dordrecht: Springer.

Hisschemöller, M., Hoppe, R., Dunn, W. N. and Ravetz, J. R. 2001. "Knowledge, Power, and Participation in Environmental Policy Analysis". *Policy Studies Annual Review 12.* New Brunswick: Transaction.

Jacob, K., Guske, A.-L. and von Prittwitz, V. 2011. "Consideration of Sustainability Aspects in Policy Impact Assessment: An International Comparative Study of Innovations and Trends". www.polsoz.fu-berlin.de/polwiss/forschung/systeme/ffu/files/SIA-Study_2011_Jacob_ex.pdf.

Jänicke, M. and Jörgens, H. 2000. "Strategic Environmental Planning and Uncertainty: A Cross-national Comparison of Green Plans in Industrialized Countries". *Policy Studies Journal* 28(3): 612–32.

Jasanoff, S. 2004. *States of Knowledge: The Co-Production of Science and Social Order.* London: Routledge.

Jordan, A. and Lenschow, A. (eds) 2008. *Innovation in Environmental Policy? Integrating the Environment for Sustainability.* Edward Elgar: Cheltenham.

Joss, S. and Durant, J. (eds) 1995. *Public Participation in Science: The Role of Consensus Conferences in Europe.* London: Routledge.

Kemp, R., Loorbach, D. and Rotmans, J. 2007. "Transition Management as a Model for Managing Processes of Co-evolution towards Sustainable Development". *International Journal of Sustainable Development & World Ecology* 14(1): 78–91.

Kemp, R., Avelino, F. and Bressers, N. 2011. "Transition Management as a Model for Sustainable Mobility", *European Transport/Trasporti Europei* 47(1–2): 25–46.

Kingdon, J. W. 1995. *Agendas, Alternatives, and Public Policies.* New York: Pearson.

Kydland, F. E. and Prescott, E. C. 1977. "Rules Rather than Discretion: The Inconsistency of Optimal Plans". *Journal of Political Economy* 85(3): 473–92.

Lafferty, W. M., (ed.) 2004. *Governance for Sustainable Development.* Cheltenham: Edward Elgar.

Lubell, M., Leach, W. D. and Sabatier, P. A. 2008. "Collaborative Watershed Partnerships in the Epoch of Sustainability". In Mazmanian, D. A. and Kraft, M. E. (eds), *Toward Sustainable Communities*, 2nd edn. Cambridge, MA: MIT Press, 255–88.

Luks, F. and Siebenhüner, B. 2007. "Transdisciplinarity for Social Learning? The Contribution of the German Socio-Ecological Research Initiative to Sustainability Governance". *Ecological Economics*, 63: 418–26.

Maggioni, E., Nelson, H. and Mazmanian, D. A. 2009. "Stakeholder Participation and Climate Change Policies". *Environment & Sustainablity*, WP-November 2009-1.

Moe, T. M. 1990. "Political Institutions: The Neglected Side of the Story". *Journal of Law, Economics, and Organization* 6 (special issue): 213–53.

Newig, J., Voß, J.-P. and Monstadt, J. (eds). 2008. *Governance for Sustainable Development: Steering in Contexts of Ambivalence, Uncertainty and Distributed Power.* London: Routledge.

Nill, J. 2009. *Ökologische Innovationspolitik: Eine evolutorisch-ökonomische Perspektive.* Marburg: Metropolis-Verlag.

North, DC 1991. "Institutions". *Journal of Economic Perspectives* 5(1): 97–112.

OECD. 2009. Promoting Consumer Education, Trends, Policies and Good Practices, www.oecd.org.

Ostrom, E. 2009. "A General Framework for Analyzing Sustainability of Social-ecological Systems". *Science*, 325: 419–22.

Pellizzoni, L. 2003. "Uncertainty and Participatory Democracy". *Environmental Values* 12(2): 195–224.

Pindyck, R. S. 1991. "Irreversibility, Uncertainty, and Investment". *Journal of Economic Literature*, 39, 1110–48.

Reich, N. 1992. "Diverse Approaches to Consumer Protection Philosophy". *Journal of Consumer Policy*, 14: 257–92.

Reisch, L. A. 2004. "Principles and Visions of a New Consumer Policy: Discussion Paper by the Scientific Advisory Board for Consumer, Food, and Nutrition Policy to the German Federal Ministry of Consumer Protection, Food, and Agriculture". *Journal of Consumer Policy*, 27: 1–42.

Renn, O., Webler, T. and Wiedemann, P. 1995. *Fairness and Competence in Citizen Participation*. Dordrecht: Kluwer.

Rowe, G. and Frewer, L. J. 2004. "Evaluating Public Participation Exercises: A Research Agenda". *Science, Technology and Human Values* 29(4): 512–57.

Sabatier, P. A. and Weible, C. M. 2007. "The Advocacy Coalition Framework: Innovations and Clarifications". In Sabatier, P. A. (ed.) *Theories of the Policy Process*, 2nd edn. Boulder, CO: Westview Press, 189–220.

Siebenhüner, B. 2004. "Social Learning and Sustainability Science: Which Role Can Stakeholder Participation Play?" *International Journal of Sustainable Development* 7(2): 146–63.

Siebenhüner, B. 2008. "Learning in International Organisations in Global Environmental Governance". *Global Environmental Politics* 8(4): 92–116.

Smith, A. and Stirling, A. 2007. "Moving Outside or Inside? Objectification and Reflexivity in the Governance of Socio-technical Systems". *Journal of Environmental Policy and Planning* 9(3/4): 351–73.

Solow, R. M. 1974. "The Economics of Resources or the Resources of Economics". *The American Economic Review* 64(2): 1–14.

Sprinz, D. F. 2009. "Long-Term Environmental Policy". Guest Editor. *Special Issue of Global Environmental Policy* 9(3): 1–8.

Stecker, R., Pechan, A., Steinhäuser, J. M., Rotter, M., Scholl, G. and Eisenack, K. 2011. *Why are Utilities Reluctant to Adapt to Climate Change?* Technical Report, Oldenburg: University of Oldenburg, www.climate-chameleon.de/htm_engl/publications_engl.html [3.12.2012].

Stigler, G. J. 1971. "The Theory of Economic Regulation". *Bell Journal of Economics* 2(1): 3–21.

Thaler, R. H. and Sunstein, C. R. 2008. *Nudge: Improving Decisions about Health, Wealth and Happiness*. New Haven, London: Yale University Press.

The Social Learning Group. 2001. *Learning to Manage Global Environmental Risks: A Comparative History of Social Responses to Climate Change, Ozone Depletion, and Acid Rain*. Cambridge, MA: MIT Press.

Voß, J.-P., Smith, J. and Grin, J. 2009. "Designing Long-term Policy: Rethinking Transition Management". *Policy Science*, 42: 275–302.

WCED, World Commission on Environment and Development. 1987. *Our Common Future*. Oxford: Oxford University Press.

WBGU (2011) *Welt im Wandel–Gesellschaftsvertrag für eine Große Transformation Wissenschaftlicher*. Wissenschaftlicher Beirat der Bundesregierung für Globale Umweltveränderungen, Berlin.

Williamson, O. E. 2000. "The New Institutional Economics: Taking Stock, Looking Ahead". *Journal of Economic Literature* 38(3): 595–613.

Yates, L. 2008. "Sustainable Consumption: the Consumer Perspective". *Consumer Policy Review* 18: 96–9.

Young, O. R., King, L. A. and Schroeder, H. (eds). 2008. *Institutions and Environmental Change: Principal Findings, Applications, and Research Frontiers*. Cambridge, MA: MIT Press.

Young, O. R., Berkhout, F., Gallopin, G., Janssen, M. A., Ostrom, E. and van der Leeuw, Sander. 2006. "The Globalization of Socio-ecological Systems: An Agenda for Scientific Research". *Global Environmental Change*, 16: 304–16.

Zafonte, M. and Sabatier, P. A. 2004. "Short-term versus Long-term Coalitions in the Policy Process: Automotive Pollution Control 1963–1989". *Policy Studies Journal* 32 (1): 75–107.

Ziesemer, T. and Michaelis, P. 2011. "Strategic Environmental Policy and the Accumulation of Knowledge". *Structural Change and Economic Dynamics* 22(2): 180–91.

Zollo, M. and Winter, S. G. 2002. "Deliberate Learning and the Evolution of Dynamic Capabilities". *Organisation Science* 13(3): 339–51.

Part I

Institutions and governance mechanisms

2 The role of expertise in environmental governance

Theoretical perspectives and empirical evidence

Michael Pregernig and Michael Böcher

Introduction

Environmental policy making has experienced some major changes over the last decades. One marked change has been the effort to find alternatives to command and control regulation, a trend which has been captured by the term "governance". New modes of governance – as contrasted with traditional modes of "governmental" steering – call for non-hierarchical forms of guidance, such as persuasion and negotiation, in which public and private actors are engaged in policy formulation and implementation (Peters 2000; Pierre 2000; Kooiman 2003; Petschow *et al.* 2006; Benz and Papadopoulos 2006; Bäckstrand *et al.* 2010; Bevir 2011; Hogl *et al.* 2012).

Closely connected to that, there is a second trend that could be paraphrased as the *"scientification of politics"* (Weingart 2002: 704). As policy issues are becoming more and more complex, science and expertise have come to play an increasingly influential role in their contribution to the formulation of policy and regulatory decisions (Banthien *et al.* 2003; Juntti *et al.* 2009). The demand for scientific expertise is especially strong in questions of environmental and natural resource policy, not least because of the long-term character and resulting uncertainties of many environmental problems (Fischer 2001). As a result of the growing pervasiveness of science-related issues there has been a corresponding increase in the use of expert scientific advice to inform decision-making at all levels of policy making (Glynn *et al.* 2003).

Also the scholarly literature has attended to the interaction between science and politics. Ever since Vannevar Bush's seminal 1945 report on "Science, the endless frontier", a number of theoretical perspectives on the role of science and expertise in policy making have been elaborated (Pregernig and Böcher 2012). To date, those different theoretical frameworks have mostly been standing side-by-side in a more or less unrelated way or, now and again, they have been antagonizing on an ideological basis (cf. the debate between Schelsky and Habermas on the appeal of a technocratic model of the 1960s). Few authors have reflected on the empirical usefulness of different theoretical conceptualizations.

In this chapter, we want to contribute to at least partly closing this gap. In the following, we strive to answer two basic questions: First, we address the *empirical* question of what role science and expertise play in environmental governance processes. More explicitly, our aim is to critically assess the expectation that in a governance context, science and expertise play distinct, new roles that go beyond the mere content-wise input of scientific knowledge in political decision-making processes. Second, we touch upon the *analytical* question of which conceptual perspectives are apt to depict science–policy interactions in a governance context.

Our investigation is based on empirical findings of the EU-FP6 research project "New Modes of Governance for Sustainable Forestry in Europe" (GoFOR)[1] that analysed evolving practices of governance in various land-use related fields (e.g. forestry, nature conservation, rural development) in ten European countries. Besides procedural elements typically accounted for in the governance discourse (like participation, intersectoral coordination, multi-level coordination, and procedural adaptivity and iterativity), GoFOR put a special focus on the role of science and expertise in governance processes. The normative concept of "democratic and accountable expertise" was used to address the question of how the relationship between science and society is organized in governance processes and how it could be developed in both a more effective and a more democratically legitimate way.

The chapter is structured as follows: the first section introduces exemplary theoretical perspectives for the analysis of science–policy interactions; this is followed by a report on empirical insights from the GoFOR governance case studies; the next section discusses and evaluates the validity and usefulness of the different theoretical perspectives introduced before; and the final section draws some conclusions.

Analytical perspectives on expertise in governance processes

The interaction between science and politics can be conceptualized theoretically in a number of ways. Below, we introduce three different conceptualizations following important recent discussions in the scholarly literature, i.e. an instrumental, a strategic, and a co-productionist conceptualization. For us these conceptualizations seem to be especially relevant against the empirical background of European environmental governance.

Instrumental perspectives on the interaction between science and policy

Classically, the role of science in policy making has been perceived from an instrumental perspective, with scientists being brought into policy processes to impart their unique knowledge and wisdom to policy makers. Science and politics are linked in a way that could be best described with the phrase "speaking truth to power" (Price 1981).

One of the standard, ideal-type conceptualizations is the so-called *knowledge transfer model* (which has also been referred to as the "linear model" (Neilson 2001; Pielke 2004, 2007) or the "modern model" (Liberatore and Funtowicz 2003)). Here, scientific expert advice is believed to make a direct contribution to the increased effectiveness and rationalization of political action. Under the transfer model, scientific advice is conceptualized as the simple transmission of ready-made scientific results (Weingart 1999). First, there is knowledge closure on the side of science, meaning that scientific questions are completely resolved and a finished product is handed over to policy makers; after that, policies are formulated ("*get-the-facts-then-act model*", Pielke 2004: 406).

In the light of recent scholarship, the naïve hopes of the cascade-like "*scientification of the non-scientific world*" (Beck and Bonß 1984: 382) turned out to be untenable, both in a theoretical and an empirical perspective. The discouraging findings of an insufficient translation of innovative ideas into practical action led more sociologically oriented scholars to renounce the notion of a simple transfer of science into politics. *Knowledge diffusion models* are built on the assumption that the immediate and direct conversion of science into practice is the exception rather than the rule, particularly when the issues are complex, the consequences are uncertain, and a multitude of actors are engaged in the decision-making process (Oh 1996). Carol H. Weiss (1980) coined the term "*knowledge creep*" to describe the way in which ideas gradually spread, enter into use, and sometimes become the conceptual framework of entire policy debates. Therefore, even though research findings are not directly employed in a specific policy, diffusion scholars assume that they on the whole can still exert a powerful influence over the terms used and the way issues are framed and understood (Hisschemöller *et al.* 2001).

Strategic perspectives on the interaction between science and policy

Political scientists argue that there are inherent limitations to the simple transfer or diffusion of scientific knowledge into political practice due to the different "codes" under which the scientific and the political system are operating. While science is oriented towards finding "the truth", the principles of politics are oriented towards the distribution of power (Mayntz 2009). This consequently leads to a more strategic view of the way expertise is used in politics and by political actors. A set of approaches, commonly termed "group politics models" (Martin and Richards 1995), put the focus on the more "political" or strategic aspects of the interaction between expertise and politics. Here, contending groups use scientific knowledge as an additional resource to increase their authority or legitimation. Advisors are selected not only for their knowledge but also for the legitimation that they provide for policies as well as for policy makers and interest groups involved in policy processes. Peter Weingart succinctly notes: "The assumption that science is always disinterested and transmits only objective knowledge is obviously a myth. Science has become one of the actors to support [policy makers'] specific interests." (Weingart 2002: 704)

Group politics models also point to the fact that in political conflicts science is often used in a selective way. Competing parties choose advice that supports their own policy choices and overlook advice which does not. Sonja Boehmer-Christiansen (1995), for example, outlines a number of different *functions* that scientific knowledge can fulfil in the policy process: scientific expertise can serve as a source of authority and hence legitimacy for official actors, as justification for unpopular policies, as instruments of persuasion in debates and negotiations (with the parties tending to select the advice that best fits their own interests), as a mechanism for delaying or avoiding action or substituting for action (since conducting more research gains time and passes the responsibility to somebody else) and as a scapegoat and cover-up for policy change (since science may be used to allow politicians to change their minds without losing face or having to admit error).

Co-productionist perspectives on the interaction between science and policy

The conceptual models described thus far proceed on the assumption that the inherent logic of either science or politics is dominating science–policy interactions: while instrumental models see – or rather: would like to see – the technical-rationalist logic of science as dominant, group politics models accentuate the power-strategic logic of politics. Studies in the fields of post-positivist policy analysis (Hisschemöller *et al.* 2001; Fischer 2003; Hoppe 2005) and science and technology studies (STS) (for an overview: Jasanoff *et al.* 1995; Hackett *et al.* 2007) have convincingly challenged both the conventional assumption that scientific governance is merely about "speaking truth to power" as well as the determinist idea that social controversies around science are "really" all about politics (Irwin 2007). Rather than presenting either science or politics as preeminent, the model of "co-production" looks at the question of "how knowledge-making is incorporated into practices of [. . .] governance [. . .], and, in reverse, how practices of governance influence the making and use of knowledge." (Jasanoff 2004: 3)

While conceptual models that follow a realist tradition distinguish in an a priori fashion between "science" and "politics", between "facts" and "values", the co-productionist model, like other socio-constructivist approaches, is more sensitive to the difficulties of making analytical distinctions between the two realms (Gieryn 1995; Guston 2001). In recent years, political and social studies of science have questioned the notion that the scientific part of decision making can be completely separated from the political part, and delegated to independent experts (Ezrahi 1980; Jasanoff 1990). Especially in complex problem settings, knowledge relevant to policy decisions is a complex intermixture of "values" and "facts" that will resist being untangled. The concept of co-production emphasizes that "[. . .] the study of scientific governance is not concerned with the interaction between two separate processes ('expertise' and 'power') but precisely the manner in which knowledge of the natural world and political action have become mutually embedded and co-constituted." (Irwin 2007: 586)

Empirical results: expert involvement in environmental governance processes

After having sketchily depicted three partly antithetic, partly complementary conceptual perspectives on the role of science and expertise in governance processes, this section will put an empirical focus on the roles and functions of experts and expertise in governance processes. The empirical basis for analysis comes from the EU-FP6 research project GoFOR which analysed 16 case studies on evolving practices of governance in various land-use related fields (e.g. forestry, nature conservation, rural development) in ten European countries. Table 2.1 gives a brief characterization of the case studies.

At first glance, the governance cases analysed look rather heterogeneous; still there are various thematic clusters. There are two sector-related clusters: one focusing on forest policy, the other one on nature conservation and biodiversity. There are also two clusters as regards the type of processes: we have six political strategy formulation and implementation processes and four processes which are heavily driven by international (including EU) commitments. Those clusters are, of course, overlapping. As regards their "inherent time horizons", the processes analysed range from strategies of sustainable development or land-use planning processes which are – more or less by definition – expected to take a long-term perspective to the very ad hoc revamping of legal and institutional frameworks following political crises. The following sub-sections will unearth the overall character of expert involvement in the case studies.

Relative weight of experts and expertise

A first aspect relevant to understanding the overall character of expert involvement is the relative weight that experts and expertise have in political processes. In principle, political processes can be located on a theoretical continuum between purely *expert-driven* processes on the one extreme and purely *politics-driven* processes on the other extreme. The case studies fall – as most real-world processes – somewhere in between those two extremes and, thus, serve the rationalities of both science and politics. Most cases tend towards the politics rather than the expertise end of the spectrum. None of the cases can be characterized as a purely or even predominantly expert-centered process. But at the same time, experts of different backgrounds have been involved at different levels in almost all the processes. For example, the Norwegian Living Forests process can be seen as a paragon in the use of expertise. Experts of different backgrounds have been involved at different levels throughout the process. Nevertheless, it cannot be called an expert-driven process as it was clearly marked by a political tug-of-war especially between environmental and economic

Table 2.1 Brief characterization of GoFOR case studies

Case title	Brief characterization
Austrian Implementation Strategy for the Convention on Biological Diversity	National strategy process mainly driven by international obligations
Austrian Forest Dialogue	Participatory and sector-integrated national strategy process
Implementation of the Habitats Directive in Denmark	National implementation of EU policy
National Park Pilot Projects in Denmark	Participatory planning processes at regional level as non-binding input to policy formulation at national level
Territorial Forest Charters in France	Participatory and sector-integrated strategic planning approach at the regional level
Relief Plan for Forests in France	*Ad hoc* governmental assistance programme in the aftermath of devastating storms
Integrated Rural Development policies in Germany (with three embedded sub-cases): • LEADER + • REGIONEN AKTIV • Joint Task "Improvement of Agricultural Structures and Coastal Protection" (GAK)	Integration of new policy approach (regional governance) in three programs: • EU pilot programme for sustainable rural development • national pilot programme for sustainable rural development • mainstream funding instrument of agricultural policy
Restructuration of management agencies for protected areas in Greece	Reorganization of administration and management of protected areas mainly driven by EU policies
National Forest Programme Hungary	Participatory and sector-integrated national strategy process
Norwegian Living Forests Project	Participatory and sector-integrated strategy process initiated and promoted by private actors
"Nature for People, People for Nature" program in the Netherland	Formulation and implementation of strategic policy document
Nature policy in the Groene Woud area, NL	Long-term policy development around nature conservation
Nature policy in the Utrechtse Heuvelrug area, NL	Same as above
Anti-corruption policies in Romania	Policy formulation and implementation driven by international obligations and pressures
Implementation of *Acquis Communautaire* in Nature Protection Policies in Romania	National implementation of EU policy
Forest Policy General Plan of Catalonia, Spain	Participatory and sector-integrated regional strategy process

Source: Compiled by authors.

interests. In this context, experts and expertise have been mobilized for different purposes (Ouff *et al.* 2008).

Only few case studies were explicitly framed as "technical" processes or were otherwise dominated by scientific reasoning. From the set of case studies, especially the implementation of the EU Habitats Directive (Council Directive 92/43/EEC), which was investigated in three countries (Denmark, Greece, and Romania), falls into this category. In Greece, management and administration of the protected area network has been firmly in the hands of public administration with numerous scientific committees and individual experts giving input on science-laden questions (Papageorgiou *et al.* 2008). Similarly in Denmark and Romania, the implementation of the Directive has been characterized by extensive use of expertise in the policy process (Boon *et al.* 2009a; Bancu 2007). The great degree of expert involvement in the implementation of the Habitats Directive seems to be mainly attributable to the highly "technical" character of this EU directive (Alphandery and Fortier 2001). In the course of implementation, however, expert opinions have frequently been broken up along the lines of conflict of the underlying political cleavages (especially between nature conservationists and land-users).

The majority of governance cases studied can be classified as *"political"* processes where expertise played a minor (but nevertheless clearly identifiable) role. In some processes, expert input was brought in solely in the form of commissioned studies dealing with rather specific, technical questions. Scientists and other experts were represented in a number of political bodies (in a wider sense) but the underlying political processes, in most cases, were still operating more or less in a *modus operandi* that can be characterized as political deliberation or negotiation.

Linking of expertise and politics in the course of policy processes

Having seen that in none of the case studies experts and expertise played an outstanding and dominant role but that, on the other hand, all 16 cases left some room for expert involvement, it is interesting to ask how expertise and politics have been sequentially linked in the course of political decision-making processes. In the science–policy literature, this linking is typically represented in a dichotomy between two ideal-type models: decisionism and technocracy. In the decisionist model, which goes back to the sociologist Max Weber, politicians should have the ultimate authority in determining policy whereas experts are confined to selecting the most appropriate means by which the politicians' goals could be attained, and for their efficient implementation ("science on tap") (Hulme 2009: 100 ff.). In the technocratic model, which goes back to Helmut Schelsky, scientific rationality is (or in a normative reading: should be) the guiding principle for political decisions; responsibility for policy making should be assigned to experts, since only they possess relevant knowledge and objectivity ("science on top") (Millstone 2007).

The Danish National Park Pilot Process, which aimed at identifying options for establishing national parks in Denmark, is a good example of a decisionist setup. The process was initiated by the Minister of Environment who sketched out rough guidelines for the organization of the pilot projects to the counties and municipalities. The subsequent local processes were marked by extensive participation of landowners and other local stakeholders, but also expert knowledge was attributed a significant role (Boon *et al.* 2009b; Lund 2009).

The process around the French Territorial Forestry Charters (CFTs) is another example for decisionism (Buttoud and Kouplevatskaya-Yunusova 2007; Kouplevatskaya-Buttoud 2009). Here, state actors were complemented by non-state actors to set the political guidelines for subsequent "technical" implementation. In the creation of this new policy instrument political aspects have been dominant with politicians and timber producers (and their representatives) driving the processes. In the implementation phase different types of expertise were mobilized, e.g. traditional forest specialists' expertise, local actors' insider knowledge, and scientific expertise.

At first sight, there is no example of the contrasting "technocratic" model in the set of case studies. This might be attributable to the fact that technocratic ideas and ideals are hardly ever called for or even explicitly spelled out in the political discourse. Millstone, however, notes that "[n]owadays, explicit and enthusiastic endorsements are rarely articulated by policy-makers or by policy analysts, but whenever policies are represented as if based on, and only on, 'sound science' then technocratic assumptions are implicitly being relied upon." (Millstone 2007: 488)

But also measured against this more differentiated perspective, the case studies provide little evidence for technocracy. In some cases, as for example the implementation of Natura 2000, one sees a rather strong influence of experts, but the setup is still far from genuine technocracy since experts rarely have other resources than their knowledge to convince policy makers (Lund 2009) and since the problem framings of scientists are – often fiercely and successfully – contested by alternative problem framings of societal stakeholders.

Institutional integration of expertise and politics

A third aspect relevant to describe the overall character of expert involvement in governance cases is the institutional integration of expertise and politics. Basically, expert advice processes can be located on a theoretical continuum between experts being fully part of political bodies, on the one hand, and expert bodies and political bodies being strictly separated, on the other hand. Under the first model, which could be called the "absorption model", scientists are fully integrated into a political body and the scientific logic is subordinated under the logic of politics. The second model, which could be named the "separation model", makes great effort to divide "technical" issues from "political" ones. Here typically, "expert working groups" focus on the former while "policy groups" deal with the latter (Farrell *et al.* 2001; Pregernig 2004).

In the set of governance cases studied the integration of science and expertise into policy processes neither fully corresponds to the absorption nor to the separation model, but rather constitutes a mixture of the two models. In most processes one finds "mixed" bodies in which policy makers, administrative officers, interest group representatives, and scientists have been sitting side by side without a clear separation of roles. Examples of such integrated bodies are the Austrian National Biodiversity Commission, the National Scientific Natura 2000 Committee and regional Park Boards in Greece, and the Editor Board in charge of the Catalonian General Plan of Forest Policy. In those bodies, scientists and other experts cooperated "at arm's length" with political actors. The role of scientists has not been exclusively restricted to providing expert inputs while also policy makers (in the widest sense) have contributed to the knowledge base on which negotiation processes could build upon. In only a few cases experts were kept in a more peripheral position.

Political functions of experts and expertise

Science and expertise can fulfill various functions in governance processes. In the set of governance case studies, a number of different functions could be found. The following is an empirically derived typology of functions coming out of our analysis of 16 governance processes.

1 First, experts have, of course, provided *content-wise input* into policy processes. Numerous examples for that could be found in the set of governance cases studied. In almost all case studies, experts gave input in the form of written reports, in hearings, or by actively participating in expert bodies.
2 In some governance processes, experts have served as *(co-)producers of dominant discourses* or "schools of thought". By introducing innovative concepts or general approaches, experts could lay the foundations for or push ahead a governance process. For example, in German rural development policies, experts played a key role in developing and propagating the overall discourse on "Integrated Rural Development" as a "policy idea" (Giessen and Böcher 2008, 2009).
3 Experts have occasionally acted as *initiators* and *driving forces* in the early phases of governance processes. Experts as "policy entrepreneurs" helped to generate, design, and implement innovative ideas in the public domain. In Austria and Hungary, for example, university scientists assisted in bringing the idea of developing a "National Forest Program" (NFP) on the political agenda.
4 In many case studies, experts have performed special organizational or procedural tasks, especially acting as *consultants on process-related questions*. In the Hungarian and the Catalonian Forest Program processes scientific experts were involved in the overall design of the processes and acted as general coordinators and organizers. In the Austrian NFP, scientists were involved in formulating the "code of conduct" for the dialogue process and, later, also served as co-moderators in working group sessions.

5   Especially in the context of political dialogue processes and strategy formulation processes, experts have frequently functioned as *builders of political consensus*. By acting as mediators or interest brokers, experts' knowledge could contribute to overcome conflicts of interest between different political actor groups and thus lay the ground for subsequent participation and negotiation processes. It seems, for example, that the main purpose of the mobilization of expertise in the Norwegian Living Forests process was to create a common and legitimate point of departure for consensus preceding the actual negotiations of the policy document (Ouff *et al.* 2008)

6   In a number of case studies, experts have played a role as *creators of political arguments and counter arguments*. In some instances, experts deliberately provided political actor groups with "suitable" arguments to make their point in political deliberations; in other instances, political actors used – some would say misused – scientific studies to argue their case with the authors of those studies not having any influence on that.

7   Last but not least, one aspect that seems to be somewhat conspicuous for new governance processes is the heightened importance of *process reviews* and *evaluations* and the key role that experts play therein. In a number of case studies, scientific experts were involved in carrying out evaluations of the setup and/or outcomes of the respective processes. A possible reason for that could be that policy makers strive to legitimate their policies by including external, "neutral" authorities, and science seems to be perfectly apt to symbolize this neutrality (Pregernig *et al.* 2012).

Discussion: validity and usefulness of instrumental, strategic, and co-productionist perspectives

In the previous section, we have tried to substantiate in an empirical way what distinct roles and functions experts and expertise can play in environmental governance processes based on the analysis of 16 case studies on evolving practices of governance in various land-use related fields. In this section, our empirical findings will be linked back to the different conceptual lenses introduced in the previous section. Thereby, it should be possible to check the validity and usefulness of either taking an instrumental, a strategic or a co-productionist perspective on science–policy interactions.

From an *instrumental* perspective, expectations for the usefulness of advisory knowledge are high. Under the classical "knowledge transfer model", experts are brought into policy processes to impart their unique knowledge and wisdom to policy makers, and expert advice is, thus, believed to make a direct contribution to the increased effectiveness of political action. In a more "enlightened" reading, the strict assumption of direct, immediate use is given up. In the "knowledge diffusion model", scientific expertise is assumed to spread in a gradual way, and it can change decision-makers' conceptual thinking over time.

Science and expertise fulfilled various functions in the environmental governance processes analysed. Only the first function mentioned above, i.e. the content-wise input of expertise into policy processes, corresponds with the knowledge transfer model according to which expertise has a direct, cognitive impact on policy. The next two functions (framing of dominant discourses and policy initiation) find their correspondence in knowledge diffusion models which point to the fact that the use of scientific findings typically does not come in the form of direct but rather in the form of indirect, conceptual use. Both the transfer and the diffusion model still have in common that they take a rather technical-rationalist look at the role of science and expertise in social and political processes, and with that bring with it the danger of technocratization, that is science gaining too much influence on policy making.

In the set of case studies, science and expertise have frequently played a prominent role, nevertheless not in a narrower sense of any "scientification of politics", i.e. that scientific expertise is dominating or even replacing politics. As outlined above, none of the cases analysed can be characterized as an expert-centred process dominated by scientific reasoning, but most cases were predominantly influenced by "political" factors. So in general, the analysis of 16 governance cases does not provide too much evidence in support of the above-mentioned thesis of the "scientification of politics" and the related danger of "technocratization".

A possible explanation for that could be that these phenomena cannot be generalized to all policy settings and that the science–policy literature hitherto has looked at a different type of policy problems than the GoFOR project did. In the science–policy literature, the "scientification of politics" has typically been accounted for in a very special class of policy problems, namely problems characterized by a high degree of system uncertainties and high decision stakes (cf. the concept of "post-normal science" by Funtowicz and Ravetz 1993). Most of our case studies do not fall into this category. They do not, for example, deal with the adoption and implementation of cutting-edge technologies (like biotechnology or stem-cell research) but rather with different forms of land use which are, of course, sometimes contested but the consequences of which are more or less predictable. In addition, a number of case studies have looked at a special class of political processes, namely "strategy processes". With their long-term perspective this type of political process is probably more detached from pressing political questions which call for immediate political action; strategy processes somehow take a more "distanced" view on policy problems. In this type of setting political and societal actors have seemingly less incentive to draw on science as a problem-solver and/or a source of political legitimacy.

All in all, our research shows that in the governance cases studied expertise is actually brought in to a certain degree in an instrumental way, but that is still not leading to constellations where science replaces politics.

From a *strategic* perspective, science is no longer seen as the neutral conveyor of substantial truths but science and scientific knowledge are rather perceived as a resource of power for different political actors. In "group politics models" (Martin and Richards 1995), contending groups use scientific knowledge simply as an additional resource to increase their authority or legitimation.

In the list of functions that experts and expertise provided in the governance processes studied, at least three functions clearly reflect the strategic perspective: when experts perform special organizational or procedural tasks, such as acting as consultants on process-related questions; when experts function as builders of political consensus, e.g. by acting as mediators or interest brokers; and when experts serve as creators of political arguments that they provide – intentionally or unintentionally – to various political actor groups who use those arguments to make their point in political deliberations. The empirical relevance of these three functions can be identified in many of our cases. They clearly reflect the strategic role of science in politics in which expertise is seen mainly as a power resource for political actors who try to realize their interests by mobilizing "appropriate" expertise.

The third conceptual perspective on the interaction between science and politics is that of "*co-production*". In the broadest sense, co-production deals with the *interrelationship* between the realms of science and political action. Rather than presenting either science (as the instrumental perspective does) or politics as predominant (as the strategic perspective does), a co-productionist model avoids both political and scientific determinism (Irwin 2007). The concept of co-production calls for a more interactive accounting, in which expert knowledge and political order are co-produced through a common social project (Jasanoff and Wynne 1998).

The 16 governance case studies provide ample evidence for the validity of a co-productionist perspective. In most of the cases analysed, expertise and politics have been tightly interwoven. Inter-linkages could be seen with respect to three types of dimensions: procedural, institutional, and functional.

With regard to a *procedural* dimension, the governance processes analysed, especially the more expert-centred ones, demonstrate that scientific closure and political closure are not independent of each other but are rather co-produced. Scientific agreement on "facts" can, under certain circumstances, contribute to the settlement of a related political dispute; but this connection often is a fragile one, with momentous changes in the political environment, like a change of government, easily breaking this link again. As shown with the highly technical – if not to say technocratic – processes surrounding the creation of the EU nature conservation network Natura 2000, the problem framings of scientists, which have dominated the early designation phase, have often been fiercely – and successfully – contested by alternative problem framings of societal stakeholders, in the later phases of the programme's implementation.

With regard to an *institutional* dimension, aspects of co-production could particularly be seen in the organizational setups chosen. The institutionalization of expert advice often neither resembles the classical "absorption model", in which scientists are fully integrated into political bodies, nor the typical "separation model", in which science and politics are strictly kept apart. In most of the cases, science–policy advice has built on multipartite bodies made up of experts and policy makers that are capable, simultaneously, of negotiating differences regarding scientific and political questions. In those "mixed" bodies policy makers, administrative officers, interest group representatives, and scientists sit side by side without a clear separation of roles. In only a few cases, experts were kept in a more separated position.

With regard to a *functional* dimension, facets of co-production could mainly be discerned in the last of the functions listed above, i.e. scientists and experts serving as *process reviewers* and *evaluators* in new governance processes. From a rationalist-instrumental perspective, review and evaluation would be regarded as instruments for rational, effective and efficient policy formulation and implementation. Here, monitoring the progress of a policy, learning from evaluation results, and adapting accordingly, constitute the necessary feedback loop that closes the cycle of strategic management (Swanson *et al.* 2004). From a co-productionist perspective, in contrast, review and evaluation are not (only) seen as stimuli for policy change but are (also) perceived as symbols of acceptability, indicating transparency and administrative willingness to learn and, thus, being central to the legitimation of state and non-state actors (Power 2000; Pregernig *et al.* 2012). From this perspective, the credibility and legitimacy of governance processes and their "products" are co-produced by science and politics through a common social project. Here, the concept of co-production "offers new ways of thinking about power, highlighting the often invisible role of knowledge, expertise, technical practices and material objects in shaping, sustaining, subverting or transforming relations of authority" (Jasanoff 2004: 4).

Conclusions

There seems to be a scholarly consensus that science has come to play an increasingly influential role in policy making, especially in the field of environmental policy. In the political debate as well as in the scientific discourse the concept of the "*science–policy interface*" has become quite prominent in recent years (e.g. Engels 2005; Pereira *et al.* 2006; Lange and Garrelts 2007; Wardekker *et al.* 2008). While the current debate mostly perceives the interaction between science and policy making from a rather narrow, instrumental perspective often calling for or propagating "cookbook approaches" for linking science and policy in a more effective way, we strove with our analysis to broaden the debate. In this chapter, we asked two basic questions: first, we addressed the empirical question of what role science and expertise play in environmental governance processes; and second, we touched upon the analytical question of which conceptual perspectives are better apt to depict science–policy interactions in a governance context.

In regard to the first, empirical question, our analysis started out with the common expectation that in a governance context, science and expertise play distinct new roles that go beyond the mere content-wise input of scientific knowledge in political decision-making processes. In the 16 governance processes analysed, this expectation could be confirmed only in part. The case studies show that there is not *the one* function that experts and expertise play in governance processes but different types of experts fulfil a variety of strategic and instrumental functions. In the set of cases, experts played a strategic role when the expertise that they provided served as a power resource for political actors, but they also played an instrumental role when their scientific insights were more or less directly integrated into policies.

In regard to the second, conceptual question, our analysis also provides a mixed picture. Even though we found some empirical indications for scientists and scientific knowledge having a verifiable impact on political decisions, a purely *instrumental* perspective on the role of science in policy making is still insufficient. Scientists can no longer – and probably never could – simply do the science and hope that someone else uses the information to make "good policies" (Cortner *et al.* 1999). Our case studies showed that science–policy interactions can be better understood if the roles of experts and expertise are also viewed from a *strategic* perspective which better sensitizes for the fact that the political use of expertise is often dependent on political actors' interests which they try to realize by choosing and using the "right" source of expertise. Finally, also the *co-productionist* perspective adds to a more comprehensive understanding of processes of scientific policy advice as it highlights that processes of knowledge making and policy making are often mutually embedded and co-constituted. The concept of co-production calls for a more interactive accounting, in which expert knowledge and political order are co-produced through a common social project (Jasanoff and Wynne 1998).

So, by way of conclusion, it can be said that there is not a single conceptual framework which is apt to depict processes of science–policy interaction within European environmental governance in an encompassing and conclusive way. Each of the three conceptual perspectives introduced in this chapter focuses on specific aspects and, thus, each of the partial models only provides an incomplete description of the interaction between science and politics. But applied together in parallel they still give a sufficiently broad picture about the specifics of the role of science and expertise in European environmental governance.

Note

1 The GoFOR project was funded by the European Commission under the Sixth EU Framework Program for Research and Technological Development. More information on the project can be found at www.boku.ac.at/GoFOR. The authors wish to thank the GoFOR project partners for their valuable contributions.

References

Alphandery, P. and Fortier, A. 2001. "Can a Territorial Policy be Based on Science Alone? The System for Creating the Natura 2000 Network in France". *Sociologia Ruralis* 41(3): 311–28.

Bäckstrand, K., Khan, J., Kronsell, A. and Lövbrand, E. (eds). 2010. *Environmental Politics and Deliberative Democracy: Examining the Promise of New Modes of Governance*. Cheltenham, Northampton: Edward Elgar.

Bancu, D. 2007. "The Implementation Process of the *Acquis Communautaire* in the Nature Protection Policies in Romania". *GoFOR Main Assessment Report, July 2007*. Suceava: Forestry Faculty, University Stefan cel Mare.

Banthien, H., Jaspers, M. and Renner, A. 2003. "Governance of the European Research Area: The Role of Civil Society". Final Report, Bensheim, Berlin, Brussels: IFOK.

Beck, U. and Bonß, W. 1984. "Soziologie und Modernisierung: Zur Ortsbestimmung der Verwendungsforschung". *Soziale Welt* 35(4): 381–406.

Benz, A. and Papadopoulos, Y. (eds) 2006. *Governance and Democracy: Comparing National, European and International Experiences*. London: Routledge.

Bevir, M. 2011. "Governance as Theory, Practice, and Dilemma". In Bevir, M. (ed.). *The Sage Handbook of Governance*. Los Angeles: Sage: 1–16.

Boehmer-Christiansen, S. 1995. "Reflections on Scientific Advice and EC Transboundary Pollution Policy". *Science & Public Policy* 22(3): 195–203.

Boon, T. E., Lund, D. H. and Nathan, I. 2009a. "Implementation of the Habitats Directive in a Governance Perspective: The Case of Denmark". *Research Report 2-2009*. Vienna: Institute of Forest, Environmental, and Natural Resource Policy.

Boon, T. E., Lund, D. H. and Nathan, I. 2009b. "The National Park Pilot Process Introducing New Forms of Governance in Danish Nature Politics". *Research Report 1-2009*. Vienna: Institute of Forest, Environmental, and Natural Resource Policy.

Buttoud, G. and Kouplevatskaya-Yunusova, I. 2007. "Territorial Forestry Charters and Relief Plan for Forests". *GoFOR Main Assessment Report*. July 2007. Nancy: Laboratory of Forest Policy, French Institute for Environment and Life Sciences & Industries.

Cortner, H. J., Wallace, M. G. and Moote, M. A. 1999. "A Political Context Model for Bioregional Assessments". In Johnson, K., Swanson, F., Herring, M. and Greene, S. (eds.). *Bioregional Assessments: Science at the Crossroads of Management and Policy*. Washington, DC: Island Press: 71–82.

Engels, A. 2005. "The Science-Policy Interface". *Integrated Assessment* [Online] 5(1): 7–26.

Ezrahi, Y. 1980. "Utopian and Pragmatic Rationalism: The Political Context of Scientific Advice". *Minerva* 18(1): 111–31.

Farrell, A., VanDeveer, S. D. and Jäger, J. 2001. "Environmental Assessments: Four Under-Appreciated Elements of Design". *Global Environmental Change* 11(4): 311–33.

Fischer, F. 2001. "Beyond Technocratic Environmentalism: Citizen Inquiry in Sustainable Development". In Hisschemöller, M., Hoppe, R., Dunn, W. N. and Ravetz, J. R. (eds.). *Knowledge, Power, and Participation in Environmental Policy Analysis*. New Brunswick, London: Transaction: 29–45.

Fischer, F. 2003. *Reframing Public Policy: Discursive Politics and Deliberative Practices*. Oxford: Oxford University Press.

Funtowicz, S. O. and Ravetz, J. R. 1993. "Science for the Post-Normal Age". *Futures* 25 (7): 739–56.

Gieryn, T. F. 1995. "Boundaries of Science". In Jasanoff, S., Markle, G. E., Peterson, J. C. and Pinch, T. (eds.). *Handbook of Science and Technology Studies*. Thousand Oaks, London, New Delhi: Sage: 393–443.

Giessen, L. and Böcher, M. 2008. "Integrated Rural Development Policy in Germany and its Potentials for New Modes of Forest Governance". *Research Report 5-2008*. Vienna: Institute of Forest, Environmental, and Natural Resource Policy.

44   *Michael Pregernig and Michael Böcher*

Giessen, L. and Böcher, M. 2009. "Rural Governance, Forestry, and the Promotion of Local Knowledge: The Case of the German Rural Development Program 'Active Regions'". *Small-Scale Forestry* 8(2): 211–30.

Glynn, S., Cunningham, P. and Flanagan, K. 2003. "Typifying Scientific Advisory Structures and Scientific Advice Production Methodologies (TSAS): Final Report". PREST, Manchester: University of Manchester.

Guston, D. H. 2001. "Boundary Organizations in Environmental Policy and Science: An Introduction". *Science, Technology, and Human Values* 26(4): 399–408.

Hackett, E. J., Amsterdamska, O., Lynch, M. and Wajcman, J. (eds.). 2007. *The Handbook of Science and Technology Studies*. 3rd edn. Cambridge, MA, London: MIT Press.

Hisschemöller, M., Hoppe, R., Groenewegen, P. and Midden, C. J. H. 2001. "Knowledge Use and Political Choice in Dutch Environmental Policy: A Problem Structuring Perspective on Real Life Experiments in Extended Peer Review". In Hisschemöller, M., Hoppe, R., Dunn, W. N. and Ravetz, J. R. (eds.). *Knowledge, Power, and Participation in Environmental Policy Analysis*. New Brunswick, London: Transaction: 437–70.

Hogl, K., Kvarda, E., Nordbeck, R. and Pregernig, M. (eds) 2012. *Environmental Governance: The Challenge of Legitimacy and Effectiveness*. Cheltenham: Edward Elgar.

Hoppe, R. 2005. "Rethinking the Science–Policy Nexus: From Knowledge Utilization and Science Technology Studies to Types of Boundary Arrangements". *Poiesis & Praxis* 3(3): 199–215.

Hulme, M. 1990. *Why We Disagree About Climate Change. Understanding Controversy, Inaction and Opportunity*. Cambridge: Cambridge University Press.

Irwin, A. 2007. "STS Perspectives on Scientific Governance". In Hackett, E. J., Amsterdamska, O., Lynch, M. and Wajcman, J. (eds): *The Handbook of Science and Technology Studies*. 3rd edn. Cambridge, MA, London: MIT Press: 583–607.

Jasanoff, S. 1990. *The Fifth Branch: Science Advisers as Policymakers*. Cambridge, MA, London: Harvard University Press.

Jasanoff, S. 2004. "The Idiom of Co–production". In Jasanoff, S. (ed.). *States of Knowledge: The Co-production of Science and Social Order*. London: Routledge: 1–12.

Jasanoff, S. and Wynne, B. 1998. "Science and Decisionmaking". In Rayner, S. and Malone, E. L. (eds): *Human Choice and Climate Change. The Societal Framework 1*. Columbus, Ohio: Battelle Press. 1–87.

Jasanoff, S., Markle, G. E., Peterson, J. C. and Pinch, T. (eds.). 1995. *Handbook of Science and Technology Studies*. Thousand Oaks, London, New Delhi: Sage.

Juntti, M., Russel, D. and Turnpenny, J. 2009. "Evidence, Politics and Power in Public Policy for the Environment". *Environmental Science & Policy* 12(3): 207–15.

Kooiman, J. 2003. *Governing as Governance*. London et al.: Sage.

Kouplevatskaya-Buttoud, I. 2009. "Adaptation to Change and Re-designing of Governance Systems: Cases from Small-Scale Rural Forestry". *Small-scale Forestry* 8(2): 231–47.

Lange, H. and Garrelts, H. 2007. "Risk Management at the Science-Policy Interface: Two Contrasting Cases in the Field of Flood Protection in Germany". *Journal of Environmental Policy & Planning* 9(3): 263–79.

Liberatore, A. and Funtowicz, S. O. 2003. "'Democratising' Expertise, 'Expertising' Democracy: What Does this Mean, and Why Bother"? *Science & Public Policy* 30(3): 146–50.

Lund, D. H. 2009. "Metagovernance of the National Park Process in Denmark". *Local Environment* 14(3): 245–57.

Martin, B. and Richards, E. 1995. "Scientific Knowledge, Controversy, and Public Decision Making". In Jasanoff, S., Markle, G. E., Peterson, J. C. and Pinch, T. (eds) *Handbook of Science and Technology Studies*, 506–26. Thousand Oaks, London, New Delhi: Sage.

Mayntz, R. 2009. "Speaking Truth to Power: Leitlinien für die Regelung wissenschaftlicher Politikberatung". *Der moderne Staat* 2(1): 5–16.

Millstone, E. 2007. "Can Food Safety Policy-making be both Scientifically and Democratically Legitimated? If So, How?". *Journal of Agricultural and Environmental Ethics* 20(5): 483–508.

Neilson, S. 2001. *Knowledge Utilization and Public Policy Processes: A Literature Review*. Evaluation Unit, IDRC, Ottawa.

Oh, C. H. 1996. *Linking Social Science Information to Policy-making*. Greenwich, CT, London: Jai Press.

Ouff, S. M., Yttredal, E. R. and Halvorsen, L. J. 2008. "The Living Forests Process: A Laboratory for New Modes of Governance in Forest Policies". *Research Report*. 4-2008. Institute of Forest, Environmental, and Natural Resource Policy, Vienna.

Papageorgiou, K., Kassioumis, K. and Vakkas, M. 2008. "Restructuring of Management Bodies for Protected Areas in Greece". *Research Report* 3-2008. Institute of Forest, Environmental, and Natural Resource Policy, Vienna.

Pereira, Â. G., Vaz, S. G. and Tognetti, S. S. (ed.) 2006. *Interfaces between Science and Society*. Sheffield: Greenleaf Publishing.

Peters, B. G. 2000. "Governance and Comparative Politics". In Pierre, J. (ed.). *Debating Governance: Authority, Steering, and Democracy*. Oxford: Oxford University Press: 36–53.

Petschow, U., Rosenau, J. and von Weizsäcker, E. U. (eds.). 2006. *Governance and Sustainability: New Challenges for States, Companies and Civil Society*. Sheffield: Greenleaf Publishing.

Pielke, R. A. Jr 2004. "When Scientists Politicize Science: Making Sense of Controversy over The Skeptical Environmentalist". *Environmental Science and Policy* 7(5): 405–17.

Pielke, R. A. Jr 2007. *The Honest Broker: Making Sense of Science in Policy and Politics*. Cambridge: Cambridge University Press.

Pierre, J. 2000. "Introduction: Understanding Governance". In Pierre, J. (ed.). *Debating Governance: Authority, Steering, and Democracy*. Oxford: Oxford University Press: 1–10.

Power, M. 2000. "The Audit Society: Second Thoughts". *International Journal of Auditing* 4(1): 111–9.

Pregernig, M. 2004. "Linking Knowledge and Action: The Role of Science in NFP Processes". In Glück, P. and Voitleithner, J. (eds.). *NFP Research: Its Retrospect and Outlook*. Vienna: Institute for Forest Sector Policy and Economics: 195–215.

Pregernig, M. and Böcher, M. 2012. "Normative and Analytical Perspectives on the Role of Science and Expertise in Environmental Governance". In Hogl, K., Kvarda, E., Nordbeck, R. and Pregernig, M. (eds) *Environmental Governance: The Challenge of Legitimacy and Effectiveness*. Cheltenham: Edward Elgar: 199–219.

Pregernig, M., Hogl, K. and Nordbeck, R. 2012. "The Politics of Sustainability Evaluation: Analysis of Three Austrian Strategies for Sustainable Development". In Sedlacko, M. and Martinuzzi, A. (eds) *Governance by Evaluation for Sustainable Development: Institutional Capacities and Learning*. Cheltenham, Northampton: Edward Elgar: 21–44.

Price, D. K. 1981. "The Spectrum From Truth to Power". In Kuehn, T. J. and Porter, A. L. (eds.). *Science, Technology, and National Policy.* Ithaca, London: Cornell University Press: 95–131.

Swanson, D. A., Pintér, L., Bregha, F., Volkery, A. and Jacob, K. 2004. *National Strategies for Sustainable Development: Challenges, Approaches and Innovations in Strategic and Co-ordinated Action.* Berlin: IISD, GTZ.

Wardekker, J. A., van der Sluijs, J. P., Janssen, P. H. M., Kloprogge, P. and Petersen, A. C. 2008. "Uncertainty Communication in Environmental Assessments: Views from the Dutch Science-policy Interface". *Environmental Science & Policy* 11(7): 627–41.

Weingart, P. 1999. "Scientific Expertise and Political Accountability: Paradoxes of Science in Politics". *Science & Public Policy* 26(3): 151–61.

Weingart, P. 2002. "The Moment of Truth for Science. The Consequences of the "Knowledge Society" for Society and Science". *EMBO reports* 3(8): 703–6.

Weiss, C. 1980. "Knowledge Creep and Decision Accretion". *Knowledge: Creation, Diffusion, Utilization* 1(3): 381–404.

3 A third industrial revolution?

Martin Jänicke and Klaus Jacob

Introduction

Concepts of a far reaching system transformation of industrialism in order to meet the challenges of scarcity of resources, environmental degradation and climate change have been taken up as a normative concept by many politicians and academics throughout the world (e.g. Barroso 2007; Gabriel 2006; Jackson 2010; Köhler 2009; Asian Academies of Science 2011; UNEP 2011; OECD 2011; World Bank 2012). Without question: industrial mass production based on cheap raw materials, which became the dominant economic and societal model in the twentieth century and fundamentally changed the face of the world, has indeed reached its critical limits. Fossil fuels played a specific role in the development of industrialism, lending an immense and steadily increasing productivity to labor since the first industrial revolution. Fossil fuels profoundly changed the technological and economic conditions for transport, production and consumption. However, there are many indications that this era is coming to an end: the impacts of fossil fuels on the environment and climate have proven to be destructive. Furthermore, the scarcity of oil is becoming evident in the skyrocketing of prices. Resource-intensive mass production in general is subject to massive pressure towards innovation. At the same time, technological breakthroughs regarding the utilization of renewable energies have been achieved. The unexpectedly strong growth of renewable energies and eco-efficient technologies are the most visible manifestations of an upheaval.

In this chapter, we analyse how the long-term development of industrial production could look under these circumstances. In particular we explore the challenges for the governance of such transformation. We argue that the current dynamics can be compared with the previous industrial revolutions. We underline that such transformations are not limited to shifts in dominant technologies, but that they have to be seen as comprehensive societal changes. We also argue that the transformation is likely to emerge from specific countries which take the lead on this. The old industrialised countries are increasingly challenged by the new emerging economies. However, it is quite open whether the new economies will take over the lead in the transformation towards green industrialism. Europe also has excellent perspectives if it keeps its leading role in setting the pace of environmental and in particular climate policies.

The concept of "Industrial Revolution"

The term "Third Industrial Revolution" (see also Schellnhuber 2007; Hawken *et al.* 2008; Rifkin 2008) refers to a comprehensive upheaval, which was already labeled by other authors as a "green industrial revolution", "efficiency revolution" and a fundamental transformation towards "green capitalism" (Schmidheiny 1992; von Weizsäcker, Lovins *et al.* 1997; Hawken, Lovins *et al.* 1999, McKinsey 2011). The IEA (2008) advocates a global "energy technology revolution", McKinsey (2011) a "resource revolution". Such contributions sometimes refer to the "Great transformation" as described by Polanyi (1944).

The term industrial revolution is taken up by politicians as well: US President Obama postulated a "green energy revolution". Similarly, the term has been used by the president of the European Commission, Manuel Barosso, the former German president Koehler, and others. Some authors have used the term "industrial revolution" without addressing the environment as a central theme. (e. g. Greenwood 1999; Freeman and Louca 2001). These different contributions all stress the radical nature of both the necessary and possible technical change. Furthermore, they all share an expectation of phases of abrupt change, which will subsequently be followed by a new equilibrium. These contributions are marked by two different concepts of the term "Industrial Revolution". Whereas a narrow understanding only refers to the change of the energy base and the related technologies, the broader understanding includes the expectation of comprehensive changes in energy base, technological systems, ecological and social conditions and the role of governments.

In our understanding, "Industrial Revolution" should be perceived as a radical and abrupt but also long-lasting ("secular") change at all levels of society: It refers to the leading industrial sectors, to the regions in which these sectors are dominant, to workers and their qualification employed in these sectors, and their institutional context. It is not limited to single technologies only, but affects comprehensive "innovation cluster" (Grübler 1998; Mokyr 1999). Reciprocal initiation, multiplication and acceleration effects within the cluster lead to economic growth, employment and a broad modernization of national economies. Industrial revolutions have always had a critical preceding phase in which traditional technologies and production methods depleted their potential for further improvements while new technologies were developed. In this phase, both radically new technical and social inventions entered the stage which lead in the course of the transformation to a radical "paradigm change" and afterwards enable a stable development over a longer period. Thus, industrial revolutions are also the result of radically innovative answers to development crises in the global economy.

Innovations are core to the long-term development of industries and the industrial structure of an economy. What are the driving forces of innovation which lead to disruptive changes? The theory of development in long waves developed by Kontradieff and Schumpeter is core to an explanation. Both refer to the introduction of the steam engine as the initial point of industrialization. "Long waves" refer to cyclical fluctuations of growth rates, which are linked to a broad spectrum of fundamental innovations, and are not restricted to the energy sector. As early as the 1920s, Kondratieff (1926), using statistical analysis of economic data, identified long-term growth cycles with a length of 40–60 years in industrialized countries. What was remarkable about this finding was that the author was only able to analyse a few countries and could not yet identify three completed "long waves" since the beginning of industrialization. At the end of the 1930s, Joseph Schumpeter continued the work and after detecting a downturn of the third wave since the early period of industrialization (including the crash of 1929), he began to speak of "Kondratieff cycles". Schumpeter and later Gerhard Mensch (1975) explained the cycles with basic innovations such as the steam engine. Such innovations and their market exploitation show typical phases of innovation, before in the last phase all potentials for improvement and cost reduction have been exploited and a new cycle begins. In the 1980s, the conditions of the socio-political framework were increasingly drawn upon as an additional explanation (overview in Huber 1985). Similarly, another, now fifth, Kondratieff "wave" is assumed to be behind the positive development of the global economy since the beginning of the 1990s (Freeman and Louca 2001). It is questionable whether this approach can explain different regional and sector-specific dynamics. However, the proven statistical regularities of long-term growth fluctuations and the high plausibility of its theoretical explanation offer an important basis for estimating industrial cycles and their need for action.

Apart from the Kontradieff cycles, numerous other suggestions for categorizing and dividing long-term transitions can be found in the literature. These terms are especially meaningful if they define the relevant differences between the transitions. Transitions which affect the energy and resource base of the economy are a subset of the identified Kontradieff cycles and the underlying technological paradigm. However, such transitions have an enormous impact on all aspects of the economy and society. The term "industrial revolutions" may be justified for this. So far, two industrial revolutions can be identified, and we are currently witnessing a third revolution of this kind. The new production methods, means of transportation, raw material, energy base, and social changes of the First Industrial Revolution in the eighteenth century are very different from the mass production, mass communication and mass democracy of the Second Industrial Revolution in the twentieth century, with its development of electrification, motorization, chemicalization, and use of concrete. Exactly these modes of industrial production have become shaky since the end of the twentieth century. The limitations of the fossil energy base, which carried the first two industrial revolutions, has become apparent. The fact that clear alternatives have already been heralded justifies the concept of another, third, industrial revolution, thus emphasizing the growing urgency of this transformation and the dramatic need for political steering.

The need for political intervention to steer the direction and the pace of transitions can be derived from the rich literature on ecological modernization. Numerous case studies have demonstrated that environmental innovations can be economically successful, but that they require initially strong political intervention and support to be successful over the existing resource intensive technologies (e.g. Jänicke *et al.* 2000; Jacob *et al.* 2005; Jänicke 2008; Jänicke 2012a). (Table 3.1)

The current crisis of resource intensive growth extends beyond the current capabilities of markets and civil society to manage the crisis. The time horizon of the markets, their inabilities to develop radical innovations and the limitations of civil society in providing sufficient incentives to overcome this market failure requires a radical change in the framework conditions for markets. This also applied to the first two industrial revolutions. The first one, through its new requirements of free trade, property rights, market development and societal division of labor increased the pressure for the creation of the rule of law and the political participation of citizens and the bourgeoisie ("liberal revolution"). The second – with its transition to mass production – necessitated a minimum of social standards and thus, social redistribution ("social revolution") occurred. With the introduction of social security systems the social costs of industrial labor, which had previously been largely externalized, were internalized or

Table 3.1 From the first to the third industrial revolution

	1st Industrial Revolution: approx. 1780-	2nd Industrial Revolution: approx. 1890-	3rd Industrial Revolution approx. 1990-
Dominant technology and raw material	Steam engine, power loom, iron processing	Electricity, chemistry, combustion engine, assembly line, synthetic materials	ICT, microelectronics, new materials, renewable raw materials, cleaner technology, bio-technology, recycling.
Dominant energy source	Coal	Coal, oil, nuclear power	renewable energies, energy efficiency
Transport/ communication	Railway, telegraphy	Car, airplane, radio, TV	High-speed railway systems, internet, mobile telecommunication
Society/state	'Bourgeoisie', freedom of trade, constitutional state	Mass production, mass society, parliamentary democracy, welfare state	Civil society, globalization, global governance
Core countries	UK, Belgium, Germany, France	USA, Japan, Germany	EU, China, USA, Japan

Source: Compiled by authors.

compensated to a certain degree. As a result, purchasing power emerged, which in turn allowed for vast growth.

The emergence of both the liberal state and the welfare state were characterized by serious conflicts, expressed by parties, social groups and ideologies. An important part of these conflicts was a re-evaluation of physical and human capital: Innovations regularly devalue investments, resources, and skills connected to them. Often those who are negatively affected fight against these changes politically.

Similarly, the Third Industrial Revolution is not only a broad wave of innovation potentially accompanied by welfare effects. It is about typical innovation conflicts. Economic sectors, which have defined the exploitation of natural resources as their commercial basis, have come under strong pressure. They perceive this threat to be the competitive resource-saving and environmentally friendly technologies currently favored by civil society actors and regulatory measures. At the same time compared to the innovators, the old sectors often have an advantage in terms of political influence, which they were able to gather in the previous boom phase. That is why "old industries" are often quite powerful. However, with the increasing technical and economic maturity of competing technologies, the political pressure on the affected sectors will increase, and in the end the capital flows reorient themselves in favor of new technologies. Continuing to generate electricity from coal, to promote nuclear power, and to disregard energy-saving and environmental protection in the automobile industry clearly show that there are relentless influential advocates for the conventional model of growth. These advocates are avoiding the pressure of innovation – sometimes with political support.

All industrial revolutions were accompanied by the development of new functions and capacities of the state apparatus. The Second Industrial Revolution, for example, was connected with the extension of national state activity and public finance. This tendency was embodied in "Wagner's law", which was the remarkable long-term forecast of an "increased need for state activity" (Wagner 1893). Social core functions have been added to the economic core functions of the liberal state, both functions being represented also in the structure of interest groups and the political party spectrum.

Since the 1970s in industrialized countries and the 1990s on a global level, a third basic state function in addition to the core economic and social duties has emerged. This new undertaking is in many countries even anchored in the constitution: the protection of the natural bases of human life. In this sense many industrialized countries and the EU have taken important steps towards an "environmental state". This movement again is grounded in the political party spectrum as well as in the social institutional arrangement – German environmental organizations have nearly as many members as the trade unions (Jänicke 2007). Pioneering states which are leaders in this respect participate more intensively in international political processes and have political systems that tend to be more open towards new interests. Interestingly enough, these states are also more competitive on a global scale (Esty and Porter 2000).

All three industrial revolutions also represent significant gains in importance of the global market. Already in the Communist Manifesto (1948) it had been stated that the big industries were the ones that created the global market. Industrialization in its current state was only possible by building infrastructures that could transport energy sources, raw materials and final goods to and from remote areas of the world at low prices unimaginable until then. The emergence of an international (however fragmented) legal system is connected with this globalization, and through standardization, regulation of cash and commodity flows, etc., it represents another functional basis for global markets. These regional and international regimes are increasingly including environmental standards.

At the same time, shifts of dominant countries and regions occur during the long-term cycles of industrial growth, a phenomenon which resulted in the theories of the "rise and decline of nations" (e.g. Olson 1982). The important centers of economic development in the early period of industrial development were England, Germany, France the Netherlands, and later Belgium. The USA took a central role in the technological dynamic with the Second Industrial Revolution. After the Second World War, Japan with its automobile, electrical and electronic industry also became one of the most important countries, shaping mass production and consumption.

There are high expectations for China and India in the third growth cycle. The success of countries and regions cannot be explained by their innovation activities only. In fact, in previous industrial revolutions, the innovations which cause the economic boom in a country, were not necessarily developed in that country. Even the pioneers of industrialization in England introduced inventions that were developed in France and Germany but not successfully merchandised there. The Japanese industrial strategy of the 1950s and 1960s of *reverse engineering* is another good example of the successful early adoption and marketing of foreign innovations (Okimoto 1990). These examples show that it is not only the ingenuity of the invention that is relevant for their success, but also the general economic and political framework. A suitable example of this may be China, which seems to be studying technological developments in Western industrialized societies while building its own industries domestically. The research, development, and testing of new technologies are often left to the industrial centers of Western Europe, North America or Japan.

Challenges of a "Third Industrial Revolution"

After a long-term decline since the first oil crisis (1973) the growth rates of the global economy have increased significantly since the 1990s. This has been expected by advocates of long-term cycles with reference to Kondratieff (Mensch 1975; Prognos Schröder *et al.* 1982; Wallerstein 1983). The basic innovations for a long-term cycle are also visible – especially in the area of renewable energies, energy autarky buildings and recycling technologies. As early as the beginning of the 1970s, innovative concepts towards a knowledge-intensive, resource and environmentally friendly production method were presented (MITI 1974), which are only now starting to be broadly accepted (SRU 2008). However, so far, this development is nothing more than an opportunity. Unless the innovation process and the economic dynamics are given a direction towards environmentally friendly and resource saving technologies, and unless the speed of the technical change is accelerated, the economic and ecological problems of resource-intensive mass production will not be overcome. In addition, the required scale of innovation exceeds previous experiences in the area of climate, energy, and resources as well as the existing steering capacities of states and companies.

The recessions (1975, 1982, 1993, 2009) during the previous decades have demonstrated that the production methods of the twentieth century have reached their limits, both economically and ecologically (strikingly addressed by Meadows, Meadows *et al.* 1972). Support for this conclusion has dramatically increased due to the alarming climate change and the renewed energy price explosion. This situation can be compared to the challenge facing Western democracies during the Second World War and their tremendous achievements defending themselves against a deadly aggression. The increasingly unequal income distribution further strengthens the general demand for change.

However, these challenges are also accompanied by opportunities and an impressive potential for innovation (see Part 4). Instead of former anarchic and crisis-driven, destructive upheavals we are now – for the first time – looking at the possibility of a targeted, politically enforced and structured change on a broad social basis and at all levels of the global system. Such an organized transition would meet the economic, environmental and the social challenges, which are causal for such a transition. It requires however, sufficient steering capacities. These aspects will be discussed in greater detail in the following.

Economic challenges: resource scarcity and increasing environmental cost

The economic risks of resource scarcity are meanwhile receiving attention of the mainstream economic policies – possibly the OECD Green Growth Strategy is the most visible indication for this. Also, the high economic dynamics of the newly industrialized countries are impacting the development of prices: oil, copper, and steel are spectacular examples. Similar demand and price surges are expected for other raw materials in the near future. The recent economic crisis relaxed the situation for some time and declines can be expected at least temporarily. Nevertheless, markets react to long-term scarcities of raw materials and fossil energies. Resource efficiency becomes imperative for economic development, and is an indicator of success in the competition for innovations.

Even with renewable raw materials we can see limits of availability: The land-use competition between food and bio-fuels is just one example. The extension of farmland at the expense of unspoiled natural lands another. However, the struggle for land is not limited to competition between food and fuels alone. Renewable raw materials play an ever-greater role in the production of chemicals. Traditional users of biotic raw materials, be it the paper, furniture or building industries, are also interested in growth.

The scarcity of water is another limiting factor for further economic growth. According to the UN Global International Water Assessment (UNEP and GIWA 2006) the availability of water will dramatically shrink due to changes in land use, climate change, pollution, overuse of drinking water, and further increases in industrial and agricultural demand in many parts of the world. Steppe formation and desertification are expected in numerous regions, which further increase the strain on the remaining fertile areas. Already current weather events have repeatedly devastated the food resources of many countries and regions. The scarcity of sinks for environmental pollutants presents the discernible limit to economic growth. Environmental costs threaten to neutralize economic gains in wealth. In countries like China, but also in Spain, the overuse of natural capital is a perceptible limit to economic development.

Ecological challenges: climate change and critical loss of natural capital

Global assessments of the state of the environment show that the carrying capacity of the Earth in many regions, and the impacts of climate change on a global level have reached critical (UNEP 2012, IPCC 2007). The OECD explicitly has supported the statement, that three of 10 "Planetary boundaries" have already been surpassed (OECD 2011). Yet, the deterioration of the environmental situation is not a steady development. Instead, there are "tipping points" – at which point limits are exceeded, and developments possessed of an incalculable and volatile self-perpetuating momentum are set in motion. The drying out of the Amazon Basin, the melting of the Antarctic ice, the cease of the Gulf Stream and the melting of the permafrost in Siberia with large-scale emissions of embedded methane are all critical areas affected by such self re-enforcing feedback mechanisms.

The United Nations Millennium Ecosystem Assessment in 2005 concluded that most of the ecosystem services are in a state of advanced or continuous degradation (Millennium Ecosystem Assessment 2005). Central functions of nature, essential to both the preservation of life and economic systems, seem to be threatened. We live from the very substance of the planet itself.

All of the current major assessments of the state of the environment, in spite of the regional differences, expect a serious global economic-ecological crisis and are calling for major changes to avoid the economic impacts. The costs of the damage due to climate change, including loss of biodiversity and natural resources, were calculated global GDP will decrease by 5–20 percent according to the Stern Report (Stern 2007) and by an additional 6 percent until 2050 due to global deforestation (European Communities 2008). Despite the judgment of the accuracy of the calculation of costs for this global environmental change there can be no doubt that the resource-intensive growth pattern of the Second Industrial

Revolution, particularly when its counterproductive economic effects are taken into account, cannot be sustained.

Social challenges: supporting the processes of modernization with social policy

The Second Industrial Revolution at the beginning of the twentieth century allowed mass production to be accompanied by mass income, which supported the requisite trend of demand. As a result, a radical change of income distribution, the introduction of union rights and social security were necessary; these often emerged after political upheavals, such as in many European countries in 1918. The worldwide development of mass markets from the 1950s onwards, led to a rapid increase in the use of natural resources and emission releases. The promises of freedom through mobility, home ownership, and other symbols of the "Western" economic miracle have spread worldwide–up to the limits of natural resources that now have become visible.

The internalization of social costs of labor with the help of social security systems gave a strong incentive to reduce the labor factor. This was accompanied by a rapid development of labor productivity which caused structural unemployment in the twentieth century. Economic crises and their social impacts not only pose a threat to mass purchasing power, but also often deter the acceptance of more ambitious efforts to protect the environment and resources. Furthermore, a broad redistribution at the expense of those with lower incomes has been pushed through in the name of globalization. The question of fairness in the distribution of wealth and resources is also relevant to the fact that the increasing consumption of luxury goods (e.g. vehicles) is linked to additional environmental pollution. The age pyramid of developed industrialized countries also creates critical challenges for social security systems. Another challenge of the twenty-first century is the dramatically increasing knowledge intensity of production in the face of critical deficits in human capital.

At the same time, the necessary change does not come without a price. The transformation causes a collision of conventional perspectives of development and growth in traditional economic branches. Traditional business sectors, their investments, their employees, and their skills are in danger of being questioned due to the rise in energy and raw material prices, and more demanding standards. In the long-term renewable energies and renewable raw materials are potential sources of prosperity. Yet, the necessary funds for development threaten to aggravate current inequality. The costs of environmental pollution and the costs of solutions could easily be dumped on those social classes, which only have a limited opportunity to raise concerns (Weidner 2007). This does not only threaten the acceptance of environmental policy but also the long-term purchasing power of lower socio-economic classes. Thus, the broad acceptance of comprehensive industrial modernization also has to be secured on a socio-political level.

Excessive demands on the steering mechanisms

The first two industrial revolutions were characterized by a profound change of the concept of statehood. The present industrial revolution again represents fundamental changes in the political system and ways to respond to newly emerged problems and claims. This could already by observed in the multi-level-system of global politics, especially since the 1990s (e.g. the proliferation of international agreements following the UN summit in Rio 1992). But the extend of the challenges and the resistance of conventional interests show an excessive demand on steering mechanisms. This is demonstrated by striking contradictions in the area of climate protection. On the one hand, the global public and politicians acknowledge the warnings of the scientific community on climate change, most recently since the 4th IPCC report (2007). At the same time many countries invest primarily in coal-power and investments in energy-efficiency and renewable energies remain at a low level in many countries. Although most states have institutionalized environmental targets, they are mostly in a weaker position compared to the liberal rights of economic actors. In general, there is now a broad societal consensus that environmental protection is needed, but in reality, when there is a conflict of interest decisions are often made at the expense of the environment. So far, environmental policy has rather focused on "win-win" situations in which efficiency gains and environmental benefits can also be obtained from a microeconomic perspective.

The particular difficulties of environmental policy – limited capacity for intervention in the case of private property, spatial and temporal divergence of cause and effect in the case of environmental problems, and the difficulty in coordinating players from different political fields and operational levels – have created numerous policy innovations that extend the capacity for action. Environmental policy, with its new forms of policy innovation and new instruments, is a prime example when it comes to political modernization in advanced countries (Jacob, Feindt *et al.* 2007). This includes the significance of calculable target-setting, the internationalization of environmental policy, the inclusion of private players and the development of new market-based and regulative instruments (Jänicke 2007). While the areas of modern environmental policy are broadened, the complexity of actor constellation has dramatically increased. Therefore, the question of final responsibility and accountability for decisions has become critical. Nation states, both individually and collectively, can assert that they have adopted a responsible role, but their role in the European and global context is not clear so far.

By and large, the challenges of the Third Industrial Revolution prove to be challenges for governmental and societal steering. The radical change requires (1) competent and globally networked governments capable of strategic action, (2) informed voters and consumers open to innovation, (3) a significantly higher degree of readiness for innovation on the part of companies and national economies, and (4) a highly productive national system of innovation. These prerequisites first need to be met.

Competent and strategic governments

The Third Industrial Revolution requires multi-level political systems with an extraordinary capacity to act. It is first and foremost a matter for states, as there is no alternative to their legitimate powers and responsibility to pursue long-term public interests. Even though governments have more and more become active players at the international level, it does not change their importance as legitimate national players. States still possess considerable resources and expertise. In a crisis, the population always holds the state responsible first. Nevertheless, there is a lack of necessary strategic capability. Such capabilities are the ability of states to establish long-term public interest policies in spite of short-term special interests. Short-term special interests are often concerns of traditional industries and social groups which consider the long-term change to be a threat. Such persistent interests often have attained an influential position, which innovative new sectors have not yet been able to achieve. In fact, large shares of the Green Economy remain invisible, as it is absorbed by the traditional sectors of machinery, car industry, chemicals, energy, etc. Technologies for renewable energies are nowadays well accounted, while the vast majority of efficiency technology is not subject to national accounting. Thereby, there are also hardly reliable data on employment in the new green technologies, while traditional sectors, which are well represented in official statistical accounts are still able to claim alleged job losses because of environmental policies.

Thus, in many countries providers of fossil fuels are capable of hindering an active climate policy. Innovations are ambivalent processes during which innovators face the resistance of the "dinosaurs", or established interests. There is no other explanation for the remarkably slow innovation process in the areas of eco-efficient technologies over the last 30 years (Jänicke 2012). In many states the conditions for action are impaired due to unsolved social problems which dominate public awareness, such as unemployment. This has worsened following the financial crisis. Also, in many places the role of the commercial media hampers an adequate understanding of the need for intervention measures in energy policy. Long-term policy orientation is a challenge for the traditional policy inclination towards short-term economic and political cycles.

A policy that affects people's lives and interests must be able to legitimize its interventions and distinguish between different protected commodities. Democratic governments often succumb to self-restriction which was created two centuries ago to protect private actors against the absolute state. Another common obstacle effective worldwide is the neo-liberal doctrine of "deregulation", "denationalization", or "tax cuts", which is based on the assumption that a general retreat of state influence would improve economic growth, innovation and wealth. This doctrine – regularly ignoring irrational actions in the business sector (banks, automobile or power industry) – is the wrong answer to the increasing steering demands of states because markets are not able to solve the long-term problems of a comprehensive industrial transition. Although the neo-liberal doctrine has reasonably broached the issue of bureaucracy, it has largely underestimated the function of governmental regulation in the market economy. Hence, what is needed is smart regulation and a more active state, which acts as a trustee for the environment and future generation. The general discrediting of government influence is questionable, particularly considering that many studies deem the imminent environmental and energy-technical revolution to be especially policy-driven (European Commission DG Environment and Ernst & Young 2006; IPCC 2007; Jänicke 2007; IEA 2008). Against this background the re-discovery of the regulatory role of the state ("regulatory capitalism") is hardly astonishing (Majone 1997; Moran 2003; Levi-Faur 2005).

Voters and consumers open to innovation

The basic conditions for a radical shift in awareness are still largely missing. The redistribution of income at the expense of the middle and lower income groups in the last 30 years has produced an unfavorable condition to begin innovation among voters and consumers. People suffering in poverty have priorities other than climate protection. Together with deficits in education, the risk of social decline is a feeding ground for the populist media and their routine witch-hunts of "the politicians". The role of the media as a transport mechanism for relevant knowledge is as important for handling the industrial revolution as for the new knowledge-based production model. The media must contribute to the knowledge that is necessary for consumers as well as voters to support innovative products and policies.

If policies fail to address the challenges of climate change and resource scarcity, the mechanisms of democratic decision-making could be called into question. The impending economic and ecological crises could be attributed to the alleged slowness of the democratic decision-making process, and thus encourage authoritative forms of statehood. Such a reaction, however, underestimates the innovative potential contained in political competition and opportunities for civil society to participate. It is no coincidence that authoritative systems failed to protect the environment. The openness of political systems to new is a central prerequisite for policy innovation and problem solving.

Innovative enterprises with a long-term perspective and good governance

Shortsightedness, the orientation towards shareholder-value, and short-cycles also present an obstacle to innovation in the business sector. But innovations are essential in the present economic crisis. The assumption that rational, informed companies will use their efficiency potential in production out of self-interest, and adapt their energy and resource consumption accordingly, is not generally confirmed by reality. Empirical studies regularly show that investments in energy-efficiency are not made because missing information, prevailing priorities or organizational blockades in a company hamper reorientation (e.g. KfW 2005).

It should be mentioned that powerful corporations often have the privilege to ignore even obvious innovation needs. Many automobile corporations are reacting to the current development of oil prices and the need for climate protection in the same way as they already did in the 1970s. For a short time, smaller, energy efficient cars were developed, but basically the trajectory of increasing the horsepower, weight, comfort and speed of cars was not put into question (DeLorean 1980). Certainly, this has contributed to the difficulties which many car manufacturers have faced in the past few years, most notably the US producers.

Another obstacle to innovation occurs when companies with products with high environmental impacts, for example in the electricity industry, do not have effective economic incentives to help to reduce energy consumption in their field. The normal reaction to energy saving of consumers will be new marketing strategies to generate more energy consumption.

Furthermore, financial markets primarily favor short-term profits. An orientation towards long-term development of the company is impaired by having to demonstrate profit in a very short period. Some countries have begun experimenting with reporting commitments to long-term environmental effects of financial assets (e.g. for pension funds in Great Britain). In any case, stronger additional incentives are necessary to encourage the actual use of these mechanisms. Meanwhile there are many governance mechanisms that are being developed such as environmental labels, standards for environmental management systems or report- and information duty. However, only in combination with regulatory standards can these mechanisms be effective (Hey *et al.* 2008).

A powerful innovation system

The challenges of a comprehensive technical-economic change require the development of adequate education and science systems to increase our human-capital, knowledge, and qualifications. The PISA study on the education system and numerous evaluations of the science system prove, however, that many countries (e.g. Germany) are not taking advantage of this potential. For example, it has been reported that the lack of well-trained skilled workers is an obstacle to further development of environmental technologies. The demographic change will aggravate this problem even further if education and research institutions do not do a better job of orientating themselves towards the new challenges. This applies to both vocational courses and further training.

The importance of educational, science and technology policy for the successful development of technologies, sectors and industrial development cannot be stressed enough. There is also a need for increased public spending on R&D and flexibility to advance (i.e. through a broad pre-structuring in funding) relevant future innovations.

Many countries have committed themselves to what is in some cases a remarkable increase in spending on research and development. The best example of this is the ambitious goal of the Lisbon strategy of the European Union to increase spending for research and development to 3 percent of GDP. However, approaches which only add further innovation programs for environmental technologies to the existing ones, will fail to meet the challenges. Apart from promoting environmental technologies in the narrower sense, it is also necessary to consider environmental aspects in all technology fields and ultimately decrease the budgets and subsidies for environmentally harmful technologies.

Possibilities of failure

Given the extent of the crisis of the resource-intensive model of growth, failure is certainly possible. Markets, societies and states may not react sufficiently and may constrain themselves to the usual level of innovation. Thereby, they will overstep the natural limits, and thus cause irreversible damage. Increasing the amount of electricity generated by coal will lead in that direction (as far as CCS is not technically possible and a legal requirement). It may well raise the belief, that the potential of the existing technologies is sufficient. There is the tendency to leave dominant large scale structures and trajectories untouched or even praise them as the solution to the problem. One example is the discussion about a renaissance of nuclear power before the Fukushima catastrophe. In some countries, renewed investments in nuclear power are still in discussion. Another example is the so called "geo-engineering" to either increase the capacity of absorbing climate gases or to reduce solar radiation. Such approaches are very risky and apparently comparatively expensive. In addition, this idea postpones solving the urgent crisis and ignores the complexity of resource and environmental problems.

An innovation-oriented industrial policy which only promotes incremental innovation without supporting radically new innovation is likely to fail. This would reinforce the past and ancient industries. This will finally affect the rise and decline of nations and regions.

Opportunities

In order to avoid undesirable development, the structure of opportunities and its possibilities to enforce the trend should now be outlined. As has been the case in previous long-term growth cycles, the crises of the current resource-intensive growth model, stands face-to-face with the opportunities of a new development model. For the first time there is an opportunity to politically shape this radical industrial change without the destructive forms of past breaks in development.

Opportunities for economic-technological development

Environmentally-friendly, resource-efficient technologies have the potential to become a lead industry. This is comparable to the textile and iron industry in the early phase of the industrial revolution or the electro-technic and automobile industry in later phases. Environmentally-friendly innovations are important because they are the basic condition of long-term industrial growth. To avoid environmental damage and deadweight loss, a growth process for technological environmental relief is needed. This goal can be met by a long-term innovation process, which is comparable to the constant gain of labor productivity. Since environmental efficiency is a condition for long-term growth it offers at the same time the advantage of stable global markets.

From an ecological standpoint, new basic innovations in the area of mobility, energy supply, agriculture, recycling, chemistry and telecommunications, which are linked to a radically lower energy and resource consumption, are necessary. A measure of the real opportunities of such a development can be found in the unusually high global growth in this sector (Table 3.2). After a short period of stalemate due to the 2008/09 economic recession, the markets for environmental technologies have regained momentum and have passed through the economic crisis much better than many other sectors (BMU 2012).

Industrial transformations have previously taken shape around industry clusters and their related key technologies. The clusters contribute above average to economic growth and as a result, their share in overall economic output increases. At the heart of these innovation and growth processes were "macro-innovations" (Mokyr 1993), which in turn were supplemented or improved by a series of "micro-innovations". Such innovations form the basis of new industrial sectors. A typical diffusion curve includes a long warm-up with low growth rates before the rapid take-off phase occurs. In the initial phase improvement innovations have to be made, the necessary skills have to be taught, if applicable the infrastructures have to be built or adjusted, and the required capital has to be collected. In this phase, providers of new technologies also have to prevail against traditional technologies.

An industrial transformation on this scale is inevitably connected to an economic structural change. Companies, which do not engage in the new dynamics and re-invest their capital stocks as usual, face the risk of losing ground in future markets. Radical innovation processes, too, are always ambivalent. They inevitably trigger oppositions, which have been overcome until now by a process of "creative destruction" (Schumpeter 1942). Another opportunity of the Third

Table 3.2 Worldwide growth of eco-efficient technologies

Annual growth 2006–08:	
PV (on-grid capacity):	60%
Biodiesel:	41%
Investment in renewables:	38%
Wind power (capacity):	28%
Forecast (2020)	
Solarthermal energy:	23%
Hybrid vehicles:	22%
Bioplastics:	22%
Automatic sorting:	15%

Source: based on: Roland Berger & BMU 2009; REN21 2008.

Industrial Revolution is that these oppositions can be overcome in more constructive ways, with less destruction of capital, and thus a higher acceptance. Within their investment cycles companies can diversify into new, more environmental-friendly fields of production.

Opportunities for environmental concerns

Resource conservation is always environmental protection, whether it concerns the consumption of energy, resources, water, soil or "nature". Climate change, in particular, calls for a broad new concept of resource use. Resource conservation also offers profitable solutions to a considerable extent – covering and exceeding the costs of damage prevention.

Renewable energies and an increase in energy efficiency are crucial contributions to climate protection. At the same time, they offer the possibility of substituting expensive energy imports, and providing energy at an affordable price. If renewable energies and energy efficiency are firmly promoted and fossil energies are charged for their external damage, possibly through an emissions trading system, learning effects and economies of scale in favor of new efficient and renewable technologies would be induced.

Similarly, an efficient use of raw materials not only assists in increasing productivity but also environmental protection. The environment benefits from the reduction or substitution of material flows in many ways. Not least because these are related to diverse burdens (transportation, secondary energy consumption, storage, dissipative losses) which are difficult to control without further regulations.

The development of a new energy and raw material base not only affects environmental and energy technologies, but impacts the ecological modernization of the entire industry. However, it is particularly important to modernize the energy, automotive, air traffic, chemical, construction and agricultural sectors. In the modernization of the construction sector, Germany can serve as an example. Germany has invested 40 billion euros into energy-saving buildings and government support is expected to increase massively (Jochem, Jaeger *et al.* 2008). Most remarkably, the investment in climate friendly technologies and products alone amounts to 5 percent of the German GDP (2005). The share is even rising due to the new climate and energy program (2007). So far a statistically quantifiable area of "environmental technology" of about 4 percent of the GDP and 1.934 million employees (2008) was "visible" which, however, excluded many environmental protection activities such as organic farming and eco-tourism. A more recent study shows that alone the area of "green-tech" has reached 11 percent of the GDP (2011). The economic potentials for innovations and growth are notoriously underestimated in economic models, and only recently studies have been published that account for these potentials (Jaeger *et al.* 2011).

Beyond this, there is a broad ecological modernization of the whole industry that cannot be quantified and proceeds usually within the enterprises. Due to the breadth of the environmental industry, an English governmental study called it an "invisible industry" (DTI and DEFRA 2006). Such a mainstreaming of environmental concerns is also not restricted to the technological products of a certain environmental sector. The potential is considerably higher if efficiency improvements are not only undertaken within technology lines, but also if innovations occur within basic functions and systems. The needs of habitation, sustainability, energy, and mobility have to be met, but this must not occur through existing environmental-intensive technologies. For example, mobility is not limited to the road traffic system and energy provision can be met through technical savings, etc.

Opportunities for social reforms

It seems that the redistribution of income during former economic recessions at the expense of the lower-income groups has reached the limit of social acceptance. The social unrest in countries which are hit worst by the financial crisis are an indication of this. The price increase of both energy and necessary provisions exacerbates the situation even further. As a result, there is a lack of readiness for innovation, and this is possibly the most serious obstacle to an ambitious innovation strategy. Fortunately, positive experiences with reform concepts in this context already exist. The cutting of subsidies, which contribute to environmental pollution and the over-use of resources, is not just a potential improvement to the public spending structure of states, but can also stimulate innovations. The implementation of such spending improvements to sector specific innovation processes can be a sensible solution.

Moreover, the basic question is whether the future decisive basis for public revenue should be labor income or resource consumption. If labor income is the main basis, the problem of mass unemployment will remain. Therefore, it is in general sensible to direct taxation towards environmental and resource consumption. The Germany eco-tax reform (2000) has resulted in about 250,000 jobs together with a push for environmental innovation. Environmentally related luxury taxes can be considered an additional source of revenue, which can assist in income redistribution policies. Such approaches further legitimize environmental policy. In the long run, it will be essential that those in the higher income brackets, who have received favorable treatment for a long time, will have to make a greater contribution to the investment in sustainable development.

The accelerated transfer towards more knowledge-based and value-added productive methods is a challenge for the education sector. The previously mentioned bottlenecks in the educational sector and in the vocational training of human capital also have to be overcome to ensure employment. In this respect, the first steps have already been made. Last but not least, the rapid growth in eco-efficient technologies clearly shows how future technological breakthroughs will be connected with qualification requirements and a broad employment potential.

Opportunities for an improved steering capacity

Reconsidering the relationships between markets, civil society and statehood in a multilevel system has the potential to overcome government failures that have been mentioned. Political globalization, with its indisputable restrictions on sovereignty, has repeatedly been interpreted as generally limiting steering capacities of nation states. What this interpretation does not consider is that the transfer of sovereignty rights occurs mostly voluntarily in the interest of collective action. Also, nation states have constructed a multi-level-system that has important steering capacities in the areas of technology standardization and the regulation of transport and trade. These steering potentials, as seen in Europe (EU), between industrialized countries (OECD) and also globally (G8, G20, UN), need to be expanded and put to use for ecological modernization. The countries of the world under the auspices of the UN summit in Rio (1992), i.e. at the start of the current industrial cycle, introduced a broad spectrum of new regulations for environmental protection. These regulations apply to international agreements (on climate, biodiversity or Agenda 21) as well as to political innovations within the countries themselves. In the year 2000, for instance, 60 percent of all countries had a ministry of the environment and 70 percent had a sustainability strategy (see Figure 3.1). These innovations should be the starting point for future strategies.

The need to enhance the *strategy capacity* of governments and intergovern-mental organizations benefits from a wide international network of policy actors. Nowadays, ministries of the environment are more connected to international politics and policies than most other departments. Another advantage of this wide network is the increasing number of players with potentially long-term perspectives: international institutions, scientific institutions (e.g. climate research), environmental associations, as well as the participating state machineries, are relatively independent of the short-term nature of election or business cycles. Finally, this also applies to jurisprudence. These institutions can meaningfully complement the short-term perspectives of enterprises and democratic systems.

Alongside the international institutions of environmental policy, other international systems and agreements can be used as mechanisms to promote and establish environmental policy (Oberthür and Gehring 2006).

Environmental targets are accepted in development collaborations and, in many cases, they form an integral part of corresponding programs. Also the World Bank, despite being rightly criticized for individual projects, has taken important steps towards environmental integration (World Bank 2012). Other international institutions, such as the WTO, which regulates trade and transport, still have a long way to go. Often the WTO requires ambitious product regulations by international trendsetters to be justified because they supposedly present an obstacle to competition. Because of that, their global expansion and the subsequent diffusion of ecologically advanced technologies still meets obstacles. But the mechanism of policy diffusion also provides a decisive opportunity to overcome this obstacle (Vogel 1995; Oberthür and Gehring 2006; Holzinger,

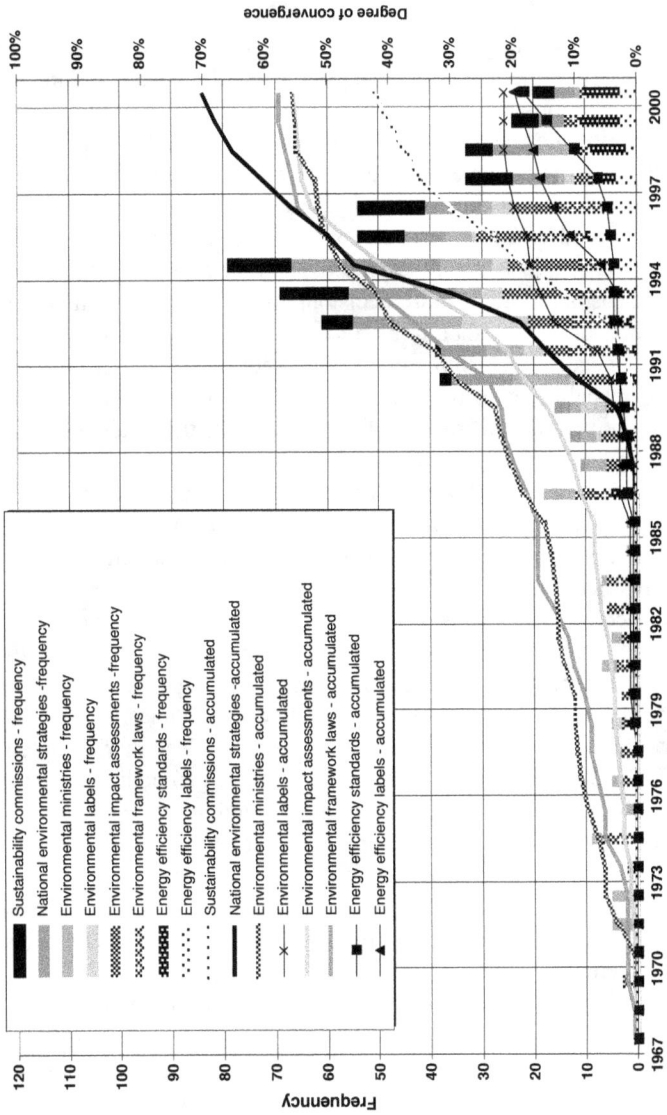

Figure 3.1 Global diffusion of environmental innovations.

Source: Busch and Jörgens 2005.

Knill *et al.* 2007). The European Union, which began as an economic union and has become a central player in environmental policy, serves to a certain extent as an example for the incremental greening of trade regimes. The World Bank has characterised the "European model" of "golden growth" as follows: "Europeans want economic growth to be smarter, kinder, and cleaner, and they are willing to accept less for 'better' growth" (World Bank 2011).

The potential for steering can also lie in a re-evaluation of the concept of statehood. Contrary to the neo-liberal paradigm the role of state administrations, finances and regulations has to be re-determined. The necessary expansion of statehood does not mean an arbitrary expansion of state budget. But not all options of state regulation have been fully exploited. The quality of governance changes in the era of knowledge-intensity. Above all, better regulation (smart regulation) is needed and less deregulation. A singular focus only on the cost estimate of regulation, as is commonly used, should be avoided.

The general suspicion, that future decisions made by the government have a high probability of error, should be reconsidered: long-term planning and investments are needed, and neither civil society nor enterprises dispose of better information or capabilities to take these decisions. However, what is correct is that a strong governmental role in the Third Industrial Revolution merits precautionary rules. The shortcomings of state action can be reduced through broad networking and evaluations on both the national and international levels. There are many lessons learned from the past to ensure "smart" regulations (e.g. Gunningham and Sinclair 1998): state laws should be made as simple as possible, flexible and restricted to a certain period of time. They should enable learning processes and corrections (Voss 2006). Integrated assessment and stakeholder consultation (also via the internet) should play an important role. Investment cycles should be respected – overheating of the economy should be avoided.

As seen in the pioneer countries of environmental policies, it is possible to promote eco-efficient innovations and diffuse them into lead markets (Beise and Rennings 2003; Jacob, Beise *et al.* 2005). This is the precondition for a global change towards nature and resource-saving technologies. Paramount is that developed countries and regions develop their internal markets for eco-efficient technologies and products. Various instruments are needed to promote innovation. Experience already demonstrates that a flexible mix of instruments that cover the entire innovation process from invention until diffusion and back to invention is beneficial.

The Japanese Top-Runner Program, in which after a certain amount of time the most efficient products in each category define the standards for all manufacturers, shows that ambitious and innovation-promoting regulation for the development of specific improvements is possible. But it always depends on the general steering through the increasing costs of energy and raw material; the policies should not only favor a broad and efficient search process for better solutions, but also reduce rebound-effects.

Environmental innovations are no subject for dogmatism towards economic instruments or state regulation. Both types of instruments are necessary:

regulation to exploit *specific* potentials for innovation – and taxes, charges or emissions trading to stimulate a *general* trend.

The emerging lead-markets for eco-efficient technologies could play a global role. These countries not only demonstrate that it is technologically and economically possible, but also politically. By designing its own markets in the area of environmental friendly technologies, the EU has gained regulative dominance (e.g. the EURO-norms for vehicles, the chemical legislation REACH or the recycling of electronic devices). These examples have often been copied in other regions of the world. This is the case also with some support programs, such as the German Renewable-Energy-Law, which was copied worldwide, including in some US states.

It is quite open which region of the world keeps this position to lead both the technology development and the creation of markets, as well as the ambitious regulatory framework to enable such development. China, India, Brazil and others are increasingly challenging the leading role of Europe in this regard. At the same time, in Europe and in the US, the political ambitions to protect the climate and to take far-reaching measures to innovate in climate neutral technologies is fading to a certain degree. It is still open whether other regions and countries can take over in the role of innovators, dispose of the necessary capital and develop the political means to organize an industrial transformation. It cannot be questioned that such efforts are needed.

References

AASA (The Association of Academies of Sciences in Asia). 2011. *Towards a Sustainable Asia – Green Transition and Innovation*. Beijing: Science Press/Springer.

Barroso, J. M. 2007. *Europe's Energy Policy and the Third Industrial Revolution*. Loyola de Palacio energy conference Madrid, 1 October 2007.

Beise, M. and Rennings, K. 2003. *Lead Markets for Environmental Innovations: A Framework for Innovation and Environmental Economics*. Mannheim: ZEW.

BMU. 2012. Bundesministerium für Umwelt, Naturschutz und Reaktorsicherheit. Greentech made in Germany 3.0. Umwelttechnologieatlas für Deutschland. Berlin, BMU.

Busch, P.-O. and Jörgens, H. 2005. Globale Ausbreitungsmuster umweltpolitischer Institutionen. In Tews, K. and Jänicke, M. (eds). *Die Diffusion umweltpolitischer Innovationen im internationalen System*. Wiesbaden: VS Verlag, 55–193.

DeLorean, J. Z. 1980. "Die Autokäufer zahlen drauf". *Der Spiegel* 2.6.1980.

DTI and DEFRA. 2006. "Environmental Innovation: Bridging the Gap between Environmental Necessity and Economic Opportunity". First Report of the Environmental Innovations Advisory Group. London.

Esty, D. C. and Porter, M. E. 2000. *Measuring National Environmental Performance and Its Determinants. The Global Competitiveness Report 2000*. Harvard University and World Economic Forum, New York/Oxford: Oxford University Press, 60–75.

European Commission DG Environment and Ernst & Young. 2006. *Eco-Industry, its Size, Employment, Perspectives and Barriers to Growth in an Enlarged EU. Report to the European Commission*, DG Environment. Brussels.

European Communities. 2008. *The Economics of Ecosystems and Biodiversity: An Interim Report*. Presented at the Ninth Conference of the Parties to the Convention on Biological Diversity in Bonn, Germany.

Freeman, C. and Louca, F. 2001. *As Time Goes By. From the Industrial Revolutions to the Information Revolution*. Oxford, New York: Oxford University Press.

Gabriel, S. 2006. *Ökologische Industriepolitik*. Memorandum für einen "New Deal" von Wirtschaft, Umwelt und Beschäftigung.

Greenwood, J. 1999. "The Third Industrial Revolution: Technology, Productivity, and Income Equality". *Economic Review – Federal Reserve Bank of Cleveland*, 35: 2–12.

Grübler, A. 1998. *Technology and Global Change*. Cambridge: Cambridge University Press.

Gunningham, N. and Sinclair, D. 1998. "Instruments for Environmental Protection". In Gunningham, N. and Grabosky, P. (eds), *Smart Regulation: Designing Environmental Policy*. Oxford: Oxford University Press.

Hawken, P., Lovins, A. B. and Lovins, L. H. 1999. *Natural Capitalism: Creating the Next Industrial Revolution*. Little, Brown and Company.

Hawken, P., Lovins, A. B. and Lovins, L. H. 2008. *Natural Capitalism: The Next Industrial Revolution*. London: Earthscan.

Hey, C., Jacob, K. and Volkery, A. 2008. "REACH als Beispiel für hybride Formen von Steuerung und Governance". In Schuppert, G. F. and Zürn, M. (eds), *Governance in einer sich wandelnden Welt*. PVS Sonderheft: 430–51.

Holzinger, K., Knill, C. and Sommerer, T. 2007. "Konvergenz der Umweltpolitiken in Europa? Der Einfluss internationaler Institutionen und der ökonomischen Integration". In Holzinger, K., Jörgens, H. and Knill, C. *Transfer, Diffusion und Konvergenz von Politiken*. PVS-Sonderheft 38. Wiesbaden: VS Verlag. 377–406.

Huber, J. 1985. "Modell und Theorie der langen Wellen". In Jänicke, M. *Vor uns die goldenen neunziger Jahre? Langzeitprognosen auf dem Prüfstand*. München: Piper, 51–78.

Intergovernmental Panel on Climate Change. 2007. Climate Change 2007: Mitigation. *Contribution of Working Group III to the Fourth Assessment Report of the Intergovernmental Panel on Climate Change*. Cambridge, New York: Cambridge University Press.

International Energy Agency. 2008. Energy Technology Perspectives 2008: Scenarios and Strategies to 2050. Paris: International Energy Agency.

Jackson, T. 2009. *Prosperity without Growth*. Sustainable Development Commission.

Jacob, K., Beise, M., Blazejczak, J., Edler, D., Haum, R., Jänicke, M., Loew, T., Petschow, U. and Rennings, K. 2005. *Lead Markets of Environmental Innovations*. Heidelberg and New York: Physica Verlag.

Jacob, K., Feindt, P. H., Busch, P.-O. and Biermann, F. 2007. "Einleitung: Politik und Umwelt: Modernisierung politischer Systeme und Herausforderung an die Politikwissenschaft". In Jacob, K., Biermann, F., Busch, P.-O. and Feindt, P. H. *Politik und Umwelt*. PVS Sonderheft 39. Wiesbaden: VS Verlag.

Jaeger, C. C., Paroussos, L., Mangalagiu, D., Kupers, R., Mandel, A. and Tàbara, J. D. 2011. *A New Growth Path for Europe. Generating Prosperity and Jobs in the Low-carbon Economy Synthesis Report*. Study commissioned by the German Federal Ministry for the Environment, Nature Conservation and Nuclear Safety.

Jänicke, M. 2007. "'Umweltstaat': eine neue Basisfunktion des Regierens. Umweltintegration am Beispiel Deutschlands". In Jacob, K., Biermann, F., Feindt, P. H. and

Busch, P.-O. (eds), *Politik und Umwelt* – Politische Vierteljahresschrift, Sonderheft 39/2007. Wiesbaden: Verlag für Sozialwissenschaften.

Jänicke, M., Blazejczak, J., Edler, D. and Hemmelskamp, J. 2000. "Environmental Policy and Innovation: An International Comparison of Policy Frameworks and Innovation Effects". In Hemmelskamp, J., Rennings, K. and Leone, F. (eds): *Innovation-oriented Environmental Regulation. Theoretical Approaches and Empirical Analysis.* Heidelberg: Physica-Verlag, 125–152.

Jänicke, M. 2012. *Megatrend Umweltinnovation: Zur ökologischen Modernisierung von Wirtschaft und Staat.* München: Oekom Verlag.

Jänicke, Martin (2012a): "Dynamic Governance of Clean-energy Markets: How Technical Innovation could Accelerate Climate Policies". *Journal of Cleaner Production*, 22: 50–9.

Jochem, E., Jaeger, C. C. *et al.* 2008. *Investitionen für ein klimafreundliches Deutschland.* Studie im Auftrag des BMU (Bundesministerium für Umwelt, Naturschutz und Reaktorsicherheit) Available online: http://www.bmu.de/fileadmin/bmu-import/files/pdfs/allgemein/application/pdf/studie_klimadeutschland_endbericht.pdf.

Köhler, H. 2009. "Berliner Rede von Bundespräsident Horst Köhler am 24. März 2009 in Berlin: Die Glaubwürdigkeit der Freiheit". Bulletin der Bundesregierung, Nr. 37-1 vom 24, März 2009.

Kondratieff, N. D. 1926. "Die langen Wellen der Konjunktur". *Archiv für Sozialwissenschaften und Sozialpolitik*, 56: 573–609.

Kreditanstalt für Wiederaufbau (KfW). 2005. KfW-Befragung zu den Hemmnissen und Erfolgsfaktoren von Energieeffizienz in Unternehmen, Frankfurt/M.: KfW.

Levi-Faur, D. 2005. "The Global Diffusion of Regulatory Capitalism". *The ANNALS* 598 (March 2005): 12–32.

Majone, G. 1997. "From the Positive to the Regulatory State: Causes and Consequences of Changes in the Mode of Governance". *Journal of Public Policy* 17(2): 139–67.

McKinsey Global Institute. 2011. Resource Revolution: Meeting the Worlds Energy, Materials, Food, and Water Needs.

Meadows, D. H., Meadows, D. and Zahn, E. 1972. *Die Grenzen des Wachstums: Bericht des Club of Rome zur Lage der Menschheit.* Stuttgart: Deutsche Verlags-Anstalt.

Mensch, G. 1975. *Das technologische Patt. Innovationen überwinden die Depression.* Frankfurt am Main: Umschau.

Millennium Ecosystem Assessment. 2005. *Ecosystems and Human Well-being: Synthesis.* Washington, DC: Island Press.

MITI (Ministry of International Trade and Industry). 1974. *Directions for Japan's Industrial Structure.* Tokyo: MITI.

Mokyr, J. (ed.). 1993. *The British Industrial Revolution: An Economic Perspective.* Boulder: Westview Press.

Mokyr, J. 1999. "Innovation and Selection in Evolutionary Models of Technology: Some Definitional Issues". In Ziman, J. (ed.). *Technological Innovation as an Evolutionary Process.* Cambridge: Cambridge University Press.

Moran, M. 2003. *The British Regulatory State: High Modernism and Hyper-Innovation.* Oxford: Oxford University Press.

Oberthür, S. and Gehring, T. (eds). 2006. *Institutional Interaction in Global Environmental Governance: Synergy and Conflict Among International and EU Policies.* Cambridge, Mass.: MIT Press.

OECD. 2011. *Green Growth Strategy Synthesis Report.* OECD Paris 2010 (C(2011) 29REV1.

70   *Martin Jänicke and Klaus Jacob*

Olson, M. 1982. *The Rise and Decline of Nations*. New Haven: Yale University Press.
Okimoto, Daniel, I. 1990. *Between MITI and the Market: Japanese Industrial Policy for High Technology*. Stanford University Press.
Polanyi, K. 1944. *The Great Transformation*. New York: Rinehart.
Prognos, A. G., Schröder, D. and Bundesministerium für Forschung und Technologie. 1982. *Politik, Wertewandel, Technologie: Ansatzpunkte für eine Theorie der sozialen Entwicklung: eine Untersuchung*. Düsseldorf: Econ Verlag.
REN21. 2008. *Renewables 2007 Global Status Report*. Paris: REN21 Secretariat and Washington, DC: Worldwatch Institute.
Rifkin, J. 2008. Europe can Lead the Third Industrial Revolution. *EurActiv* (31.1.2008).
Sachverständigenrat für Umweltfragen. 2008. *Umweltschutz im Zeichen des Klimawandels*. Berlin: Erich Schmidt Verlag.
Schellnhuber, H. J. 2007. Europas Dritte Industrielle Revolution. In Schulte-Noelle, H. T. and M. M. (ed.). *Abendland unter? Reden über Europa*. Kreuzlingen: Hugendubel, 90.
Schmidheiny, S. 1992. Changing Course: a Global Business Perspective on Development and the Environment. Cambridge, Mass.[u.a.]: MIT Press.
Schumpeter, J. A. 1942. *Capitalism, Socialism, and Democracy*. New York, London: Harper & Brothers.
Stern, N. 2007. *The Economics of Climate Change: The Stern Review*. Cambridge and New York: Cambridge University Press.
United Nations Environment Programme and Global International Waters Assessment. 2006. *Challenges to International Waters: Regional Assessments in Global Perspective*. Nairobi: United Nations Environment Programme.
UNEP 2011. *Towards a Green Economy: Pathways to Sustainable Development and Poverty Eradication*.
UNEP 2012. *GEO 5: Global Environmental Outlook*.
Vogel, D. 1995. *Trading Up: Consumer and Environmental Regulation in a Global Economy*. Cambridge, London: Harvard University Press.
Von Weizsäcker, E. U., Lovins, A. B. and Lovins, L. H. 1997. *Faktor Vier: Doppelter Wohlstand – Halbierter Naturverbrauch: der neue Bericht an den Club of Rome*. München: Droemer Knaur.
Voss, J.-P. (ed.). 2006. *Reflexive Governance for Sustainable Development*. Cheltenham: Edward Elgar.
Wagner, A. 1893. *Grundlegung der politischen Ökonomie*. Leipzig.
Wallerstein, I. M. 1983. *Historical Capitalism*. London: Verso.
Weidner, H. 2007. Deutsche Klimapolitik: Erfolgreich und gerecht? Zur Rolle von Fairnessnormen. In Jacob, K., Biermann, F., Feindt, P. H. and Busch, P.-O. (eds) *Politik und Umwelt. Politische Vierteljahresschrift-Sonderheft*. Wiesbaden, Verlag für Sozialwissenschaften. 39/2007: 452–78.
WBGU. 2011. *Welt im Wandel – Gesellschaftsvertrag für eine Große* Transformation Wissenschaftlicher, Wissenschaftlicher Beirat der Bundesregierung für Globale Umweltveränderungen, Berlin.
World Bank 2011. *Golden Growth – Restoring the Lustre of the European Economic Model*. Washington, D.C.: The World Bank.
World Bank 2012. *Inclusive Green Growth. The Pathway to Sustainable Development*. Washington, D.C.: The World Bank.

4 Governance in the face of socio-ecological change

A legal response

Anél du Plessis

> Through the centuries, men have grappled with the problems posed by their changing environment. In modern society, this task takes on a new sense of urgency as scientific and technological advances occur in a geometric progression. Law and legal institutions play a vital role in this process of change by influencing the extent to which interests favoring or opposing change are recognized, encouraged or impeded. Thus perceived, law is a social institution for achieving desired ends, and a prime consideration in legal analysis must be the capacity of legal institutions to adjust to the changing social environment.
>
> (Dienes in Nagel 1970: 3)

> The very function of law as a social institution demands that change be managed.
>
> (Dienes in Nagel 1970: 41)

Introduction

It seems impossible to aptly define and pinpoint the parameters of socio-ecological change (SEC). It can arguably best be described as an ever-present phenomenon that involves progress and/or recoil in the composition and functioning of, and relationships in communities of people as well as in the natural environment (Nagel 1970: 8).[1] Bearing this description in mind, the notion of SEC is certainly not an invention of our time. However, some of the unsustainable effects of SEC are unquestionably now much more prominent than before and captivate the minds, *inter alia*, of the scientific community (Kirdar 1992: 3).[2]

Law, social and environmental sciences are often explored and presented as separate disciplines and bodies of knowledge. These disciplines emanate, *inter alia*, from different ideologies and are traditionally focused on divergent facets of (regulated) life on earth. The distinction of each of these from the other in scientific thought may therefore be merited. It is, however, not unthinkable for some of the challenges of our time (inclusive of those related to SEC) to require a fusion and intersection of law, social and environmental sciences to arrive at generally acceptable solutions and responses (see Steiner: 19–21 on the interrelatedness of humans, human activities and the environment). Kirdar (1992) observes that:

> (t)he emerging conception that environment and development are very closely linked shows that the world is increasingly confronted with issues that affect people as a whole. It also shows that most of these issues are interlinked and multidimensional ... Their solutions require multidisciplinary joint undertakings.
>
> (Kirdar 1992:7)

Until recently, focus areas in law such as that of human rights, have received little attention in sociology and environmental sciences (Anleu 2000: 200). One of the reasons for this could be rooted in the (somewhat distorted) view that rights are mere "legal constructions or philosophical abstractions" (Anleu 2000: 200) but another could be that, until recently, no real need existed for these disciplines to traverse the domain of law, or human rights *per se*. The governance of SEC may arguably require a change to this position as is explained below.

Governance is part of regulated life on earth. In essence it refers to the management of the relations between government and its populace within a given constitutional order (Ginther *et al.* 1995: 157). Governance refers to government "in action" and deals with the relationship between authorities and the communities that they are responsible for. It is the backbone of, and reason for government, where "governance" is the basic verb to describe the demeanour or activities of government. Governance in the face of widespread SEC devolves largely on the state, leaving ordinary people exposed to its effects. The power of state authorities is, however, accompanied by responsibilities in as far as governors are bound by the rules and principles of international and domestic law, for example (c.f. Anleu 2000: 227). Constitutional and administrative law, specifically, should be a direction indicator and barometer for governors in this context. In the area of SEC specifically, rights-based constitutional *environmental* law seems particularly important[3] if one bears in mind, as an example, the wording of the often referred to section 24 of the Constitution of the Republic of South Africa, 1996:

Everyone has the right:

(a) to an environment that is not harmful to their health or well-being; and
(b) to have the environment protected, for the benefit of present and future generations, through reasonable legislative and other measures that:
   (i) prevent pollution and ecological degradation;
   (ii) promote conservation; and
   (iii) secure ecologically sustainable development and use of natural resources while promoting justifiable economic and social development.

(Constitution of the Republic of South Africa, 1996)

South Africa is an example for many countries with constitutions that contain one or more substantive provision related to peoples' environment.[4] Provisions such as section 24 in the South African Constitution, raise the question to what extent substantive environmental rights assist in conceptualizing and directing states" domestic governance efforts, the latter also embracing states' governance of SEC. In response, this chapter conceptually evaluates the dimensions of the positive obligations that may result from constitutional environmental rights or provisions such as the section 24 environmental right in South Africa as a case in point. In doing so, attention is paid to the types of activities that state governments may be expected to engage in, in order to fulfill peoples' environmental rights and constitutional claims. A conceptual string gets woven through the fulfillment of (constitutional) environmental rights and claims and states' governance of SEC in the domestic or national context. It is thus not the objective of this chapter to provide a comparative overview or analysis of constitutional environmental provisions in different countries or to discuss in detail the related national laws, policies or (best) practices one may expect to accompany these constitutional provisions.

The scene set by international law

International environmental law (IEL)[5] and regional environment law[6] often trigger and/or influence domestic environmental law developments (Dugard 2005: 27). Compared to other domains of law, environmental protection is a fairly recent addition to most national law frameworks. In instances where the domestic environmental law objectives, principles, rights or duties (whether it be entrenched in constitutional law, ordinary law or policy) must be applied, domestic courts could turn to corresponding jurisprudence, principles, guidelines or law that exist at the international level. "Rights" are common legal constructions that capture entitlements. Judges and critics may accordingly make normative sense of "rights" as a generic phenomenon in law – whether it be international, regional or domestic law. For this reason, international law (IL) could illuminate and reinforce ill-defined and inadequate or still emerging domestic constitutional law.[7] Bodansky (2004) holds in this regard that international sources are useful in constitutional interpretation for two reasons: they can be sources of good ideas and they can provide empirical evidence of how a prospective legal rule operates in practice (Bodansky 2004: 425; Birnie and Boyle 2002: 257).

One of the areas of IL that is of particular relevance for making sense of the normative content of domestic constitutional law is international human rights law. This holds true generally, but also for constitutional environmental law. Literature on international human rights and IEL agree on the need for fundamental protection of the environment and highlight a number of links between peoples" environment and their human rights, for example (see *inter alia*: Lavrysen and Theunis 2007: 363–382; Burns 1993: 13; Picolotti 2003: 48). IL in fact transcends mere esoteric agreement on these issues and various of its sources offer rules, principles, guidelines and criteria by means of which to take the protection of fundamental environmental interests of people further – also in national contexts (Birnie and Boyle 2002: 259). The most prominent IEL and human rights law instruments (many of which are soft law) that imply or reflect on fundamental environmental rights protection specifically, include, for example: the Stockholm Declaration of 1972; the United Nations World Charter for Nature of 1982; the United Nations World Commission on Environment and Development (WCED) Report on Sustainable Development (Brundtland Report) of 1987; the Rio Declaration (including Agenda 21) of 1992; the United Nations Vienna Declaration and Programme of Action of 1993; the United Nations Ksentini, Special Rapporteur's Report on Human Rights and the Environment and the Draft Declaration of Principles on Human Rights and the Environment of 1994; the Copenhagen Declaration (World Summit on Social Development) of 1995; the Convention on Access to Information, Public Participation in Decision-making and Access to Justice in Environmental Matters (Aarhus Convention) of 1998 and the United Nations Millennium Declaration (Millennium Development Goals) of 2000.

These and other instruments confirm a contemporary environmental rights explosion in IL. It was accompanied and in some cases, followed by a constitutional environmental rights boom in various national law systems and today various countries have environmental rights and principles/norms entrenched in their constitutions (Bakshi 2000: 88; Nair and Jain in Bakshi: 32).

The primary difference between constitutional environmental rights and constitutional environmental principles of state policy, lies in the fact that the former is justiciable where often the principles serve to provide constitutional *direction* to the state without being enforceable by individuals before a court of law. Directive principles are contained, *inter alia*, in the constitutions of Spain, Ireland, Germany, India, China, Yugoslavia and Czechoslovakia. Directive principles generally require primarily positive action and have less of a negative character than, for example, traditional civil and political rights. It is generally accepted that it is the duty of state authorities to respect, protect and fulfill constitutionally entrenched environmental provisions. Yet, they are often open-ended, imprecise and rather vague (e.g. Kamenka and Erh-Soon Tay 1978: 43; Merrills in Bodansky *et al.* 2007: 673–674). One of the ways in which one could estimate what authorities are expected to do in relation to constitutional environmental provisions is to look at how similarly constructed provisions are generally understood and interpreted in the IL milieu. IL developments are valuable in, *inter alia*, identifying and understanding what exactly it is that state governments may be expected to do (through the taking of positive action) in fulfilling constitutional environmental rights and claims.[8]

Constitutional environmental rights specifically are often categorised as socio-economic rights and constitutional environmental principles/norms may similarly have a socio-economic nature where their realization depend on the availability of state resources (amongst others: Verschuuren 1993: 31; Brand in Brand and Heyns 2005: 3). The Limburg Principles on the Implementation of the

International Covenant on Economic, Social and Cultural Rights (ICESCR) of 1987 (the Limburg Principles), the Maastricht Guidelines on Violations of Economic, Social, and Cultural Rights of 1997 (the Maastricht Guidelines) as interpretative texts as well as IL jurisprudence (decisions of international courts)[9] are all aids that assist in clarifying the meaning and structural analysis of the fulfillment of socio-economic rights in a general sense (United Nations 1987; Human Rights Quarterly 1987; Human Rights Quarterly 1998).[10]

From these two principle and guideline documents it is derived that the requirement for fufillment of constitutional environmental provisions implies that governments should: employ legislative, administrative, judicial, economic, budgetary, social and educational measures to this effect;[11] ensure equality for right-holders;[12] that activities which are expressly required should be conducted progressively, without delay and within the powers of the state;[13] that any obstacles in the way of such fulfillment should be removed;[14] that the identification of a minimum substantive standard should be maintained; that targets should subsequently be set and monitoring mechanisms developed[15] and that states should employ policy-making as a medium to facilitate fulfillment.[16]

A number of steering decisions *inter alia* by the European Court of Human Rights (ECHR) and the African Commission on Human and Peoples" Rights[17] have been made at the international level. Some of the most pertinent decisions that addressed the positive duties of governments in terms of environmentally relevant rights include *Social and Economic Rights Action Centre for Economic and Social Rights (SERAC) v Nigeria* (2001),[18] *López Ostra v Spain* (1994),[19] *Guerra and Others v Italy* (1998),[20] *Hatton and other v UK* (2001)[21] and *Taskin and others v Turkey* (2004),[22] for example. In each of these cases the judicial bodies raised certain issues that illuminated what governments" fulfillment of environmental rights obligations may entail. Some of the key dicta arising from these deliberations were that environmental rights: compel public participation in environmental decision-making, require the gathering and sharing of environ-mental information,[23] pursuance of compliance with and enforcement of environmental law;[24] that a government should "move its machinery towards the actual realization" of environmental rights;[25] that authorities may be expected to order or permit independent scientific monitoring of threatened environments,[26] that authorities should conduct and make known environmental and social impact studies prior to major developments;[27] that environmental information must feed into decision-making processes and policy development;[28] that authorities should protect their citizens from exposure to the dangerous effects of activities when these are indicated by an environmental impact assessment (EIA);[29] that governments are obliged to prevent serious damage to citizens" health caused by pollution (inclusive of noise pollution) from industrial sites or caused by incidents at industrial sites – even where the industries are privately owned and managed,[30] and that governments should weigh up individuals" rights against those of communities, an action which could require individual economic benefit with environmental impact to be weighed up against the environmental, social and cultural rights of a broader community.[31]

These duties have all been derived from rights protected in international law – rights that, at least as far as its formulation are concerned, correspond with rights and claims to be found in domestic constitutional law. The question arises as to what we could learn from these internationally recognized duties in relation to the positive action necessary for the state to fulfill constitutionally entrenched environmental duties "at home" or in the national domain – especially in the face of widespread SEC.

What do we learn from IL?

An evaluation of the IL instruments referred to above shows that authorities (specifically the makers and implementers of the law) may have to actively engage in at least seven kinds of activities in order to comply with the duties usually generated by constitutional environmental law.[32] These include:[33]

1 public participation;
2 collection and dissemination of environmental information;
3 development and implementation of environmental law, policy and programmes;
4 compliance with and enforcement of environmental law;
5 the provision of environmental infrastructure;
6 the establishment of partnerships; and
7 environmental education (Leckie and Gallagher 2006).

Each activity stands open for in-depth analysis. For the purposes of this chapter these are, however, only briefly described.

Public participation[34]

In order to ensure that constitutional environmental rights and provisions are realized and meaningfully contribute to effective governance of SEC, governments must ensure accessible and procedurally sound public participation in decision-making processes.[35] However, public participation should not be narrowly defined but should be understood to include community involvement in specialized environmental governance activities such as the monitoring of environmental performance and SEC, environmental needs analysis and the collection of environmental data.[36] Public participation processes are often thought to hamper and delay decision-making[37] and this opinion may be well founded. Therefore innovation and creativity of authorities are required in facilitating participation and in aligning public input *inter alia* with the state's governance endeavours, planning and use of resources. Public participation is two-sided. It is process-related where it is viewed as an end in itself, and it is substantive where it contributes to some further important outcomes/achievements (Pring and Noé in Zillman *et al.* 2002: 22). Participation in environmental decision making is an effective tool to establish long- and short-term environmental priorities, to offer solutions to environmentally relevant challenges (inclusive of SEC), and to prepare, execute and apply the most practicable environmental option (Picolotti and Taillant 2003: 50ff).[38]

Collection and dissemination of environmental information[39]

In order to ensure that constitutional environmental rights and provisions are realized and meaningfully contribute to effective governance of SEC, governments must collect and make available environmental information. Consensus exists that the collection and dissemination of environmental information, the provision of access to such information, and the incorporation thereof in the design of policy, law and decision-making processes are all equally important considerations (Kimber in Jewell and Steele 1998; Belotsky 1998; Kiss in Picolotti and Taillant 2003; Birnie and Boyle 2002; Verschuuren 2005; Earthrights 2002). Environmental information stands at the core of estimating, *inter alia*, the extent and impacts of ecological change (Robinson in Jewell and Steele 1998).[40] The type of information required may vary from, amongst other measurable factors, data on environmental impacts, the properties of hazardous substances, pollution and emission levels to the success rate of conservation strategies, the state of environmental infrastructure and the rate of resource consumption (Robinson in Jewell and Steele 1998: 53). It is important for the most appropriate means or methods for data collection to be explored and to establish the most suitable medium by means of which to fairly disseminate environmental information. An extended positive obligation of government may be to compel private industries to collect and disseminate environmental information and to report in public on environmentally relevant impacts and footprints (Du Plessis 1999: 9). Environmental information may not be filtered to reveal only "what is good for people to know" and should be factually correct and valid. Authorities should of course also ensure that environmental information remains at all times non-discriminatory and accurate. Access to accurate environmental information could be a crucial pre-requisite, *inter alia*, for well-informed public participation, environmental law, policy and programmes development, compliance and enforcement efforts and environmental education.[41] It may arguably be impossible also to plan governance strategies and to effectively govern in the face of SEC in the long or short term, without information being available on, for example, baseline environmental status and longitudinal ecological and social trends.

Development and implementation of environmental law, policy and programmes[42]

In order to ensure that constitutional environmental rights and provisions are realized and meaningfully contribute to effective governance of SEC, governments must *develop* and *implement* environmental law, policy and programmes. The positive obligations posed by constitutional environmental provisions are to a large extent directed at the legislative and executive branches of government.[43] It follows that fulfillment of environmental rights in the third place requires suitable supplementary domestic environmental law, policy and programmes within these branches (De Wet 1996).[44] The idea of having an obligation to design and implement laws, policies and programmes is in itself, rather woolly. The question that begs to be answered is what type of issues should these instruments address? How comprehensive must they be? How many of what? When is it appropriate to address an issue in an enforceable law, and when is it preferable to address it by means of an unenforceable policy or programme? The answers to these questions are directly related, amongst other aspects, to a government's structure, the extent of legislative and executive decentralization, the constitutional powers of the legislature and executive, the state of the environment, and the socio-economic conditions of a country. It is therefore impossible to provide clear and generically applicable answers. A few observations should, however, be made in this regard.

The development, subsequent to the inception of a constitutional environmental provision, of a framework of environmental *laws (legislation)* on broad areas and sectors such as environmental management, environmental impact assessment, integrated planning, integrated pollution control, water, air, biodiversity etc may be inevitable. These laws should arguably be aligned, to an extent appropriate to a particular country, with internationally recognized environmental principles, standards, management systems, best practical environmental options and mechanisms for compliance and enforcement. Framework environmental laws should also be clear on who is bound by them and who is accountable for their implementation and enforcement. Furthermore, environmental laws must provide clear definitions, for example, of "the environment" or "pollution". The mentioned issues could be addressed in *policy documents* instead, in which instance at least two factors need to be borne in mind: (1) policies are generally unenforceable before a court of law and usually only public entities can in some way be held accountable in terms thereof, and (2) policy is more flexible than legislation in the sense that it can usually be amended more easily (Ferreira 1999).[45] The development of *programmes*[46] (such as, for example, programmes related to climate change mitigation or adaptation that involve the public and private sector, programmes aimed at improved corporate social responsibility or projects on greening supply chain management) may at times be particularly useful in furthering constitutional environmental provisions. They need not necessarily be developed by organs of state or exclusively by organs of state. Programmes are generally less formal and fixed than laws or policies and often have an envisaged beginning and end as well as a very particular goal. The usefulness of programmes to advance the fulfillment of constitutional environmental provisions lies in the fact that these instruments can be used to achieve, *inter alia*, the aims of different laws or policies – including cross-sectoral laws and policies (Leckie and Gallagher 2006). Programmes can, however, also have extended aims that are not necessarily based on the objectives of other laws or policies.

The detail, scope and suitability of different laws, policies and programmes will depend on *inter alia* the government structure and conditions in a particular state. What may, however, hold generally true is that the development of law, policy and programmes as a generic activity for the fulfillment of environmental rights should be viewed as a crucial means to introduce guidelines, commitments, objectives, targets, indicators, substantive standards and requirements and specific duties to facilitate the fulfillment of constitutional environmental provisions and effective governance of SEC.[47] The framing of legislation and policy and subsequent environmental programmes may furthermore be crucial to establish an acceptable minimum standard of environmental performance. Laws, policies and programmes can be designed so as to have short or long-term goals and can therefore facilitate the long-term and sustained governance of SEC, for example. They can also be the means to amalgamate most of the generic activities inherent in the fulfillment of constitutional environmental provisions.

Compliance and enforcement[48]

In order to ensure that constitutional environmental rights and provisions are realized and meaningfully contribute to effective governance of SEC, authorities must pursue compliance and enforcement as governor and as governed organs of state. Compliance in this context refers to the meeting of obligations in terms of environmental law, whilst compliant behaviour is behaviour that conforms to legal rules (Crossen 2004: 477; Hutter 1997: 13). Enforcement seeks results, and refers to the set of actions that authorities and/or others take to achieve legal compliance within a determined regulated community and to correct or halt situations that arise from activities beyond the confines of the law.[49] Enforcement therefore relates to the "implementation of consequences" of non-compliance. These consequences may vary from financial penalties (e.g. taxes) to legal action following inspections or declaratory orders. In his reflection on the duties generated by environmental rights, Nickel (1993) remarks that an effective system of environmental protection requires a governmentally enacted system of environmental regulation that, *inter alia*, sets safety standards for all processes and substances. This system must encourage or pressure those using these processes and substances to comply with its regulations, and impose penalties on those who fail to comply. For example, violations of environmental rights may occur through the direct actions of government or the activities of other entities insufficiently regulated by government. As a generic activity in the fulfillment of environmental rights, compliance and enforcement therefore apply to the private sphere as a community regulated by government, but also to government as a public entity regulated and governed by the law. In other words, when it comes to compliance with and enforcement of environmental law, the state or government is simultaneously a regulated entity and an entity responsible for regulation. Compliance and enforcement of law generally, but environmental law in particular, may be one of the means through which state authorities may control the negative consequences of SEC and prevent avertable detrimental SEC caused by illegal behaviour. As far as it pertains to positive action, government may also be expected to develop, for example, licencing or incentive mechanisms to induce compliance, and to establish well-equipped and trained enforcement agencies. It is important to acknowledge the crucial role of the courts in deciding environmental law cases. The entire compliance and enforcement structure of a state collapses if people do not believe in a strong and reliable judiciary and if judges are hesitant to protect the environmental entitlements that people have in terms of constitutional law for the sake of economic development, for example.

Provision of environmental infrastructure[50]

In order to ensure that constitutional environmental rights and provisions are realized and that it meaningfully facilitates SEC, governments must provide environmental services/infrastructure. Environmental infrastructure in this context directly relates to strategic planning whilst environmental service delivery relates to the provision of potable water supply and management, energy, solid waste management, waste-water collection and treatment, and sanitation, for example. Perhaps at the heart of the fulfillment of environmental rights in developing or under-resourced countries is government's provision of sufficient, non-discriminatory environmental infrastructure. Environmental infrastructure is an important part of the immediate physical environment of people and it is often the primary means by which people get access to natural resources such as clean water and air and as such potentially creates one of the vulnerabilities that could accompany SEC. Their access to environmental infrastructure, as well as the efficiency and maintenance of environmental infrastructure by government, more often than not determines peoples' sense of government's fulfillment of their constitutional environmental claims. The Maastricht Guidelines refer to the "minimum core obligation to ensure the satisfaction of, at the very least, minimum essential levels" of rights. The minimum essential level for the fulfillment of constitutional environmental provisions (if this can in fact be established) arguably relates to the provision of environmental infrastructure. An environmental right is void of any meaning for people where they do not even have access to basic environmental amenities. In so far as environmental infrastructure is crucial, *inter alia*, in access to sanitation and hygienic living conditions, it is also directly related to peoples' right to human dignity and the notion of environmental justice. It should be added that to provide sufficient and sustainable environmental infrastructure that will be sustainable in the long term and in the face of SEC, public bodies may require public input (participation) as well as, *inter alia*, statistical information on the parameters and extend of peoples' needs.

Partnerships

To ensure that constitutional environmental rights and provisions are realized and meaningfully contribute to effective governance of SEC, authorities should further establish multi-level partnerships and coordination in public and private domains. It is deduced from IL that the sixth generic activity for the fulfillment of environmental rights is authorities' establishment of partnerships with a number of parties inclusive of: right-holders; other organs of state (different spheres and line-functionaries of government as well as traditional or indigenous authorities where applicable); the private sector; public bodies in foreign jurisdictions; non-governmental organizations (NGOs); community based organizations (CBOs); and international organizations. Streck (2002) is of the view that the positive obligations derived from environmental rights cannot be the mandate of a single sector (the public sector) or a single level (national government) alone. Instead, to fulfil the obligations imposed by constitutional environmental provisions, governments may inevitably have to work on a long-term basis with partners from other sectors at a variety of levels, including local, national, regional and global levels. The long-term governance of SEC may similarly depend on cross-disciplinary relationships and partnerships (typically in the fields of sociology, law and natural sciences) and on maintaining open communication channels, generally.

Environmental education

Education is an often neglected albeit potentially very important aspect of the fulfillment of socio-economic rights and of understanding and dealing with SEC, generally. Provision and promotion of environmental education (not merely environmental awareness) not only form part of the promotion of environmental rights amongst people, but should also constitute the last of the generic activities for the fulfillment of constitutional environmental provisions and the effective governance of SEC. According to Symonides (1992) "(t)he progress in environmental education which goes beyond cognition (awareness and comprehension) into valuation and attitudinal formation can be seen as a very important factor for the implementation of the right to a healthy and balanced environment". The notion of environmental education takes the element of environmental information sharing further by implying that, apart from only sharing facts and data with environmental rights-holders, people should be educated on what to do with the information they receive. The positive duty of governments is hence two-fold: (1) people should be comprehensively educated on issues related to their environment (including change) and (2) people should be capacitated to act upon the environmental knowledge gained. For the long-term governance of SEC it may be crucial to educate people (children, adult learners, civil society in general, public office bearers and politicians) on the long-term effects of SEC and measures to prevent detrimental SEC and also to build systematically on existing knowledge bases.

Discussion

IEL and international human rights law (even where contained in international soft law) serve as direction indicators pertaining to what may be expected of governments in fulfilling positive obligations imposed by constitutional environmental provisions. With reference to a number of key IL instruments at least seven elements for the fulfillment of constitutional environmental provisions were highlighted above. There might be more, but, as was indicated, these elements direct attention to the need for action or "deeds" on the part of government, and hence translate into what can be referred to as a set of necessary "generic activities". It is proposed that these generic activities: (1) provide clarity as to what it may mean for governments to satisfy the obligation to fulfil constitutional environmental provisions and (2) should be viewed as, at least, some basic legal "requirements" for the process of governing SEC on a long-term basis. The first part of the proposal is factually based on what is contained in the IL instruments discussed. The second, more inventive part of the proposal is based on the idea that the long-term and effective governance of SEC requires concerted positive action on the part of the executive and legislative branches of state governments. It requires of authorities actions to meet certain "criteria". The governance of SEC can arguably be sustainable only with the direct participation of governed entities and communities; when governance strategies and decisions are based on sound environmental information that can foretell future trends and challenges; in as far as it is captured and planned for in resilient and apt legislation, policy or programmes; to the extent that governing and governed communities are committed to compliance with and enforcement of related legislation; where environmental infrastructure is provided in equal fashion to all who are entitled thereto; in so far as good inter-governmental working relationships and strong partnerships between government and other sectors are established for the sharing of resources, knowledge and capacity and to prevent overlap in functions; and to the extent that people exposed to (and perhaps also to some extent responsible for) SEC are sufficiently and coherently educated, *inter alia*, on good environmental practices and the severe consequences of leaving prolonged environmental footprints.

A look at the way forward

The law should not be underestimated as an important building block in understanding and especially addressing SEC. It is argued that a fusion and intersection of law, social and environmental sciences are required to arrive at generally acceptable solutions and responses to the challenges posed by SEC. "The law" is, however, a very broad field. A number of issues/phenomena related to "the law" have generally come to the fore thus far, and can be summarised as follows:

- the law is at the disposal of people (inclusive of governors) to establish order and the law is a means to achieve order under particular and changing circumstances;
- constitutional law is of a fundamental kind with superior power and often embraces environmental provisions of a deep-seated nature as in the case of,

for example, section 24 in the Constitution of the Republic of South Africa, 1996;

- constitutional environmental provisions in and by themselves are not clear on what exactly governments are compelled to do in order to fulfil the obligations they impose;
- a vast array of IL instruments offers indications and guidelines as to what may be required of national authorities to fulfil not only the internationally entrenched rights of citizens, but also constitutional provisions of a fundamental nature;
- as far as it specifically pertains to the fulfillment of constitutional environmental provisions, IL and IEL reveal at least seven key elements that give substance to these provisions; and
- the elements for fulfillment of environmental rights or fundamental constitutional provisions represent and require motion and affirmative behaviour and can hence be translated to a set of necessary "generic activities".

Based on the above it is proposed that constitutional environmental law (especially the positive obligations imposed by it) as preset and predetermined be employed by state governments as a key direction indicator in their governance of often volatile SEC. This seems justified in the light of the inextricable link between the environment, environmental law and the phenomenon of SEC. This legal response is, however, based on (1) the supposition that a constitutional environmental provision indeed exists in a particular country, and (2) that countries clearly define what SEC means within its specific socio-economic and environmental context. The proposal may still be widely applicable in as far as contemporary state constitutions generally do include an environmental provision or a variant thereof. The legal response proposed suggests that the legislative and executive branches of governments deliberately consider the implications and meaning of fundamental environmental provisions contained in constitutional law. At times, clear positive obligations can be derived from the constitutional provisions themselves, but governments usually have to rely on judicial interpretation – especially in common law countries. In the absence of judicial interpretation or to complement the decisions of courts, authorities can (and are encouraged to) turn to IL developments for an improved understanding of the positive action required by constitutional environmental provisions generally. An (inverse) enquiry into whether or not global environmental governors may learn from domestic experiences is highly relevant and likely to produce interesting results, but falls beyond the scope of what has been the focus in this chapter.

The generic activities that were extracted from IL in this contribution may at times be almost as broad as constitutional environmental provisions themselves. Clearly, however, they appear to be dynamic. Each of the generic activities carries equal weight, and no one of them should be regarded as more significant than another. Hence, it may be necessary for national government to design a means through which to ensure that all of the generic activities are attended to. It may similarly be necessary for domestic courts to understand and buy into the idea that, generally speaking, these activities resemble the type of entitlements that people have in terms of constitutional environmental law.

SEC needs to be regulated or "governed" for the detrimental impacts (although not suggesting that all the impacts of SEC are necessarily negative) thereof to remain manageable over time. The law should be regarded as a key part of this governance endeavour. Constitutional environmental law in particular can create flexible parameters for the governance of SEC – but should not be impervious to scientific knowledge or social demands.

This chapter has aimed to show that the long-term and effective governance of SEC ultimately requires not only an intersection of legal, social and natural sciences but also of the fields of IL, constitutional law and planning. It furthermore showed that the challenges posed by SEC, at least from a legal perspective, may demand a fusion of activities at different levels. In the final instance a case was made that those possessing state authority, as but one group among many SEC stakeholders, should take cognizance of the need to take the lead in the preservation of our socio-ecological environment, while acknowledging the equally important need to welcome all of the other stakeholders into an equal partnership in this important endeavour. The route to follow towards this end would seem already to have been mapped out in international and constitutional environmental law.

Notes

1 According to Nagel (1970) "social change" may be viewed as a restructuring of the basic ways in which people in a society relate to each other with regard to government, culture, family life and the environment, for example. Kirdar (1992) (holds that "ecological change" relates to continuing deterioration of the world ecology and environment as evidenced in climate change and depletion of natural resources and is primarily caused by unsustainable patterns of production and consumption (particularly in industrialised countries) and persistence of poverty and restricted economic opportunities (particularly in developing countries).
2 See Kirdar (1992) on the historic development of environmental degradation and change generally.
3 This chapter focuses on constitutional environmental law. Yet, as far as the environment is in anthropocentric style defined to embrace also social concerns, the final proposals made embrace the notion of SEC and not only *ecological* change as the title to this chapter suggests.
4 Other countries with constitutional environmental rights or provisions include, but are not limited to: India, the Philippines, Colombia, the United States of America, Peru, Portugal, South Korea, Honduras, Uganda, Bangladesh, Spain, Belgium, Hungary, Norway, Brazil, Argentina, Chile, Costa Rica, Greece, the Netherlands, Namibia and Kenya.
5 The sources of international law generally include international conventions, international custom, the general principles of law recognized by civilised nations, judicial decisions and the teachings of valued publicists.
6 The environmental law of the European Union, the African Union, the Southern Africa Development Community or the Inter-American regional system, for example.
7 This thinking is supported in De Wet and Du Plessis (2010).

8 The judiciary in different countries will obviously not adopt concepts or elements from non-binding international instruments that are inconsistent with their constitutions.

9 Judiciaries and adjudicating bodies often strengthen the law by reflecting on veiled meanings and by construing directives. In the absence to date of an international environmental court, existing international tribunals and domestic courts remain to strengthen and interpret environmental rights. Adjudicating bodies may be crucial in assessing states' "margin of discretion" and in enlightening, *inter alia*, the role of the executive in fulfilling environmental rights.

10 Eide (1999: 132) states that the obligation to fulfill can be divided twofold: the obligation to facilitate and the obligation to provide. The obligation to facilitate requires states to take measures creating conditions by which individuals can take the necessary steps to take care of their own needs and the obligation to provide corresponds with the idea of providing a "safety-net".

11 The idea is conveyed that legislative measures alone are insufficient for the fulfillment of socio-economic rights. See principles 17 and 18 of the Limburg Principles.

12 Principles 27 and 28 of the Limburg Principles.

13 Principle 72 of the Limburg Principles and guideline 8 of the Maastricht Guidelines. The notion of "progressive realization" does not, however, serve as a pretext for the non-fulfillment of environmental rights. Similarly, states will not be able to justify derogations from or limitations of environmental rights because of, for example, different social, religious and cultural backgrounds.

14 Guideline 7 of the Maastricht Guidelines. For specific violations through acts of commission and acts of omission, see guidelines 14 and 15.

15 Guidelines 9 and 11 of the Maastricht Guidelines.

16 Guidelines 16, 18 and 19 of the Maastricht Guidelines.

17 The basis for action in these cases was not exclusively environmental rights or provisions. Environmental issues have been addressed also by making use of rights contained in IL instruments such as the rights to life, association, expression, information, political participation, personal liberty, equality, health, decent living conditions, decent working environments, family life and legal redress. Shelton in Picolotti and Taillant 2003 at 3 remarks that "international organs and tribunals expanded or reinterpreted" many of these guarantees "in light of environmental concerns". (See further Shelton in Picolotti and Taillant 2003: 11–13).

18 In the decision by the African Commission on Human and Peoples" Rights on Communication 155/96, the Nigerian government was found to be in violation of the article 24 environmental right contained in the African Charter on Human and Peoples" Rights.

19 *López Ostra v Spain* (1994), Strasbourg, application 16798/90. In this case the government of Spain's inaction resulted in non-fufilment of the environmental obligations imposed by article 8 of the European Convention on Human Rights.

20 *Guerra and Others v Italy* (1998), Strasbourg, application 14967/89. In this case the Italian government was found in contravention of the environmental claims that are read into article 8 of the European Convention on Human Rights, where it failed to provide timely and essential environmental information on a hazardous chemical factory enabling participants to assess the risk of living nearby this plant.

21 *Hatton and Others v UK* (2001), Strasbourg, application 36022/97. In this case the European Court of Human Rights addressed the issue of noise pollution (as a form of environmental pollution) in the context of the regulation of night flights at Heathrow Airport.

22 *Taskin and Others v Turkey* (2004), Strasbourg, application 46117/99. In this case the government of Turkey was successfully challenged before the European Court of Human Rights based on an alleged violation of citizens' environmental rights due to authorized gold mining activities that had serious environmental and health impacts.

23 *Social and Economic Rights Action Centre for Economic and Social Rights (SERAC) v Nigeria* (2001); *Taskin and Others v Turkey* (2004) and *Guerra and Others v Italy* (1998).

24 *Hatton and Others v United Kingdom* (2001) and *Social and Economic Rights Action Centre for Economic and Social Rights (SERAC) v Nigeria* (2001).

25 *Social and Economic Rights Action Centre for Economic and Social Rights (SERAC) v Nigeria* (2001) at para. 47. The machinery of a state can be interpreted to include legislative and administrative functionaries as well as other organs of state inclusive of the different spheres or levels of government and of course the governance endeavour itself.

26 *Social and Economic Rights Action Centre for Economic and Social Rights (SERAC) v Nigeria* (2001).

27 *Social and Economic Rights Action Centre for Economic and Social Rights (SERAC) v Nigeria* (2001) and *Taskin and Others v Turkey* (2004).

28 *Social and Economic Rights Action Centre for Economic and Social Rights (SERAC) v Nigeria* (2001); *Taskin and Others v Turkey* (2004) and *Guerra and Others v Italy* (1998).

29 *Taskin and Others v Turkey* (2004).

30 State authorities may, for example, be expected to remove residents from a dangerous or exposed site. See *Social and Economic Rights Action Centre for Economic and Social Rights (SERAC) v Nigeria* (2001); *Fadeyeva v Russia* (2005), Strasbourg, application 55723/00; *Moreno Gomez v Spain* (2004), Strasbourg, application 4143/02 and *Oneryildiz v Turkey* (2004), Strasbourg, application 48939/99. The latter case was, however, decided in terms of article 2 of the European Convention.

31 *Social and Economic Rights Action Centre for Economic and Social Rights (SERAC) v Nigeria* (2001) and *López Ostra v Spain* (1994). The ECHR found in the latter case that the aims intended with an environmental provision (a right) are important considerations in this balancing act.

32 This chapter is focused in the particular on the positive obligations of the executive and legislative branches of the state. Accordingly, no attention is paid to the obligations that may befall the judicial branch of government. However, the fulfilment of environmental rights, when taking into account the role of judicial bodies, may necessitate the addition of an eighth element that focuses on access to justice and issues related to *locus standi*.

33 In the context of this chapter, environmental justice and equality are not regarded as separate elements but are perceived as inextricably intertwined with each of the seven elements proposed.

34 Public participation in relation to environmental rights is expressly or implicitly called for, *inter alia*, in the Rio Declaration (principles 10, 20 and 22); Agenda 21 (chapter 23); Local Agenda 21; the Ksentini Report (para. 70 and principle 18 of the Draft Principles thereto); the Brundtland Report (principle 6); the Earth Charter (principle 13 (b)) and the Aarhus Convention (articles 6–8). It features also in international environmental case law. See par 2 above.

35 See on the importance of public participation, Pring and Noé in Zillman 2002: 11.

36 This links with the idea that participation embraces both the rights to know and to review. See Saladin in Picolotti and Taillant (2003: 57).

37 Verschuuren with reference to Ebbesson remarks that participation is costly, time-consuming and obstructive and could to some extent even repress differences. See Verschuuren (2005: 40–48) and Robinson in Jewell and Steele (1998: 54).

38 Picolotti (2003) outlines four basic modalities of public participation, namely: informative participation, consultative participation, participation in decision making and participation in management. The four conditions to ensure the enjoyment of the right to participate are said to be access to information, autonomy, political willingness and stakeholder identification.

39 Collection and dissemination of environmental information in relation to environmental rights are expressly or implicitly called for, *inter alia*, in the Aarhus Convention; the Rio Declaration (principle 10); Agenda 21 (chapter 23); Local Agenda 21 and the Ksentini Report (principle 15 of the Draft Principles thereto). They feature also in international environmental case law. See par 2 above.

40 Robinson in Jewell and Steele (1998) remarks with reference to Dovers that "(g)iven the pervasive uncertainty" surrounding environmental decision-making, we need a profound increase in ecological research and monitoring, and stronger statutory and informational bases for gathering, co-ordinating and communicating information."

41 The right to claim access to environmental information will, however, not under all circumstances be absolute – it could at times be subject to limitation in terms, for example, of the right to privacy.

42 The development and implementation of environmental law, policy and programmes in relation to environmental rights is expressly or implicitly called for, *inter alia*, in Agenda 21; Local Agenda 21 and the Ksentini Report (principle 22 of the Draft Principles thereto). It featured also as a particular point of importance in the SERAC decision. See par 2 above.

43 Although not in detail discussed in this contribution the very important role of innovative and progressive judicial decisions (the work of the judicial branch of government) in realizing constitutional environmental entitlements cannot be over-emphasised. If any of the generic activities discussed in par 3 fails the people, it is up to the courts to see that justice be done in as far as the separation of state powers (the *trias politica*) allows.

44 De Wet (1996: 38) contends that legislation is often needed "to give a more concrete shape to constitutional rights."

45 Ferreira (1999: 92, 106, 291) holds that the implementation of socio-economic rights (inclusive of environmental rights) can be vastly dependent on matters of policy. He proceeds to state that environmental policy may serve a particularly important role as a means to hold governors accountable for commitments made. He also makes a strong case that the implementation of socio-economic rights largely depends on policy considerations. Several advantages and disadvantages exist pertaining to the use of legislation or policy documents. Due to length constraints these will not be elaborated upon in this chapter.

46 The notions of programmes and projects can for the purpose of this chapter be viewed as two sides of the same coin and to carry the same meaning. Programmes and projects in the context used here are indicative of activities other than law and/or policy making.

47 The inception and use of accurate and scientifically validated environmental information and interdisciplinary cooperation may be fundamentally important in the development of law, policy and programmes.

48 Compliance and enforcement in relation to environmental rights are expressly or implicitly called for, *inter alia*, in guidelines 16, 17, 19 and 25 of the Maastricht Guidelines. Compliance and enforcement also features as a particular point of importance in the López Ostra decision. See par 2 above.

49 International Network for Environmental Compliance and Enforcement (INECE) Principles of Enforcement 2005.

50 Provision of environmental infrastructure in relation to environmental rights is expressly or implicitly called for in, *inter alia*, principle 28 of the Limburg Principles and guideline 9 of the Maastricht Guidelines.

References

Anleu, S. L. R. 2000. *Law and Social Change*. London: Sage.
Bakshi, P. M. 2000. *The Constitution of India*. 4th edn. Delhi: Universal Law Publishing.

Belotsky, L. 1998. "Freedom of Access to Environmental Information: A Survey of Problems and Legislative Developments". *Tel Aviv University Studies in Law*: 287–304.

Birnie, P. and Boyle, A. E. 2002. *International Law and the Environment*. 2nd edn. New York: Oxford University Press.

Bodansky, D. 2004. "The Use of International Sources in Constitutional Opinion". *Georgia Journal of International and Comparative Law*: 421–8.

Bodansky, D., Brunnée, J. and Heyet, E. (eds) 2007. *The Oxford Handbook of International Environmental Law*. New York: Oxford University Press.

Brand, D. and Heyns, C. (eds) 2005. *Socio-Economic Rights in South Africa*. Pretoria: Pretoria University Law Press.

Burns, Y. 1993. "South Africa in Transition Green Rights and an Environmental Management System". Paper delivered at a workshop of a conference on South Africa in Transition held on 15 October 1993 by the VerLoren van Themaat Centre Environmental Law Division of the University of South Africa and Published in the Environmental Law Series no 2.

Crossen, T. 2004. "Multilateral Environmental Agreements and the Compliance Continuum". *Georgetown International Law Review*: 473–500.

De Wet, E. 1996. *The Constitutional Enforceability of Economic and Social Rights*. Durban: Butterworths.

De Wet, E. and Du Plessis, A. 2010. "The Meaning of Certain Substantive Obligations Distilled from International Human Rights Instruments for Constitutional Environmental Rights in South Africa". *African Human Rights Law Journal*: 345–67.

Du Plessis, W. 1999. "'n' Reg op Omgewingsinligting in Nederland". *Stellenbosch Law Review*: 36–55.

Dugard, J. 2005. *International Law: A South African Perspective*. 2nd edn. Cape Town: Juta.

Earthrights. 2002. "The Need to Recognise the Right to a Satisfactory Environment". *Yearbook of Human Rights and Environment* 2: 221–62.

Eide, A. 1999. "The Right to an Adequate Standard of Living under International Human Rights Law". *Norwegian Institute of Human Rights Human Rights Report* 2: 131–47.

Fadeyeva v Russia. 2005. Strasbourg, application 55723/00.

Ferreira, G. M. 1999. "Omgewingsbeleid en die Fundamentele Reg op 'n Skoon en Gesonde Omgewing". *Journal of South African Law* 1: 90–113.

Ginther, K., Denters, E. and de Waart, P. J. I. M. (eds). 1995. *Sustainable Development and Good Governance*. Dordrecht: Martinus Nijhoff.

Guerra and Others v Italy. 1998. Strasbourg, application 14967/89.

Hatton and Others v UK. 2001. Strasbourg, application 36022/97.

Human Rights Quarterly. 1987. "The Limburg Principles on the Implementation of the International Covenant on Economic, Social and Cultural Rights". *Human Rights Quarterly* 9(2): 122–35.

Human Rights Quarterly. 1998. "The Maastricht Guidelines on Violations of Economic, Social and Cultural Rights". *Human Rights Quarterly* 20(3): 691–704.

Hutter, B. 1997. *Compliance: Regulation and Environment*. Oxford: Clarendon Press.

Jewell, T. and Steele, J. (eds). 1998. *Law in Environmental Decision-Making: National, European and International Perspectives*. Oxford: Clarendon Press.

Kamenka, E. and Erh-Soon Tay, A. 1978. *Human Rights*. London: Edward Arnold Publishers.

Kirdar, U. 1992. *Change: Threat or Opportunity for Human Progress*. New York: United Nations Publications.

Lavrysen, L. and Theunis, J. 2007. "Het Recht op de Bescherming van Een Gezond Leefmilieu: Een Blik over de Grenzen en Een Blik Actherom" *Liber Amicorum Paul Martens*: 363–82.

Leckie and Gallagher (eds) 2006. *Economic, Social and Cultural Rights: A Legal Resource Guide*. Philadelphia: University of Pennsylvania Press.

López Ostra v Spain. 1994. Strasbourg, application 16798/90.

Moreno Gomez v Spain. 2004. Strasbourg, application 4143/02.

Nagel, S. S. (ed.). 1970. *Law and Social Change*. California: Sage Publications.

Nickel, J. W. 1993. "The Human Right to a Safe Environment: Philosophical Perspectives on Its Scope and Justification" *Yale Journal of International Law Volume* 18: 282–95.

Oneryildiz v Turkey. 2004. Strasbourg, application 48939/99.

Picolotti, R. 2003. "Agenda 21 and Human Rights: The Right to Participate". In Picolotti, R. and Taillant, Jd. (eds) 2003. *Linking Human Rights and the Environment*. Tucson, Arizona: The University of Arizona Press.

Picolotti, R. and Taillant, Jd. (eds) 2003. *Linking Human Rights and the Environment*. Tucson, Arizona: The University of Arizona Press.

Social and Economic Rights Action Centre for Economic and Social Rights (SERAC) v Nigeria 2001.

Streck, C. 2002. "The World Summit on Sustainable Development: Partnerships as New Tools in Environmental Governance". *Yearbook of International Environmental Law*: 63–95.

Symonides, J. 1992. "The Human Right to a Clean, Balanced and Protected Environment". *International Journal of Legal Information Volume* 20: 24–40.

Taskin and Others v Turkey. 2004. Strasbourg, application 46117/99.

United Nations 1987. Limburg Principles on the Implementation of the International Covenant on Economic, Social and Cultural Rights. UN doc. E/CN.4/1987/17, Annex.

Verschuuren, J. 1993. *Het Grondrecht op Bescherming van Het Leefmilieu*. LLD Thesis. The Netherlands: University Tilburg.

Verschuuren, J. 2005. "Public Participation regarding the Elaboration and Approval of Projects in the EU after the Aarhus Convention". *Yearbook of European Environmental Law Volume* 4: 29–48.

Zillman, D. N., *et al.* 2002. *Human Rights in Natural Resource Development*. New York: Oxford University Press.

Part II
Economics

5 Assessing financial adaptation strategies to extreme events in Europe

*Stefan Hochrainer-Stigler and
Reinhard Mechler*

Introduction

The increase in natural disaster losses from floods, storms, droughts, and other climate-related hazards, both in developed and developing countries, over the past decades has only been recently analysed in the context of longer run economic development (Gurenko 2004; Hochrainer and Mechler 2009). While the increase as of today may be explained largely by socio-economic factors such as increases of wealth and exposure (Munich Re 2009), there is mounting evidence of a climate-change signal in hazard intensity and frequency too (Schönwiese *et al.* 2003; Emanuel 2005; Parry *et al.* 2007).

Already today many regions and sectors in Europe seem very vulnerable to (increasing) disaster risk, partly due to a lack of resources to implement cost-effective loss reduction and novel risk transfer instruments, and the consequent inability to recover in a timely manner. While there has been little (with important exceptions) research on economic vulnerability as well as economic and fiscal risks of disasters, these risks can be very large (Mechler 2004; Hallegatte 2008, Hochrainer and Mechler 2009) and in order to provide an adequate basis for adaptation policies including such risk estimates seems crucial. Mostly due to a lack of reliable data, assessments of adaptation measures and their impacts within a risk-based manner are complicated and the inherent uncertainties can be very large. Yet, while specific weather extremes are unpredictable beyond a few days in the future, they can be best grasped in a risk-based manner by deriving probability distributions identifying events and losses in terms of return periods such as 10-, 50- or 100-year events (e.g. a 100 year event happens on average every 100 years, or in other words with 1 percent annual probability; see Grossi and Kunreuther 2005). In this manner, all possible loss scenarios can be analyzed and most robust strategies determined (Pflug and Römisch 2007).

Several economic and other sectors are already today rather exposed to climate variability and face planning problems with regard to climate change. Factoring in climate change (or failing to do so) will have important long term implications, as time horizons associated with investment decisions can be very large. For example, water infrastructure, dykes and dams, are often planned and built for decades, if not centuries (see Table 5.1).

Table 5.1 Planning for climate change in different sectors

Sector	Economic agent	Time scale (years)	Exposure to climate variability & change
Water infrastructure	Public sector	30–200	+++
Land-use planning	Public	>100	+++
Coastline & flood defences	Public	>50	+++
Building & housing	Public & private	30–150	++
Transportation infrastructure	Public & private	30–200	+
Energy production	Private	20–70	+
Financial risk management planning	Public (budget) & private (insurance)	1–5	+++

Source: Extended from Hallegatte 2009.

Contrary to most of the sectors mentioned in Table 5.1, decisions pertaining to the management of financial risks are different as the time scales involved are shorter – insurance is generally renewed annually, and budgets are planned on an annual basis, while planning implications, revenue and expenditures are often projected forward another 5 to 10 years. Consequently given the large uncertainties and knowledge gaps, there is more flexibility for pro-actively revisiting projections and decisions as compared to, e.g. land use planning or water infrastructure planning.

Our chapter suggests that the assessment of and the implementation of pro-active adaptation options for extremes should be analysed and modelled in a risk-based manner including a consideration of future projections (say, up to 10 or 20 years into the future depending on the time horizon of the adaptation measures). Although there are major methodological and data-related hurdles to overcome, such modelling is increasingly being made possible due to recent innovations and improvements in the relevant theory, especially extreme value theory and related fields in statistics (Embrechts *et al.* 1997), as well as modelling techniques and data provided by the climate change and natural hazards modelling communities (Hochrainer 2006; Hallegatte 2009; Feyen and Watkiss 2011). Running such assessments should eventually lead to a better and more consistent assessment and management of natural disaster risk in the long run, while better accounting for the inherent aleatoric (chance) variability of the relevant hazard phenomena (Kunreuther 2002; Oberkampf *et al.* 2004).

One of the key issues we address in this chapter is the quantification of economic vulnerability of governments including possible long-term conse-quences (here up to 10 years into the future). Economic vulnerability is defined as the capacity to refinance and absorb losses without major long-term consequences. We use an extended version of the CatSim (Catastrophe Simulation) modelling approach (Hochrainer 2006, Mechler *et al.* 2006; Hochrainer and Mechler 2009; Hochrainer, Mechler and Pflug 2009; Mechler, Hochrainer and Pflug 2012) to describe recent examples of assessments of *economic* impacts of natural disasters within a *risk-based* economic framework helping to study the costs and benefits of adaptation measures for reducing the longer run impacts of disasters. Such evaluation should not only be beneficial for the adaptation and risk management communities dealing with quantifiable approaches, but also for a general audience interested in an understanding of the most important components and interactions within an adaptation framework, including current caveats and emerging problems which have to be solved in the near future.

The chapter is organized as follows. In order to provide motivation for our analysis, the next section outlines disaster loss statistics and then discusses the issue of funding disaster losses in Europe. The following section presents possible adaptation strategies for the short as well as the long run which could be used in principle. Modelling approaches for assessing adaptation strategies in the longer run, which in the following are applied within the CatSim methodology are then discussed. The next section provides applications on long term implications, as well as key remaining problems with a special focus on Europe. The chapter ends with conclusions.

Natural disaster losses, financing strategies and climate change in Europe

Loss experience in Europe

Globally natural disaster impacts both in terms of human and economic effects are on the rise (CRED 2009; Munich Re 2009; Swiss Re 2009). This holds true for Europe, where especially flooding, but also wind storms and extreme temperature events seem to be increasing substantially (Figure 5.1). It is important to note that Europe is mostly affected by hazards which can be altered in their frequency and intensity through climate change (Figure 5.1). Hence, climate change is an

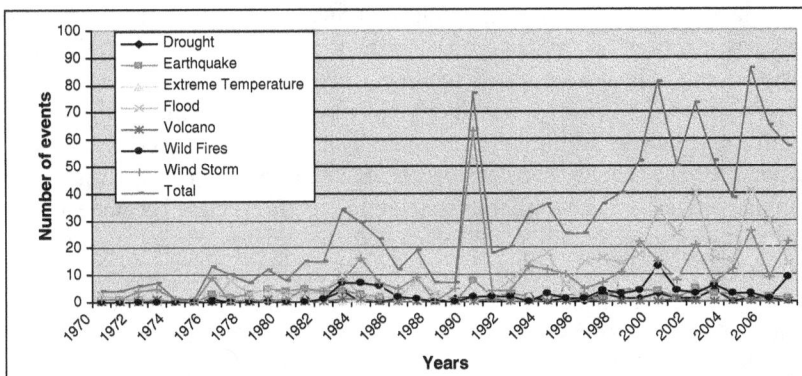

Figure 5.1 Number of natural disaster events for different hazards for the time period 1970–2007.

Source: CRED 2009.

important topic when it comes to determining the future developments of natural extreme phenomena.

Most of the natural hazards in Europe, especially flooding, have the potential to affect several countries at the same time, causing even higher losses simultaneously. For example, the Odra flood in 1997 affected the Czech Republic, Germany, Poland Slovakia at the same time, causing more than 100 casualties, economic losses of around €5 billion and insured losses of about €0.8 billion. Furthermore, more than 300,000 people had to be evacuated. Another large scale event was the flooding of 2002 in Austria, the Czech Republic, Germany and Slovakia causing 112 casualties, more than €14.4 billion in economic losses and more than €3.4 billion insured losses with more than 400,000 evacuations (EEA 2003).

Financing the losses

Beyond the immediate destruction and direct losses, disaster events may lead to a variety of adverse consequences, including the problem of financing the losses, from the household to the country level and finally to the European scale. To indicate the problems risk bearers may have in financing losses of large loss events, we examine the government natural disaster reserve fund in Austria, which is the national funding vehicle of last resort, and the European Solidarity Fund, which is the European sponsor of last resort for public sector risk accruing to member states. Both funds have been stressed after recent events. We start with the Austrian reserve fund.

After years with small losses, in 1998 the Austrian fund had been restricted legally to €29 million annually (for a full discussion see Hochrainer and Mechler 2009). In the wake of heavy flooding in 2002, relief and reconstruction expenses vastly exceeded the capital, and the fund had to be rescued by fresh capital to the extent of over €100 million in 2002 and nearly €200 million in 2003. Overall, the reserve fund as the government mechanism of financing public and private sector losses has not been an effective mechanism for coping with the aftermath of disaster events. Other sources of funding had generally to be sought, and a discussion ensued in Austria on the need and government's ability in light of this calamity to continue with certain large-scale investment projects such as the upgrading of the country's defensive air shield by means of the purchase of additional aircraft. Eventually, frictions within the government became so large, that the government coalition fell apart and the aircraft project was reduced substantially.

Given country financial vulnerability, countries may turn to the European Solidarity Fund (EUSF) as the European funding vehicle of last resort for natural and technological disasters (for a full discussion see Hochrainer, Bayer and Mechler 2010). The EUSF was actually funded after the 2002 floods and entered into force on 15 November 2002. Member states and accession countries can request aid in the event of a major natural disaster. It provides financial aid for emergency measures in the event of a natural disaster with direct losses above

€3 billion (at 2002 prices) or 0.6 percent of the gross national income (GNI). Thus, in case of a substantial national disaster event, the EU fund provides a mechanism for assistance and solidarity within the EU and has been accessed frequently over the last years. Although in relative terms the support granted is still small (for example, €134 million for the Austria floods in 2002 compared to a total direct damage of €2,900 million), the funding is sizeable and above all comes at no cost. There is a discussion to change the threshold levels to €1 billion and 0.5 percent of GNI as well as widening the definition of events to incorporate industrial disasters, public health emergencies and terrorism (Commission Report 2006), which at constant funding puts the viability of the fund at risk. What is more, the fund may be heavily exposed to one event only, as experienced in 2002 with three-quarters of the fund depleted due to the flooding event. With a large number of new very hazard-prone members and disaster losses likely to rise, the Solidarity Fund is likely to be severely underfunded in the future.

The role of climate change

Climate change with a projected significant climate-change related contribution to losses in the future, creates additional challenges (see Parry *et al.* 2007; Alcamo *et al.* 2007). Although losses are expected to rise, there is high uncertainty as regards to its spatial and sectoral distribution, a major problem for assessing impacts and losses on an aggregate basis. Because regions with lower economic development can be expected to experience larger adverse economic impacts (Benson and Clay 2000), it follows that from an adaptation perspective the question is not only where increases/decreases of natural hazard intensity and frequency are likely to occur in the future, but additionally whether exposed agents with their current set of shorter-term adaptation strategies are able to cope after the events without longer-term negative consequences. In the next section we therefore separate out options according to short- and long-run time scales.

Adaptation to climate variability and change

Disaster risks can be reduced or financed. As a first step for any systematic approach, it is important to identify who bears the risk. In the aggregate, risk bearers are the government and the private sector (business and households). Private sector stakeholders include property owners, insurers, reinsurers and the capital market. Additionally, as risks are effectively handed on further given low capacity to finance losses and little formal insurance and reinsurance, international financial institutions such as the World Bank, but also the European Union are exposed as funders of last resort (Miller and Keipi 2005). Each stakeholder mentioned above may implement a wide range of risk management and adaptation strategies, including risk reduction, preparedness and transfer. The most important options for climate variability (adaptation in the short run) and climate/global change (adaptation in the long run) are presented in the next subsections.

Instruments for adapting to climate variability

Generally speaking, risk management strategies can be separated into risk reduction techniques, risk financing instruments and loss absorption. The latter is called an *ex-post* or after-the-fact approach, while the former two are proactive (*ex-ante*) approaches. Risk reduction techniques (also called risk mitigation measures in the disaster community) are directed at lessening the direct impacts of a natural disaster. Risk reduction can take place before, during or after the disaster during the reconstruction phase. Measures may be both physical or structural and non-structural (Benson and Twigg 2004). While structural risk reduction reduces the physical susceptibility of the exposed elements at risk and includes measures such as building codes, non-structural risk reduction measures include, among others, the training of people in response to disasters and land use regulation.

Risk financing instruments can be categorized into risk transfer and risk spreading instruments. The dominant risk financing instrument is risk transfer through insurance. Alternative insurance instruments include, catastrophe bonds, contingent surplus notes, exchange traded catastrophe options, catastrophe equity puts, swaps and weather derivatives (Pollner 2001). There is also the possibility for inter-temporal risk spreading by means of contingent credit arrangements, reserve funds or micro-credit and micro-savings (see Table 5.2 for an overview for different risk bearers).

Table 5.2 Pre- and post-disaster risk financing arrangements

	Security for loss of assets (households/ businesses)	Food security for crops/livestock loss (farms)	Security for relief & reconstruction (governments)
Post disaster (ex post)	Emergency loans; money lenders; public assistance	Sale of productive assets, food aid	Diversions; loans from World Bank & other IFIs
Pre disaster (ex ante)			
Non-market	Kinship arrangements	Voluntary mutual arrangements	International aid
Inter-temporal	Micro-savings	Food storage	Catastrophe reserve funds, regional pools, contingent credit
Market-based risk transfer	Property & life insurance	Crop & livestock insurance (also index based)	Insurance or catastrophe bonds (also index based)

Source: Linnerooth-Bayer and Mechler 2005.

There are also government catastrophe (insurance) programs to increase insurance density in the country by supporting insurance companies after hazard events, which caused huge losses. The programs differ widely amongst each other and reflect the underlying exposures and the social milieu of the country (see Guy Carpenter 2003).

Adaptation to climate change and global change in the longer run

While the adaptation measures introduced above are important ones to decrease current and near future risk, for example a decade into the future, other, more long term adaptation options are equally important. For example, land use planning is seen as particularly important for addressing flooding in the long run. Relevant decisions include options as different as (i) the introduction of changes in land-use planning and management, (ii) the introduction of zoning – the delineation of areas where certain land uses are restricted or prohibited, (iii) the development of control of flood hazard areas leaving floodplains with low-value infrastructure, (iv) buy-out of land and property located in floodplains and stimulating relocation, (v) the introduction of flood protection for buildings, flood proofing installations and flood protection devices for cars, (vi) awareness raising, (vii) the building of flood defense infrastructure such as dams and flood control reservoirs, flood dykes, diversions, flood ways, improvement of channel capacity to convey a flood wave, enhancing source control via watershed management, (viii) enhancing storage – implementing floodplains and wetlands, polders and washlands, enhancing infiltration – permeable pathways and parking lots, (ix) managing vegetation like afforestation, cropping pattern avoiding bare soil during precipitation season, (x) promoting terracing and contour ploughing as well as (xi) various forms of techniques and options using probabilistic approaches for new insurance schemes.

In the case of droughts, which cause losses in agriculture, shape species distributions and abundance in tropical forests, and increase fire risk in temperate, Mediterranean and tropical systems, there are also different options possible. One can differentiate between low-cost, farm level technologies, and economy scale adjustments to droughts. Examples of the former include: choice of crop variety, change of planting date and local irrigation. Economy scale adjustments include: the availability of new cultivators, large scale expansion of irrigation, widespread fertilizer application, regional/national shift in planting date and the building of water reservoirs (McEvoy *et al.* 2008).

It seems evident that the quantification and modelling of long term adaptation instruments within a risk-management framework is difficult because of the dynamic nature of these adaptation measures and the explicit spatial approach necessary. Yet, modelling adaptation to climate variability is less problematic as measures can be built around other concepts used in relevant research areas like extreme value theory (Embrechts *et al.* 1997), dynamic financial risk analysis (Malevergne and Sornette 2006) and (probability-based) risk functional approaches (Pflug and Römisch 2007).

Modelling impacts and adaptation in the longer run

To a considerable extent, the management of disaster risks falls within the realm of local and regional authorities, and above all central governments, which will be discussed next.

Climate extremes and the role of the public sector

Not all losses due to extreme natural events can be efficiently reduced and market effects may not efficiently help to spread losses across a population or an economy. For coping with the residual impacts, there are many funding modalities helping to share and finance disaster losses: private and public (tax revenue) savings, insurance, and international assistance. For example, Figure 5.2 shows a cross-country sample of major disasters. In addition to insurance markets, governments as 'insurers of last resort' have an important role in supporting infrastructure reconstruction and relief support for households and businesses. Spending as a share of direct losses has ranged from 11 percent (drought in Portugal) to 48 percent (flooding in Poland). The only outlier in Europe has historically been the UK, with a large insurance penetration and almost no relief provided to the affected[1] (Linnerooth-Bayer and Mechler 2005).[2]

In the following, we focus on the financial implications on the public sector and options for sharing risks nationally. Disaster risk emanates from explicit and implicit contingent public sector liabilities, classified in Table 5.3. The explicit liability consists of rebuilding damaged or lost infrastructure, which is due to the public sector's allocative role in providing public goods. Implicit liabilities are related to the commitment of providing relief due to the distributive function in

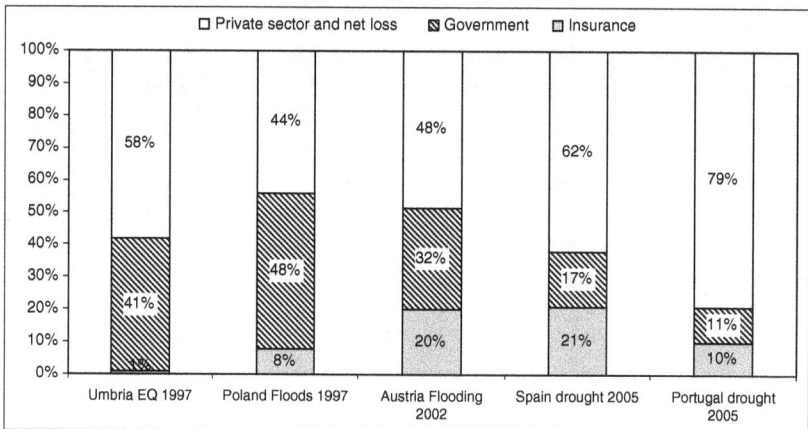

Figure 5.2 Cross-country sample of financing modalities of disaster losses by insurance, government assistance, and private sector and net loss (as a percentage of direct losses).

Source: Hochrainer and Mechler 2009.

Table 5.3 Government liabilities and disaster risk

Liabilities	Direct: obligation in any event	Contingent: obligation if a particular event occurs
Explicit Government liability recognized by law or contract	Foreign and domestic sovereign borrowing. Expenditures by budget law and budget expenditures	State guarantees for nonsovereign borrowing and public and private sector entities, reconstruction of public infrastructure
Implicit A 'moral' obligation of the government	Future recurrent costs of public investment projects, pension and health care expenditure	Default of subnational government and public and private entitites, disaster relief

Source: Modified after Schick and Polackova Brixi 2004.

reallocating wealth and providing support to the ones who cannot cope by themselves.

In order to study the relevance of contingent liabilities some illustrations may be useful. Figure 5.3 charts out flood risks in terms of average losses the government is responsible for financing from its budget compared to the regular deficit for key flood prone eastern European countries as well as Austria (as a reference point). Note that the 3 percent deficit line indicates the Maastricht criterion for sustainable budgeting. An implication of the charted results is that some governments seem unable or will fail to replace damaged infrastructure and to provide assistance to those in need post-disaster.

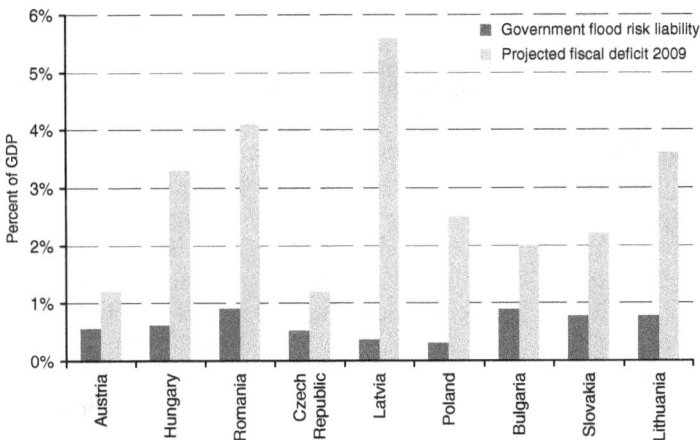

Figure 5.3 Government deficits and contingent disaster liabilities in flood-prone European countries.

Source: Hochrainer and Mechler 2009.

Framework and modelling approach

To assess the (macro) economic effects due to natural disasters in the long run an economic model has to be used. To address the main limitations within the economic modelling area we distinguish between the economic modelling in the disaster risk management field and the climate adaptation community (for a full discussion see Hochrainer and Mechler 2009; Mechler, Hochrainer and Pflug 2012). While the former focuses more on disaster risk represented in terms of average effects or the remodelling of singular events in the past, which may lead to a serious underestimation of the potential consequences of disasters due to its low probability/high consequence nature, in the latter extreme event risks are represented in a rather ad-hoc manner usually via add-on damage functions that are based on average past impacts and contingent temperature increases. Furthermore, there are usually no feedbacks considered within the climate change impacts to the socio-economic drivers (production, demographics). Finally, adaptation is not considered explicitly. This subsection lays out how to overcome these problems in a systematic manner on the country level.

The model framework we use is the CatSim (Catastrophe Simulation), which in a risk-based framework accounts for the macroeconomic impacts due to natural disasters as well as outlines the costs and benefits of measures for reducing those impacts (Mechler *et al.* 2006; Hochrainer 2006, Hochrainer and Mechler 2008; Hochrainer, Mechler and Pflug 2009; Mechler, Hochrainer and Pflug 2012). The innovation of CatSim is that it explicitly models direct and indirect risks as well as the inherent uncertainty of those estimates from a probability based perspective and helps the decision maker to define and analyse risk management strategies on a country level. In the following we focus on financial and economic vulnerability and risk to natural hazards. However, it should be kept in mind that our approach assesses only one dimension of risk, namely the economic one, neglecting important ecological and social effects. Figure 5.4 shows the overall methodological approach in a nutshell.

Direct monetary risks to public and private sector assets are estimated as a function of the frequency and intensity of hazards (floods, storms), the assets exposed and their physical vulnerability. Economic vulnerability is a function of economic resilience and direct risk and relates the susceptibility of the economic system to potential disaster damage in terms of monetary losses and return periods. A key objective of fiscal policy is to ensure sufficient *fiscal space*, which can be defined as the flexibility in a government's budget to fund new and emerging items subject to keeping the fiscal position sustainable (see Heller 2005). It can be assessed by simulating asset risks and estimating the government and private sector ability to finance these risks.

In the model, disaster risk is mainstreamed into national development planning by incorporating direct disaster risk and potential resource gaps for funding these losses into macroeconomic projections of the country. These consequences can be analysed on variables, such as on the budget or on economic growth, which are *flow* indicators as compared to impacts on *stocks* addressed by the direct asset risk

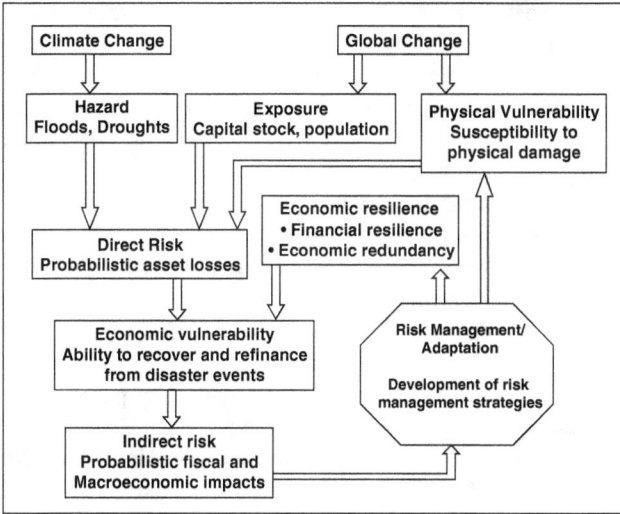

Figure 5.4 CatSim framework.
Source: based on Hochrainer, Mechler and Pflug 2009.

estimation. Taking these risks into account one can look at proactive (risk management/adaptation) options to strengthen the economic resilience and/or decrease physical vulnerability by means discussed already above.

The macroeconomic specifications are based on a simple Solow-type growth framework and the model's focus is on the potential for medium to longer term growth and development of aggregate economic variables given the explicit consideration of disaster risks. One key consideration here is the path dependence of the modelling approach. As disasters can happen any time (and more than once over a given time frame) and such occurrences will change the economic trajectory going forward, all possible disaster occurrence situations have to be considered, e.g. it will make a difference in year 10 if in year 2 and year 7 an event occurs, or if it occurs in year 5 and year 7 (Hochrainer 2006). As the adaptation instruments and their availability are also dependent on the current economic situation in an non-linear way (e.g. outside help is dependent on media attention, deficit financing is dependent on current indebtedness levels etc.), analytical solutions are not tractable and therefore simulation type of approaches have to be used. To account for uncertainty confidence bounds and different model outcomes (where possible) are used to reflect aleatoric and epistemic uncertainty (Kunreuther 2002; Oberkampf *et al.* 2004; Grossi and Kunreuther 2005).

Applications of the model framework

We focus on different angles of our assessment approach (Figure 5.4) in order to suggest the relevance of a risk based assessment of extremes and adaptation measures, including the necessity of stakeholder involvement.

We start with the European Solidarity fund (EUSF), which is an important financing instrument for EU governments after large disaster events. A government aiming at a fiscally sustainable risk financing strategy for its contingent and hidden liabilities would include this instrument in its ultimate chosen portfolio, as it comes at no price. However, to assume the liquidity of the fund one has to assume that the €1 billion capacity is never reached, which is merely an optimistic assumption not based on any assessment of corresponding risk. Hence, we wanted to answer the question what the annual ruin probability of the Fund is, i.e. the annual probability that payments from the Fund would exceed the 1 billion threshold. We therefore had to estimate loss distributions on the country scale for each European country, i.e. direct risk had to be estimated (a very complex and difficult task, see Lugeri *et al.* 2009). This was only possible for flood hazards, which caused the largest damages; 75 percent of the Fund payments were due to this type of hazard in the past (see Hochrainer, Bayer and Mechler 2010). Using a stochastic simulation approach (Hochrainer 2009), it was calculated that the Fund may already be underfunded today as the annual probability of ruin was estimated to be around 8 percent, or in other words, one could expect that on average every 12 years there will be an expected shortfall (Hochrainer, Bayer and Mechler 2010). This in other words means that, assuming the fund cannot be used anymore, additional help from the EUSF would not be available for governments. As a consequence, governments are more highly financially vulnerable than previously thought.

As always, there are several limitations associated with the assessment approach:

- While this was the first time country direct loss distributions have been used to make a risk assessment of the Fund, one key disadvantage of the approach was that only one (flood) hazard was looked at. Looking at the recent history of the EUSF, 75 percent of payments were due to flood events, which indicates that our estimate could neglect as much as 25 percent of expected EUSF payouts.
- Only single events for each country were looked at, i.e. no flood events which are happening simultaneously over more than one country were considered. Hence, the estimates have to be treated as at the lower bounds. The possibilities of large scale events affecting several countries has therefore to include some dependency measures.
- Global change, including the increase in wealth, could further increase total losses and therefore decrease the robustness of the Fund in the future. Furthermore, while climate change was only incorporated in a way of sensitivity analysis it additionally showed a further decrease in the robustness (Hochrainer, Bayer and Mechler 2010).

Regarding adaptation options rendering the fund sustainable in the long run, but recognizing that the risk of depletion cannot be decreased to zero, the funds risk could be decreased in principle, either by an increase of the Fund or via novel reinsurance arrangements (Hochrainer, Bayer and Mechler 2010).

As a second application, we give an example for determining the *economic vulnerability* and *macroeconomic risk* of natural disasters on the country scale. As a case study we select Hungary. Hungary, encompassing the Tisza River basin to the east, is an interesting case for several reasons. In Europe, Hungary ranks only behind the Netherlands with respect to geographical area exposed to floods. Over half of the country's territory, two-thirds of its arable land and a third of its railways are exposed to riverine, ground water and flash floods. Adding to the geographical scale of the problem, floods appear to be worsening in their intensity and frequency. With increasing losses, the Hungarian government is concerned about continuing its tradition of taking almost full responsibility for flood risk management, including flood prevention, response, relief and public infrastructure repair. With membership in the European Union Hungarians have committed to a program of fiscal austerity.

Direct risk (Figure 5.4) was used as an input parameter and defined in terms of loss exceedance curves, i.e. the probabilities (y axis) that given losses (x-axis) are exceeded. Figure 5.5 shows the loss exceedance curve for Hungary. Note that three distributions are given, due to modelling uncertainties.

Economic vulnerability was measured as the resource gap year event, and macroeconomic (fiscal) risk in terms of decrease of budget resources in the next 10 years due to natural disaster events. It was found that Hungary could have problems of financing losses for events happen on average less then every 100 years. Furthermore, it could expect a 10 percent decrease of their fiscal space in the next 10 years due to natural disaster events compared to the no-disaster event case (Hochrainer and Mechler 2009). Hence, the analysis suggests that disasters may importantly add to fiscal volatility today and in the future, and fiscal planning may be necessary to avoid these impacts. While in the CatSim approach (local) optimal financing portfolios could be calculated (dependent on the objective

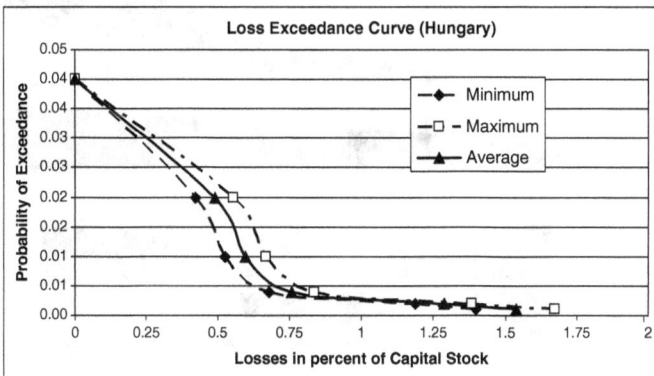

Figure 5.5 Loss exceedance curve for Hungary.
Source: Hochrainer and Mechler 2009.

function) we already noted that these numbers show only one dimension (the economic one) of the whole problem. To arrive at sustainable solutions in the long run, participatory processes are useful; these are discussed next.

It is a challenge to bridge the gap between the scientific assessment and risk management strategies (see Figure 5.4), as well as policy-relevant and more practical issues. For this purpose, CatSim also has a graphical user interface and can be used as a stand-alone application which makes it possible to assess expert opinions within the model approach. The results and interrelationships of important variables such as probability, losses and risk financing are used to express complex ideas in an understandable manner. Figure 5.6 may serve as an example, which shows the user interface for assessing the financial vulnerability. The parameters which can be changed are listed on the top, while the graphical results are shown in the main part of the window. Without using any terminologies and modelling explanation, the user can easily understand the relationship between loss financing and the probability level of the disasters, if he knows that the x-axis is the graphical representation of the impact level of the disasters and the y-axis is the damages due to disasters separated into different financing resources available. Issues of global and climate change can be assessed in this manner too, e.g. by shifting loss distributions or increasing the exposure

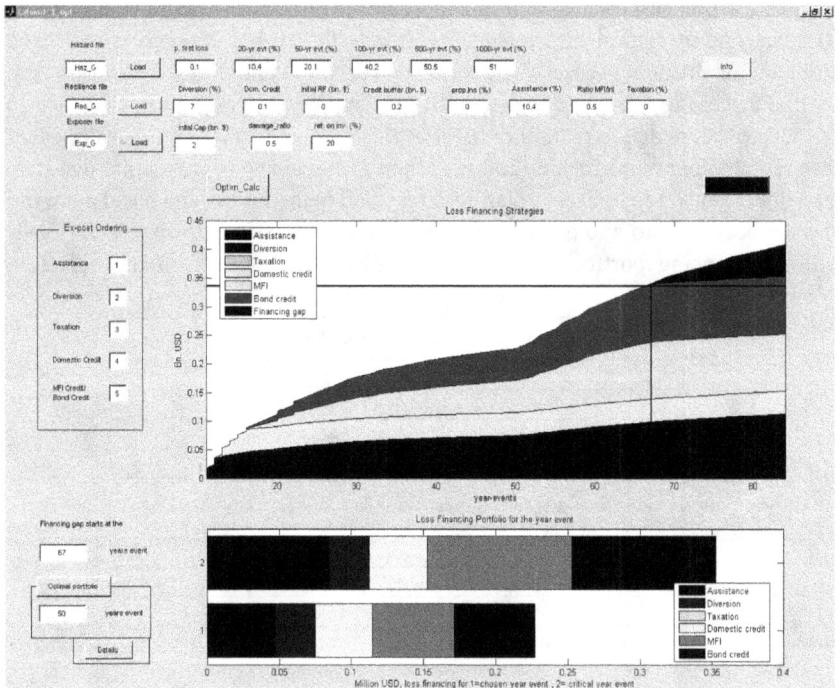

Figure 5.6 CatSim user interface to determine the financial vulnerability.
Source: Hochrainer and Mechler 2008.

over time. As already indicated it is important to keep in mind that the model shows one dimension of the threat only, namely the economic vulnerability of the government and the implications for the future via a set of indicators. It is clear, that other dimensions in the context of extreme events and global changes are equally important, e.g. environmental effects or protection of human lives to name but a few, and in the process of assessing the financial vulnerability, such questions of adapting to global *and* climate change naturally arises because of the interrelationship of the different dimensions (Hochrainer and Mechler 2008).

The model can assist policy makers in assessing one piece of the problem, but results are not optimal in the sense that they solve the problems for all dimensions. Hence, rather than presenting the results an open process and discussion is always required when it comes to decision making (Hochrainer and Mechler 2008). This is, for Europe, no exception.

The last key component is the dynamics of direct risk and economic vulnerability due to climate and global change. However, for (not only) Europe such analysis is difficult due to the following.

- Most important is the lack of detailed spatial data information of land use changes in the future. However, such spatial maps of exposed elements are not yet available.
- Also detailed spatial information about the increase/decrease of natural hazards in the near future on the European scale is missing. More information is available for specific regions, but on larger spatial scales changes are often only expressed in terms of changes of some impact levels, e.g. the 100 year event or in terms of averages (Feyen and Watkiss 2011).
- Furthermore, physical vulnerability may change over time. Currently, with some exceptions (Hochrainer, Mechler and Pflug 2009) in the most advanced models, only changes in the probability of first loss are considered yet (Feyen and Watkiss 2011).

Conclusions

Irrespective of future changes, weather-related disasters already today pose substantial burdens for households, businesses, and governments in Europe, and adaptation to those hazards and changes therein is already ongoing. The starting point for the analysis was the fact that we find evidence seemingly refuting the common belief, that European countries due to their level of development can efficiently deal with disaster risk and are risk-neutral towards such risk due to their ability to pool and spread risks; therefore they would not need to account for disaster risks in their economic planning. After presenting possible adaptation options in the short and in the long run, we suggested tackling the problem from a (quantitative) risk based perspective, and to include indirect and possible macroeconomic effects explicitly within the analysis of different adaptation options.

We assessed the question how much risk the European Union and member states should take on. Financial risk management and adaptation options come with a price, usually higher than the expected losses (see for example Froot 2001). While risk cannot efficiently be reduced to zero, a consensus is needed to identify how much risk to absorb and how much to finance or transfer. Hence, as a part solution to this decision problem, the cost and benefits or the effectiveness of adaptation options may be quantified in a risk-based approach to make better decisions for the long run.

We proposed that it is inevitable to bridge the gap between science and policy to make progress in finding an efficient solution where not all decision variables can be quantified and therefore 'process based' approaches should be used instead in this stage. Based on a probability-based framework, we presented recent applications and suggested that it is indeed possible to assess adaptation options in the long run in a risk-based manner. We would argue that such approaches are preferable as they can incorporate all possible future scenarios in their assessment of given adaptation options. However, there are large uncertainties to be accounted for. Not all important variables can be reasonably well quantified or even should be quantified in monetary terms and therefore these non-quantifiable variables have to be taken into account differently, e.g. in stakeholder workshops for example.

Important limitations of such a risk-based approach are mainly due to lack of data needed to undertake estimates within reasonable confidence bounds. In other areas there is even no data at hand which could be used for assessing future effects due to extreme natural phenomena. Hence, risk estimates should also be updated from time to time to reflect changes in our knowledge of risk and associated patterns as well as adapt adaptation options (Bettencourt *et al.* 2006).

Especially in the light of the current debt crisis, including the downgrading of EU countries as well as the slowing of economic growth, the results presented above can be considered rather optimistic. Today, the European Union and its member states are much more vulnerable to natural disasters than in the past and it is just a question of time when the next catastrophe will occur which, in case of no action, will cause considerable fiscal and economic consequences which may reach far into the future.

Notes

1 This can be attributed to an (unwritten) compact holding that the government is responsible for structural risk management while households and business need to take action in terms of insurance.
2 Data on private sector spending are not available, and thus are lumped together with the net loss.

References

Alcamo, J., Moreno, J. M., Nováky, B., Bindi, M., Corobov, R., Devoy, R. J. N., Giannakopoulos, C., Martin, E., Olesen, J. E. and Shvidenko, A. 2007. 'Europe. Climate

Change 2007: Impacts, Adaptation and Vulnerability. Contribution of Working Group II to the Fourth Assessment Report of the Intergovernmental Panel on Climate Change'. In Parry, M. L., Canziani, O. F., Palutikof, J. P., van der Linden, P. J. and Hanson, C. E. (eds). *Climate Change 2007: Impacts, Adaptation and Vulnerability*. Cambridge, UK: Cambridge University Press, 541–80.

Benson, C. and Clay, E. 2000. 'Developing Countries and the Economic Impacts of Catastrophes: Managing Disaster Risk in Emerging Economies'. In Kreimer, A. and Arnold, M. (eds). *Managing Disaster Risk in Emerging Countries*. Washington, DC: World Bank Publication.

Benson, C. and Twigg, J. 2004. *Measuring Mitigation: Methodologies for Assessing Natural Hazard Risks and the Net Benefits of Mitigation. A Scoping Study*. Geneva: ProVention Consortium.

Bettencourt, S., Croad, R., Freeman, P., Hay, J., Jones, R., King, P., Lal, P., Mearns, A., Miller, G., Pswarayi- Riddihough, I., Simpson, A., Teuatabo, N., Trotz, U. and Van Aalst, M. 2006. *Not if but When: Adapting to Natural Hazards in the Pacific Islands Region: A Policy Note*. Washington DC: East Asia and Pacific Region, Pacific Islands Country Management Unit; the World Bank.

Commission Report 2006. *European Union Solidarity Fund Annual Report 2005*. COM (2006) 444 final, Brussels, 7.8.2006.

CRED. 2009. *The OFDA/CRED International Disaster Database*, www.em-dat.net – Université catholique de Louvain – Brussels – Belgium.

EEA. 2003. 'Mapping the Impacts of Recent Natural Disasters and Technological Accidents in Europe'. *Environmental issue report* 35. Copenhagen.

Embrechts, P., Klüppelberg, C. and Mikosch, T. 1997. *Modelling Extremal Events for Insurance and Finance*. Berlin: Springer.

Emanuel, K. 2005. 'Increasing Destructiveness of Tropical Cyclones over the past 30 Years'. *Nature*, 436: 686–68.

Feyen, L. and Watkiss, P. 2011. 'Policy Briefing Note 6: River Floods. The Impacts and Economic Costs of River Floods in Europe and the Costs and Benefits of Adaptation'. ClimateCost Project.

Froot, K. A. 2001. 'The Market for Catastrophe Risk: A Clinical Examination'. *Journal of Financial Economics*, 60: 529–571.

Grossi, P. and Kunreuther, H. (eds). 2005. *Catastrophe Modeling: A New Approach to Managing Risk*. New York: Springer.

Gurenko, E. 2004. *Catastrophe Risk and Reinsurance: A Country Risk Management Perspective*. London: Risk Books.

Guy Carpenter 2003. *The World Catastrophe Reinsurance Market 2003*. New York: Guy Carpenter.

Hallegatte, S. 2008. 'An Adaptive Regional Input-output Model and its Application to the Assessment of the Economic Cost of Katrina'. *Risk Analysis*, 28: 779–99.

Hallegatte, S. 2009. 'Strategies to Adapt to an Uncertain Climate Change'. Global *Environmental Change Part* doi:10.1016/j.gloenvcha.2008.12.003.

Heller, P. 2005. *Understanding Fiscal Space*. IMF Policy Discussion Papers 05/4, Wahington DC: International Monetary Fund.

Hochrainer, S. 2006. *Macroeconomic Risk Management against Natural Disasters*. Wiesbaden: German University Press (DUV).

Hochrainer, S. 2009. 'The European Union Solidarity Fund: Assessing its Risk of Depletion due to Catastrophe Flood Events', Annals. *Economic Science Series* 15(1): 35–41.

Hochrainer, S. and Mechler, R. 2008. 'Assessing Financial and Economic Vulnerability to Natural Hazards: Bridging the Gap between Scientific Assessment and the Implementation of Disaster Risk Management with the CatSim Model'. In Patt, A., Schröter, D., Klein, R. and de la Vega-Leinert, A. (eds) *Assessing Vulnerability to Global Environmental Change*. London: Earthscan, 173–94.

Hochrainer, S. and Mechler, R. 2009. *Report on Europe's Financial and Economic Vulnerability to Meteorological Extremes*. A.2.3. final deliverable, Brussel, Belgium: ADAM.

Hochrainer, S., Mechler, R. and Pflug, G. 2009. *Assessing Current and Future Impacts of Climate-related Extreme Events. The Case of Bangladesh*. IIASA Interim Report, IR-09-030, Laxenburg, Austria.

Hochrainer, S., Linnerooth-Bayer, J. and Mechler, R. 2010. 'The European Union Solidarity Fund: Its Viability, Legitimacy and Efficiency'. *Mitigation and Adaptation Strategies for Global Change*, 15: 797–810.

Kunreuther, H. 2002. 'Risk Analysis and Risk Management in an Uncertain World'. *Risk Analysis*, 22: 655–64.

Linnerooth-Bayer, J. and Mechler, R. 2005. 'Financing Disaster Risks in Developing and Emerging-Economy Countries'. *Policy Issues in Insurance* No. 08: Catastrophic Risks and Insurance, Paris: OECD, 105–62.

Lugeri, N., Kundzewicz, Z. B., Hochrainer, S., Genovese, E. and Radziejewski, M. 2009. 'River Flood Risk and Adaptation in Europe: Assessment of the Present Status'. *Mitigation and Adaptation Strategies for Global Change* (accepted).

Malevergne, Y. and Sornette, D. 2006. *Extreme Financial Risks*. New York: Springer.

McEvoy, D., Matczak, P., Heller, A. and Banaszak, I. 2008. *Adaptation and Mitigation Strategies: Supporting European Climate Policy*. A2.4. 18 month deliverable.

Mechler, R. 2004. *Natural Disaster Risk Management and Financing Disaster Losses in Developing Countries*. Karlsruhe: Verlag Versicherungswirtschaft GmbH.

Mechler, R., Hochrainer, S., Linnerooth-Bayer, J. and Pflug, G. 2006. 'Public Sector Financial Vulnerability to Disasters: The IIASA-Catsim Model'. In Birkmann, J. (ed.). *Measuring Vulnerability and Coping Capacity to Hazards of Natural Origin. Concepts and Methods*. Tokyo: United Nations University Press.

Mechler, R., Hochrainer-Stigler, S. and Pflug, G. (forthcoming). *The CATSIM Model for Assessing Policy Responses to Disasters on the Country Level*. Advances in Natural and Technological Hazards Research, Springer.

Miller, S. and Keipi, K. 2005. *Strategies and Financial Instruments for Disaster Risk Management in Latin America and the Caribbean*. Sustainable Development Department Technical Paper Series, Washington DC: IDB.

Munich, Re. 2009. Topics Geo. Natural Catastrophes 2008. Analyses, Assessments, Positions, Munich: Munich Reinsurance Company.

Oberkampf, W. L., Helton, J. C., Joslyn, C. A., Wojtkiewicz, S. F. and Ferson, S. 2004. 'Challenge Problems: Uncertainty in System Response given Uncertain Parameters'. *Reliability Engineering and System Safety*, 85: 11–19.

Parry, M. L., Canziani, O. F., Palutikof, J., van der Linden, P. and Hanson, C. (eds). 2007. *Climate change 2007: Impacts, adaptation and vulnerability*. Contribution of Working Group II to the Fourth Assessment Report of the Intergovernmental Panel on Climate Change, Cambridge, UK: Cambridge University Press.

Pflug, G. and Römisch, W. 2007. *Modeling, Measuring and Managing Risk*. Singapore: World Scientific.

Pollner, J. D. 2001. *Catastrophe Risk Management. Using Alternative Risk Financing and Insurance Pooling Mechanisms*. Research Working Paper 2560, Washington DC: World Bank.

Schick, A. and Polackova Brixi, H. (eds). 2004. *Government at Risk*. Washington DC: World Bank and Oxford University Press.

Schönwiese, C. D., Greaser, J. and Trowel, S. 2003. 'Secular Change of Extreme Monthly Precipitation in Europe'. *Theoretical and Applied Climatology*, 4: 132–9.

Swiss, Re. 2009. *Natural Catastrophes and Man-made Disasters in 2008*. Sigma 2/2009, Zurich: Swiss Reinsurance Company.

6 Demographic changes, sustainability, and the regulation of supply systems

Diana Hummel, Alexandra Lux and Cedric Janowicz

Introduction

Demographic changes represent specific challenges for long-term sustainability policies and governance: current population dynamics will have significant effects in the distant future, yet estimates of future demographic trends are only partially reliable. The impact of demographic changes on society and the environment is frequently the subject of debate within science and politics, as are possibilities to control population development in terms of 'demographic sustainability'. However, it is generally difficult to determine the connection between demography and sustainability itself, since the problems associated with population dynamics are complex, and include ecological, economic and societal aspects.

This chapter deals with demography from a transdisciplinary social–ecological perspective, which relates population dynamics to supply systems based on natural resources such as water, food and energy. If one considers the growing heterogeneity of demographic characteristics, this approach conceptualizes the interactions between demographic changes and provisioning as 'social–ecological systems'.[1] In this way, the analysis of population dynamics can be related to the problem of societies' capability to adapt to demographic changes, the shaping of social–ecological transformations, and societies' capacity to develop. From this perspective, regulatory and governance problems can be addressed differently: Instead of examining the preconditions for 'sustainable population development' and political attempts to control demographic development, one can focus upon the conditions for the regulation of supply.

The chapter starts with a discussion of the diversity of population dynamics and their impact on sustainable development. Against this background, the theoretical assumptions of the social–ecological approach will be described. The concept of supply systems serves as a methodological tool for empirical analyses. We discuss results drawn from empirical research in order to illustrate the governance challenges resulting from the interactions between demographic processes and provisioning structures. We present two case studies which investigate the challenges various demographic changes pose in terms of water supply systems. We then identify some properties of governance that can contribute to supply systems being better able to adapt.

Demography and sustainability

Efforts to understand the relationship between demographic and environmental changes have a long tradition, beginning with Thomas Malthus' famous 'Essay on the Principle of Population' (1798). In the 1970s, the debate largely concentrated on the impact of global population growth and high fertility rates in developing countries. For example, Paul Ehrlich's book 'The Population Bomb' (1968) focused on the issue of population growth, food production, and the environment, and gained wide public attention. By 1972, the Club of Rome's World Model predicted an 'overshoot and collapse' of global carrying capacity over the next 100 years. In the context of sustainable development, the issue of demographics was for a long time widely related to population growth, mainly in developing countries. For example, the World Commission on Environment and Development stated that 'rapidly growing populations can increase the pressure on resources and slow any rise in living standards; thus sustainable development can only be pursued if population size and growth are in harmony with the changing productive potential of the ecosystem' (WCED 1987: 9).

Today, the scientific debate about population, development and environment (PDE research) widely agrees that demographic developments depend on socio-cultural, economic and ecological conditions, and in turn impact upon societal and economic development, resource use, and ecosystem services in each specific context (de Sherbinin *et al.* 2007; Lutz *et al.* 2002; Charbit and Petit 2011). Mono-causal explanations and a focus on population size and growth are thus inadequate. Likewise, a recent report from The Royal Society emphasizes the diversity of demographic changes and their impact on sustainability, consumption and human wellbeing. 'The interactions between population, development and environment vary globally and regionally, and there are important differences among countries at different stages of development' (The Royal Society 2012: 63). It is not only population size that affects people's contribution to ecosystem changes and sustainable development; one should not ignore other demographic differences such as age composition, people's characteristics (such as educational attainment, health and nutrition status, place of residence), the density and distribution of a given population and household structures. Demographic diversity must therefore be taken into account, since these varying demographic patterns each have specific impacts on (non-) sustainable development, and different demographic transformations require differentiated political responses.

Social–ecological perspective: Provisioning the population

By systematically relating population dynamics to provisioning structures based on natural resources such as water, food or energy, the social–ecological approach allows an integrative, problem-oriented analysis of social and ecological problems caused by demographic changes.

From a theoretical perspective, population dynamics can be viewed as part of the interactions between 'nature' and 'society': Diverse demographic changes indicate transformations of *societal relations to nature*, that is, the relational network formed by individuals, societies and nature in interaction (Becker and Jahn 2006). This concept represents the historically and culturally specific structures and practices whereby individuals and societies regulate their relationship with nature, both with respect to material-energetic dimensions as well as cultural-symbolic aspects.

Provisioning structures are essential in terms of sustainable development issues: Each society must address the task of providing its population with food, energy, water, housing, and education and health services in such a way that it simultaneously meets basic human needs, ensures a decent quality of life, and preserves the natural foundations of life itself. Population dynamics are thus of crucial importance because the number, composition and needs of people in a given society (and their changes) imply regulatory requirements for supply systems. Furthermore, these interconnections result in social–ecological problems. From this perspective, regulatory and governance problems can be addressed in a new way: Instead of examining the preconditions for 'sustainable population development', this perspective focuses on the conditions needed for the sustainable provisioning of a population (Hummel *et al.* 2008a). Correspondingly, research questions can be posed differently: How do demographic changes and transformations of supply systems interact? What are the major challenges? What are the prerequisites for their adaptation and sustainable regulation?

As an analytical concept, supply systems aim at conceptualizing structures which provide the population with basic goods such as water, food, energy, transportation or housing as being societal regulated. Supply systems based on ecosystems are thus focused upon, so that links between natural resources and their utilization can be emphasized in the analysis. Accordingly, supply systems cover material-energetic dimensions (e.g. environmental conditions, resources, technical artifacts, etc.) as well as cultural-symbolic aspects of life (lifestyles, gender roles, forms of knowledge, etc.). The 'social' and the 'natural' are linked in a certain way, and develop specific problem dynamics in which economic, technical, political and ecological problems closely interact. In this context, demographic developments are vitally important: The scale and functional capability of supply systems such as water and food depend on present and future numbers of people who have to be provided for, together with their needs and income plus consumption and lifestyle patterns. The functioning of supply systems is therefore closely correlated with population dynamics, differentiation in social structures and culture, as well as macro-economic trends.

Supply systems as social–ecological systems

Supply systems can be conceived as complex social–ecological systems (SES) characterized by a coupling of natural and social elements and processes (Figure 6.1; see also Hummel *et al.* 2008a; Lux *et al.* 2006):

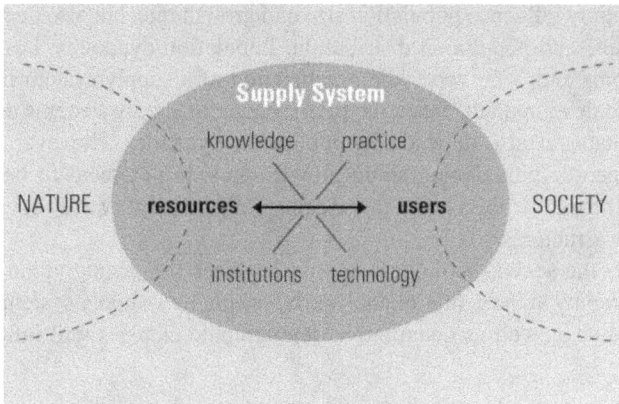

Figure 6.1 Supply systems as social–ecological systems.
Source: Hummel 2008a: 48.

Natural resources and their users are major components in the process of resource utilization for particular purposes. *Resources* comprise material-energetic, organic and spatial structures within an ecological and biophysical complex that are relevant and useable for supply systems such as food, water and energy. Renewable and non-renewable natural resources as well as further ecosystem services such as climatic regulations or sinks for pollutants and waste are considered as resources. Regulating the access to resources determines the level of provisioning and the degree of provisioning security. However, the *users* of supply system's goods and services are not synonymous with a given population; each group of users must be analysed for specific supply systems. Different user categories correspond to different parts of the population: For instance, groups of water supply system users include various sub-groups such as individuals, households, public water utilities, industry and agriculture. Depending on each specific supply system, distinctions must be made between (and within) different user groups (individual preferences, household structures, urban or rural dwellers, consumer sectors, etc.).

How do users obtain provisional services from supply systems? Interactions between users and resources are determined by forms of knowledge, practices, institutional arrangements, and technology. These elements determine the scope for action and possible options, and describe ways and means of accessing and allocating resources.

Demographic changes and the organization of provision are mutually dependent. Changes in numbers, distribution and social composition of the population in a given area influence the spatial-temporal dynamics of supply systems. However, there is no linear causal relationship between demographic processes and transformations of supply systems; instead, each mutually affects the other by means of feedback. Demographic processes are dynamic shifts that arise from changes in mortality, fertility and migration, and the effects of these changes not only influence population size and growth rate, but also age structure, household size and population distribution. Population dynamics thus influence supply systems and, vice versa, the organization of a supply system impacts on demographic development. Since the performance of supply systems depends on societal demand, it also depends on population dynamics. However, the sheer number of people plus demographic growth rates do not seem to be adequate indicators if one is to assess the quality of different ways of regulating provisioning structures.

Therefore, the social–ecological approach places the demographic *dynamics* and their diversity at the center of analysis by asking how supply systems together with qualitative as well as quantitative demographic changes will influence one another.

Demographic changes and the regulation of water supply systems

Different empirical case studies have been carried out in the *demons* project (see Note), applying the general conceptual model of supply systems. These empirical studies have examined supply systems for water or food. In order to take appropriate account of the temporal and spatial heterogeneity described above, the studies concentrated on selected demographic aspects: migratory movements, population distribution, population growth, urbanization, and decreases in population size. For the purposes of this chapter, we briefly sketch the results of the Middle East case study and the one relating to Germany, which both focus on water supply. Although these regions differ greatly with respect to their historic and political context, as well as their socioeconomic and environmental conditions, we identified some common patterns with respect to the interactions of demography and transformations of water supply.

Population growth and water resource management in the Middle East

Israel, the Palestinian Territories and Jordan are neighbours within the common geography and hydrology of the Jordan River Basin, and their residents depend on shared water resources. At the same time, their respective demographic development is closely interlinked as a result of historical and political developments within the region. Since the 1970s, the region has suffered from an ever-increasing water shortage while at the same time experiencing enormous population growth and rapidly increasing urban agglomerations. In addition, these transformations have taken place within an extremely complicated political situation – the Arab-Israeli conflict (Lipchin *et al.* 2007). Geopolitical conditions, the hydrological situation, and changes in ecosystems as well as social, economic and demographic transformations have been condensed into a conflict constellation that makes governance extremely difficult. Due to this set of issues, predictions about future demographic changes are very uncertain, particularly forecasts of interregional and intraregional migration processes. As our case study revealed, it is these migratory movements rather than natural population growth due to high fertility that have proved the most decisive demographic factor affecting the precarious state of the water supply (Hummel 2008). For example, Jordan has hosted several waves of refugees caused by the Middle East conflict. These migratory movements have led to enormous pressure on the country's water supply systems. Research and public debate usually concentrate on the interstate disputes over water resources in the region. If one takes the relevance of population dynamics into account, increasing intrastate tension must also be considered. This includes conflicts concerning the distribution of scarce water resources and how these resources are to be used – on the one hand between urban and rural residents, and on the other hand between water usage sectors, in particular agriculture and municipalities.

It is here that the relationship between supply systems for water and food becomes clear, since irrigated agriculture accounts for the lion's share of water use while contributing scant added value. From the point of view of economic efficiency, the best strategy to deal with water scarcity and a growing demand for drinking water would be to reallocate water from irrigated agriculture to sectors with greater added value such as industry and tourism and to urban households too. However, this transformation of the water supply system may lead to unintended consequences such as a marginalization of rural regions, which in turn would encourage migration to the cities and thus aggravate the strain on urban water supply systems (Shuval and Dweik 2007). This raises the question of an appropriate form of regulation, one which takes account of population dynamics as well as the relationship between water and food security. Strategies for demand-oriented resource management are required here – not only concerned with water availability in terms of quantity, but also with types of demand and the purpose for which water resources are used. Integrated water resources management would include new forms of resource utilization such as desalination, water re-use, and water-saving technologies, together with the involvement of relevant groups of players in decision-making processes. One therefore requires a set of policies that allows for the participation of different stakeholders at the intersectoral level (agriculture, industry, municipal water sector) and intergroup level (e.g. urban/rural residents, small farmers/agribusiness), see Figure 6.2.

Given these governance structures and forms of social–ecological regulation, population dynamics and limited water resources would not be an impediment; on the contrary, they could constitute the driving force for the development of more sustainable and adaptive supply systems – at the national level at least.

Population decline and water supply in Eastern Germany

Social–ecological problems arising from the interactions between supply systems and demographic developments can also be found in more developed regions. A wide body of literature on water, sewage, energy or waste infrastructure has highlighted the fundamental transformations that European infrastructure management is undergoing due to changes such as the liberalization of utility

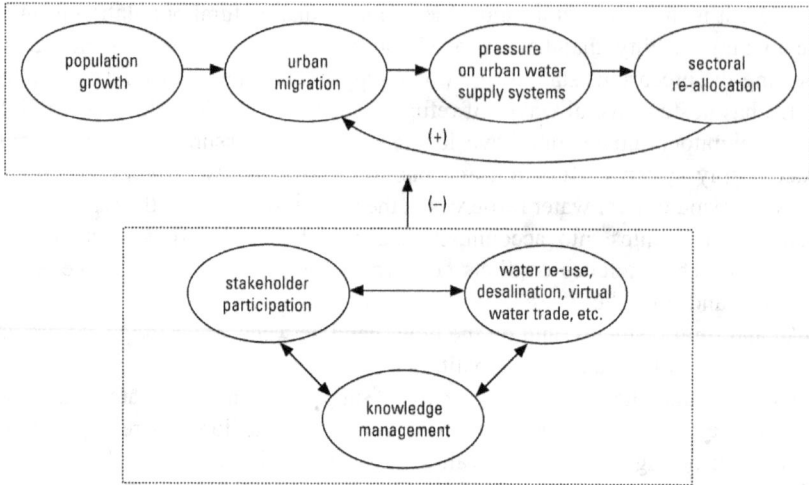

Figure 6.2 Social–ecological regulation.
Source: Hummel 2008: 207.

service markets, high costs of network modernization, uncertainty over future consumption patterns and over-capacity in networks (Guy *et al.* 2001; Loske and Schaeffer 2005; Juuti and Katko 2005). The study by Lux (Lux 2008, 2009) illustrates how decreasing populations impact on the water supply.

Eastern Germany experienced shrinking populations, the result of a decline in birth numbers and a high rate of migration to Western Germany (especially in the early 1990s), together with other demographic changes such as increasing household numbers and decreasing household sizes. This demographic situation is combined with the region's overall tendency to use less water. If the population of a municipality decreases, so does the number of its consumers; total demand for water falls, and its spatial distribution changes. This has technological, ecological and economic effects. These effects interact with demographic changes, thereby resulting in reciprocal reinforcement: Technical problems that may arise from underutilization are superimposed on economic consequences. Thus prices rise for individual households: the number of customers falls, so fewer people must bear the high fixed costs of water supply pipelines and facilities. There is a time lag before this effect appears, with repair and modernization work on the technical facilities only strengthening it. Different feedback loops can thus be identified, characterized on the one hand by demographic changes and consumer behaviour, and on the other hand by path dependency in relation to technical infrastructure and the economic basis of water supply (see Figure 6.3).

The study made clear that demographic shrinkage represents a many-sided phenomenon which cannot simply be reduced to a fall in population size. It includes the concurrence of decreasing population and a fall in population density as well as changes in household structures. A growing heterogeneity is apparent in

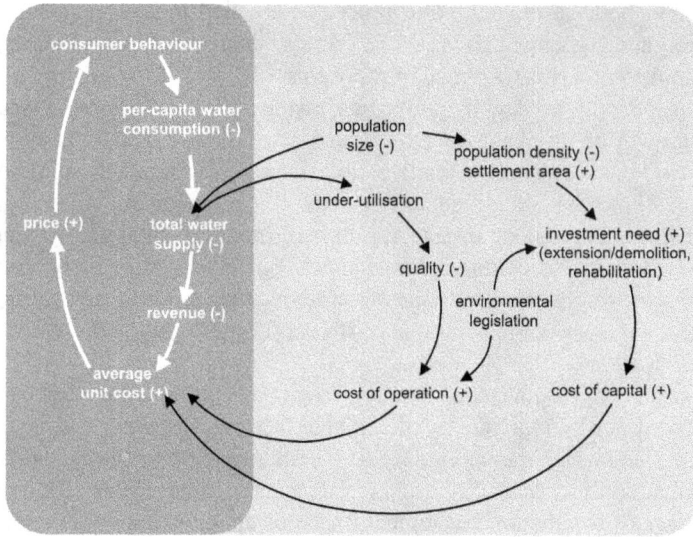

Figure 6.3 Feedback loops of reduced water consumption.
Source: Lux 2008: 173.

the region we studied: a juxtaposition of demographic growth, stability, and shrinkage. A central conclusion of the study was that fewer people do not necessarily mean less water will be used. It is far more the case that the structural effects of changes in population and household structures are superimposed on one another. Thus one can expect higher levels of water use with a growing number of smaller households and an increase in the total number of households. Moreover, changes in household technology and consumer's behaviour also play an important role in the relationship between population size and water use.

Challenges for the adaptive capacity of supply systems

As both case studies revealed, there is no linear or proportional relationship between decreases/ increases in the number of residents to be supplied and a fall/ rise in water use. Although they differ markedly in terms of their historical and cultural contexts, there are some striking similarities with respect to the impact of demography: demographic patterns are quite heterogeneous, containing asynchronous and sometimes contrary processes. Changes in household structures, i.e. the trend towards a growing number of households coupled with a reduction in the average household size, could be found in both regions. They significantly affect water demand and consumption. As a result, new demands are made on the adaptive capacity and regulation of the water supply systems. Both case studies revealed the key importance assigned to the factor of migration. In the Middle East, serious challenges for supply systems arise from sudden immigration, whereas in Eastern Germany it is emigration that has been causing problems. In both cases, migration processes are tied to changing population distribution and settlement patterns, which represents a challenge for the short- and medium-term adaptivity of supply systems.

What is often described in public discussions of demographic changes as harmful growth or shrinkage becomes (from a social–ecological perspective) a problem of unsuccessful adaptation to altered demographic and societal conditions. Somewhat simplified, one can say: it is not population developments as such that are the problem; instead, it is the inability of societal supply structures to adequately adapt to demographic changes. Societies can actively shape the effects of demographic changes. One therefore requires governance concepts that recognize the relevance of institutions, different forms of knowledge, technology, and social practices.

Crisis-prone developments of supply systems are produced neither by direct causal impact nor by individually identifiable factors. However, it is possible to determine – and weigh the importance of – certain driving forces that are critical to the formation of particular kinds of social–ecological problems which emerge in the course of population development. One of the most important findings of the case studies in the *demons* project is that migration and changes in population distribution and density present particular challenges to supply systems. Such changes are accompanied by specific problems of adaptation and governance, since they are associated with fluctuations in demand for goods and services, and are therefore difficult to predict. Moreover, special challenges arise as a result of divergent and asynchronic demographic developments and the superimposition of short-term and long-term processes. Depending on the historical context and specific geographic, economic and social-cultural conditions, these factors may contribute to regionally specific problems and crisis-prone changes that can threaten the security of provisioning. A major challenge for supply systems such as water supply is to consider long-term as well as short-term demographic developments because of the long life-cycles of supply and disposal networks and their high costs. One problem is that past decisions, especially in the area of material infrastructure, are difficult to rectify in the short or medium term. Any attempts at governance thus have to deal with the inherent uncertainty. For instance, predictions of future water demand are limited due to unexpected developments such as price structures and changing consumption patterns. The future flexibility and limited reversibility of planning decisions must therefore be taken into account (cf. Hummel and Lux 2007). A high degree of path dependency – that is, the irreversible nature of current structures and processes due to past decisions – diminishes the ability of supply systems to react to changes in demand. In this way, path dependencies can trigger feedback effects which impact on the population structure as well as supply systems.

Properties of governance

Sustainable or non-sustainable development of supply systems is not exclusively determined by demographic developments, but by economic and institutional structures too. It is impossible to provide a general description of sustainable conditions for supply systems and to formulate precise instructions for concrete action that could directly be put into practice. However, we can identify certain basic conditions for the regulation capabilities of supply systems. Specific 'guiding principles' have been developed for integrated strategies concerning resource regulation in infrastructures: functionality, transformation openness, adaptivity and integration (Kluge *et al.* 2007; Kluge and Schramm 2006). When it comes to the governance of water supply systems responding to the challenges presented by demographic changes, they can be formulated as follows (see also Hummel *et al.* 2008b: 442 ff.; Hummel 2012: 134 ff.):

- *Functionality* refers to the stability of supply systems and a system's economic and (in particular) managerial requirements, its need to ensure the fulfillment of its goals, and the requirement that its quality standards be met, e.g. the quality of drinking water. Both the functionality of ecosystem services and societal supply structures must be reflected.
- *Transformation openness* also refers to the ability to ensure supply services' reliability, as well as the ability to react to changes in demand in a timely manner – which often means quickly.
- *Integration:* Decisions about resource management must incorporate different knowledge and expertise from different groups of players. One therefore needs a participatory approach which allows the interested parties to develop a shared understanding of the problem at hand. This implies that conflicting interests among stakeholders are revealed, and alternative options for action are developed.
- *Adaptivity* refers to a system's capacity to evolve in order to accommodate changes and to expand its range of variability and ways of reducing vulnerability (Smit and Wandel 2006; Adger 2006). When it comes to designing sustainable supply systems, this means that the system is flexible enough to revise decisions that have already been made when faced with possible future changes in initial conditions. The capability of supply systems to adapt to demographic changes particularly means dealing with path dependencies and tendencies to persistence, as described above. For example, one needs flexible structures which are able to adapt to changed settlement patterns. Adaptivity also includes the efficient use of resources, and a resource productivity that takes account of various usage purposes and different consumption practices. In terms of sustainability, ecological, economic and social aspects must be combined. This could lead to a broader view in traditional supply sectors and open up new perspectives. For example, if water supply and sewage systems are merged at a decentralized level, their provisional services could be enhanced: It is not only possible to produce drinking water and water for sanitation and industrial use, but one can also gain recycled water and transfer it back into the water supply, or nutrients from sewage can be extracted and fed into agriculture.

Conclusion

Focusing on the relationships between diverse demographic changes and provisioning structures helps to highlight specific challenges for the long-term governance of sustainability. Population dynamics are associated with social–ecological problems: They are interdependent, difficult to predict, and not isolated in particular sectors. In fact, they unfold simultaneously along various temporal, spatial and social scales, from present events to far-reaching consequences. In order to regulate supply systems, one needs enhanced management practices which are geared toward predictive uncertainty, feedback, and the interference of short-term and long-term processes. The consequences of the unintended side-effects of steering actions or sectoral regulations must therefore be reflected. Policy instruments for the sustainable regulation of supply systems should include participative forms of feedback which allow the inclusion of players' perceptions of the effects of actions taken, such as monitoring or decision support systems. Long-term governance can then be seen as an iterative, adaptive learning process – a process that must always maintain and continually replenish its own natural and social foundations.

Note

1　The chapter refers to the major findings of the interdisciplinary research project entitled 'Supplying the Population. Interactions among Demographic Trends, Needs & Supply Systems' (*demons*), which was carried out between March 2002 and November 2007 (Hummel 2008). The research group was a joint project of ISOE (Institute for Social–Ecological Research) and the Goethe University, Frankfurt/Main, and was sponsored by the German Ministry of Education and Research (BMBF) as part of the 'Social–ecological Research' (SOEF) program.

References

Adger, W. N. 2006. 'Vulnerability'. *Global Environmental Change*, 16: 268–81.
Becker, E. and Jahn, Th. (eds). 2006. *Soziale Ökologie. Grundzüge einer Wissenschaft von den gesellschaftlichen Naturverhältnissen*. Frankfurt/ Main: Campus.
Bongaarts, J. 2006. 'How Long Will We Live?'. *Population and Development Review* 32 (4): 605–28.
Brown, L. R. 2006. *Plan B 2.0: Rescuing a Planet under Stress and a Civilization in Trouble*. New York: W.W. Norton & Company.
Caldwell, John C. 2001. 'The Globalization of Fertility Behavior'. *Population and Development Review* Suppl. 27: 93–115.
Chaimie, J. 2000. 'Demographic Issues of the 21st Century: The New International Population Order'. *Zeitschrift für Bevölkerungswissenschaft* 25(3, 4): 365–73.
Charbit, Y. and Petit, V. 2011. 'Toward a Comprehensive Demography: Rethinking the Research Agenda on Change and Response'. *Population and Development Review* 37 (2): 219–39.
de Sherbinin, A., Carr, D., Cassels, S. and Jiang, L. 2007. 'Annual Review of Environment and Resources'. *Population and Environment* 32(5) 5. July 2007, 21:47.
Ehrlich, P. 1968. *The Population Bomb*. New York: Ballantine Books.

Guy, S., Marvin, S. and Moss, T. (2001): *Urban Infrastructure in Transition: Networks, Buildings, Plans*. London/Sterling: Earthscan.

Hummel, D. 2008. 'Demographic Changes, Water Conflicts and Governance in the Middle East'. In Hummel, D. (ed.): *Population Dynamics and Supply Systems: A Transdisciplinary Approach*. Frankfurt/ Main: Campus, 181–210.

Hummel, D. 2012. 'Population Dynamics and Adaptive Capacity of Supply Systems'. In Glaser, M., Krause, G., Ratter, B. and Welp, M. (eds): *Human-Nature Interactions in the Anthropocene*. London: Routledge, 123–36.

Hummel, D., Hertler, C., Niemann, S., Lux, A. and Janowicz, C. 2008a. 'The Analytical Approach'. In Hummel, D. (ed.). 2008. *Population Dynamics and Supply Systems: A Transdisciplinary Approach*. Frankfurt/Main: Campus, 11–69.

Hummel, D., Hertler, C., Niemann, S., Lux, A. and Janowicz, C. 2008b. 'Synthesis'. In Hummel, D. (ed.). *Population Dynamics and Supply Systems: A Transdisciplinary Approach*. Frankfurt/ Main: Campus, 213–53.

Hummel, D. and Lux, A. 2007. 'Population Decline and Infrastructure: The Case of the German Water Supply System'. *Vienna Yearbook of Population Research*, 5: 167–91.

Juuti, P. and Katko, T. S. 2005. *WaterTime. D45: City in Time*. University of Tampere, Finland. www.watertime.org, retrieved 30/11/2011.

Kaufmann, F.-X. 2005. *Schrumpfende Gesellschaft. Vom Bevölkerungsrückgang und seinen Folgen*. Frankfurt/Main: Suhrkamp.

Kluge, Th., Liehr, S. and Schramm, E. 2007. Strukturveränderungen und neue Verfahren der Ressourcenregulation. Frankfurt/Main: ISOE–Diskussionspapiere No. 27.

Kluge, Th. and Schramm, E. 2006. 'Transformationsmanagement in Kommunen'. In Kluge, T., Liehr, S. and Schramm, E. 2007 (eds). *Strukturveränderungen und neue Verfahren der Ressourcenregulation*. ISOE-Diskussionspapiere 27, Frankfurt/Main: ISOE.

Kuckshinrichs, W. and Schlör, H. 2005. 'Challenges for the German Water Sector: The EU Water Framework Directive, National Infrastructure and Demography'. *Economic Business Review* 7(4): 291–309.

Lipchin, C., Pallant, E., Saranga, D. and Amster, A. (eds) 2007. *Integrated Water Resources Management in the Middle East*. Dordrecht: Springer.

Loske, R. and Schaeffer, R. (eds.) 2005. *Die Zukunft der Infrastrukturen. Intelligente Netzwerke für eine nachhaltige Entwicklung*. Marburg: Metropolis.

Lutz, W., Prskawetz, A. and Sanderson, W. C. (eds) 2002. 'Population and Environment: Methods of Analysis' *Population and Development Review*. A Supplement to Vol. 28, 2002, New York: Population Council.

Lutz, W., Sanderson, W. C. and Scherbov, S. (eds) 2004. *The End of World Population Growth in the 21st Century*. London/Sterling: New Challenges for Human Capital Formation & Sustainable Development.

Lutz, W., Sanderson, W. and Scherbov, S. 2008. 'The Coming Acceleration of Global Population Ageing'. In *Nature* published online 20 January 2008.

Lux, A. 2008. 'Shrinking Cities and Water Supply'. In Hummel, D. (ed.). *Population Dynamics and Supply Systems: A Transdisciplinary Approach*. Frankfurt/ Main: Campus, 161–79.

Lux, Alexandra 2009. *Wasserversorgung im Umbruch*. Der Bevölkerungsrückgang und seine Folgen für die öffentliche Wasserversorgung, Frankfurt/New York: Campus.

Lux, A., Janowicz, C. and Hummel, D. 2006. 'Versorgungssysteme'. In Becker, E. and Jahn, Th. (eds) *Soziale Ökologie*. Grundzüge einer Wissenschaft von den gesellschaftlichen Naturverhältnissen. Frankfurt/Main.

Malthus, Th. R. 1798. *An Essay on the Principle of Population*. London: J. Johnson. Library of Economics and Liberty. Available at www.econlib.org/library/Malthus/malPop1.html.

Roca, M. N. O. and Nuno Leitão, N. 2005. *Demographic Sustainability in Portugal*. Paper presented at 14th European Colloquium on Theoretical and Quantitative Geography, 9–13 September 2005 in Tomar/ Portugal. Hosted by Universidad Nova de Lisboa. Available at http://ceged.ulusofona.pt/Publicacoes/2005/2RocaMNO_LeitaoN_Text.pdf.

Royal Society (2012): *People and the Planet*. London: The Royal Society Science Policy.

Speidel, J. J., Weiss, D. C., Ethelston, S. A. and Gilbert, S. M. 2009. 'Population Policies, Programmes and the Environment'. *Philosophical Transactions of the Royal Society*, 364: 3049–65.

Shuval, H., and Dweik, H. (eds) 2007. *Water Resources in the Middle East: Israel-Palestinian Water Issues- From Conflict to Cooperation*. Berlin/Heidelberg: Springer.

Smit, B. and Wandel, J. 2006. 'Adaptation, Adaptive Capacity and Vulnerability'. *Global Environmental Change*, 16: 282–92.

Swiaczny, F. 2005. 'Aktuelle Aspekte des Weltbevölkerungsprozesses. Regionale Ergebnisse der UN World Population Prospects 2004'. Materialien zur Bevölkerungswissenschaft, No. 117. Wiesbaden.

United Nations 2011. *World Population Prospects*. The 2010 Revision Highlights and Advance Tables, New York: UN.

WCED – World Commission for Environment and Development 1987. *Our Common Future*. Oxford: Oxford University Press.

7 Innovation dynamics as lever for adaptive long-term policies

An evolutionary approach

Jan Nill

Introduction

Long term ecological changes such as climate change, which endangers at least the exisiting quality of life in many societies, involve two main governance challenges. First, due to the long-term and less visible character of those ecological changes which often span over more than one generation, proactive and long-term oriented policy strategies are necessary before the full consequences are visible. Second, according to the state of knowledge, the current development of economy and society in industrialised countries is not ecologically sustainable and there is a need for considerable technological, institutional and social changes to reach sustainable social–ecological pathways (e.g. Luks 2005; Meadowcroft 2005). For example greenhouse gas emissions of industrial countries would need to be reduced by 80 to 95 per cent between 1990 and 2050 if dangerous climate change is to be avoided (e.g. IPCC 2007).

How can the necessary adaptation process of technical, political and social systems be directed and the two governance challenges related to long-term environmental problems be addressed? Both challenges are difficult to tackle in democratic political systems, as e.g. the screening study "Political Strategies for a Sustainable Dynamics of Social–ecological Transformations" at the start of the research programme "Social–ecological Research" of the German Federal Ministry for Education and Research (Nill *et al.* 2002) has shown. Hence it is no surprise that, for example, the implementation of long-term oriented "sustainability strategies" often falls short of their ambitious policy objectives. This chapter proposes that the design of long-term policies should put more conceptual scrutiny on levers for changes in social, political and economic systems in order to improve their effectiveness. One challenge is that an important lever for changes in social and political systems, the direct problem feedback, can only partly be used due to the long-term character of the ecological changes.

This contribution therefore investigates the potential and possibilities for innovation-oriented strategies to meet these challenges by exploiting the dynamics of technological innovation as another important lever for changes of social and economic systems (as already forcefully argued by Schumpeter 1934). It is increasingly argued that for substantial improvements of environmental sustainability incremental innovation is not sufficient and radical or system innovation ("path changing" innovation) is needed instead (e.g. Freeman 1992; Kemp 1994; Weaver *et al.* 2000; Meadowcroft 2005). Innovation research shows that therefore also corresponding innovation-oriented strategies need a long-term perspective, in particular if the lock-in of environmentally harmful technologies needs to be overcome.

In the last decade, several innovation-oriented policy approaches have been developed which contain fruitful elements for addressing long-term problems (for an overview see Nill and Kemp 2009). The approach of "strategic niche management" highlights the importance of protected spaces and of user involvement in early technological development to create new paths which are able to replace unsustainable technologies (e.g. Kemp *et al.* 1998; Hoogma *et al.* 2002). These insights informed the concept of "transition management" with its broader scope on system changes and system innovation, and reliance on evolving adaptive portfolios (e.g. Rotmans *et al.* 2001; Kemp *et al.* 2007). In parallel, the concept of "time strategies" has been proposed which focuses on the political preparation and utilisation of time windows of opportunities in unstable phases of technological competition (e.g. Nill and Zundel 2001; Zundel *et al.* 2005a). Some authors even argued for a concept of technological forcing, i.e. to enforce innovation by setting environmental standards which cannot be met with available technologies (e.g. Ashford 2000). However, there is a danger that problematic solutions are enforced and the few existing examples only provide evidence for the inducement of incremental innovation – if at all given political and informational constraints on the implementation of such policies (for a discussion see Nill 2009).

In the following, an integrative evolutionary-economic policy approach to address long-term problems such as climate change is set out, which builds and extends upon the mentioned approaches. The analysis draws on relevant results of a PhD dissertation on ecological innovation policy (Nill 2009). The focus is on techno-economic levers and corresponding policy criteria, but also links to relevant aspects of the political system are taken into account. Of course, the tackling of environmental long-term problems cannot be reduced to the question of the development and diffusion of path-changing technological innovations, but as will be shown they can play an important role. Nevertheless, due to income and ecological rebound effects, policies addressing changes in consumption pattern and life-styles also remain important (e.g. Luks 2005). The next section starts with a more detailed problem analysis and sketches a qualitative process model of overcoming lock-in, which takes into account inertia of innovation trajectories and supporting institutions as well as drivers of change linked to knowledge creation, dynamic markets and democratic societies. Based on this, in the following section a new conceptualization of path- and phase-oriented environmental innovation policy is set out. The core criterion for policy success in a dynamic perspective is not efficiency but path effectiveness, accompanied by adaptive flexibility to cope with uncertainty and learning and to preserve the economic system's capacity to adapt. Path-effective policy strategies are distinguished according to phases of path competition. Next the implementation of the policy approach will be illustrated with results from a case study on housing policy, a sector of high relevance for climate protection in which both problems and solutions are marked by high relevance of the long-term. The last section concludes and discusses the potentials and limits of innovation-oriented long-term policy strategies as well as further research needs.

A dynamic problem analysis: inertia and lock-in and remaining levers for change

Non-incremental technological innovations with the desired ecological benefits do not easily succeed due to the lock-in of established technology paths. In particular the neo-Schumpeterian and complex system theoretic strands of evolutionary economics (building on the seminal work of Dosi 1982; Nelson and Winter 1982; David 1985 and Arthur 1989), allow for a substantive perspective on technologies, technological competition and socio-technical systems beyond mere input-output relations, taking into account trajectories and different types of innovation. Freeman and Perez (1988) established the useful distinctions between incremental and radical technological innovation and system innovation. The notion system may refer in this context either to large technological systems (Hughes 1983) with a huge impact of the availability infrastructures for technology performance (e.g. energy production and distribution system, transport system) and/or systems or technological regimes of which the configuration is to a large extent shaped by institutions and social norms.

   Also the role of path dependence in technological competition has been put to the forefront, and circumstances have been described under which technologies might persist even though they might be inferior to their competitors (a situation which Arthur (1989) termed lock-in). One result of corresponding barriers to change may be a spillover between selection and variation that inhibits in general the chances of radical new technologies. Existing environmentally problematic technologies diffused under conditions in which their ecological aspects were not yet considered as problematic – problems related to resource use often only come to the forefront when a high level of diffusion is already reached. In such environmentally problematic lock-in situations, the barriers irreversible investment and switching costs due to technological complementarities (e.g. in energy and transport systems) gain systematically even more importance. Moreover, some of the static environmental externalities highlighted by environmental economics do not vanish over time but related coordination problems add to the forces leading to lock-in and barriers to technological regime shifts offering sustainability benefits (e.g. Ayres 1991; Kemp and Soete 1992).

   Nevertheless, an evolutionary economic analysis also highlights several factors which contribute to the unlocking of lock-ins and the emergence of techno-economic guideposts, niches and transition windows for path changes, on which also policies to tackle long-term environmental problems can build. However, not all of such levers are applicable for environmental innovations. Even if long-term environmental problems are recognized, their direct feedback into the economy, e.g. by increasing natural resource prices, is delayed and the adaptation of the economic system is slowed down (Pasche 1994). Also, new technological breakthroughs are less probable in many environmentally important sectors which are characterized by quite mature technological paradigms. Technical bottlenecks might not be reached yet either. However, deviating ecological demand and supporting environmental regulation can contribute to destabilize lock-ins.

Taken together, these considerations explain why the unlocking of environmentally problematic lock-ins is more difficult than assumed in several general evolutionary economic models of technology competition. This is also the result from the few existing models which take the environmental dimension into account (Kemp 1994; Reichel 1998; Unruh 2000; Polenz 2004). In the following an evolutionary economic conceptual framework is sketched which synthesizes the literature and puts barriers and levers for overcoming lock-in and their respective influence into a temporal and phase-dependent perspective (for details see Nill 2009).

Extending upon a concept introduced by Sahal (1985), new "techno-economic guideposts" are the basis for radical innovation. They emerge from search processes, which are constrained by uncertainty and fostered mainly by performance limits of established technologies and new technological opportunities, but partly also by different demand. In the case of search for environmentally beneficial guideposts technological opportunities are rather of lesser and different demand requirements are rather of higher importance.

"Innovation paths" that start from these new techno-economic guideposts are initally stabilized by the combination of different demand, new technological opportunities and actor coordination around the guidepost. Corresponding new innovation directions can only become competitive with locked-in established paths if they can benefit from niche protection in their instable early development phase. "Niches" provide specific resources which are positively affected by entrepreneurs, political support and local input availability and help to overcome barriers. It is useful to distinguish development niches and application niches, because some main determinants vary. The extent of resource provision for development niches depends strongly on technological opportunities and is constrained by irreversible investment, switching costs, set-up cost and technical uncertainty. Specific resources provided by application niches are strongly determined by different demand and sometimes also by converters, while niche dynamics are here mainly constrained by service uncertainty.

Ecologically promising innovation paths can benefit from similar development niche determinants, although for some types the maintenance of a longer term niche dynamic might be more difficult. For eco application niche dynamics it is decisive that a significant ecological demand is available, otherwise political support is of crucial importance. Even if ecological demand is strong, a problematic issue is an endogenous dynamisation of the application niche by the interaction of network effects, information effects and learning effects, because it requires invasion into less stable and less ecologically motivated demand segments (see also Smith 2007a). Further determinants vary according to path types. For details see Nill (2009), who distinguishes four relevant types of techno-economic guideposts and innovation paths as well as two types of application niches. Taken together, while also ecological innovation paths can use niches for a first path stabilization, it is more difficult for them to gain sufficient dynamics to reach the next "transition window" phase.

Only after an extended niche dynamics phase which may last a decade and longer, as empirical studies have shown, a "transition window" in the competition between innovation paths may emerge. In this phase, dynamics and results of the competition are determined mainly by irreversible investments, switching costs due to technological complementarities and coordination problems as barriers and input price changes, policies and increasing returns due to learning and network effects as levers for change. This implies at the same time that all barriers and levers which differ between normal and ecological innovation paths – including the determinants highlighted by environmental economics, are relevant in the transition window phase. This phase is hence of crucial importance for the success of ecological paths, except if it was to be jumped over by a political ending of old paths, which is, however, politically very demanding and empirically rarely observed.

It is hence not at all certain that the existence of ecological innovation dynamics is sufficient for the success of new innovation paths in the market selection process. The perception of environmental problems and related changes in functional requirements as well as new technological opportunities can induce the search for and emergence of new, environmentally promising techno-economic guideposts. Ecological demand of some users can support eco application niches and hence counter the problem of insufficient variation, but does not suffice to overcome the selection problem in the broader market, if there are not substantial increasing returns or significant changes in the ecological requirements of general user demand. This holds in particular, if also additive or "end of pipe" innovations on the established path are available and compete with new environmentally less problematic innovation pathes (see also Oltra and St. Jean 2003; Frenken *et al.* 2004). Environmentally beneficial path changes are a difficult and by no means "automatic" process and are crucially influenced by political support. It justifies the need for political intervention. This holds in particular for the transition window phase and partly also for the niche dynamics phase, while it is less important for the search phase of new techno-economic guideposts. A corresponding policy framework for path changes or transitions is set out in the next two sections.

Strategies and assessment criteria for adaptive evolutionary long-term policies

This analysis of problems of path changes justifies policy intervention, given that there is a clear policy case that innovation beyond established technology paths is necessary to meet long-term environmental goals like avoiding dangerous climate change. Thus environmental goals are transformed into ecological innovation goals. Given the complexity of dynamics of ecological systems and uncertainty of ecological-economic interactions (see e.g. Beckenbach 2001), the substantive policy goal itself is not determined by economic theory but by societal prioritisation, in this an evolutionary approach follows the lines of classical economics as well as pragmatic environmental economics (see also Baumol and Oates 1971; Wegner 1997). Once such environmental goals and the corresponding acceptable level of risk have been defined in a societal articulation and problem evaluation process (see, e.g. Beckenbach 2001), the policy framework presented here covers choice of strategy and implementation options and their limits. Hence, policy analysis does not follow the approach of neoclassical environmental economics which reduces its scope to the analysis of instrument choice – or naïve instrumentalism in the view of political scientists (e.g. Böcher and Töller 2007).

Instead, in line with approaches suggested in policy analysis (e.g. Jänicke 1997), a strategic policy framework is presented which takes account of inertia and constraints which stabilize lock-ins and makes targeted use of path changing forces of dynamic markets and democratic societies. Core characteristics are process-oriented normative evolutionary economic criteria for the assessment of path oriented innovation policies and the distinction of policy strategies in line with phases of technology path competition. Building on the time strategic approach (Zundel *et al.* 2005a), policies to support the search for new techno-economic guideposts, policies to prepare transition windows and policies to utilize transition windows are distinguished, while policies to enforce path changes are evaluated critically. With a phase-specific analysis of policies, design timing, dosage and design of policy instruments become more important than the choice of instrument as such. Dealing with constraints to policy implementation is also part of the framework. In line with the evolutionary approach, the focus is on knowledge constraints (Wegner 1997; Moreau 2004). Constraints related to the political process which are e.g. highlighted by political science approaches are not systematically covered but referred to where relevant. Nevertheless, political scientists also highlight that the analysis of problem structure and possible policy solutions is key for policy analysis (e.g. Böcher and Töller 2007) – or, with Lowi (1972), "policies determine politics".

The environmental innovation goal consists in contributing to the emergence, development and competitiveness of innovation paths which enable the achievement of the environmental goal. The key normative evolutionary economic criterion for the assessment of such path-oriented innovation policies is hence *path effectiveness*: Policy interventions are path effective if they contribute to overcoming inflexibilities of established innovation paths which turn out to be problematic in the context of new functional requirements, and if they enable that changed innovation paths, which correspond potentially better with new ecological functional requirements, can develop and become competitive in technology competition. This comprises both competition between old and new innovation paths as well as between new innovation paths. Path-effectiveness can remain the key policy success criterion as long as the economic system's capacity to evolve is not endangered by policy interventions and its adaptability is hence preserved, and as long as policies themselves are adaptive and flexible and contain mechanisms of learning and revision to cope with knowledge constraints concerning characteristics of innovation paths and changes in the selection environment (for more details see Nill 2009). Hence unlike neoclassical approaches the framework does not include an efficiency criterion because the latter's analytical substance is bound to a static framework.

These considerations allow already for one important policy conclusion and a caveat. A confinement to solely variety enhancing policies as suggested e.g. by Rammel and van den Bergh (2003) does not comply with the path effectiveness criterion. It is necessary to also focus on the quality and balance of alternatives (Stirling 1998) and the selection mechanisms of the transition window phase. Second, "technology forcing" policies which try to force specific path changes, without the ground being prepared by corresponding economic innovation dynamics, may be assessed sceptically with regard to the transition costs implied which might endanger the economic system's adaptability and the flexibility to react to changes in knowledge. Against this background, it is not surprising that empirical examples of such path change forcing policies are lacking. The Californian zero emission mandate for verhicles, which is sometimes cited as an example, is an interesting border case (see Nill 2009).

For achieving path-effectiveness, policy strategies have to be differentiated according to phases of innovation path competition. First considerations in this direction can be found by Sahal (1985: 81). Theoretical and empirical analysis reported in the last section has shown that policies can have the highest effects in the transition window phase and also in the late niche dynamics phase if set-up costs are high or application niches are not very dynamic due to particularities of ecologically beneficial innovation paths. Also Rip and Schot (2002) distinguish three "loci" to influence technological change. In my terminology, the first two can be related to development and application niches, which are addressed by window preparation, and the third one to transition windows (niche branching in Rip and Schots terminology). Correspondingly, three phase-specific strategic angles seem promising:

1 *Policies to support the search for new techno-economic guideposts* in phases in which an established innovation path dominates and no new techno-economic guidepost has emerged. Main targets are to improve problem recognition of actors involved in search processes and if necessary enable the pursuit of corresponding search processes.

2 *Policies to prepare transition windows* in phases in which new techno-economic guideposts have emerged but corresponding innovation paths are not competitive yet. Main targets are to foster niche dynamics and to avoid a too early restriction of competition between new technologies.

3   *Policies to utilize transition windows* aim primarily at making use of an open
    selection phase of innovation path competition for improving the competi-
    tiveness of ecologically better paths and at avoiding premature lock-in of
    specific new paths.

Under the perspective of appropriate governance of long-term problems, in
particular the first two strategies, policies to support the search for new techno-
economic guideposts and policies to prepare transition windows are important
and will be the focus of the following.

In phases in which an established innovation path dominates and no new
techno-economic guidepost has emerged, a path change is not achievable – or at
least not with efforts which are both politically and economically feasible in
democratic socities with market economies. This resonates well with the finding
of Zundel *et al.* (2005a) that in all successful policy cases of time strategies
studied, there was already a techno-economic guidepost or, in their terms, a
promising alternative. More patience and hence a long term focus of policies is
needed and the *support of the search for new techno-economic guideposts* is the
main feasible strategy. The support of search processes is in particular needed if
the context is problematic with regard to the extent of technological opportunities
and the availability of divergent demand. A main option is the financial support of
problem-oriented basic research. If sufficient knowledge over long-term
environmental problems is available, the establishment of and a credible political
commitment to ambitious long-term environmental goals is also helpful to foster
innovation (see also Jänicke *et al.* 2000a, Nill *et al.* 2002). If it is ambitious
enough, it orients actors and their search processes and reduces uncertainty if
investments into costly search processes for new techno-economic guideposts are
worthwhile.

Committing to long term environmental targets is also a complementary
element of policies to prepare transition windows once a techno-economic
guidepost has emerged, because it has also a signalling effect for actors which are
bound to established paths, e.g. by devaluating switching costs. It also gives
orientation for competition between new paths and the diversity of options to be
explored. In this phase, such long-term targets should be result-oriented
concerning the environmental and hence also technological performance aspired.
At the same time it should be sufficiently realistic to be taken seriously by market
actors and foresee sufficient time for non-incremental innovation and path
stabilization. Empirical studies show that announcement effects of credible
measures lead to innovation (Klemmer *et al.* 1999).

Nevertheless, it is difficult for policy to induce direct path changes in phases in
which new techno-economic guideposts and niches have emerged, but alternative
innovation paths are not yet competitive and hence no transition window exists.
But policy can *prepare the emergence of such windows*, mainly by strengthening
niche dynamics which can be used by the new innovation paths. It is in this phase
that a strategic approach, advocated as crucial part of innovation friendly policy
patterns e.g. by Jänicke *et al.* (2000b), is particularly important. The aim is to

transform technological variation into economically viable variation or, in the words of Schot (1992), a bridge between variation and selection. Also new-new-competition is fostered and a too early restriction of options is avoided. If the performance of new innovation paths is not sufficient with regard to an approaching transition window or due to problems in the development process, policy has to adapt. Three implementation strategies can be distinguished taking account of specifics of niche dynamics and the influencing factors of lock-in and its overcoming:

- A process-oriented *stabilization of the dynamics of development niches* for alternative innovation paths is in order if they are constrained by important barriers which reinforce the lock-in of established paths, e.g. high set-up costs.
- The *strategic management of application niches* is the appropriate implementation strategy if some demand pull is available but application niche dynamics are problematic due to the lack of drivers to overcome lock-in. It can build on the insights generated by the literature on strategic niche management (e.g. Kemp *et al.* 1998; Hoogma *et al.* 2002; Raven 2005) and puts the results and their limits into context.
- As complement, and also as substitute, if neither barriers nor drivers are particularly problematic and hence the lock-in problem is not very substantial, changing the selection environment by *environmental policy "framework" instruments* can be a path-effective element of window preparation.

More details of appropriate innovation policy implementation strategies to address long-term environmental problems, in particular the latter two variants, are discussed in the following section concerning the example of sustainable housing with a focus on Germany.

Policy implementation strategies: the example of sustainable housing in Germany

Housing contributes substantially to long-term environmental problems linked to resource and soil consumption and in particular climate change through energy consumption. One-third of German carbon dioxide emissions can be attributed to the final demand sector construction and living (Coenen and Grunwald 2003). Single family dwellings as the currently preferred form of living are characterised by the worst environmental performance (Huber 2004). Thermal insulation is one of the decisive emission determinants besides heating technologies and temperature requirements of users. While short-term emission reductions can be mainly achieved by refurbishment of old dwellings, innovation is mostly driven by new buildings. Even if they only slowly diffuse broadly, they are decisive for the enlargement of mitigation options, the achievement of long-term environmental goals and as an innovation source for solutions which can also be implemented in the existing building stock.

The most relevant environmental target is the commitment to reduce German greenhouse gas emissions compared to 1990 by 21 per cent 2008/12 and by 40 per cent by 2020. In view of these targets, and in particular the envisaged climate targets for the longer term (−80–95 per cent by 2050 for industrialised countries like Germany, see IPCC, 2007 and confirmed by the European Council in October 2009), established innovation paths are not sufficient, and changes need to start early due to the slow diffusion in this sector. However, while some measures, mainly refurbishment subsidies, have always been reported in national climate protection programmes, a specific contribution of construction and living to target achievement is only mentioned since 2005. Building regulations and investment subsidies and loans are the dominant policy instruments targeted at the sector. The innovative effects of regulatory policies are usually limited. This is particularly true for building regulation in Germany, where rather the opposite causal chain, i. e. from innovation with a large time lag to regulation, can be empirically observed (Lehr 2000).

Concerning the innovation path competition in Germany, conventional innovation paths for small dwellings have been gradually improved towards a kind of low energy standard, in the definition of the energy saving ordinance of 2002 representing 70–110 kwh end energy per m^2 per year. Given rather low technological opportunities in this technologically rather mature field, there is in general scarcity of new techno-economic guideposts, notwithstanding that at the innovation frontier much larger steps have come into sight (for details see Haum and Nill 2004; Nill 2009). In particular passive housing emerged in the early 1990s as a new techno-economic guidepost enabling much lower energy consumption (below 15 kwh/m^{2}a) for heating at a reasonable cost. Other technical options like zero energy housing were also explored, but lacked economic potential to become a techno-economic guidepost. Technologically, a passive house is a non-incremental innovation of the architectural type, a new combination of technologies with some new components and a changing functional performance. It reduces the end energy use for heating purposes to less than 15 kwh/m^{2}a and hence makes the omission of conventional heating systems feasible. To achieve this requires a combination of strong thermal insulation, a utilization of passive solar gains by solar-oriented windows and internal savings, a special type of three-layer windows and a ventilation system with heat recuperation which provides for the necessary rest of energy. In parallel, and partly in reaction to progress on the passive housing innovation path, incremental and add-on improvements of established innovation paths towards "three litre houses" (30 kwh/m^{2}a) have been explored, by improving insulation while keeping conventional heating systems.

Policies to support the search for new techno-economic guideposts have been of very limited importance in Germany. The techno-economic guidepost passive housing was developed in the late 1980s in a Swedish-German collaboration. It is an example that search processes are undertaken by economic and scientific actors themselves if problem recognition is sufficient and there is some direct demand envisageable (for an account of the early phase see e.g. Feist 2001). The feasibility was shown on the basis of newly developed computer simulation programmes. The prototype was constructed in 1991 in Darmstadt-Kranichstein by the Institute for Living and Environment, led by Wolfgang Feist. Technologically it made use of a recombination of insulation and ventilation technologies developed for low energy housing which had been pioneered by Scandinavian countries, also in response to regulation. The main actors were outsiders to the construction industry, and strongly motivated by environmental concerns. The main component innovations required were integrated planning approaches by architects and better insulated three-layer windows. In Germany, regional policy support in the Land Hesse started with the first demonstration project in Darmstadt.

However, *policies* played an important role after the emergence of the passive housing techno-economic guidepost and *supported the emergence of a transition window* at least in some market segments. German support for new low energy houses can at least ex-post be regarded on the implementation side as appropriate window preparation strategy. Its dominant form was that of a strategic application niche management, which is well suited to architectural innovation paths, which due to lower cost of technology development and differing performance characteristics are less dependent on development niches. They are hence less constrained by high barriers – with the important exception of coordination problems – to but rather by the lack of sufficiently strong levers for path changes, such as dynamic deviating demand. The following elements contributed to the path-effectiveness of the window preparation policy pattern:

First, some German Länder contributed to the stabilization of the application niche in the early phase of the new passive housing innovation path. For example the Land Hesse already in the mid 1990s supported financially the first settlement concept which followed this path. In general, Länder and local authorities supported both low energy houses and passive houses. The main aims were to demonstrate feasibility and to get people to know the concept. Applied research on passive solar systems and components was supported from the mid 1990s by the federal ministry of economics as part of the research programme on solar optimised construction. Other research areas were solar supported heating and cooling systems and solar optimised buildings with ultra low energy consumption, hence the competition between new options was not restricted. Traditional construction research, however, remained oriented towards components and not towards building concepts (Ebel *et al.* 2000).

Second, low energy houses including passive houses were financially supported by an ecological bonus to an existing investment subsidy for house owners. Between 1996 and 2002 an additional maximum of €1,600 was paid for the construction of a low energy building and an additional maximum of €2,000 for energy saving technology components like solar thermal water boilers, heat pumps or heat recovery in new buildings as well as for the refurbishment of old buildings. All these components can be used for passive houses but also for other types of environmentally friendly buildings. An evaluation showed, however, that the support only made low energy buildings economically competitive, but not passive houses nor the supported technology components. The use of the support measure for technology components was with only 7 per cent of all beneficiaries of the investment subsidy correspondingly low (IWU 2001). The use of renewable energy for heating, which is compatible with several, and also established, innovation paths has been additionally supported by a technology adoption subsidy since 1999.

Third, in 1998, when the number of passive housing units was still below 50, the federal public loan agency Kreditanstalt für Wiederaufbau started an own-initiative loan programme for passive houses. The programme was part of the general carbon dioxide reduction programme financially supported since 1996 by the German government, and supported the new innovation path by redirecting an existing premium loan programme for new private housing from low energy housing to passive housing. The criteria followed the so called passiv house standard which had been developed by the Passiv House Institute in cooperation with field actors and hence leveraged the self-organization of the field actors to overcome coordination problems. The programme provided loans for more than 300 houses in 1999 and more than 500 houses in 2000 and thus supported stabilization and expansion of the niche by fostering and encouraging differentiated demand.

Together with the ecological bonus and partly still available parallel support by Länder and local authorities, the loan programme contributed significantly to a first boost of the new path in 1999, in a crucial phase for the dynamisation of architectural innovation paths. The extent of the effect is assessed differently by the interviewed experts. Economic calculations show that the incentive is significant but that the support is not too generous (for details see Nill 2009). The instrument has also been sufficiently flexible to be adapted to changing regulatory conditions and has been adapted several times over the years. For example, in 2001 the building performance standards changed from end energy to primary energy use, creating more favorable conditions for the integration of renewable energy heating systems. The loan programme was adapted and since then also the more incremental new option of three litre houses ($30\,kwh/m^2a$) has been backed, albeit with less favorable interest rate conditions.

Some of the remaining Länder programmes added other niche management specific elements such as support of networks and coordination as well as user inclusion and advice. Again Hesse can be named as example which ended its subsidies but continued support for coordination in the working group cost-efficient passive houses and for information and advice to users. It also sponsored research projects on user acceptance and corresponding learning effects. Hence it is not surprising that a relatively high share of the loan programme went to beneficiaries in this region.

A certain, albeit according to interviewed experts limited, contribution to window preparation was provided by the moderate rise of taxes on gas and heating oil since 1999 in the framework of the so-called ecological tax reform. The tax reform, which affected both new and established paths was characterized by one-off and partly irregular increases of tax rates. Hence it gave a certain signal but for a real impact it would need to rise predictably over a longer time period in the view of sector experts.

Summing up, an appropriate window preparation strategy in form of application niche management could be observed at least until 2002, and a transition window emerged in the segment of quality housing. However, this was not achieved by a coordinated political strategy but by separate activities of different political levels. The political and administrative actors were well informed about techno-economic dynamics, so that the UK-informed sceptical view by Smith (2007b) in this respect cannot be confirmed for Germany. Federalism turned out to be a supportive institutional framework, which added important non-financial policy elements of niche management. Nevertheless, the lack of consideration of regional experiences in federal research support and the lack of a corresponding coordination has been criticised by Ebel *et al.* (2000), which points to further room for improvement.

If we briefly compare the German case with the contrasting case of the United Kingdom, we can conclude that in the United Kingdom crucial elements of a niche oriented window preparation strategy were lacking. Demonstration buildings with very low energy consumption have been taken up by policy makers as good examples. However, there was a lack of systematic activities to support niche dynamics and expansion (Lovell 2007; see also Smith 2007b). Until 2006 support programmes focused on the use of renewable heating in buildings.

Finally, it should be briefly noted that policies from 2002 onwards to utilize the emerging transition window, which would have been crucial for a successful path change, have been less path-effective (for a detailed account see Nill 2009). The problem was not that the window would not have been used. In October 2002 the re-elected red-green German government stated the ambition to create an incentive programme for 30,000 passive houses and thus to utilize the emerging techno-economic window. Originally it was intended as capital subsidy. Problems related rather to a lack of a transition framework and implementation problems. For example, due to budget constraints and administrative problems in creating a new scheme, it was implemented only to a limited extent, by way of changing the financial conditions of the premium loan scheme in May 2003. The incentive was better than before, but with some State schemes being reduced at the same time and the ecological bonus being stopped, the effects remained below the ambition. Moreover, in the decentralized housing market, the critical phase of competition is diffusion beyond a niche, and for this subsidies are a quite expensive instrument.

Energy taxes as a potentially path effective framework instrument were not used as an additional signal for transition needs. Only later, in the German climate action programme 2005, was a concrete emission target for private households set. Further implementation steps then became part of the integrated energy and climate programme at the end of 2007 which, however, chose the established regulatory pathway to improve the energy performance of buildings. The energy concept of 2010 has set targets for 2020 and 2050 and has envisaged for 2012 the implementation of the recast EU energy performance directive and its efficiency standard for new buildings which comes close to enabling a path change.

Nevertheless, the case shows that phase-oriented policy interventions are feasible. The niche dynamics phase of 13 years duration and, in this case, also the transition window phase, since 2002 have been long enough to enable political responses to emergent critical dynamics. Also limits of knowledge have not been as important as constraints as they are sometimes pictured in the innovation policy debate (e.g. Collingridge 1980; Wegner 1997) and the state was not a "blind giant" as David (1987) famously put it. Rather, policy makers had to cope with distributed power (Voß et al. 2007) and partly, once a transition window in important market segment was reached, also with opposition from established actors who stand to lose from path changing policies (see e.g. Unruh 2002). Given such constraints and its necessary long-term orientation, path changing innovation policy will remain to a certain degree experimental. But as also visible in the construction case, in particular political multi-level governance systems like federal states or the European Union enable experimental policies at least to a certain extent in practice.

Conclusion and outlook

This chapter has investigated the potential and possibilities of innovation-oriented strategies to address governance challenges related to long-term environmental problems and to modulate the necessary adaptation process of technical, political and social systems. It has set out a politically feasible evolutionary policy approach which builds on and modulates innovation dynamics as a key policy lever and at the same time does justice to the long-term horizon required to overcome the lock-in of environmentally harmful technologies. Based on a dynamic problem analysis of technological path changes, an evolutionary justification of active long-term policies to address long-term problems is provided and a phase-specific policy design is proposed and illustrated at the example of construction policies.

The approach shows that an appropriate phase-specific policy-mix or innovation-friendly policy pattern combining framework instruments and appropriate timed and designed specific impulses is more important for policy success than instrument choice. This resonates well with contributions of political scientists (e.g. Jänicke 1997). Before concrete instruments are chosen, a monitoring of innovation paths and their potential in relation to the long-term policy goals should uncover the status and phase position of technology competition. Policy can play an important role in shaping niche dynamics and preparing transition windows, by stabilizing development niches, managing application niches – as illustrated in some detail in the case study – and/or influencing the selection environment with framework instruments. In the case of environmental problems, policy retains a crucial role once a transition window emerges. As the case study has also pointed out, it is far from certain that policy will succeed in such an endeavour, even if is not significantly hindered by knowledge constraints.

A successful policy approach needs to be adaptive to changing circumstances and will remain to a certain degree experimental. A technology forcing policy in the sense of creating new innovation paths is in this perspective neither politically feasible nor desirable. It might also not be path effective because the danger of neglecting endogenous economic innovation dynamics is too big. What remains possible is a more moderate variant of a policy which accelerates technology development, as long its design retains adaptive flexibility. Key elements of the approaches should also remain valid if the innovations in question are dominantly (social-) organizational, i.e. strongly change actor relations or use patterns. Early niche protection is here primarily based on value-based deviating behaviours and hence less amenable to targeted political support. However, practical experiments in application niches to enable learning effects and the support of their dynamics by strategic niche management should even gain importance. This is because technological self-reinforcing mechanisms like scale effects become less and user-related dynamics more important (see Nill *et al.* 2002), and endogenous niche as well as broader diffusion dynamics through a virtuous cycle of learning and cost reduction cannot be expected but need specific drivers and support.

Despite the huge potential of innovation-oriented approaches, addressing long-term environmental problems such as climate change cannot be reduced to the question of enabling the emergence and success of path changing environmental innovations. This would imply a direct causality between techno-economic innovation characteristics and ecological effects instead of ecological potentials. However, ecological as well as finally also economic effects also crucially depend on how promising innovation paths are shaped, if complementary changes take place and if the innovations are broadly diffused (e.g. Grübler 1998). Also the question remains open to what extent path changing innovation can over-compensate environmental damages due to perhaps even thus induced economic growth. However, even sceptics on these grounds concede a lack of viable alternative strategies (e.g. Luks 2005).

The presented dominantly economic policy approach assumes a certain level of political intervention capacity, which enables a strategic approach and an adaptive implementation. While focusing on the "policy" dimension of the approach and the policy enabling potential of innovation dynamics, it has not addressed in detail the "politics" dimension. However, if policy aims at path changes, the effect of policy on path competition might not be unidirectional. There might be relevant lock-in reinforcing co-evolutionary processes with the institutional and political framework, in particular because there are economic incentives of actors behind established paths to prevent such policies (e.g. Berg 1995; Unruh 2000). Of course, building on ongoing innovation dynamics will ease corresponding policy constraints because alternatives are at least in principle available. Hence a relevant impact is mainly to be expected if there are strong technological complementarities and correspondingly high switching costs and institutional switching barriers. However, even if such factors are less important, constraints related to the political process will not disappear.

Hence there is a need for further research on co-evolutionary and governance dynamics when addressing policy responses to long-term environmental problems. On the co-evolutionary part, Nill (2002) and Zundel *et al.* (2005b) provide some first steps in this direction, building on the temporally defined process model of agenda setting by Kingdon (1995). On governance dynamics see e.g. Voß *et al.* (2007). However, such research and the generation of general results is complicated by important national specificities of "polities" and their impact, as well as by the difficulties of empirical research beyond case-studies. Nevertheless, as long as an evolutionary approach such as the one set out here is not understood as a universal theoretical paradigm but as an heuristical starting point, it may be a well-suited bridging concept for the necessary inter- and trans-disciplinary dialogue to better understand and foster necessary adaptation processes of technical, political and social systems.

References

Arthur, W. B. 1989. "Competing Technologies, Increasing Returns, and Lock-in by Historical Events". *Economic Journal* 99: 116–31.

Ashford, N. A. 2000. "An Innovation-Based Strategy for a Sustainable Environment". In Hemmelskamp, J., Rennings, K. and Leone, F. (eds) *Innovation-oriented Environmental Regulation*. Heidelberg and New York: Physica-Verlag, 67–108.

Ayres, R. U. 1991. "Evolutionary Economics and Environmental Imperatives". *Structural Change and Economic Dynamics* 2: 255–73.

Baumol, W. J. and Oates, W. E. 1971. "The Use of Standards and Prices for Protection of the Environment". *Swedish Journal of Economics* 73: 42–54.

Beckenbach, F. 2001. *Beschränkte Rationalität und Systemkomplexität. Ein Beitrag zur Ökologischen Ökonomik*. Marburg: Metropolis-Verlag.

Berg, C. 1995. *Technologischer Fortschritt und ökonomische Regulierung*. Frankfurt a.M.: Peter Lang.

Böcher, M. and Töller, A. E. 2007. "Instrumentenwahl und Instrumentenwandel in der Umweltpolitik: Ein theoretischer Erklärungsrahmen". In Jacob, K., Biermann, F., Busch, P. O. and Feindt, P. H. (eds) *Politik und Umwelt*. PVS Sonderheft 39/ 2007, Wiesbaden: VS Verlag für Sozialwissenschaften, 299–322.

Coenen, R. and Grunwald, A. 2003. *Nachhaltigkeitsprobleme in Deutschland: Analysen und Lösungsstrategien*. Berlin: edition sigma.

Collingridge, D. 1980. *The Social Control of Technology*. London: Pinter.

David, P. A. 1985. "Clio and the Economics of QWERTY". *American Economic Review, Papers and Proceedings* 75: 332–37.

David, P. A. 1987. "Some New Standards for the Economics of Standardization in the Information Age". In Dasgupta, P. and Stoneman, P. (eds) *Economic Policy and Technological Performance*. Cambridge: Cambridge University Press, 206–39.

Dosi, G. 1982. "Technological Paradigms and Technological Trajectories: A Suggested Interpretation of the Determinants and Directions of Technical Change". *Research Policy* 11: 147–62.

Ebel, W., Eicke-Hennig, W., Feist, W. and Groscurth, H. M. 2000. *Energieeinsparung bei Alt- und Neubauten*. Heidelberg: C.F. Müller Verlag.

Feist, W. 2001. *10 Jahre Passivhaus in Darmstadt-Kranichstein*. Darmstadt, Germany: Passive House Institute.

Freeman, C. 1992. *The Economics of Hope: Essays on Technical Change, Economic Growth and the Environment*. London and New York: Pinter.

Freeman, C. and Perez, C. 1988. "Structural Crises of Adjustment, Business Cycles and Investment Behaviour". In Dosi, G., Freeman, C., Nelson, R. R., Silverberg, G. and Soete, L. (eds) *Technical Change and Economic Theory*. London and New York: Pinter, 38–66.

Frenken, K., Hekkert, M. and Godfroij, P. 2004. "R&D Portfolios in Environmental Friendly Automotive Propulsion: Variety, Competition and Policy Implications". *Technological Forecasting and Social Change* 71: 485–507.

Grübler, A. 1998. *Technology and Global Change*. Cambridge: Cambridge University Press.

Haum, R. and Nill, J. 2004. *Zeitstrategien ökologischer Innovationspolitik bei Wohngebäuden*. policy paper. Berlin: Institute for Ecological Economy Research.

Hoogma, R., Kemp, R., Schot, J. and Truffer, B. 2002. *Experimenting for Sustainable Transport: The Approach of Strategic Niche Management*. London and New York: Spon Press.

Huber, J. 2004. *New Technologies and Environmental Innovation*. Cheltenham: Edward Elgar.

Hughes, T. 1983. *Networks of Power: Electrification of Western Society 1880–1930*. Baltimore: John Hopkins University Press.

IPCC 2007. *Climate Change 2007: Synthesis Report*. Contribution of Working Groups I, II and III to the Fourth Assessment Report of the Intergovernmental Panel on Climate Change. [Core Writing Team, Pachauri, R. K. and Reisinger, A., eds.], Geneva, Switzerland: IPCC.

IWU – Institut für Wohnen und Umwelt (ed.). 2001. *Evaluation der Ökozulage*, final report, IWU, Darmstadt.

Jänicke, M. 1997. *Umweltinnovationen aus Sicht der Policy-Analyse: vom instrumentellen zum strategischen Ansatz der Umweltpolitik*. FFU-report 97/3, FU Berlin.

Jänicke, M., Jörgens, H. and Koll, C. 2000a. "Elemente einer deutschen Nachhaltigkeitsstrategie. Einige Schlussfolgerungen aus dem internationalen Vergleich". In Jänicke, M. and Jörgens, H. (eds) *Umweltplanung im internationalen Vergleich: Strategien der Nachhaltigkeit*. Berlin *et al.*: Springer, 221–30.

Jänicke, M., Blazejczak, J., Edler, D. and Hemmelskamp, J. 2000b. "Environmental Policy and Innovation: An International Comparison of Policy Frameworks and Innovation Effects". In Hemmelskamp, J., Rennings, K. and Leone, F. (eds) *Innovation-Oriented Environmental Regulation*, Heidelberg: Physica Verlag, 125–52.

Kemp, R. 1994. "Technology and the Transition to Environmental Sustainability: The Problem of Technological Regime Shifts". *Futures* 26: 1023–46.

Kemp, R. and Soete, L. 1992. 'The Greening of Technological Progress: An Evolutionary Perspective'. *Futures* 24: 437–57.

Kemp, R., Schot, J. and Hoogma, R. 1998. Regime Shifts to Sustainability through Processes of Niche Formation: The Approach of Strategic Niche Management. *Technology Analysis and Strategic Management* 10: 175–95.

Kemp, R., Loorbach, D. and Rotmans, J. 2007. "Transition Management as a Model for Managing Processes of Co-evolution". *International Journal of Sustainable Development and World Ecology* 14: 78–91.

Kingdon, J. W. 1995. *Agendas, Alternatives, and Public Policies*. New York: Pearson.

Klemmer, P., Lehr, U. and Löbbe, K. 1999. *Environmental Innovation. Incentives and Barriers*. Berlin: Analytica.

Lehr, U. 2000. "The Example of the Thermal Insulation in Germany". In Hemmelskamp, J., Rennings, K. and Leone, F. (eds) *Innovation-oriented Environmental Regulation*. Heidelberg and New York: Physica, 221–33.

Lovell, H. 2007. "The Governance of Innovation in Socio-technical Systems: The Difficulties of Strategic Niche Management in Practice". *Science and Public Policy* 34: 35–44.

Lowi, T. 1972. "Four Systems of Policy, Politics and Choice". *Public Administrative Review* 32: 298–310.

Luks, F. 2005. "Innovationen, Wachstum und Nachhaltigkeit. Eine ökologisch-ökonomische Betrachtung". In *Jahrbuch Ökologische Ökonomik, Band 4: Innovationen und Nachhaltigkeit*. Marburg: Metropolis-Verlag, 41–62.

Meadowcroft, J. 2005. "Environmental Political Economy, Technological Transitions and the State". *New Political Economy* 10: 479–98.

Moreau, F. 2004. "The Role of the State in Evolutionary Economics". *Cambridge Journal of Economics* 28: 847–74.

Nelson, R. R. and Winter, S. G., 1982. *An Evolutionary Theory of Economic Change*. Cambridge, MA, and London: Belknap Press.

Nill, J. 2002. "Wann benötigt Umwelt (innovations) politik politische Zeitfenster? Zur Fruchtbarkeit und Anwendbarkeit von Kingdons "policy window"-Konzept". Discussion paper No. 54/02 of the Institute for Ecological Economy Research, IÖW, Berlin.

Nill, J. 2009. *Ökologische Innovationspolitik. Eine evolutorisch-ökonomische Perspektive*. Marburg: Metropolis-Verlag.

Nill, J. and Kemp, R. 2009. "Evolutionary Approaches for Sustainable Innovation Policies: From Niche to Paradigm?" *Research Policy* 38: 668–80.

Nill, J. and Zundel, S. 2001. "Die Rolle von Vielfalt für Zeitstrategien ökologischer Innovationspolitik". *Zeitschrift für angewandte Umweltforschung*, special issue 13/2001: 148–57.

Nill, J., Einacker, I., Korbun, T., Nordbeck, R. and Peine, A. 2002. "Nachhaltigkeitsstrategien. Neuere Ansätze für innovative politische Langfriststrategien und Probleme ihrer Anwendung im Handlungsfeld Mobilität und Verkehr", Schriftenreihe Nr. 158/01 des Instituts für ökologische Wirtschaftsforschung, Berlin.

Oltra, V. and Saint-Jean, M. 2003. *The Dynamics of Environmental Innovations: Three Stylised Trajectories of Clean Technology*. Cahier du GRES 2003-3, Pessac.

Pasche, M. 1994. "Ansätze einer evolutorischen Umweltökonomik". In Beckenbach, F. and Diefenbacher, H. (eds) *Zwischen Entropie und Selbstorganisation – Perspektiven einer ökologischen Ökonomie*. Marburg: Metropolis-Verlag, 75–118.

Polenz, C. 2004. *Zur Diffusions- und Wettbewerbsdynamik ökologischer Produktinnovationen. Eine Untersuchung am Beispiel des Hypercars*. Kassel, Germany: Kassel University Press.

Rammel, C. and van den Bergh, J. C. J. M. 2003. "Evolutionary Policies for Sustainable Development: Adaptive Flexibility and Risk Minimising". *Ecological Economics* 47: 121–33.

Raven, R. P. J. M. 2005. *Strategic Niche Management for Biomass*. PhD Thesis, Eindhoven, Netherlands: Eindhoven University of Technology.

Reichel, M. 1998. *Markteinführung von erneuerbaren Energien. Lock-out-Effekte und innovationspolitische Konsequenzen für die elektrische Wind- und Solarenergienutzung.* Wiesbaden, Germany: Deutscher Universitätsverlag.

Rip, A. and Schot, J. 2002. "Identifying Loci for Influencing the Dynamics of Technological Development". In Williams, R. and Sørensen, K. (eds) *Shaping Technology, Guiding Policy.* Cheltenham: Edward Elgar, 158–76.

Rotmans, J., Kemp, R. and van Asselt, M. 2001. More Evolution than Revolution: Transition Management in Public Policy. *Foresight* 3: 15–31.

Sahal, D. 1985. "Technological Guideposts and Innovation Avenues". *Research Policy* 14: 61–82.

Schot, J. 1992. "The Policy Relevance of the Quasi-Evolutionary Model: The Case of Stimulating Clean Technologies". In Coombs, R., Saviotti, P. and Walsh, V. (eds) *Technological Change and Company Strategies.* London: Academic Press, 185–200.

Schumpeter, J. A. 1934. *The Theory of Economic Development.* Cambridge, MA: Harvard University Press (original in German 1911).

Smith, A. 2007a. "Translating Sustainabilities Between Green Niches and Socio-technical Regimes". *Technology Analysis & Strategic Management* 19: 427–50.

Smith, A. 2007b. "Governance Lessons from Green Niches: The Case of Eco-housing". In Murphy, J. (ed.). *Governing Technology for Sustainability.* London: Earthscan, 89–109.

Stirling, A. 1998. *On the Economics and Analysis of Diversity.* SPRU Electronic Working Paper Series No. 28, Brighton: University of Sussex.

Unruh, G. C. 2000. "Understanding Carbon Lock-in". *Energy Policy* 28: 817–30.

Unruh, G. C. 2002. "Escaping Carbon Lock-in". *Energy Policy* 30: 317–25.

Voß, J. P., Newig, J., Kastens, B., Monstadt, J. and Nölting, B. 2007. "Steering for Sustainable Development: A Typology of Problems and Strategies with respect to Ambivalence, Uncertainty and Distributed Power". *Journal of Environmental Policy & Planning* 9: 193–212.

Weaver, P., Jansen, L., van Grootveld, G., van Spiegel, E. and Vergragt, P. 2000. *Sustainable Technology Development.* Sheffield: Greenleaf.

Wegner, G. 1997. "Economic Policy from an Evolutionary Perspective: A New Approach". *Journal of Institutional and Theoretical Economics* 153: 485–509.

Zundel, S., Erdmann, G., Kemp, R., Nill, J. and Sartorius, C. 2005a. "Conclusions – A Time-Strategic Ecological Innovation Policy". In Sartorius, C. and Zundel, S. (eds) *Time Strategies, Innovation and Environmental Policy.* Cheltenham: Edward Elgar, 322–48.

Zundel, S., Erdmann, G., Kemp, R., Nill, J. and Sartorius, C. 2005b. "Conceptual Framework". In Sartorius, C. and Zundel, S. (eds) *Time Strategies, Innovation and Environmental Policy.* Cheltenham: Edward Elgar, 10–54.

Part III
Participation

8 From interest consultation to collective knowledge production

The influence of participation on EU environmental governance

Hui-Yin Sung and Ho-Ching Lee

Introduction

Participation is nowadays essential in the policy cycle[1] of long-term environmental policymaking. Long-term policies, defined as "institutions where current actions have effects in the (far) future, or that respond to problems resulting from current actions that have effects in the (far) future", have to address long-term problems whose causes and effects have long time lags, which cannot be solved rapidly and involve intergenerational equity and trade-offs (Siebenhüner *et al.* Chapter 1 in this volume). These features of long-term problems undermine the authority of scientific knowledge regarding environmental problems. On the one hand, the complex interaction between human society and earth ecosystems makes scientific confirmation difficult. On the other hand, as Ulrich Beck (1998: 12–14) claims, scientific knowledge can only provide more or less uncertain factual information about probabilities, but never answer whether risk is acceptable. As a result, scientific knowledge concerning long-term environmental problems has been questioned and the policies based on it have also been challenged.

In a modern democratic society, government's decision of risk taking must be accepted by stakeholders as legitimate, otherwise there will be acute opposition against it (Yearley 2008: 929). As a remedy, environmental assessment which aims at evaluating the risk of certain policies or actions and whether the risk is acceptable therefore becomes a common tool and necessitates the participation of stakeholders. With the publication of *The White Paper on European Governance in 2001* (European Commission 2001a), actors at different levels with different concerns gradually acquire the access to each stage of policy cycle in the EU. They articulate not only their interests but also provide local or practical knowledge about the impacts of the long-term problems and the potential consequences of intended long-term policies. Accordingly, participation in EU environmental assessments has transformed from interest consultation to the inclusion of collective knowledge production.

However, as one of the conclusions from the project of Global Environmental Assessments, the salience, credibility and legitimacy of environmental assessments are necessary but not sufficient for assessment's influence because participants view salience, credibility and legitimacy differently (Clark *et al.* 2006: 16). This chapter reconfirms this conclusion. Furthermore, drawing insights from social studies of science and systems theory, it tries to explain why participants view the three elements differently by pointing out participants' differing risk-taking logic.

This chapter focuses on participation in environmental assessments and its impact on the effectiveness on EU environmental governance. We argue that the enlargement and better design of participation in the environmental assessment has positive effects on EU environmental governance in many ways. However, its influence on the effectiveness of EU environmental governance in terms of policy acceptance remains indeterminate. The enlargement and better design of participation in environmental assessments may broaden the scope and quantity of knowledge. However, it does not change its nature as science whose logic of risk taking is based on the truth of cost-benefit evaluation over different policy choices. When policies based on environmental assessments enter into the stage of decision making, the logic of risk taking entails a political consideration according to which policymakers have to balance different interests of stakeholders in order to retain their office by attracting enough votes.

In the next section, we discuss the relationship between participation, risk, and EU environmental governance, and then develop a simplified framework of EU policy making process to illustrate differing participants' risk-taking logic. The third section illustrates the processes and the outcomes of EU environmental assessments regarding air pollution and climate change to validate our arguments. Finally, we conclude that the enlargement and improved design of participation in environmental assessments are necessary, but by no means sufficient to improve the effectiveness of EU environmental governance, because the outputs of EU-level policies are determined by political bargaining among EU policy makers.

Risk, participation, and EU environmental governance

Risk is a potential danger that has negative consequences for those who take it. In daily life, individuals take risks voluntarily to acquire what they want. With the increasing complexity of modern society, the internal differentiation of functional systems develops in order to maintain the performance of the society as a whole. These systems – including political, economic, scientific, legal, art and educational – separate people into different groups and lead to their distinct forms of risk-taking logic. Accordingly, each group's evaluation of risk taking varies in the face of the same policy. Different groups in society, like individuals, also spend their limited resources on selected issue areas that they consider worthwhile to take risks. However, risks accepted by one group might not be accepted by others. Accordingly, any government which is elected by the governed has to balance the distribution of risk and benefits of environmental policies when these environmental policies involve different types of stakeholders.

Participation is a major element in EU environmental governance. Governance, according to the *White Paper*, refers to "rules, processes and behaviour that affect the way in which powers are exercised at European level, particularly as regards openness, participation, accountability, effectiveness and coherence" (European Commission 2001a: 8). Suffering from a democratic deficit, the EU wants to establish a closer relationship between government and civil society (MacCormick 2008:160–161). At the same time, the EU also emphasizes "shared responsibility" between the public and private sectors, encouraging broader participation in the environmental policy cycle since the fifth environmental programme (1992–2000).[2]

Environmental assessment as a tool of risk evaluation uses the resulting knowledge for making environmental policy design more acceptable to the majority. Therefore, the participation of stakeholders is necessary for making policy proposal more legitimate, and thus more acceptable. While the literature on environmental assessments disagrees on how participation should be undertaken, they all agree that broader and more effective participation is desirable (e.g. Hartley and Wood 2005; Doelle and Sinclair 2006; Stewart and Sinclair 2007; O'Faircheallaigh 2010; Pohjola and Tuomisto 2011). Subsequently, participation in environmental assessments has become a common practice in EU environmental governance.

Jasanoff and Wynne (1998: 117) depict an intricate framework on the relationship between science and politics. They point out that knowledge about nature does not belong to any specific domain of society. Each domain, as understood as an ideal type of culture – including bureaucratic, economic, scientific, and civic – have their own beliefs, goals, discourses and practices which formulate their distinct knowledge about nature. These cultures are highly interdependent, connecting together through different organizations (Jasanoff and Wynne 1998: 16). Accordingly, scientific knowledge and environmental policies are co-produced through a complex form of interaction among these different cultures. A similar idea proposed by Ortwin Renn (2004), aims to improve the risk assessment in a pluralist society. According to Renn (2004: 294), a society needs effectiveness, efficiency, legitimacy, and social cohesion, with each task handled by four major functional systems, including science, economics, politics and social structure. The two frameworks are common in the sense that they distinguish distinct operating logic from different culture/societal systems. This feature links to a systems theory developed by a German sociologist Niklas Luhmann who distinguishes different societal systems by different codes that each system holds.

According to Luhmann (1982: 168), "[a] code [...] is a structure with specific characteristics: it has a special capacity for guiding selection". For example, a political system operates with the binary code of government/opposition. Economic systems operate with the binary code of payment/no payment. Scientific systems operate with the binary code of true/not true. In other words, an issue will get the attention of policy makers only when policy makers can relate the issue to political competition. Economic actors will notice an issue when it has implications for their profits. Scientists are interested in an issue when they try to prove it as true or not true. Each system cares only about its own continuity and tries to preserve it without considering others. Consequently, political actors may adopt a policy that will induce more votes in the short-term regardless of whether the policy is detrimental to the economy. Factories do not care about long-term impacts of their activities on the environment as long as they can benefit from the status quo. Scientists may provide a solution to pollution without considering the cost overrun of polluters. However, these systems are interdependent to maintain the function of a society as a whole. In environmental policy making, political, economic, scientific and social systems are the four systems most affected by environmental policies. Accordingly, the communication between these systems will take place when they are affected by the actions or non-actions of others. Environmental assessment thus becomes an arena for the inter-communication among stakeholders from the four systems.

The source of ruling power in political systems is legitimacy. Seeking legitimacy is its operational logic in dealing with environmental risks. Therefore, decisions of political system should be made on the basis of institutionalized procedures consented by the governed. With the economic system, efficiency (i.e. allocating optimal resources to maximize interests) is its operational logic in dealing with environmental risk. Decisions within the economic system should be made on the basis of a cost-benefit calculation to attain efficiency. In the realm of scientific systems, pursuing effective solutions by identifying the causal relationship of an environmental risk is its operational logic. This logic directs actors to adopt a series of methodological procedures to evaluate the validity of scientific knowledge. The operational logic of a social system is to pursue social welfare, fairness, and common values among diverse actors in order to sustain social cohesion. Decisions of a social system should be made through an exchange of values. It helps actors to reach a fair distribution of values and information when dealing with environmental risks.

It is worth noticing that the complex institutional design of the EU discourages European individuals to continuously engage in environmental governance. Therefore, the inter-system communication in EU environmental governance takes on the characteristics of an "organized civil society" (Greenwood 2007), in which different organizations from the four societal systems represent different demands of European individuals. Therefore, EU environmental governance can be viewed as network governance by sophisticatedly interconnected societal systems (Kohler-Koch 1999). In this context, the representatives of political system include EU decision-making institutions, namely the Commission, European Parliament (EP) and the Council of Ministers (hereafter, the Council). The representatives of the economic system include commercial companies and associations of industries. The representatives of the social system include various non-governmental organizations (NGOs). The representatives of the scientific system include scientists and experts who conduct research on the implementation of policies and their impacts in assumed scenarios of application.

During inter-system communication, the four societal systems contribute to a more comprehensive knowledge base regarding the risk-benefit distribution under different scenarios. However, the final policy design and decisions are inevitably matters of political judgment according to EU policy making system.

In EU policy making system, environmental policy usually starts with the communications of the Commission in the form of Green Paper, White Paper, or various programs, strategies and reviews. The environmental policy then proceeds to the discussions in EU institutions or public forums. After a consultation process, the Commission will present formal legislative proposals to the EP and the Council. The EP then assigns a committee to prepare a report with amendments of the Commission proposal and the report will be adopted as the EP position after the reading process. The Council discusses the Commission's proposal and adopts a common position after EP amendments. The process goes back and forth in different policy-making procedures. EU environmental policy making is mainly under the co-decision procedure. Accordingly, the participation of the four societal systems creates a flow of inter-system communication through which each system conveys different observations according to their respective operation logic and then enters into the stage of decision making in the EU policy cycle (shown in Figure 8.1).

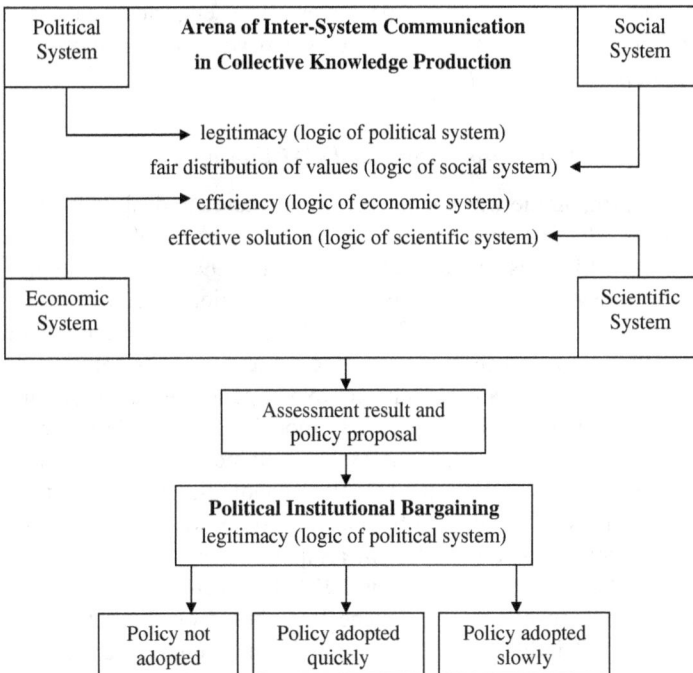

Figure 8.1 Simplified framework of EU policy-making process.
Source: Jasanoff and Wynne 1998; Renn 2000: 295. Redesigned by the authors.

Participation in environmental assessments and the effectiveness of EU environmental governance

With the initiation of the Fifth Environmental Action Plan (EAP) in 1993, more and more actors are increasingly involved in the policy cycle at the EU level. Ten years later, the launch of the Sixth EAP in 2002 recognized that EU environmental policy should be based on sound science, economic cost-effectiveness, and engagement of stakeholders in a manner of transparent partnership (European Commission 2001b). This transformation exemplifies the broadening scope and scale of participation in the process of risk management at the EU level.

The Auto-Oil programme, Clean Air for Europe (CAFE)[3] programme, and European Climate Change Programme (ECCP)[4] were large-scale collaborations launched by the Commission to facilitate environmental policy formulation and decision making at the EU level regarding air quality and climate change. In this section, we analyse the design of participation and its effectiveness in the three programmes. We conduct case studies with the following steps. First, we elucidate the mandates of these three environmental programmes. Second, instead of identifying distinct participants in the programmes, we code them into different societal systems according to their functional attributes and then identify their participatory scales. Third, we identify their participatory forms according to the organizational structure of these programs. The empirical data relies on unclassified documents from EU institutions and working group reports of the three programmes.

Air quality: the Auto-Oil programme and CAFE programme

The Auto-Oil programme was conducted in two phases to deal with the problem of air pollution. The first phase (AOI) was conducted from 1992 to 1996, and the second phase (AOII)[5] was conducted from 1997 to 1999. It was an attempt by the Commission to develop a new environmental legislation model.

The Commission launched the AOI in 1992 to identify cost-effective measures in order to reduce road transport emissions to the levels consistent with clean air. It included three research areas: technical-experimental research, an air quality modelling study, and a cost-effectiveness modelling study. The experimental technology research was carried out by the automobile and oil industries to investigate the effects of different vehicle technologies and fuel qualities on emission performance. The air quality modelling study was led by the Directorate General (DG) Environment to predict the air quality in seven European cities and the ground level ozone across the EU in 2010. The cost-effectiveness study was conducted by the consultancy of Touche Ross based on the data supplied by automobile and oil industries. Participation in the AOI was called "tripartite dialogue", including automobile industry, oil industry, and three DGs (Environment, Energy, and Transport) of the Commission (Friedrich *et al.* 2000: 597–8).

The air quality modelling study includes only economic actors and scientific actors, which made this study only take the general impact of air pollution on human health into consideration, but ignored other local environmental problems. The cost-effectiveness modelling study did not take social cost and environmental damage into account. The scale of participation in this program was limited: EU member states, the EP and the Council were excluded from this programme. As a result, policy legitimacy was undermined by the lack of participation of the major EU policy making institutions, member states and NGOs. The Commission proposed two legislative proposals regarding passenger car emission standards and fuel quality (European Commission 1996) and they were adopted as Directive 98/69/EC and 98/70/EC. However, the standards for car emission and fuel quality provoked intensive debates among EU member states during the policy making process. The EP further advanced more stringent standards in the final legal act.

The AOII aimed to establish a consistent framework of policy options to reduce the emission of pollutants by assessing air quality and identifying all emission sources. After the experience of AOI, the participants in AOII included relevant stakeholders such as EU member states, industries and NGOs. The AOII established a management group, a contact group and seven working groups. The management group included the chair of working groups and staff from the Commission. It was to facilitate the interface between different working groups and coordinate the administrative details relating to organization of meetings and contracts. The contact group served as an exchange platform, all interest groups could express their concerns and received reports from working groups. The seven working groups conducted studies on environmental objectives, vehicle technology, fuels, inspection and maintenance, non-technical measures, fiscal instruments and cost-effectiveness. Each working group consisted of a number of experts nominated by the stakeholders and was chaired by the Commission official.

The AOII involved participation including scientists/experts, economic actors, NGOs and EU policy making institutions. Each working group contained actors from different societal systems according to respective assessment items. All the results produced by them were integrated into the final cost-effectiveness study. The Commission proposals that refer to the results of AOII assessments are related to the reduction of air pollutants from road vehicles (European Commission 1997, 1998). These proposals were then accepted as Directive 1999/96/EC, Council Directive 2000/30/EC. There are other proposals that related to the reduction of air pollutants from road vehicles without referring to AOII but were assessment items in the AOII during 2000 and 2001 (European Commission 2000a, 2000b, 2000c, 2001c). They are also accepted as Directive 2001/1/EC, 2001/100/EC, 2002/51/EC, and 2003/17/EC.

The CAFE was a programme of technical analysis and policy development launched in May 2001 to develop an integrated long-term policy to protect human health and the environment from the effects of air pollution (European Commission 2001d). Its assessment items included setting air quality targets and policy, assessing the concentration of particulate matter in the air, reviewing the national programmes on the implementation of the national emission ceilings directive and identifying policy instruments for better implementation of air quality directives in EU member states.

At the end, the Commission initiated a thematic strategy on air pollution (European Commission 2005a) which was confirmed by the Council and the EP with requirements for legal actions and stringent standards to attain the objectives of the Sixth EAP. The proposal integrated sporadic EU directives on air pollution[6] into a single one and was adopted as Directive 2008/50/EC. The Commission also proposed a proposal on volatile organic compounds (European Commission 2002) and introduced particulate matter $PM_{2.5}$ in the proposal for the ambient air quality (European Commission 2005b). Both proposals were also accepted as Directive 2004/42/EC and Directive 2008/50/EC.

Climate change: European Climate Change Programme

Climate change has become a major issue in EU political agenda since the 1990s and the EU has developed several policies to address this problem. However, these efforts were fragmented because of the lack of a comprehensive perspective on this problem. The ECCP was launched in June 2000 to bring newly developed knowledge and policies into consideration and to integrate old policies into a coherent EU strategy to implement the Kyoto Protocol. The Commission claimed that the ECCP was a multi-stakeholder approach, which was supposed to provide a positive experience for the Commission at drafting legislative proposals (European Commission 2000d: 6). This programme was separated into two phases. The ECCP I was conducted from 2000 to 2003 to develop policies and measures on energy, transport, and industry sectors. The ECCP II was launched in October 2005 to continue the unfinished work of the ECCP I.

The ECCP I contained a steering committee and eleven working groups. The steering committee composed of all Commission services that took part in the programme and met once a month. It was in charge of managing the programme and maintaining regular contacts with stakeholders. The working groups operated according to the timetable and terms of reference developed by the steering committee, and assessed the implications of policies and measures on society according to the information provided by Commission services. The ECCP II continued the work of ECCP I. It maintained the basic framework of ECCP I but added in several new working groups. These working groups including ECCP I review (with five subgroups: transport, energy supply, energy demand, non-CO_2 gases, agriculture), aviation, CO_2 and cars, carbon capture and storage, adaptation, reducing greenhouse gas emissions from ships. In addition to meetings of working groups and stakeholders, the ECCP II provided a platform on the website for different societal actors to provide their opinion. The ECCP involves various forms of participation. Members in the working groups that represent different societal systems could express their concerns about the possible policy impact or advocate certain policy options according to their expertise. Their communication was based on the information provided by the Commission services. The records of working group meetings were available from the EU website.

At the end of the ECCP, the Commission incorporates existing policies and measures and initiates new policy instruments to deal with climate change problems. The ECCP produced over 40 EU-level policies and measures on climate change at EU-level (European Commission 2006). Some are the old policies and measures and others are new such as the introduction of flexible mechanisms, including the emissions trading scheme, the clean development mechanism and joint implementation.

Summary of case studies

The scale and form of participation varied from programme to programme. In the AOI, automobile and oil industries, functioning as representatives of economic system, both conducted technical analysis and provided data for cost-effectiveness assessment. There was no participation of the political or social system in the programme. In the AOII, all four societal systems engaged in research or acted as consultants in different working groups. In the CAFE programme, four societal systems were engaged in conducting research in working groups, and public consultations were conducted in the form of a questionnaire. Finally, all societal systems participated in the ECCP in the form of consultation. All participants in the three programmes were selected by the Commission.

Our research finds that policies based on collectively produced knowledge do not always attain policy acceptance. Prolonged debates and delayed policy implementation occur frequently. Three environmental assessment programmes demonstrate that broader and better participation does not guarantee the policy acceptance of EU environmental legislation. With a similar scale and form of participation in the AOII and CAFE programmes, as well as that in the two phases of the ECCP, the policy acceptance in different policies varied. Some were accepted very quickly, others were controversial and took a long time to be accepted as EU legislation. For example, in the issue area of air quality, it took two years for the EU to adopt Auto-oil directives based on the controversial result of AOI. However, with improved participation in AOII and CAFE, the relevant policy proposal also took two or even three years to be adopted. In the issue area of climate change, the directive for renewable energy promotion (Directive 2001/77/EC) was adopted within two years, and the first ETS directive (Directive 2003/87/EC) was passed in two years, while it took three years for the regulation on fluorinated greenhouse gases (Regulation (EC) No 842/2006) to be adopted. It shows that improved participation in environmental assessment has little effect during the institutional bargaining between policy makers (Table 8.1).

Table 8.1 Participation and the effectiveness of EU environmental assessments

	Air Quality			Climate Change	
	AOI	AOII	CAFE	ECCP I	ECCP II
Scale of participation	Economic and scientific actors	Political, economic, social and scientific actors			
Form of participation	Data provision and research	Research, working groups and consultation		Consultation working groups	
Effectiveness (Acceptance of policy proposals)	Policy adopted either slowly or quickly with amendments from the EP or the Council				

Source: Compiled by the authors.

Conclusions

The research findings of this chapter indicate that the influence of environmental assessment on political decision is indirect. As a result, improved participation in environmental assessments, which implies a more comprehensive inclusion of diverse actors and more effective participation in producing collective knowledge about environmental risks, can only enhance the legitimacy of Commission's policy proposals. However, the effectiveness of EU environmental governance is less influenced by the improved participation. The effectiveness depends more on the results of EU institutional political bargaining, which is subject to dynamic developments with EU member states, as well as at the EU and international level.

Participation is necessary but not sufficient for effective EU environmental governance

This chapter demonstrates that the enlargement and better design of participation plays an important role in improving the legitimacy of large-scale environmental assessments. However, the acceptability of policy proposals does not directly derive from the legitimacy of environmental assessments. Theoretically, more participation makes the environmental assessment more legitimate when dealing with long-term environmental problems. However, the scale and form of participation in environmental assessments do not directly link to the effectiveness of EU environmental governance. Our research findings suggest that the enlargement and better design of participation is a necessary, but not sufficient, condition for effective EU environmental governance. Accordingly, we could expect that participation in environmental assessments can improve EU environmental governance by bringing more knowledge regarding environmental problems and its solutions. However, to what extent environment assessments can influence EU environmental policy making depends on how policy makers code them with their own logic of risk taking.

Environmental assessment can be a tool to facilitate inter-system communication and has the potential to improve the effectiveness of EU environmental governance. Participation in environmental assessments can improve the information gap between policy makers and society. However, it can never resolve conflicting interests in the society. Furthermore, effective EU environmental governance still depends on the ultimate decision of the institutional political bargaining, where political actors try to gather the minimum legitimacy that can sustain their ruling power.

Further research on long-term policies

According to Reed (2008), there is already a lot of literature that identifies better design of participation in environmental management which could be also applied in environmental assessments. Based on the research findings of this chapter, effective participation is definitively an indispensable element for long-term policy making. Moreover, with effective participation in environmental assessments as a prerequisite, it is important to identify the conditions under which long-term policy making could systematically and effectively make use of collectively produced knowledge. Another important question is how do you build a bridge between different forms of the logic of risk-taking during environmental policy making? These questions link the other three themes of this book together. What form of *governance and institution* can best facilitate the use of *knowledge and policy learning* in environmental policy making? How do you integrate the various forms of risk-taking logic from other societal systems into modern society's most prevalent form of risk-taking logic, the *economic* system? Are there best practices that different societal systems work out in protecting the environment and why? Does the systemic common culture and beliefs other than those of the four systems have the potential to build bridges among the four systems? To address these questions, we require more thorough interdisciplinary dialogues.

Notes

1 Policy cycle refers to the sequences of stages in the process of policymaking, including agenda-setting, policy formulation, decision-making, policy implementation and policy evaluation. (Howlett and Ramesh 2003: 11, 13)
2 Official Journal of European Communities, No. C 138, 17, 5, 1993, p. 24.
3 Information on the CAFE is available at: http://ec.europa.eu/environment/air/cafe/index. htm
4 Information on the ECCP is available at: http://ec.europa.eu/clima/policies/eccp/index_ en.htm
5 AOII is available at: http://ec.europa.eu/environment/archives/autooil/index.htm
6 These directives are Council Directive 96/62/EC, Council Decision 97/101/EC, Council Directive 1999/30/EC, Directive 2000/69/EC, Directive 2002/3/EC, available at: http:// eur-lex.europa.eu/en/index.htm

References

Beck, U. 1998. "Politics of Risk Society". In Franklin, J. (ed.), *The Politics of Risk Society*. Cambridge: Polity Press, 9–22.

Clark, W. C., Mitchell, R. B. and Cash, D. W. 2006. "Evaluating the Influence of Global Environmental Assessments". In Mitchell, R. B., Clark, W. C., Cash, D. W. and Dickson, N. M. (eds), *Global Environmental Assessments: Information and Influence*. Cambridge: MIT Press, 1–28.

Doelle, M. and Sinclair, A. J. 2006. "Time for a New Approach to Public Participation In EA: Promoting Cooperation and Consensus for Sustainability". *Environmental Impact Assessment Review* 26(2): 185–205.

European Commission. 1996. Proposal for a European Parliament and Council Directive Relating to Measures to be Taken against Air Pollution by Emissions from Motor Vehicles and Amending Council Directives 70/156/EEC and 70/220/EEC. COM (1996) 248 final.

European Commission. 1997. Proposal for a European Parliament and Council Directive amending Council Directive 88/77/EEC on the Approximation of the Laws of the Member States relating to the Measures to be Taken against the Emission of Gaseous and Particulate Pollutants from Diesel Engines for Use in Vehicles. COM (1997) 627 final.

European Commission. 1998. Proposal for a Council Directive on the Roadside Inspection of the Roadworthiness of Commercial Vehicles Circulating in the Community. COM (1998) 117 final.

European Commission. 2000a. Proposal for a Directive of the European Parliament and of the Council amending Council Directive 70/220/EEC Concerning Measures to be Taken Against Air Pollution by Emissions from Motor Vehicles. COM (2000) 42 final.

European Commission. 2000b. Proposal for a Directive of the European Parliament and of the Council amending Directive 97/24/EC on Certain Components and Characteristics of Two or Three-wheel Motor Vehicles. COM (2000) 314 final.

European Commission 2000c. Proposal for a Directive of the European Parliament and of the Council amending Council Directive 70/220/EEC Concerning Measures to be Taken Against Air Pollution by Emissions from Motor Vehicles. COM (2000) 487 final.

European Commission. 2000d. *Towards an European Climate Change Programme*. COM (2000) 88, March 8, 2000. Brussels: Commission of the European Communities.

European Commission. 2001a. *European Governance: A White Paper*. COM (2001) 428, July 25, 2001. Brussels: Commission of the European Communities.

European Commission. 2001b. *Our Future, Our Choice: The Sixth Environment Action Programme*. COM (2001) 31, January 24, 2001. Brussels: Commission of the European Communities.

European Commission. 2001c. Proposal for a Directive of the European Parliament and of the Council on the Quality of Petrol and Diesel Fuels and amending Directive 98/70/EC. COM (2001) 241 final.

European Commission. 2001d. *The Clear Air for Europe Programme: Towards a Thematic Strategy for Air Quality*. COM (2001) 245.

European Commission. 2002. Proposal for a Directive of the European Parliament and of the Council on the Limitation of Emissions of Volatile Organic Compounds due to the Use of Organic Solvents in Decorative Paints and Varnishes and Vehicle Refinishing Products and Amending Directive 1999/13/EC. COM (2002) 750 final.

European Commission. 2005a. *Communication from the Commission to the Council and the European Parliament: Thematic Strategy on Air Pollution.* COM (2005) 446 final.

European Commission. 2005b. Proposal for a Directive of the European Parliament and of the Council on Ambient Air Quality and Cleaner Air for Europe. COM (2005) 447 final.

European Commission. 2006. *The European Climate Change Programme: EU Action against Climate Change.* Luxembourg: Office for Official Publications of the European Communities.

Friedrich, A., Tappe, M. and Wurzel, R. K. W. 2000. "A New Approach to EU Environmental Policy-making? The Auto-Oil I Programme". *Journal of European Public Policy* 7(4): 593–612.

Greenwood, J. 2007. "Organized Civil Society and Democratic Legitimacy in the European Union". *British Journal of Political Science* 37(2): 333–57.

Hartley, N. and Wood, C. 2005. "Public Participation in Environmental Impact Assessment: Implementing the Aarhus Convention". *Environmental Impact Assessment Review* 25(4): 319–40.

Howlett, M. and Ramesh, M. 2003. *Study Public Policy: Policy Cycles and Policy Subsystems*, 2nd edition. Oxford: Oxford University Press.

Jasanoff, S. and Wynne, B. 1998. "Science and Decisionmaking". In Rayner, S. and Malone, E. L. (eds) *Human Choice and Climate Change, The Societal Framework.* Columbus, OH: Battelle, 1–87.

Kohler-Koch, B. 1999. "The Evolution and Transformation of European Governance". In Kohler-Koch, B. and Eising, R. (eds) *The Transformation of Governance in the European Union.* London: Routledge, 14–35.

Luhmann, N. 1982. *The Differentiation of Society.* Translated by Holmes, S. and Larmore, C. New York: Columbia University Press.

MacCormick, N. 2008. "Constitutionalism and Democracy in the EU". In Bomberg, E., Peterson, J. and Stubb, A. (eds) *The European Union: How does it Work?* 2nd edn. Oxford: Oxford University Press, 159–76.

O'Faircheallaigh, C. 2010. "Public Participation and Environmental Impact Assessment: Purposes, Implications, and Lessons for Public Policy Making". *Environmental Impact Assessment Review* 30(1): 19–27.

Pohjola, M. V. and Tuomisto, J. T. 2011. "Openness in Participation, Assessment and Policy Making upon Issues of Environment and Environmental Health: A Review of Literature and Recent Project Results". *Environmental Health* 10(58): 1–13.

Reed, M. S. 2008. "Stakeholder Participation for Environmental Management: A Literature Review". *Biological Conservation* 141(10): 2417–31.

Renn, O. 2004. "The Challenge of Integrating Deliberation and Expertise: Participation and Discourse in Risk Management". In McDaniels, T. and Small, M. J. (eds) *Risk Analysis and Society.* Cambridge: Cambridge University Press, 289–366.

Stewart, J. M. P. and Sinclair, A. J. 2007. "A Meaningful Public Participation in Environmental Assessment: Perspectives from Canadian Participants, Proponents and Government". *Journal of Environmental Assessment Policy and Management* 9(2): 161–83.

Yearley, S. 2008. "Nature and the Environment in Science and Technology Studies". In Hackett, E. J., Amsterdamska, O., Lynch, M. and Wajcman, J. (eds) *The Handbook of Science and Technology Studies*, 3rd edn. Cambridge, MA: The MIT Press, 921–47.

9 Potential and limits for businesses to address long-term social–ecological challenges

The case of European fish processors

Franziska Wolff and Katharina Schmitt[1]

Introduction

Major present-day challenges for policy makers are characterized by complex interactions of societal and ecological aspects, often mediated by technologies. The connections between climate change or biodiversity loss with industrial and agricultural production modes, energy systems, population growth or individual lifestyles are cases in point. Many social–ecological problems require decades to deal with: not only are the problems themselves complex and dynamic in nature and knowledge about them is uncertain, but their drivers are deeply embedded in societal habits and/or technological paths (Becker and Jahn 2006; Ostrom 2007). Policy making suffers among other things from implicit goal conflicts and from long problem cycles being at odds with political attention spans (Pierson 2004; Voß *et al.* 2009; Voß and Kemp 2006). For the private sector, too, barriers exist to commitment. These include high uncertainty regarding possible business risks and opportunities linked to long-term social–ecological problems (Hoffman 2001). Also, tackling such problems typically requires changes in whole systems of provision, and "sufficiency" approaches on top of efficiency policies (Spaargarden 2003; Tukker *et al.* 2008).

Nevertheless, there is a strong case for including the business sector in the tackling of long-term social–ecological problems. First, the "polluter pays" logic stipulates that contributors to such problems should be included in their abatement. Second, companies often possess means – including know-how, resources and influence – that can significantly contribute to the solution to such problems. Third, many societies attach duties to the role of companies in the economy and society. While these are typically reflected in regulation, businesses are also expected to contribute to societal welfare on a voluntary basis and beyond regulation. Such "Corporate Social Responsibility" (CSR) activities are particularly widespread in Anglo-Saxon societies but are increasingly taking root in continental Europe as well (Habisch *et al.* 2004; Barth and Wolff 2009). We perceive CSR as one possible approach to integrate the private sector in strategies to address long-term social–ecological challenges. At the same time, through CSR businesses typically integrate civil society in their own strategy-building, making it a participatory approach that works in two directions.

The focus of this chapter is on CSR by European fish processors and on the integration of CSR into long-term political approaches. The fish processing sector has a key position in fighting the global depletion of marine resources, a persistent sustainability issue. Yet despite the sector's vested interest in maintaining its resource base, only recently did a larger number of processors start engaging in the issue. This raises the question of how effective voluntary contributions by the private sector can be for political long-term approaches. After briefly conceptualizing the relation between CSR and political long-term strategies in the second section, we present empirical insights into the potential of European fish processers to effectively address seafood sustainability through CSR. A discussion follows on how their CSR impacts contribute to achieving long-term EU policy goals. Finally, we highlight limits to the inclusion of the private sector in addressing long-term challenges. The conclusions serve to discuss the consequences on transparency and legitimacy of an integration of private sector participants in long-term policies.

CSR as an approach to integrate the private sector in strategies addressing long-term social–ecological challenges

What is CSR and how does it serve to involve business actors in the solution of social–ecological conflicts?

CSR is defined by the European Commission (2001: 6) as a "concept whereby companies integrate social and environmental concerns in their business operations and in their interaction with their stakeholders on a voluntary basis. Being socially responsible means not only fulfilling legal expectations, but also going beyond compliance [...]". CSR can relate to phenomena as diverse as labor standards, AIDS, corruption, human rights, diversity or the environment. A number of issues addressed by CSR are both social–ecological and long term in nature (e.g. climate change, poverty reduction).

CSR can address social or ecological aspects directly linked to corporate processes – product development, sourcing, production, marketing etc. ("built-in" CSR); or they can address sustainability issues in the company's wider environment ("bolt-on" CSR). In both cases, companies can make use of standardized instruments or develop own programmes. In the case of "built-in" CSR, instruments range from codes of conduct (e.g. the UN Global Compact principles) to management systems (like the Social Accountability 8000 standard), accounting practices (based, for example, on the GRI Guidelines), and interactions with stakeholders (such as the Clean Clothes Campaign). For "bolt-on" CSR, instruments encompass donating, sponsoring, cause-related marketing, volunteering and others. Finally, CSR tools exist for the areas of responsible consumption (above all product labelling, e.g. for fair trade) and responsible investment (ethical funds) (AccountAbility 2003).

Businesses make use of CSR for a number of reasons. One important motive is that CSR can be a means for them to respond to social–ecological challenges and to better cope with uncertainties resulting from these (Wheeler 2003). Let us take the over-exploitation of the seas as an example. For the fisheries sector, the erosion of its supply base involves a fundamental threat to and insecurity about the sector's commercial outlook. Promoting sustainable fisheries through CSR helps to counter these risks and provides frontrunner companies with the opportunity to distinguish their products from those of competitors. Socially, jobs can be secured and fisheries-dependent communities strengthened. Ecologically, CSR may contribute to the restoration of fish stocks and marine ecosystems.

CSR not only provides businesses, but also societal stakeholders and policy makers with a tool for sustainability governance (Wolff *et al.* 2009): non-business actors contribute to shaping and pushing CSR. Societal stakeholders can influence companies' CSR activities either through markets – by consuming sustainable goods or investing ethically – or through the "allocation" of legitimacy (Hoffmann 2001; Midttun 2005). For example, civil society organizations can participate in CSR processes or, withholding legitimacy, can name and shame wrongdoers, organize boycotts or take legal action against them.

Governments, too, can draw on CSR as part of their efforts to integrate businesses in long-term sustainability strategies (Albareda *et al.* 2007; World Bank 2002).[2] They can do so by stimulating CSR that relates to identified long-term challenges, for instance by means of capacity building, networking, financial incentives including sustainable public procurement, or providing legal frameworks for voluntary instruments (such as the EU's Environmental Management and Auditing Scheme).[3] With CSR being a voluntary activity, there is of course no guarantee that companies will align their goals with those of governments (cf. Hahn 2004). The inclusion of CSR leader companies and societal stakeholders in the development and implementation of long-term sustainability strategies, however, can be a remedy. Generally, deliberative approaches like CSR can help to change perceptions and norms and to build trust among state, business and societal actors. They are hence apt to support the cognitive, normative and technological transitions necessitated by long-term social–ecological challenges (Hoogma *et al.* 2005; Kemp and Rotmans 2005).

The implications that these two forms of actor-participation have for transparency and legitimacy of long-term political approaches will be discussed at pp. 175, while the following section provides empirical insights above all on implications for policy effectiveness.

The potential of voluntary business contributions to address long-term challenges: insights on the sustainability of fisheries

As has been pointed out above, policy makers can draw on voluntary business contributions – i.e. CSR – when devising strategies to address long-term social–ecological challenges. The acid test of this is whether CSR really is effective with regard to long-term socio-ecological problems. We will discuss this question focussing on the European fish processing sector and its voluntary activities on sustainable seafood/ sustainable fisheries. This is a long-term social–ecological challenge, with fish stocks worldwide having been under serious pressure for some three decades. In 2007 circa half of the world's fish stocks were fully exploited while about another quarter of stocks was either overexploited, depleted or recovering from depletion (FAO 2009). With seafood demand doubling in the past 30 years, fishing has been the major cause of this resource depletion and its ecological and social impacts (Pauly *et al.* 2005).

Fish processors hold an important position to help alleviate the problem of unsustainable fisheries: they can source fish from sustainable stocks, e.g. from fisheries eco-labelled by the Marine Stewardship Council (MSC). Also, their relative size and power in the supply chain allows them to require fishing companies to abandon environmentally harmful fishing practices. How European fish processors make use of this potential, and how their voluntary efforts contribute to the achievement of EU policy goals will be discussed in the following.

Research design and method

This section examines the above question on the basis of findings from the research project "Rhetoric and Realities: Analysing Corporate Social Responsibility in Europe" (RARE).[4] Its paramount question was whether CSR unfolds a positive impact on society and the environment. This topic was investigated for various European industries and social–ecological issues in a comparative fashion. The research was based on a common framework for assessing and explaining the effects of CSR policies and for linking them to public policy goals (Barth and Wolff 2009a).

The RARE research on sustainable seafood is based on a survey among eight fish processors (Schmitt and Wolff 2009) and an in-depth case study of three companies from this sample that performed particularly well with regard to CSR (Wolff and Schmitt 2009). To enable a thorough impact assessment, the case study was focused on the issue of seafood sustainability (as will be done in the following), though other ecological and social CSR issues[5] had been covered in the survey, too (Schmitt and Wolff 2006). The three companies selected for the case study were: the Dutch-British multinational *Unilever*, one of the world's largest whitefish buyers in 2005; the British processor *Young's*, UK's market leader in both frozen and chilled fish; and German *Gottfried Friedrichs* KG, a medium-sized supplier of smoked fish premium products. Interviews were carried out with different company representatives and civil society stakeholders during 2006 and 2007.

Our approach to CSR impact assessment was as follows: we qualitatively analysed and evaluated CSR effects, striving to entangle through process tracing and identification of causal mechanisms the complex relations between fish processors' CSR policies ("CSR output") and their effects ("CSR outcome" and "CSR impact")[6] (Skjærseth and Wettestad 2009). More precisely, *CSR output* describes the extent to which companies change their commitment and strategies with regard to social and environmental performance, including the adoption of specific CSR instruments. *CSR outcome* denotes concrete changes in the companies' social and environmental practices, resulting from changes in CSR output. Finally, *CSR impact* covers the substantive consequences for society and the environment outside the company, induced by the sustainability changes in corporate practices (i.e. the outcome). In our case, the path from output to outcome and impact typically looks as follows: sustainable fishing policies and purchasing guidelines (output) lead to changes in seafood sourcing practices and product portfolios (outcome). These subsequently contribute to preserving fish stocks and marine ecosystems and, indirectly, global food security and livelihoods in fishing communities (impact). Finally, we benchmarked the expected impact against policy-goals defined in EU strategies addressing the long-term problem of unsustainable fisheries.

CSR output

Unilever, Young's and Friedrichs feature rather high levels of (seafood-related) CSR output. It evolves from corporate seafood policies and sustainable sourcing guidelines.

Unilever's Fish Sustainability Initiative (FSI), established in 1996, committed the company to purchase 100 per cent seafood from sustainable sources by 2005. In order to achieve this goal, the company joined forces in 1997 with the World Wildlife Fund (WWF) to set up the MSC. Transformed into an independent not-for-profit organization in 1999, the MSC is today one of the major CSR initiatives. We will briefly describe its functioning.

The MSC provides an international product label that assures consumers that a seafood product stems from a sustainable fishery. Two distinct types of certification exist within the scheme: certification of the fishery itself and chain of custody (CofC) certification. In the fisheries certification, a fish stock is assessed against "MSC Principles and Criteria which require healthy populations of targeted species (MSC Principle 1); the integrity of ecosystems (Principle 2); and an effective (public) management system that respects local, national and international law (Principle 3). In mid-2009, 42 fisheries around the globe had been certified against these standards and over 150 underwent assessment, making up about 7 per cent of the annual global wild harvest (MSC 2009). Once a fishery is certified, the MSC label may be used on respective seafood products, provided a CofC assessment verifies that the products originate from the certified fishery.

In its early years, certification of fisheries through the MSC progressed very slowly and Unilever feared it would not be able to achieve its 100 per cent target in time. It hence developed an additional, in-house fishery assessment tool to guide its sourcing decisions. This "Traffic Light System", assesses fisheries against five criteria similar to the MSC's (though with less procedural conditions) and graded results into traffic light colours. Fisheries with an all green assessment are considered "sustainable", those with a mix of green and yellow "managed and progressing", and those with one or more red scores "poorly managed". Unilever stops sourcing from "unmanaged" fisheries that score red against all indicators.

Young's "Fish for Life" policy – developed under consultation with various environmental organizations – includes a commitment not to sell endangered species and to apply "responsible" procurement criteria. In addition, the company renounces from knowingly purchasing fish from illegal, unreported and unregulated (IUU) sources. Since the late 1990s, Young's has been MSC CofC-certified. Due to the initially low number and slow process of fishery certifications by the MSC, Young's (like Unilever) developed an own in-company tool ("Fishery Health Check") to assess the sustainability of stocks from which to source fish. The fisheries are rated to be "low", "medium" or "high" risk, with risk relating both to ecological and business exposure risk. A "high risk" assessment either requires withdrawal from that fishery or species, or definition of conditions under which an engagement with the fishery or species is upheld. By early 2007, the tool was applied to 36 fisheries or species, 14 of which were rated "low risk". Young's has not defined a concrete target for sourcing sustainable fish – MSC-certified or "low risk".

Like Young's sustainable seafood policy, Friedrichs has committed itself in its (non-public) code of ethics to refrain from using fish species that are legally protected or threatened with extinction. Based on their decision in 2002 to undergo – as the first German fish processor – a MSC CoC certification, Friedrichs also aims to expand the share of MSC-labelled products in their portfolio of wild-caught fish products. While the company does not have a formal target for the sourcing of sustainable fish, it informally strives for 100 per cent MSC fish in its portfolio of wild-caught fish.

In the development of their CSR output, the two bigger companies engaged with civil society stakeholders. Our interviewees confirmed that this not only increased the legitimacy of their initiatives at least among those groups involved, but that civil society participation tended to strengthen the ecological ambitiousness of the CSR output. It did not, however, increase the transparency of the company-specific assessment tools, whose exact criteria, application and results are not public. Policy makers were not involved at any point. Ironically, however, the failure of public fisheries' managers to sustain fish stocks – and hence the sector's supply base – had been a driver for the MSC's development and other CSR outputs (Wolff and Schmitt 2009).

CSR outcome

Changing their business practices (CSR outcome), all companies made use of the following three mechanisms to adjust seafood sourcing and product portfolios: withdrawal or abstention from over-exploited/depleted fisheries; sourcing from sustainable fisheries; and implementing supplier requirements on responsible fishing practices.

As regards the first mechanism, none of the companies sources fish from protected or threatened species. Both Unilever and Young's have withdrawn from the overexploited North Sea cod fishery. Young's has furthermore reduced its purchases from the Eastern Baltic cod stock by one third. Friedrichs renounced sturgeon caviar and dogfish.

Second, the companies have shifted from unsustainable fisheries to buy fish from sustainable fisheries. In our sample the share of MSC-sourced fish in the companies' volume of wild-capture fish (measured in tons) ranges between 40 and 90 per cent. In mid-2006, before it sold its fish business, Unilever had sourced 46 per cent of its (wild-caught) fish from certified fisheries. In particular, certification of the Alaskan Pollock fishery in early 2005 had provided the opportunity to boost the MSC share from 4 to 46 per cent. In addition, Unilever declared 10 per cent of its seafood to be sourced from "green light" fisheries according to its "Traffic Light System". At the same time, Unilever fully or partially withdrew from fisheries ranked "red" in the system. It also encouraged managers and stakeholders of "yellow" fisheries to improve their performance and those of "green" ones to undergo a MSC certification (Unilever 2003). In absolute terms, no other company sourced as many tons of fish from sustainable fisheries, though Unilever failed to achieve its target of purchasing *all* fish from sustainable sources by 2005. With a 40 per cent share of MSC fish among its wild capture purchases in early 2007, Young's achieved a somewhat lower share than Unilever. An additional part of Young's seafood was sourced from fisheries rated as "low risk" by the company's "Fishery Health Check". Finally, the share of MSC certified fish in Friedrichs' portfolio of wild-caught fish was at 90 per cent in 2007. This translated into about 1,000 tons of wild salmon, a relatively low tonnage when compared with the absolute amount of sustainable fish sourced by the other two companies.

The third mechanism to achieve CSR outcome is through "green" supplier requirements. Unilever had a set of sustainable sourcing requirements which were communicated to and discussed with its suppliers. Boats that processed fish for Unilever were regularly inspected (Porritt and Goodman 2005: 44). Young's applies supply chain audits, traceability systems and inspections to make sure that suppliers conform to their standards. These require fishermen to abstain from destructive fishing practices and from IUU fishing. For some stocks, the latter requirement is based on standardized buying guidelines by the EU Fish Processors Association (AIPCE 2006). In addition, Young's has an "open book" policy for its own records of all seafood sources. The company has stopped business relations with suppliers not willing to share Young's policies. Like the other processors, Friedrichs commits its suppliers to sustainable fishing and trading practices. However, the purchasing agreement is not tied to control or auditing mechanisms.

Civil society stakeholders contributed to behavioural changes and CSR outcomes in all companies, both through pressure and cooperation: for instance, internationally legitimising the MSC as CSR instrument (Unilever), providing advice in the implementation of in-company tools (Young's) or intervening in product development (Friedrichs). Their participation can be said to have increased the legitimacy and effectiveness of CSR outcomes. This can only partly be said for governments (focussing on those in which our companies are headquartered): their greatest contribution can probably be seen in funding MSC fisheries certifications (UK) and supporting voluntary commitment through active national CSR strategies (UK, Netherlands); none of the three governments, however, promoted sustainable seafood in its public procurement policies or in sustainable consumption campaigns (Wolff and Schmitt 2009).

CSR impact – a contribution to EU policy goals?

To what extent have the described changes in corporate behaviour (CSR outcomes) resulted in an impact on society and the environment? And to what extent do these impacts contribute to achieving the goals of public strategies which address long-term social–ecological challenges? These are key questions when pondering the integration of the private sector – through CSR – in such strategies. Note that by "integration" we do not mean active participation of businesses in public strategy formulation, but the taking into account of CSR contributions to the strategies' goal attainment. Many goals of public strategies are not immediately *directed at* companies, but are at least partly *transferable to* them – that is, businesses can voluntarily contribute to them. In this section, we review policy goals set by the EU regarding sustainable fisheries and discuss how the CSR outcomes can be expected to create an impact with regard to these goals.[7]

The EU's current strategy to address the long-term challenge of more sustainable fisheries manifests itself above all in its Common Fisheries Policy and in "neighbouring" policy fields like biodiversity conservation. Excepting more general objectives such as to "[s]afeguard the earth's capacity to support life in all its diversity" (see the 2006 EU Sustainable Development Strategy) and to halt biodiversity decline by 2010 (6th European Action Programme, EAP), the relevant long-term goals can be clustered as follows:

- to conserve and sustainably use fish stocks and feeding grounds, both within the EU and outside;[8]
- to reduce the impact of fishing on non-target species and the marine ecosystem, including achieving healthy marine populations, good environmental status, and good surface water status;[9]
- to stop illegal, unregulated and unreported (IUU) fishing.[10]

All three companies tackle these policy goals – as part of implementing CSR strategies (outcomes). The measures by which civil society has participated in the shaping of these outcomes have been described above. We will now discuss how the outcomes may create impact. Table 9.1 summarizes our findings.

Conservation and sustainable use of fish stocks

Our case study companies address the EU goal "conservation and sustainable use of stocks" through all three (outcome) mechanisms specified at the beginning of this section. The causal paths to CSR impact are as follows:

Table 9.1 CSR impact and the business sector's contribution to achieving EU policy goals

EU policy goal	Do CSR efforts by the companies support the EU policy goals?		
	Yes/No	… through the following CSR outcomes:	… which can be expected to produce the following CSR impacts:
Conservation and sustainable use of fish stocks and feeding grounds	Yes	Withdrawal from critically threatened stocks	Reduced pressure on critically threatened stocks (dependent on overall demand)
		Sourcing from MSC certified fisheries	Relatively sustainable target stocks
		Sourcing from fisheries assessed to be sustainable by in-company tools	(Impact on target stocks difficult to specify)
		Supplier requirements	(Impact on target stocks difficult to specify)
Reduction of impact on non-target species and the marine ecosystem	Yes	Sourcing from MSC certified fisheries	Relatively sustainable ecosystems
		Sourcing from fisheries assessed to be sustainable by in-company tools	(Impact on ecosystems difficult to specify)
		Supplier requirements	(Impact on ecosystems difficult to specify)
Eradicate illegal, unregulated and unreported fishing	Yes	Supplier requirements, for example based on AIPCE Guidelines	Impact not measurable so far

Source: based on Wolff, Bohn, Schultz and Wilkinson 2009: 260.

First, by reducing or refraining from seafood purchases from overexploited or depleted fisheries, fishing pressure on these stocks is reduced. Relief is created to the extent that the companies' purchasing stop is not (over) compensated by other actors' demand for the seafood in question.

Second and most importantly, the processors create positive impact on target stocks by sourcing fish from sustainable fisheries. In line with the EU policy goal, both the MSC certification as well as (complementary) company-specific tools for determining the sustainability of a fishery require target stocks to be sustained. While it is difficult to evaluate the potential impact of Unilever's and Young's own instruments – their assessments and consequences not being public – the design of the MSC scheme is rather conducive to impact: it is specific (setting quantifiable targets and requiring corrective action) and places obligations on fisheries participants that are independently verified and can be sanctioned. However, analyses of the MSC's de facto environmental impact are not conclusive, with some more sceptical accounts (Greenpeace 2006; Philipps *et al.* 2003) and some more positive ones (Agnew *et al.* 2006; Hoel 2004; Knapp *et al.* 2007). There is agreement, at least, that the MSC assures that a fisheries' sustainability is not an incidental occurrence but is monitored and fostered within a given time frame.

The third mechanism by which processors contribute to the sustainability of target stocks is by imposing specific standards on fish suppliers. The standards may, for instance, require fishermen to prevent discards and high-grading of catch, to carry out technical conservation measures, or to reduce fish waste. Among our sample companies (excepting Unilever whose supplier requirements are not publicly accessible), achievement of environmental impact seems most plausible for Young's: their supplier standards are most specific and the company is the only one that verifies compliance both through inspections and supply chain audits. Friedrichs' standards are more general with no system in place to monitor and verify that suppliers actually meet the requirements.

Reducing impacts on non-target species and the marine ecosystem

The EU policy goal to reduce impacts on non-target species and the marine ecosystem is also addressed by our processors' CSR activities. Impact can be expected through paths similar to those elaborated above:

First, processors contribute to the EU goal by sourcing fish from fisheries assessed to be sustainable by the MSC or alternative (company-specific) tools. The MSC Principle 2 requires fishing operations to allow maintenance of the ecosystem on which the fishery depends. The scheme's actual performance regarding this criterion is particularly contentious (Wildhavens 2004; Greenpeace 2006). Nevertheless, with its high levels of specificity and obligation (see above) the MSC is the most reliable CSR instrument to date to warrant that the ecosystem of a fishery is relatively sustainable. As regards company-specific assessment tools, Unilever's "Traffic Light System" requires that research on a fishery, for the fishery to be given a "green light", takes an ecosystem-based approach (Porritt and Goodman 2005: 43). Young's "Fishery Health Check" takes into account data on a fishery's levels of by-catch and the environmental impact of fishing operations. Since in both cases, the assessments are not independently verified and remedying measures are at the companies' discretion, the two instruments' impact on ecosystems is difficult to specify, and probably lower than the MSC's.

Second, the three processors selectively address ecosystem aspects in supplier standards. Activities which at least one of our processors requires their suppliers to conform with include: to minimize by-catch of fish; to reduce injuries to and mortality of by-catch other than fish; to prevent the mortality-causing loss of fishing nets; to minimize impact on the seabed; to lessen on-board pollution of the marine ecosystem. In addition, Young's explicitly reduces coastal pollution through its own on-land processing activities. Even though supplier requirements have the potential to contribute to reducing ecosystem impacts, sourcing MSC fish presently achieves a more comprehensive, reliable and verifiable contribution.

Eradicating illegal, unregulated and unreported fishing

The EU goal of eradicating IUU fishing has risen on businesses' CSR agenda only recently. The creation of Barents Sea cod and haddock and Baltic Sea cod buying guidelines by the EU Fish Processors Association (AIPCE 2006) was a major step towards this goal. The AIPCE supplier guidelines had been pushed among others by Young's and Unilever. Being an industry-wide initiative, they may reach a significant scale in the future. However, some member organizations were reluctant in developing the guidelines and may be unwilling to support them. Due to their recent development, we are unable to assess the guidelines' acceptance and impact so far. In our company sample, only Young's has included IUU aspects into both its supplier standards and its control system, suggesting a robust causal path to impact.

Summary

From among the identified policy goals, businesses have the largest potential to create sustainability impact with regard to conserving and sustainably using fish stocks and feeding grounds. Measures most likely to be effective include the voluntary withdrawal from critically threatened stocks and sourcing from MSC certified fisheries. With regard to the other policy goals identified, it is more difficult to conclude from companies' changes in behaviour to actual sustainability impacts. It is thus problematic to come to more generalised conclusions regarding the effectiveness of private sector participation in, or contributions to, long-term political approaches: even within the same policy field, effectiveness may vary from one issue to another.

Limits of voluntary business contributions to address long-term challenges

We suggested above that the private sector can contribute through CSR to alleviating long-term social–ecological problems. At the same time, our case study of seafood-related CSR in Unilever, Young's and Friedrichs points to some systematic limits for effective business contributions. By this we mean constellations that hamper the creation of CSR outcomes and impacts which it is difficult for businesses themselves to address successfully. In areas where such systematic limits exist it is not advisable to exclusively rely on CSR as a form of private sector inclusion in political long-term strategies.

Two such limits which emerge from our research on seafood-related CSR are companies' weak control over a CSR issue and the difficulties in linking necessary changes in the core business with a business case. These aspects were confirmed by other case studies (on different sectors and CSR issues) within the RARE project, which also hinted at additional CSR limits.[11] Beyond the realm of fisheries, we point to a further limit – (lacking) strategic relevance of an issue as perceived in a sector – as a possible reservation against relying too much on CSR.

Limited control over a CSR issue

The sustainability impact of CSR is affected by the degree of control that a company has over a CSR issue. Impact is more difficult to achieve when the issue lies outside the company's immediate sphere of influence.

In the case of seafood sustainability, CSR impact depends not only on fish processors, but to a large extent on the behaviour of fishers and, ironically, on public fishery management. Since fish processors neither own nor manage the fish resource from which they source, their capacity to influence actual "on the water impact" is limited, especially for smaller businesses. Fishermen need to support a fisheries' MSC certification and to actually implement "green" supplier standards required by responsible processors. Our interviews indicated that for both these aspects, a lot of convincing is necessary. This, in turn, presupposes that processors actually know who their suppliers are – which is impossible once they purchase seafood on the spot market, as the majority of the sector does. Durable and reliable supplier relations on the other hand are necessary levers vis-à-vis suppliers to accept sustainable fishing practices.

In addition to fishermen, governments and fisheries managers play a crucial role in making a fishery certifiable. As Hoel (2004: 50) points out, "ecolabelling schemes in fisheries rest on an assumption that the producers of fish products will be able to influence governments to modify management practices so as to satisfy the standards set by the label, alternatively that governments will be sensitive to the market concerns of the industry and modify resource management practices accordingly". This is often not the case: the main reason for all our sample companies not to (be able to) source all their marine inputs from certified sources was the limited availability of certified seafood, especially from the species (or close substitutes thereof) that their portfolios "required". This limit of certification schemes is exacerbated in the Global South by low data availability and weak governance capacities for stock management which make MSC certifications virtually impossible (ibid). Also, seafood labelling schemes depend on consumer demand, and such demand at least for the time being is largely limited to EU and North American markets (FAO 2009). For a more encompassing solution to the degradation of oceans, CSR will hence not suffice.

A company's core business and the business case argument

It is a special challenge when CSR requires changes in the core business, that is, in a company's portfolio of products and services. Less sustainable products or services need to be replaced by more sustainable alternatives. When such changes in core business are not seen to provide a business case at least in the long run, firms will be hesitant to realize them. This reflects the familiar problem of markets not delivering in the case of public goods (Doane 2005; Musgrave and Musgrave 1976).

For an enterprise, integrating sustainability concern into products and services implies major investments (McWilliams and Siegel 2001): it may need to adjust R&D and innovation strategies, production processes, markets and supply chains, customer relations, marketing and brands. These adjustments can translate into costs and losses with regard to a company's market positioning, customers, and supply base. Also, technical as well as social and organizational learning are required and the changes need to be legitimized vis-à-vis investors, employees and customers (Cramer *et al.* 2004).

Replacing seafood from unsustainable stocks by sustainably managed and harvested fish, our case study companies expected to meet (or create) the demand of at least a small segment of responsible consumers, i.e. create a business case. At the same time, costs had to be dealt with. These ranged from the charges of an MSC chain of custody certification, its annual reviews and label royalties, co-funding of MSC fisheries pre-/assessments (in some cases), to company-internal adjustment costs of substituting one fish species by another (certified) one. Price, quality and the reliability of supply vary when a processor sources fish from a new fishery, as do taste and performance levels.

This involves financial risks for the companies, as became apparent, for example, when European consumers did not appreciate the replacement of cod by certified hoki in Unilever's fish fingers. Moving into new fisheries furthermore requires setting up new quality control systems with newly established suppliers. Finally, focusing one's supply base to fewer (certified) stocks means that processors' bargaining power vis-à-vis their suppliers shrinks and prices threaten to go up.

The good news: where a business case allows for sustainability changes in the core business, CSR impact is not only likely to be deep, but also long term: the high costs of changing product portfolios and potential "path dependency" will stabilize the commitment to sustainable products, once taken.

Strategic relevance of an issue

The strategic relevance of an issue affects the scope and depth of CSR impact. At the most general level, sustainability is impaired when companies do not regard the tackling of a CSR issue as strategically important in the first place.

In the realm of fisheries, the sustainability of seafood supply is a core strategic concern – without shrinking marine resource, business will shrink, too. The rather positive picture of CSR performance in our case companies can to a significant share be attributed to this fact. However, in sustainability domains where there is less sense of urgency and where the feedback loops between corporate behaviour (overfishing) to a strategically critical state of the environment (depletion of fish stocks) are less direct, CSR is less likely to be helpful for addressing long-term social–ecological challenges. This insight also limits the external validity of our findings.

Conclusions

When policy makers devise strategies to address long-term social–ecological challenges, CSR can be made use of to integrate the private sector into problem-solving. CSR comprises voluntary considerations of social and ecological concerns in a company's business operations and stakeholder relations. Ideally, CSR processes involve an intense interaction between companies and their stakeholders, including civil society and (empirically less often) policy makers. If policy makers wish to draw on CSR for strategies addressing long-term social–ecological challenges, they have to deal with the fact that CSR is an essentially voluntary activity, and that they cannot determine its contents or forms. In many cases, therefore, CSR will be carried out quite independently from any public strategy and it will not be tailored to meet the strategy's concrete goals. Policy makers can, however, try to win companies to align their CSR activities with political strategies on social–ecological challenges. Possible measures include a broad communication of the strategies; the tailoring of public CSR stimulation and regulation measures towards the strategies' issues and goals; and inclusion of CSR leader companies in their development and implementation.

What does this mean with regard to transparency and legitimacy of political strategies addressing social–ecological challenges? The first two of the proposed measures are rather straightforward: the business contribution to problem solving basically emerges independently from the forging of the political strategy. As a consequence in terms of transparency, policy makers will not know the exact extent of the business contribution to their strategies' impact. This, however, is a problem of assessing effectiveness rather than of upholding democratic standards. In terms of legitimacy, none of the problems typically linked to private sector participation in policy making is likely to occur. Such legitimacy problems include "state capture" through vested business interests; marginalisation of third actors (e.g. civil society representatives) from policy-networks or neo-corporatist arrangements; emergence of a "cartel of elites" which renders parliaments powerless and so on (Mayntz and

Marin 1991; Streeck and Kenworthy 2005). The third proposed measure – inclusion of CSR leader companies in public strategy development and implementation – however, may bring about some of these hitches. There is no warranty that companies committed to CSR may not use such involvement to follow their own agendas[12] or lobby for their special interests. And not all of these will be synergetic with the public interest in social–ecological conflicts. This holds all the more in large companies, where different units often have quite different positions on sustainability issues and follow different logics of action. When designing the involvement of non-governmental actors in the development and implementation of public strategies, the very least is to balance participation of different stakeholders, so that representatives of "responsible" companies are complemented with those of trade unions, environmental organizations, women groups, etc. Inclusion of parliamentarians helps to link the strategy to the parliamentary process from the beginning.

Finally, what are the consequences arising from an inclusion of the private sector (through CSR) into political long-term strategies when it comes to the strategies' effectiveness? This question can only be answered by knowing how effective CSR is in the first place – that is, to what extent it creates sustainability impact. We tackled this question using the example of European fish processors committed to promoting sustainable fisheries. The three companies analysed have sustainable seafood policies (CSR output) in place and to a large extent adjusted their behaviour and product portfolios (CSR outcome) to them. On the basis of a causal – not empirical – analysis we expect that the CSR outcomes lead to impact. The extent of impact, however, will vary with the tools employed[13] and the exact issue tackled. By clustering the issues according to the EU strategy goals, we demonstrated that companies contribute to all three goals. While one swallow does not make a summer, the good performance of these three CSR leaders highlights the potential of voluntary business activities in tackling long-term challenges. However, there are a number of systematic limits to the effectiveness of CSR as well. A fundamental caveat regarding the role of CSR in long-term approaches concerns the fragile reliability and durability of CSR impact: due to the voluntary nature of CSR, its implementation and resulting impact depend on the discretion of corporate decision makers. For example, when the business environment changes or when CSR does not seem opportune any more, corporate leaders may dismiss CSR achievements very quickly. As was argued above, sustainability impact is most likely to be long-term when CSR leads to changes in product portfolios.

Notes

1 Öko-Institut e.V., Berlin Office, Schicklerstr. 5–7, 10179 Berlin, Germany.
2 The motivation of governments to do so may be threefold: to provide sustainability governance where so far none existed, to complement more traditional public policies or to substitute them (Moon 2002).
3 In addition, governments can *regulate* formerly voluntary CSR activities, above all by making mandatory non-financial company reporting or introducing disclosure obligations for investment funds. There is, however, a debate whether this can still be called CSR (which, by definition, is voluntary).

4 The project was funded within the EU Sixth Framework Programme (2004–2007; Contract No. CIT2-CT-2004-506043). Project results do not necessarily reflect the European Commission's views and in no way anticipate its future policy in this area.

5 These were: mitigating climate change and chemical risks, promoting gender equality, countering bribery.

6 The concepts of output, outcome and impact originate in policy analysis (see e.g. Prittwitz 2003 or Vedung 2000).

7 While we cannot empirically determine the actual on-the-water impacts produced, for instance, by processors sourcing MSC fish we can, however, analyse *causal paths* from CSR outcome to impact.

8 See Art. 2.1, Common Fisheries Policy (CFP) Framework Regulation No. 2371/2002/ EC; European Code of Sustainable and Responsible Fisheries Practices; Commission Action Plan to integrate environmental protection into the CFP; EU Council Conclusions on the Community External Fisheries Policy of July 2004; para 15, Biodiversity Action Plan (BAP) for Fisheries.

9 See Art. 2.1 CFP Framework Regulation; para 15, BAP Fisheries; Art. 2 and 6.1, 6th EAP; Art. 2, Marine Strategy Directive; Art. 1 and 4(a)(ii), Water Framework Directive.

10 See Community Action Plan for the eradication of illegal, unreported and unregulated fishing, COM (2002) 180, 28/05/2002.

11 Such as the difficulty of CSR to create sustainability impact when a CSR issue (such as corruption) is not very visible or "hidden", difficult to measure, already densely regulated or when social and environmental interests in the issue area are poorly organized (cf. Wolff, Barth, Schmitt and Hochfeld 2009).

12 A case in point is a CSR initiative of BP and Shell: with their voluntary emission trading schemes the companies strove to influence governmental regulatory processes, among others to safeguard organizational lead over competitors should an obligatory emissions trading system be implemented (Skjærseth and Wettestad 2008).

13 E.g. MSC certification vs. company-specific instruments vs. supplier standards.

References

AccountAbility. 2003. *Mapping Instruments for Corporate Social Responsibility.* Report for the European Commission. Belgium.

Agnew, D., Grieve, C., Orr, P., Parkes, G. and Barker, N. 2006. *Environmental Benefits Resulting from Certification against MSC's Principles and Criteria for Sustainable Fishing.* London: MRAG UK Ltd and Marine Stewardship Council.

AIPCE. 2006. Purchase Control Document on IUU fishing as agreed at the EU Fish Processor's Association (AIPCE) meeting on 29 September 2006.

Albareda, L., Lozano, J. M. and Ysa, T. 2007. "Public Policies on Corporate Social Responsibility: The Role of Governments". *Journal of Business Ethics* 74(4): 391–407.

Barth, R. and Wolff, F. (eds) (2009). *Analysing Corporate Social Responsibility in Europe: Rhetoric and Realities.* Cheltenham: Edward Elgar, 3–25.

Becker, E. and Jahn, T. (eds) 2006. *Soziale Ökologie.* Grundzüge einer Wissenschaft von den gesellschaftlichen Naturverhältnissen, Frankfurt/Main: Campus.

Cramer, J., Jonker, J. and Heijden, A. 2004. "Making Sense of Corporate Social Responsibility". *Journal of Business Ethics* 55: 215–22.

Doane, D. 2005. *The Myth of CSR.* Stanford Social Innovation Review.

European Commission. 2001. *Promoting a European Framework for Corporate Social Responsibility.* Green Paper, COM (2001) 366, Brussels.

FAO. 2009. *The State of World Fisheries and Aquaculture 2008.* Rome.

Greenpeace. 2006. Greenpeace position paper "Marine Stewardship Council" (MSC), available online: www.greenpeace.de/themen/meere/fischerei/artikel/das_marine_ stewardship_council_msc/.

Habisch, A., Jonker, J., Wegner, M. and Schmidpeter, R. (eds) 2004. *CSR Across Europe*. Berlin: Springer.

Hahn, T. 2004. *Why and when Companies Contribute to Societal Goals. The Effect of Reciprocal Stakeholder Behavior*. Annual Conference of the Academy of Management, 6–11 August 2004. New Orleans, USA.

Hoel, A. H. 2004. *Eco-labelling in Fisheries: An Effective Conservation Tool?* Norut Report, Tromsø.

Hoffman, A. J. 2001. *From Hersey to Dogma: An Institutional History of Corporate Environmentalism*. Stanford: Stanford University Press.

Hoogma, R., Weber, M. and Boelie, E. 2005. "Integrated Long-Term Strategies to Induce Regime Shifts towards Sustainability: The Approach of Strategic Niche Management". In Weber, M. and Hemmelskamp, J. (eds) *Towards Environmental Innovation Systems*. Berlin/ Heidelberg: Springer, 209–36.

Kemp, R. and Rotmans, J. 2005. "The Management of the Co-Evolution of Technical, Environmental and Social Systems". In Weber, M. and Hemmelskamp, J. (eds) *Towards Environmental Innovation Systems*. Berlin/Heidelberg: Springer, 33–55.

Knapp, G., Roheim, C. and Anderson, J. L. 2007. "Analysis of Marine Stewardship Council Certification of Alaska Salmon". In Knapp, G., Roheim, C. and Anderson, J. L. (eds) *The Great Salmon Run: Competition between Wild and Farmed Salmon*. Washington: TRAFFIC North America/WWF, 247–59.

Mayntz, R. and Marin, B. (eds) 1991. *Policy Networks: Empirical Evidence and Theoretical Considerations*. Frankfurt a.M.: Campus.

McWilliams, A. and Siegel, D. 2001. "Corporate Social Responsibility: A Theory of the Firm Perspective". *Academy of Management Review* 26: 117–27.

Midttun, A. 2005. "Realigning Business, Government and Civil Society: Emerging Embedded Relational Governance Beyond the (Neo) Liberal and Welfare State Models". *Journal of Corporate Governance* 5(3), 159–74.

Moon, J. 2002. "The Social Responsibility of Business and New Governance". *Government and Opposition* 37(3), 385–408.

MSC. 2009. *Net Benefits – The First Ten Years of MSC Certified Sustainable Fisheries*. www.msc.org/documents/fisheries-factsheets/net-benefits-report/Net-Benefits-report.pdf.

Musgrave, R. A. and Musgrave, P. B. 1976. *Public Finance in Theory and Practice*. Prentice Hall: McGraw-Hill Books.

Ostrom, E. 2007. *Sustainable Social-Ecological Systems: An Impossibility?* Paper presented at 2007 Annual Meetings of the American Association for the Advancement of Science, San Francisco, 15–19 February.

Pauly, D., Watson, R. and Alder, J. 2005. "Global Trends in World Fisheries: Impacts on Marine Ecosystems and Food Security". *Phil Trans R Soc B*, 360: 5–12.

Phillips, B. T. W. and Chaffee, C. 2003. *Eco-labelling in Fisheries: What Is It All About?* Oxford: John Wiley & Sons.

Pierson, P. 2004. *Politics in Time: History, Institutions, and Social Analysis*. Princeton: Princeton University Press.

Porritt, J. and Goodman, J. 2005. *Fishing for Good*. London: Forum for the Future.

Prittwitz, V. von 2003. *Politikanalyse*. Stuttgart: Leske and Budrich.

Schmitt, K. and Wolff, F. 2006. *CSR in the Fish Processing Industry: Evidence from a Survey among Selected European Companies*. www.rare-eu.net.

Schmitt, K. and Wolff, F. 2009. "CSR in the European Fish Processing Industry: Not Just Fishing for Compliments". In Barth, R. and Wolff, F. (eds) *Analysing Corporate Social Responsibility in Europe: Rhetoric and Realities*. Cheltenham: Edward Elgar, 80–94.

Skjærseth, J. B. and Wettestad, J. 2008. *EU Emissions Trading: Initiation, Decision-making and Implementation*. Aldershot: Ashgate.

Skjærseth, J. B. and Wettestad, J. 2009. "A Framework for Assessing the Sustainability Impact of CSR". In Barth, R. and Wolff, F. (eds), *Analysing Corporate Social Responsibility in Europe: Rhetoric and Realities*. Cheltenham: Edward Elgar, 26–37.

Spaargaren, G. 2003. "Sustainable Consumption: A Theoretical and Environmental Policy Perspective". *Society and Natural Resources* 16: 687–701.

Streeck, W. and Kenworthy, L. 2005. 'Theories and Practices of Neo-Corporatism'. In Janoski, T. et al. (eds). *Handbook of Political Sociology*. Cambridge: Cambridge University Press, 441–60.

Tukker, A., Charter, M., Vezzoli, C., Sto, E. and Munch Andersen, M. (eds). 2008. *Perspectives on Radical Changes to Sustainable Consumption and Production*. System Innovation for Sustainability 1. *Sheffield*.

Unilever (2003). *Unilever's Fish Sustainability Initiative (FSI)*. Rotterdam/London.

Vedung, E. 2000. *Public Policy and Program Evaluation*. New Brunswick: Transaction.

Voß, J.-P. and Kemp, R. 2006. "Sustainability and Reflexive Government: Introduction". In Voß, J.-P. and Kemp, R. (eds) *Reflexive Governance for Sustainable Development*. Cheltenham: Edward Elgar, 3–27.

Voß, J.-P., Smith, A. and Grin, J. 2009. "Designing Long-Term Policy: Rethinking Transition Management". *Policy Sciences* 43(4): 275–302.

Wheeler, D. 2003. "The Successful Navigation of Uncertainty: Sustainability and the Organization". In Burke, R and Cooper, C (eds) *Leading in Turbulent Times*. Oxford: Blackwell, 182–207.

Wildhavens (2004). "An Independent Assessment of the Marine Stewardship Council". Report by Highleyman, S., Amos, A.M. and Cauley, H., prepared for the Homeland Foundation, Oak Foundation and Pew Charitable Trust. Available at www.zibycom. com.ru/aboutus/documents/WildhavensMSC.pdf, 25 April, 2008.

Wolff, F. and Schmitt, K. 2009. "Hunt for Sustainable Seafood: Sustainability Effects of CSR in Three Fish Processing Companies". In Barth, R. and Wolff, F. (eds), *Analysing Corporate Social Responsibility in Europe: Rhetoric and Realities*. Cheltenham: Edward Elgar, 157–89.

Wolff, F., Bohn, M., Schultz, I. and Wilkinson, P. 2009a. "CSR and Public Policy: Mutually Reinforcing for Sustainable Development?". In Barth, R. and Wolff, F. (eds) *Analysing Corporate Social Responsibility in Europe: Rhetoric and Realities*. Cheltenham: Edward Elgar, 249–68.

Wolff, F., Barth, R., Hochfeld, C. and Schmitt, K. 2009b. 'Rhetoric and Realities in CSR: Main Findings and Implications for Public Policy and Research'. In Barth, R. and Wolff, F. (eds), *Analysing Corporate Social Responsibility in Europe: Rhetoric and Realities*. Cheltenham: Edward Elgar, 289–311.

World Bank. 2002. Public Sector Roles in Strengthening Corporate Social Responsibility: a baseline study. Washington.

10 Participation beyond the state

Why some environmental NGOs partner with business, and others do not

Kristian Krieger and M. Brooke Rogers

Introduction

In the last two decades, participation has become a key concept in environmental governance. Participation – at its simplest – means the involvement of agents, such as citizens and non-state actors, in collective decision-making processes. The relevance of this key concept is underlined by prominent policy initiatives such as UNCED's Agenda 21, with its recognition of eight major stakeholder groups in environmental governance and the UNECE's Aarhus Convention, strengthening public participation in decision making. While these two initiatives are the outcome of inter-governmental processes and invite non-state actors to contribute to the environmental policies of state actors, participation in environmental governance also occurs beyond the state. This chapter investigates one particular aspect of this environmental governance beyond the state, namely "green partnerships" between non-governmental and corporate organizations.

The analytical focus of this chapter on environmental partnerships in the energy field might seem surprising given the history of antagonism between the energy industry and environmental non-governmental organizations (NGOs). In spite of past hostilities such as the UK's anti-nuclear movement in the 1970s and 1980s, and the often-cited Greenpeace/Shell conflict over the deep-sea disposal of the oil platform Brent Spar, increasing attention is being paid to friendly relations between NGOs and the corporate sector in general. Discussions about the emergence of "green alliances" (Arts 2002), NGO-business-partnerships in pursuit of environmental goals, and alternative, non-state forms of "civil regulation" (Tully 2004) or "social regulation" through rule-setting within partnerships (Haufler 2003) suggest that NGO-business partnerships are one tool for increased participation by stakeholders in collective decision making without the involvement of a state. Overall, participation in governance is believed to improve the legitimacy of decision-making processes and enhance the effectiveness of governance through mobilizing additional resources and facilitating implementation in a more consensual way. This is particularly important in the context of long-term problems associated with uncertainty about longer term consequences and future events whose effective governance requires a broad knowledge base, as well as continuous communication and deliberation that stimulates social learning and reflexive governance.

However, questions remain about the role and benefits of participation in environmental governance. Case-study literature (see Bendell 2000) often discusses the advantageousness of partnership schemes for NGOs and corporations. Popular examples in this debate are partnerships between McDonalds and Environmental Defence (recycling), Friends of the Earth and Bodyshop (animal-friendly products), Unilever and WWF (sustainable fishery), the timber industry and NGOs (sustainable forestry), and General Motors and the World Resources Institute (research and development on engines). Beyond the case study material, the literature refers to structural shifts in the political economy and environmental discourse that drive the rise of partnerships.

This chapter takes a different approach. By exploring the variation between individual NGOs' partnership potential and examining organizational factors explaining this variation, it makes it possible to discover limitations and benefits of partnerships and participatory schemes. This contrasts with structural and case study approaches that are unable to detect variation between individual NGOs' partnership potentials and preferences and – based on the variation – gain a more systematic understanding of the variables that shape the application and consequences of participatory tools in environmental governance. Using the case of Britain's NGOs and energy industry, the authors question why some NGOs use partnerships with the corporate sector as a tool to achieve their environmental objectives whilst others do not.

Apart from the aforementioned past hostilities between NGOs and Britain's energy industry, the analytical focus on the energy industry also seems particularly relevant because the energy industry's impact on climate and environment renders this sector a significant field of interaction with NGOs. Moreover, since the deregulation of the previously largely state-owned sector commencing in the late 1980s under the Thatcher government, private corporations' decision making regarding investment and operations has become crucial, stressing the importance for NGOs to interact with the energy companies to promote their environmental objectives.

Shifts in environmental governance and the emergence of "green partnerships"

When environmental issues became important in the societies of industrialised nations in the 1960s and 1970s, the state was expected to address them. Decisions based on "certain" scientific evidence and often in consensus with the polluter enabled the hierarchical state to intervene into socio-economic processes for the purpose of reducing environmental risks and preventing environmental degradation. The emergent environmental movement was largely excluded from policy making. In short, there was little to see in the way of participation – and any inclusion of NGOs or the public was perceived as an aberration from good practice (Bulkeley and Mol 2003).

The role of stakeholders in today's environmental governance is remarkably different from the state-led environmental governance of the 1960s and 1970s. Currently, environmental governance issues are increasingly being analysed, discussed and addressed by a variety of actors, including formal government organizations (national and international), "hybrid" public-private organizations, corporations, and NGOs (Spagnuolo 2009). Additionally, new forms of "collaborative governance" have arisen in order to improve and ensure the quality of decision making and environmentally sound outcomes within these multi-player interactions. In this context, partnerships emerged, with the involvement of NGOs and other stakeholder groups being seen as a means to increase the inclusiveness of institutions (Spagnuolo 2009: 8) through the mobilization of material, information, and political resources by all participating actors. As a result, partnerships between business and environmental NGOs as a particular form of participatory governance have been discovered as an increasingly popular alternative to state-driven solutions to environmental problems, as well as to industry self-regulation and governmental regulation.

The emergence of green partnerships in particular has been argued to be a result of a number of interrelated factors. Arguing from a *structural* viewpoint, Newell (2000) points to the shifts in the power of states, corporate sector and civil society resulting from economic and political globalization as an important driver for NGO-business-collaborations. As states retreat from regulation and the corporate sector gains power as a result of globalization processes, the traditional focus of NGOs on the state as actors through which to accomplish their objectives becomes increasingly ineffective and NGOs redirect some of their attention to the corporate sector. More generally, Bulkeley and Mol (2003) point to the 1980s debates challenging the notion of a strong state which in turn led to a reconfiguration of state-market relations. These reconfigurations implied a redefinition of the "standard operating procedures", opening space for participation and non-state stakeholder forms of governance. Another structural factor which stimulates interactions between corporate and environmental organizations is the shift of the international environmental discourse towards "sustainability" and "ecological moderniz-ation", approaches to environmental issues often implying a compatibility of economy and environment (Heap 2000). The shift towards the language of sustainable development also serves an important partnership function as it has been used to create a common vocabulary on which to base a dialogue (Bendell 2000).

Other scholars, focusing on the *actors* within individual partnerships, suggest that NGOs and corporate partners are increasingly recognizing the concrete benefits of partnerships. These include, but are not limited to, commercial advantages such as reputational gains, production cost reduction, enhanced marketing, and political advantages such as increased lobbying impact and more environment-friendly business operations (Waddell 2000).

As with many other novel concepts and approaches to governance, the concept of "green partnerships" has not remained without critics for long. One issue that has been raised is the different value system that underpins civil society and corporate organizations, as illustrated by Bendell's (2000) statement, "NGOs focus on social systems and networks based on values and beliefs; they derive their power from their ability to speak to tradition, community benefit and values" (Bendell 2000: 17). In contrast, standard business concerns tend to focus on economic systems that encourage individuals to follow the organizational lead/ meet organizational objectives through financial inducements. The development of a common set of rules and procedures designed to enable cooperation beyond pure rhetoric are extremely difficult to create and enforce, thus undermining the sustainability and effectiveness of partnerships (Arts 2002).

Another issue addresses the broader implications of the rise of partnerships for environmental governance. Some scholars argue that "green partnerships" can only complement state regulations because they are built upon "soft" rules, as well as limited in scope and scale (Arts 2002). Moreover, Tully (2004) and others (Bulkeley and Mol 2003) note that by pursuing partnerships and voluntary schemes, the state may do less to mitigate environmental problems. Finally, Levy (1997) suggests that partnerships reinforce power structures and status quo by marginalizing radical environmental organizations and selecting major NGO players.

In conclusion, a number of powerful drivers have influenced and contributed to the emergence of "green partnerships" and participatory approaches in environmental governance. For some, participation promises more effective and legitimate governance. This is influenced by structural forces that create a conducive environment for the emergence of new cooperative, non-state forms of governance, in particular discursive and politico-economic shifts. Partnerships can also offer concrete benefits to participants. However, critics challenge the partnership schemes' sustainability and implications for effective and democratic governance. This in turn raises questions about the pervasiveness, nature and consequences of partnerships which will be discussed throughout the remainder of this chapter.

The case of Britain's energy sector: a conducive environment for partnerships and diversity in the NGO scene

This chapter explores how NGOs are engaging with industry partners in Britain's energy sector. The two main reasons for choosing Britain's energy sector are, on the one hand, that it provides a relatively conducive environment for partnerships, and, on the other, that Britain's NGO landscape is characterized by a significant diversity. This analysis allows the authors to gain a better understanding of the degree of pervasiveness of and barriers to the use of the partnership tool among Britain's NGOs and of the emergence of different forms of partnerships within the sector.

Whilst a legacy of antagonism over a variety of issues (e.g. nuclear power and waste) seems to lower the likelihood of partnerships, other factors create a more favorable context for partnerships between NGOs and business to emerge in Britain's energy field. First, commencing with the nuclear debate in the 1970s, environmental considerations became increasingly important in the energy field, culminating in the 2003 Energy White Paper "Our Energy Future – Creating a low carbon economy" (DTI 2003) with its identification of the energy sector as key to addressing the issue of climate change and carbon dioxide reduction. The importance of the energy industry created a strong interest and presence of environmental NGOs in energy issues. Second, the government gradually conceded its control over the British energy industry with the advent of the privatization and deregulation wave under the Thatcher government, strengthening the importance of corporate actors and their decisions (Helm 2002). Third, as an illustration of an endorsement by the industry of the corporate responsibility and sustainability discourses, the majority of Britain's largest energy companies are part of the United Nation's Global Compact, the world's largest voluntary corporate responsibility initiative, and/or are members of the Energy Savings Trust. Fourth, over half of the British public does not support the use of extreme campaign approaches against companies. In fact, members of the British public are exerting indirect pressure on NGOs to partner with business as they believe (2:1) that the most effective method for not-for-profit organizations to convince industry to be more responsible is to develop close partnerships with industrial organizations (Dawkins 2004: 6).

The case of Britain, however, is not only interesting because it suggests that its energy sector is populated by "green partnerships" but also because of the nature of its environmental movement and green NGO landscape. In contrast to relatively uniform presentations of environmental NGOs as well-established, moderate and highly institutionalised (McCormick 1991; Rootes 2003), Rawcliffe (1998) discusses four phases of the evolution of the environmental movement in Britain, each associated with different environmental NGOs, including the late nineteenth century conservationist organizations such as the Royal Society for the Protection of Birds (RSPB), the interwar organizations such as the Council for the Protection of Rural England (CPRE) with broader environmental concerns, the 1960s and 1970s mass movement organizations such as Greenpeace and the Worldwide Fund for Nature (WWF), and the loosely coordinated direct action networks such as Earth First! from the 1990s. This historical diversity is reinforced by the dynamics within the movement. Rootes and colleagues, for instance, suggest that the emergence of Earth First! and other radical groups are responses to the increasing institutionalization of some of the previously radical movement organizations such as Greenpeace or Friends of the Earth (Rootes, Seel *et al.* 2000).

The diverse nature within Britain's NGO scene makes it possible to explore whether some of the previously noted critical comments about the limitations and negative implications of partnership schemes can be vindicated through this particular empirical case study.

Classifying Britain's non-governmental organizations

The two analytical dimensions

In order to discover patterns in the use of partnerships with energy companies by Britain's environmental NGOs and thereby be able to critically review suggestions about the rise and benefits of partnerships, it is important to generate a classification of NGOs. Following earlier work (see Krieger and Rogers 2010), this chapter employs two analytical dimensions of NGOs, namely NGOs as resource-mobilizing organizations and as value-oriented movement-rooted organizations, in order to map the current landscape of British NGOs involved in the energy field.

The first analytical dimension primarily draws on the resource mobilization approach (RMA) (see Gamson 1975; McCarthy and Zald 1977; Tully 1978) which focuses on the need of NGOs to mobilize political resources in order to survive and pursue political goals. These political resources can include public support, expertise and financial resources. This dependence on political resources is reflected in their organizational structures and resources. It is, for instance, argued that more hierarchically structured and professionalized organizations are more effective in mobilizing donations and public support (see Gamson 1975; Tilly 1978; Diani and Donati 1999).

The resource mobilization approach can be extended by the political opportunity structure approach (POSA) which highlights the embeddedness of NGOs in broader political and economic structures (see Eisinger 1973; Tarrow 1988; Kitschelt 1996; Rucht 1996). It proposes that the characteristics of a political system (such as the concentration or fragmentation of decision-making systems) shape the political and organizational strategies of NGOs.

In short, RMA and POSA suggest that the nature of Britain's NGOs is strongly shaped by organizational structures and resources as means to acquire relevant political resources and operate successfully in Britain's political system. Therefore, this chapter suggests the dimension "capacity to act" compounding organizational structures and resources as one of two dimensions helping to analyse NGOs in Britain.

The second analytical dimension emphasizes value orientation and collective identities of NGOs, thereby embedding them more firmly in social movements. For the purpose of this discussion, social movements are defined as loosely coordinated networks of organizations and individuals motivated by shared environmental concern and values (see Rootes 2003: 44). It is argued that the NGOs' formative values influence political objectives and activities. In short, identity approaches (see Zald 1996; Polletta and Jasper 2001) emphasize value and ideational orientation of an NGO as shaping the NGOs' nature. Therefore, this chapter suggests the dimension "orientation of action" comprising values and policy ideas of NGOs as the other dimension used to analyse NGOs in Britain.

This chapter uses these two analytical dimensions to illustrate and order the organizational diversity in Britain's NGO landscape. However, these two dimensions are also relevant for the comparative study of the NGOs' partnership potential. The partnership literature agrees on a number of general requirements for collaborative schemes to work. The prerequisites can be distinguished into two broad categories, namely material-organizational aspects, and immaterial aspects. The material prerequisites primarily refer to a necessary professionaliza-tion of NGOs, the creation of an appropriate institutional infrastructure within each partner and for resolving conflicts between the parties, as well as the continued presence of qualified managers to manage the partnership (Miller, Chen *et al.* 2004: 405; Heap 2000: 35).

Immaterial prerequisites are also of great importance. One of the core challenges of collaborations between NGOs and industry is the fact that non-profit and for-profit organizational cultures need to be combined. Scholars stress the importance of a shared vision and goals, as well as transparency of each organization's objectives and interests, the full endorsement and dedication on both sides of and to the scheme, as well as a long-term orientation for the collaborative scheme (Heap 2000; Stafford and Hartmann 1996: 145). These two types of prerequisites, the material-organizational and the immaterial, mirror the two analytical dimensions, the "capacity to act" and "orientation of action" respectively, underlining the relevance of the two NGO dimensions to explore their partnership potential.

Operationalizing the dimensions

The previous section identified two analytical dimensions to classify the nature of NGOs which were argued to be relevant also for assessing the NGOs' partnership potential. In order to capture the diversity of Britain's NGO landscape and identify clusters of similar NGOs empirically, a questionnaire was sent out to Britain's NGOs working in the energy/environment field. Forty-one organizations were selected on the basis of existing directories of Britain's green groups (Milner 1994; Cowell 1995), complemented by and updated through NGOs mentioned in other literature (Rootes 2003; Take 2002; Rawcliffe 1998) and organizations participating in recent energy-related public consultations (e.g. the "Energy Challenge" consultation, January–April 2006, DTI). Of the 41 organizations contacted between February and September 2007, 22 NGOs responded to the questionnaire.

Eleven out of the 12 questions[1] within the questionnaire elicited information about the attitudes of NGO representatives working on energy issues within their organizations towards a range of issues that serve as proxies for the two broad dimensions (capacity to act; orientation of action). The operationalization of the two analytical dimensions through the questionnaire design and data analysis is summarized in Table 10.1 and discussed in detail below.

The "capacity to act" was broken down into four elements: (i) the decision-making structures (see question 1 in Table 10.1), (ii) number of full-time staff (see question 2), (iii) annual revenues (see question 3), and (iv) the political levels at which NGOs operate (i.e. international versus local) (see question 4). It was

Table 10.1 Analytical dimensions for NGO analysis

Dimensions	Elements	Aspects (Questionnaire question number)	Response options (Scores)
Capacity to act	Decision making (1)		Trustee Board (3), Executive Board/secretariat (3), Local groups (1), Volunteer assembly (1), Member assembly, (1) Member organizations (1)
	Staff (2)		Largest 20% of NGOs (3), largest 21–40% of NGOs (2.5), largest 41–60% of NGOs (2), largest 61–80% of NGOs (1.5), largest 81–100% of NGOs (1)
	Budget (3)		Richest 20% of NGOs (3), richest 21–40% of NGOs (2.5), richest 41–60% of NGOs (2), richest 61–80% of NGOs, richest 81–100% of NGOs.
	Operational level (4)		Local (1), regional (2), national (3), international (3)
Orientation of action	Attitudes towards energy issues	Thematic context (5)	Fuel source nuclear (1), Pollution (2), Climate change (3), energy savings (3)
		Fuel sources (6)	Promotion of fuel source (3), reduction of fuel source (2), abolition of fuel source (1)
		Industry Structure (7)	Combinations (3), non-combinations (1)
	Attitudes towards other actors	Government (8)	Partner (3), open-minded (2), industry capture (1), public campaign target (1)
		Businesses (9)	Partner (3), open-minded (2), adversary (1), public campaign target (1)
		Description of own organization (10)	Advocacy (1), service (3), info provider to NGOs (2), umbrella NGO (2)
		Main funding sources (11)	Government (2), Corporate (3), Individual, small donations (1), member fees (1), consultancy (3), merchandising (2)

Source: Based on Krieger and Rogers 2010.

assumed that the "capacity to act" is greater if decision-making structures are more concentrated and hierarchical, human and financial resources are greater, and operations take place across several political levels and/or at the higher levels. Such a greater "capacity to act" enables NGOs to provide the organizational resources, as well as reflect the appropriate professional structures that are prerequisites for partnerships between NGOs and businesses.

Whilst NGOs are differentiated by their relatively greater or smaller "capacity to act", the second dimension distinguishes NGOs by their relative degrees of "pragmatism" or "radicalism". It is assumed that the more pragmatic an NGO's orientation is, the greater its potential to partner with industry would be. A more pragmatic value and policy orientation of NGOs implies that the respective NGOs are relatively more likely to accept that, in order to pursue their objectives, compromises and collaborations with other actors (government; industry), as well as the acceptance of parts of wider politico-economic structures (existing market and industry structures; market rules; political norms, processes and structures) are required. A more radical orientation prioritizes the pursuit of NGOs' value-based objectives without compromising, collaborating or accepting parts of politico-economic structures. This differentiation broadly follows existing categorizations of NGOs such as Breitmeier and Rittbergers's (1998) fundamental versus pragmatic NGOs or Heap's (2000) differentiation between eco-activists, reformers, and supporters of market-based environmentalism.

The "orientation of action" was disaggregated into four elements: (i) The first element identified the NGOs' attitudes on various energy issues (see questions 5–7 in Table 10.1). First, it was assumed that some issues associated with energy policy and industry are linked to more confrontational attitudes vis-à-vis other actors (see question 5). For instance, NGOs working on nuclear waste and the nuclear fuel source in general can be expected to be more radical due to the historically conflictual relations with government and industry (Rüdig 1990). Similarly, pollution issues associated with energy production are also argued to have a greater affinity to radical ideas than pragmatic ones. According to Rootes (2003), a broad spectrum of urban, industrial and pollution issues have accounted for about 20 per cent of all environmental protest events in Britain between 1988 and 1997.

In contrast to these relatively conflictual issues, energy saving issues and emissions and climate change appear to be less confrontational issues in the energy field. Gough and Shackley, for instance, argue that climate change politics by NGOs is "respectable" politics: "Compared to the single-issue campaigning style generally associated with the approach of NGOs to environmental [. . .] risk issues, climate change ushers in a new era of engagement that empowers NGOs by giving them a place at the negotiating table" (2001: 329). A convergence of corporate and governmental objectives with those of NGOs in respect to energy efficiency is, for instance, reflected in the successful establishment and work of the Energy Savings Trust whose members include the majority of large energy companies of the UK.

Second, the attitudes (promotion, reduction, abolition) towards various fuel sources (renewables, gas, coal, nuclear) were investigated (see question 6). Calls for abolition point to a more radical orientation. This is based on a rationale that the complete abolition of any of the currently used fuel sources is problematic in view of current energy industry structures and energy security challenges. This reflects the DTI's argument that as a result of the abolition of any fuel source (here: nuclear), "we would be reliant on a more limited number of technologies to achieve our goals, some of which (e.g. carbon capture and storage) are yet to be proven at a commercial scale with power generation. This would expose the UK to greater security of supply risks" (DTI 2007: 17). Third, the NGOs were asked about their vision regarding the structure of the energy industry and market (see question 7). Similar to the question concerning fuel sources, pragmatism was reflected in an acceptance of a diverse structure comprising smaller and large companies, and decentralized and centralized production structures. NGOs exclusively demanding one type of industry are assumed to hold more radical attitudes.

The second element, attitudes towards other actors, investigates the attitudes of NGOs towards other actors. On the one hand, the NGOs were questioned about how they perceive corporate actors (see question 9). Pragmatic organizations were expected to perceive them as partners, more radical ones as adversaries. On the other hand, the same question is asked about the NGOs' attitude towards government where possible responses oscillate between government as partner and industry-captured government (see question 8).

The third element, description of own organization, explores the self-perception of NGOs (see question 10). The question is mainly based on the differentiation between advocacy, service and educational NGOs whereby service and educational NGOs are expected to be more pragmatic than advocacy organizations. Service organizations need to be pragmatic in order to attract assignments whilst educational organizations are assumed to consider more balanced information than advocacy organizations that can be expected to be more focused on getting their specific views across. The difference between advocacy and other types of NGOs is further reinforced by the fact that educational and service NGOs are often institutionalized as "charities" that have to abstain from public politics whilst advocacy organizations such as Friends of the Earth and Greenpeace choose the corporate form limited company (Rootes, Seel *et al.* 2000).

The fourth element, main funding sources, analyses the main sources of funding of NGOs (see question 11). Whilst predominant reliance on membership fees and individual donations is associated with relatively more radical leanings, government, corporate funding and consultancy work shows a more pragmatic attitude towards other actors in the energy/environment field.

Even though all eight elements make some contribution to exploring the NGOs' capacity to act and orientation of action, they are only proxies. By using four elements for each of the two dimensions, a relatively reliable and comparable approximation of the capacities and orientation is made possible.

Empirical findings

The NGO landscape and the three clusters

One way in which the questionnaire data were used for the analysis of varying partnership potential of NGOs was as a basis for empirically presenting the British NGO landscape and identifying clusters of similar NGOs. This is accomplished by locating individual NGOs within a two-dimensional scatterplot (see Figure 10.1), based on the assignment of scores to different response options in the questionnaire (see Table 10.1). Each of the possible answers to the questionnaire questions has been assigned a score between 1 and 3. The score of "3" means the highest value and indicates a strong capacity to act and a pragmatic "orientation of action"; "1" a relatively weak capacity to act and a relatively radical orientation. The overall score of each NGO for its "capacity to act" and "orientation of action" is derived by averaging the average values for each of the four elements of this dimension.

The figure shows the distribution of organizations along two axes. The axes in the figure represent the averaged score values for the orientation, from radical to

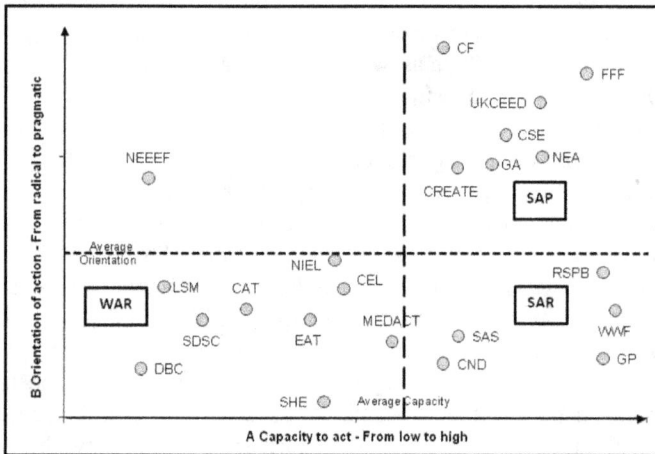

Figure 10.1 Britain's NGO in the energy/environment field surveyed.

Source: Krieger and Rogers 2010.

Notes
Organisations: Campaign for Nuclear Disarmament (CND); Centre for Sustainable Energy (CSE); Centre for Research, Education, and Training in Energy (CREATE); Christian Ecology Link (CEL); Communities against Toxics (CAT); Conservation Foundation (CF); Druridge Bay Campaign (DBC); Environmental Awareness Trust (EAT); Forum for the Future (FFF); Green Alliance (GA); Greenpeace (GP); Life Style Movement (LSM); Medact (MEDACT); National Energy Action (NEA); North East Environmental Education Forum (NEEEF); Northern Ireland Environment Link (NIEL); Royal Society for the Protection of Birds (RSPB); Shut Down Sizewell Campaign (SDSC); Stop Hinkley Expansion (SHE); Surfers against Sewage (SAS); World Wide Fund for Nature UK (WWF); UK Centre for Economic and Environmental Development (UKCEED).
Clusters: Strong and pragmatic NGOs (SAP); Weak and radical NGOs (WAR); Strong and radical (SAR).

pragmatic, on the vertical axis and for the capacity to act from low to high, on the horizontal axis, reflecting different degrees of resource endowment and organizational structures. The figure is divided by two lines, representing the average values for the two analytical dimensions. These lines help identify those organizations exceeding and falling short of the average values.

Three sufficiently populated clusters of British NGOs can be identified and differentiated on the basis of the survey. They refer broadly to those NGOs situated within the three most populated quadrants with below average values for capacity and orientation ("weak and radical" organizations (WAR) in the bottom-left quadrant), above average values for the two dimensions ("strong and pragmatic" organizations (SAP) in the top-right quadrant), and above average value for capacity and below average value for orientation ("strong and radical" organizations (SAR) in the bottom-right quadrant).[2]

The following sections elaborate on the characteristics of the three clusters and explore each cluster's partnership potential. This elaboration draws on the questionnaire data. Rather than collapsing the axes into average score values for each of the two dimensions, the data is used to identify responses shared by the majority (or a substantially greater proportion than in other clusters and on average across the whole sample) of NGOs within a cluster in order to differentiate between NGOs of different clusters in a more detailed manner and describe the nature of the member NGO of each cluster more comprehensively. Moreover, responses to a questionnaire question concerning the actual engagement of NGOs in partnerships (question 12, see Table 10.2) were included in order to relate NGO clusters to varying partnership patterns. In order to triangulate and enrich the questionnaire data, seven semi-structured interviews with senior NGO representatives working on energy issues were conducted between June and December 2007 whereby the interviewees represented NGOs from each cluster (WAR cluster: three interviews NGO WAR.1–NGO WAR.3; SAP cluster: three interviews NGO SAP.1–NGO SAP.3; SAR cluster: one interview NGO SAR.1).

The three clusters of NGOs and their varying partnership potential

Following the partnership literature, it is possible to argue that a greater potential of NGOs to engage in a partnership with the energy industry can be linked to a greater capacity to act and a more pragmatic orientation of NGOs. "Strong and pragmatic" organizations are expected to be NGO groups that engage with the energy industry most substantially whilst "weak and radical" organizations emerge as the least active group of organizations in terms of partnership.

This is confirmed by the responses to the questionnaire (question 12) in which NGOs were asked about different kinds of engagement they undertook with energy companies (see Hartmann and Stafford 1996). These different types range from the NGOs' provision of brochures and policy papers ("provision of information"), the participation in workshops and roundtables ("exchange of information", e.g. within the BNFL's National Stakeholder Dialogue), the companies' financial support for specific projects or organizations ("sponsorship", e.g. WWF's HSBC Climate Partnership), NGOs providing expertise, training and advise to companies ("consulting and services", e.g. Forum for the Future's "Leadership for Sustainability Training" program), corporate use of NGO "brand" ("licensing of NGO name", e.g. WWF's Panda symbol), an explicit endorsement of a specific product of a company by an NGO ("product endorsement", e.g. Greenpeace's endorsement of nPower's "Juice" electricity product), institutionalized collaborations to change business processes and products ("task force", e.g. Greenpeace-Wenco car "Smile") to joint, institutionalized pursuit of public policy goals vis-à-vis government ("public policy alliance", e.g. the joint call for action of Greenpeace and the World Business Council for Sustainable Development in advance of the Johannesburg "World Summit on Sustainable Development" in 2002). The responses are summarized in Table 10.2.

The "strong and pragmatic" organizations (SAP) engage with business in seven out the eight proposed ways. Moreover, the share of SAPs that engage in a particular way with business is in most cases above the share of all surveyed organizations. Mirroring this, "weak and radical" organizations (WAR) only engage in four out of eight ways and in most cases their share is below the overall share. "Strong and radical" organizations (SAR) – thanks to their greater "capacity" – are between "strong pragmatics" and "weak radicals" in terms of scope of engagement and share. However, some of the survey figures require further exploration: most conspicuously, a significant share of WAR engages in public policy alliances and product endorsement schemes with business. Furthermore, SAR engage more extensively with business in terms of lower intensity engagement than SAP. Additional interview data provide further insight into how NGOs in the different clusters engage with energy companies, and whether their specific organizational characteristics can contribute to understanding their use of partnerships, as well as resolve the questions left open by the survey data.

Table 10.2 NGOs and types of engagement with business organizations in the energy field

Question	Responses	WAR $n = 9$	SAP $n = 7$	SAR $n = 5$	All $n = 22$
Types of engagement	Provision of info	13%	42%	100%	41%
	Exchange of info	38%	57%	80%	50%
	Sponsorship	0	57%	20%	23%
	Consulting & Services	0	57%	0	14%
	Licensing of NGO name	0	0	0	0
	Product endorsement	25%	57%	40%	32%
	Task force (e.g. 'greening business')	0	42%	20%	18%
	Public policy alliance	38%	42%	20%	32%

Source: Krieger and Rogers forthcoming.

Weak and radical NGOs

The "weak and radical" organizations (WAR) include NGOs such as SHE, SDSC, DBC, and CAT (see acronyms below Figure 10.1). These organizations are closely associated with the relatively radical anti-nuclear and environmental movement of the 1970s and 1980s, e.g. through their founding generation and leadership, as reflected in their above average interest (questionnaire question 5 in Table 10.1) in the nuclear fuel source and the abolition of nuclear power (question 6). The founders of these organizations were often "local concern people" (interview with NGO WAR.1), driven by the "panic" and often single issue that new hazardous sites would be situated nearby (NGO WAR.2). This "local concern" is reflected in the emphasis of the interviewed organizations on local operations (question 4), as well as their advocacy orientation (question 10). The organizations predominantly target governments to accomplish their objectives, rather than business organizations (questions 8, 9). However, this is not necessarily because they do not perceive businesses as important. Rather, in the words of one representative, "it is just that we cannot do everything" (NGO WAR.3). The movement roots also show in the NGOs' heavy reliance on volunteers (mirrored in their relatively limited human resources) (question 2) and individual donations (question 11). Moreover, compared to the other clusters and the total sample, decision-making structures are less hierarchical and centralized, allowing members, volunteers, local groups and organizations a greater say (question 1).

Interviewees from "weak and radical" organizations point to two issues to account for their limited engagement with business. On the one hand:

> it comes down to resources. [...] It is not that we don't think business is important or partnerships cannot have benefits. [...] But we are just a bunch of volunteers so we do the things we can do and as well as we can but we leave the rest to the "bigger" people.
>
> (NGO WAR.3)

On the other hand, the need for a strong overlap in terms of values and objectives is stressed. As one NGO put it, "we have to wholeheartedly support what they are doing. And we assume that they support what we do" (NGO WAR.3). This requirement is particularly problematic given the strong interest of "weak radicals" in nuclear issues. In the words of one NGO, "I don't think in the case of the nuclear industry, this [a partnership] is ever going to be possible. I mean the whole existence of the nuclear sites is against the interests of the local community. [...]" (NGO WAR.2).

These two issues, resources and strong overlap of values and objectives, also shape the actual partnerships WAR engage in. Lack of resources and local focus of operations imply an interest in schemes that generate resources (such as an NGO-promoted energy/fuel source switching scheme linked to a donation to an NGO) and the often futile search for local partners. The strong interest in a value and objective overlap is reflected in the fact that the interviewed WAR only collaborated with renewables companies. Partnerships with renewables companies also make it possible to account for the unexpectedly strong presence of WAR in some categories of Table 10.2. In short, WAR, if partnering with business at all, engage mostly locally, on a limited scale and/or with the renewables segment of the energy industry, reflecting their limited resources and critical ideas as local groups historically focusing on controversial single issues. Their focus on policy makers as campaign targets shows in their strong presence in public policy alliances.

Strong and pragmatic NGOs

The "strong and pragmatic" organizations (SAP) include NGOs such as FFF, GA and CSE. Members of this cluster are often founded to complement the confrontational approach of other NGOs and seek partnership with the corporate and public sectors, as reflected in their relatively favorable attitude towards business (question 9). One interviewee's organization's founders reasoned that "there must be room for a different approach: As well as throwing stones at companies, [there needs to be] some place to sit down and talk constructively" (interview with NGO SAP.1). Rather than advocacy organizations, this group's organizations often define themselves as service providing organizations (question 10). This service orientation is also reflected in the choice of issues: many of the organizations work on non-conflictual issues where NGO expertise is welcomed by business and government (question 5). All organizations have operational foci on energy efficiency/savings, and the vast majority also works on climate change and emission reduction issues while nuclear fuel is only of concern to a small share of "strong pragmatics". In contrast to the WAR, "strong and pragmatic" organizations acquire resources primarily from institutional sources such as the government and corporations (question 11) but also through fees for consultancy work for public and corporate organizations, reflecting their comparatively favorable attitude towards business and their service orientation.

Interviews with "strong and pragmatic" organizations (SAP) reinforced the importance of the fact that founding rationale and organizational model of "strong pragmatics" endorse a collaborative relationship with other stakeholders such as businesses and government in the environmental policy field, thereby making the broad scope and scale of partnerships with energy companies understandable. The endorsement of partnerships and a favorable opinion of the potential role of businesses in the environment has two implications that shape the character of partnerships SAP engage in. First, NGOs are less insistent on a perfect match in terms of organizational values as long as both sides' interests are served. One interviewed NGO actively seeks partnerships with companies by trying "to find common areas of interest [. . .]; what are the issues for business with a specific environmental policy" (NGO SAP.2). Another one stresses: "I don't think we should be picky. I mean anybody can go and work with "The Body Shop". If you get a major company such as Tesco to change their ways a little, this can make quite a difference" (NGO SAP.1).

Second, partnership schemes – as an integral part of the organizational model of the NGOs – are initiated to gain financial resources. Whilst "strong and pragmatic" NGOs often provide at least expertise and dedicated human resources to the partnership, business often pays regular fees in exchange. In short, SAP engage with a broad range of companies (even if their environmental credentials are not impeccable) in a flexible, professionalized and institutionalized manner, reflecting their strong resource base, professional organization, pragmatism and founding rationale.

Strong and radical NGOs

The "strong and radical" organizations (SAR) comprise prominent organizations such as WWF UK, RSPB, GP, and CND. SAR's predominantly advocacy operations (question 10) take place on multiple levels (from local to international) (question 4) and cover multiple issues (question 5), reflecting their strong capacity often based on contributions by large memberships (question 11), substantial human resources (question 2) and professionalized organizational structures (question 3). Moreover, they target both government and business (questions 8, 9). As one representative put it, "we have teams to engage with government, for example, to look into smarter regulation; we have teams for business relations, as well. And some of our campaigns are consumer-facing" (interview with NGO SAR.1). They broadly share the critical attitude in terms of relevant issues and other stakeholders in the field of the "weak radicals".

"Strong and radical" organizations display different patterns of engagement with business. One NGO representative described its engagement as follows:

> [W]ithin business relations, our three main approaches are convening meetings where we have roundtables where industry people are grappling with the big issues, we have a partnering approach where we look at bilateral partnerships to drive the transformation of a business, and we have campaigns, as well, where we go public and criticize commercial practices.
>
> (NGO SAR.1)

This is underlined by the survey: SAR engage in low intensity engagement types such as one-way provision and exchange of information, hereby, for example, relying on their expertise, and in higher intensity ones such as public policy alliances and task forces. Moreover, the reference to the alternative option of public campaigning shows the NGOs' capacity to act, and the relative strength and independence of their position within partnerships.

The relatively strong position within partnerships is reflected in the fact that partnerships are not restricted to those with renewable companies, as partnerships such as the one between Greenpeace and the gas- and coal-fired plant owning RWE npower concerning the renewable electricity product "Juice" and "RSPB Energy" with the UK's second largest electricity generator, Scottish and Southern Energy, show. However, even though a wider range of partners is considered by

SAR, their partners face a strong NGO with relatively strict rules of engagement. As one of the interviewees noted: "We are pursuing a partnership with one of the big players [but only] if the right commitment [to forward-looking improvement, specific targets and to support our engagement with government] is in place" (NGO SAR.1). In short, if SAR engage in interactions with business beyond low-intensity information provision and exchanges, they do so with a wider range of businesses than WAR but also with stronger interest and capacity than SAP in asserting their own objectives.

Conclusions

"Green partnerships" imply co-operative relations between two of the key stakeholders in environmental governance, namely environmental NGOs and corporations. As such, partnerships need to be understood as part of the increasingly important theme of participation in environmental governance.

Participation in general has been praised as offering a remedy for the many problems and challenges in environmental governance that the traditional state-centric, "closed" governance arrangements could not address. In particular, solutions to long-term problems require a broadening of the knowledge base, as well as opportunities for social learning. Advocates claim that the integration of new actors into collective decision making means access to more resources and greater legitimacy of governance, the avoidance of policy failures as a result of the complexity and uncertainty associated with many environmental policy challenges, the resistance of stakeholders and formerly outside groups such as the environmental movement organizations, and capture by strong interest groups. However, there have also been more critical and cautious comments regarding the benefits of participatory schemes in environmental governance. This comparative empirical analysis of NGOs and partnerships in Britain's energy sector vindicates some of the critical comments.

The NGOs' use of the tool "partnership with business" and some of the characteristics of such schemes have been shown to be diverse and can be linked to each NGOs' "capacity to act" and "orientation of action". Therefore, the comparative analysis of this study shows that there are limitations to the NGOs' interest and capability in using partnerships with companies of the British energy industry as a tool to pursue their objectives. The analysis also provides an opportunity to reflect on the theoretical arguments in the partnership debate predicting the expansion of and environmental benefits from green partnerships against those questioning their sustainability and advantageousness for the environment. For example, the emergence of SAP with an often explicit partnership focus confirms that NGOs recognize the need and potential benefits of partnering with energy companies.

However, the "flexibility" in their choice of partners also vindicates critical observers that the required radical change in business behaviour will not result from partnerships based on "soft rules" and advisory services. The more "transformative" partnerships that SAR seek to establish with a wide range of partners in turn seem to point to the potential of partnerships to produce environmental benefits. However, the case of the partnership between Greenpeace and RWE npower on the green product "Juice" shows the difficulties of such schemes: In 2006, Greenpeace withdrew from the partnership that was launched in 2003 as a result of RWE's suing of the EU for an increase of RWE's carbon emission allowances and pushing for the commissioning of a new generation of nuclear power stations, highlighting the lack of sustainability of partnerships between organizations with different objectives and values. Finally, the limited range of partnership that WAR would be willing and able to engage in highlights further issues that were stressed by critical observers, namely the limited scope and scale of partnerships, as well as the marginalization of more radical voices. This limited, selective and/or biased engagement of Britain's NGO community with businesses casts doubts on the ability of NGO-business-partnerships to replace other forms of business regulation, serve as an effective solution to environmental problems and/or as a step towards systemic change towards sustainability.

The lessons from this empirical study, as well as the specific debate on "green partnerships" are also relevant in the context of the broader debates on participation. The involvement of additional actors is not enough to ensure that environmental governance becomes more effective and democratic. As Pellizoni (2003) notes, the crucial question is not how much participation, but what kind of participation, by whom, to which purpose.

Notes

1 Question 12 investigates the existing forms of NGO engagement with energy companies and is discussed at p. 192.
2 A grouping of NGOs under such broad clusters is inevitably open to contestation, e.g. placing GP and CND (as organizations with a history of antagonisms with the business communities) in the same cluster (SAR) as the more business-friendly WWF or the long-established RSPB. It is important to understand that the split is, on the one hand, specific to the policy area/industry sector of energy and, on the other hand, the values are averaged across a number of different proxies. That implies that the clustering may look different for other areas/sectors and that certain extreme values for proxies (e.g. corporate funding) are leveled out by other proxies (e.g. thematic focus on nuclear). It is important to interpret the scatterplot as a heuristic tool on the basis of which the following, more detailed discussion of organizations within clusters (and specifically their *potential to partner* with *energy* companies is undertaken.

References

Arts, B. 2002. "'Green Alliances' of Business and NGOs: New Styles of Regulation or 'Dead End Roads'?" *Corporate Social Responsibility and Environmental Management* 9: 26–36.

Bendell, J. (ed.). 2000. *Terms of Endearment: Business, NGOs and Sustainable Development.* Sheffield: Greenleaf.

Breitmeier, H. and Rittberger, V. 1998. "Environmental NGOs in an Emerging Global Civil Society". *Tübinger Arbeitspapiere zur Internationalen Politik und Friedensforschung* (32).

198   *Kristian Krieger and M. Brooke Rogers*

Bulkeley, H. and Mol, A. 2003. "Participation and Environmental Governance: Consensus, Ambivalence and Debate". *Environmental Values* 12: 143–154.

Cowell, S. 1995. *Who's Who in the Environment: England*. London: Environment Council.

Dalton, R. 1994. *The Green Rainbow: Environmental Groups in Western Europe*. London: Yale University Press.

Dawkins, J. 2004. *The Expert Perspective: Views of Corporate Responsibility among NGOs and CSR Commentators*. London: MORI.

Diani, M. and Donati, P. 1999. "Organisational Change in Western European Environmental Groups: A Framework for Analysis". *Environmental Politics* 8(1): 13–34.

DTI [Department for Trade and Industry]. 2003. *Our Energy Future: Creating a Low Carbon Economy*. London: DTI.

Eisinger, P. 1973. "The Conditions of Protest Behavior in American Cities". *American Political Science Review* 76: 11–28.

Eisinger, P. 2007. *Meeting the Energy Challenge: A White Paper on Energy*. London: DTI.

Gamson, W. 1975. *The Strategy of Social Protest*. Homewood, Ill. Dorsey Press.

Gough, C. and Shackley, S. 2001. "The Respectable Politics of Climate Change: The Epistemic Communities and NGOs". *International Affairs* 77(2): 329–345.

Hartman, C.L. and Stafford, R.R. 1996. "Green Alliances: Strategic Relations Between Businesses and Environmental Groups". *Business Horizons* 39(2): 50–9.

Haufler, V. 2003. "New forms of Governance: Certification Regimes as Social Regulations of the Global Market". In Meidinger, E., and Elliott, C. *et al.* (eds) *Social and Political Dimensions of Forest Certification*. Remagen-Oberwinter: Kessel, 237–247.

Heap, S. 2000. *NGOs Engaging with Business: A World of Difference and a Difference to the World*. Oxford: INTRAC.

Helm, D. 2002. "Energy Policy: Security of Supply, Sustainability and Competition". *Energy Policy* 30(3): 173–184.

Kitschelt, H. 1996. "Demokratietheorie und Veränderungen politischer Beteiligungsformen". *Forschungsjournal neue soziale Bewegungen* 9(2): 17–29.

Krieger, K. and Rogers, M. 2010. "Green Partnerships in Britain's Energy Sector: NGOs' Potential to Co-operate with Energy Companies". *Environmental Politics* 19(6): 910–929.

Levy, D. 1997. "Environmental Management as Political Sustainability". *Organization and Environment* 10(2): 126–147.

McCarthy, K. and Zald, M. 1977. "Resource Mobilization and Social Movements: A Partial Theory". *American Journal of Sociology* 82(6): 1212–1241.

McCormick, J. 1991. *British Politics and the Environment*. London: Earthscan.

Millar, C. J. M., Choi, C. J. and Chen, S. 2004. "Global Strategic Partnerships between MNEs and NGOs: Drivers of Change and Ethical Issues". *Business and Society Review* 109(4): 395–414.

Milner, J. 1994. *The Green Index: A Directory of Environmental Organizations in Britain and Ireland*. London: Cassell.

Newell, P. 2000. "Globalisation and the New Politics of Sustainable Development". In Bendell, J. (ed.). *Terms of Endearment: Business, NGOs and Sustainable Development*. Sheffield: Greenleaf, 31–39.

Pellizzoni, L. 2003. "Uncertainty and Participatory Democracy". *Environmental Values* 12: 195–224.

Polletta, F. and Jasper, J. 2001. "Collective Identity in Social Movements". *Annual Review of Sociology* 27: 283–305.

Rawcliffe, P. 1998. *Environmental Pressure Groups in Transition*. Manchester: Manchester University Press.

Rootes, C. 2003. "Britain". In Rootes, C. (ed.). *Environmental Protests in Western Europe*. Oxford: Oxford University Press, 20–58.

Rootes, C., Seel, B. *et al.* 2000. "The Old, the New, and the Old New: British Environmental Organisations from Conservationism to Radical Ecologism" *Paper presented at the ECPR Joint Sessions "Environmental Organisations in Comparative Perspective"*, Copenhagen, 14–19 April 2000.

Rucht, D. 1996. "The Impact of National Contexts on Social Movement Structures: A Cross-Movement and Cross-National Comparison". In McAdam, D., McCarthy, J.D. *et al.* (eds). *Comparative Perspectives on Social Movements: Political Opportunities, Mobilizing Structures, and Cultural Framings*. Cambridge: Cambridge University Press.

Rüdig, W. 1990. *Anti-nuclear Movements: A World Survey of Opposition to Nuclear Energy*. Harlow: Longman.

Spagnuolo, F. 2009. "Beyond Participation: Administrative-Law Type Mechanisms in Global Environmental Governance. Towards a New Basis of Legitimacy?" *European Public Law* 15(1): 49–64.

Take, I. 2002. *NGOs im Wandel: Von der Grasswurzel auf das diplomatische Parkett*. Wiesbaden. Opladen: Westdeutscher Verlag.

Tarrow, S. 1988. "Old Movements in New Cycles of Protest: The Career of an Italian Religious Community". In Klandermans, B., Kriesi, H. *et al.* (eds) *From Structure to Action: Comparing Social Movements across Cultures, International Social Movement Research*. Greenwich, Conn. JAI Press, 281–304.

Tilly, C. 1978. *From Mobilization to Revolution*. Reading, Ma.: Addison-Wesley.

Tully, S. 2004. "Corporate-NGO Partnerships as a Form of Civil Regulation: Lessons from the Energy and Biodiversity Initiative". *LSE CARR Discussion Paper* (22).

Waddell, S. 2000. "Complementary Resources: The Win-win Rationale for Partnership with NGOs". In Bendell, J. (ed.) *Terms of Endearment – Business, NGOs and Sustainable Development*. Sheffield: Greenleaf, 193–206.

Zald, M. N. 1996. "Culture, Ideology, and Strategic Framing". In McAdam, D., McCarthy, J. D. *et al.* (eds). *Comparative Perspectives on Social Movements: Political Opportunities, Mobilizing Structures, and Cultural Framings*. Cambridge: Cambridge University Press.

11 Participatory scenarios in developing and implementing long-term policies

Potential benefits and attributes of influence

Christian Albert

Introduction

The development and implementation of long-term policies presents society with two key challenges: the high degree of complexity and uncertainty in the evolution of the coupled economic, social and ecological systems (e.g. Gunderson and Holling 2002, NRC 1999), and the need to integrate various kinds of information and perspectives of societal actors in this process (cf. Kates *et al.* 2001; Siebenhüner *et al.* Chapter 1 in this volume).

Participatory scenario development and assessment is frequently considered a key instrument for responding to these tasks (Swart *et al.* 2004; Wiek *et al.* 2006; NRC 1999). While numerous definitions for scenarios exist, a broad and generally agreed-upon consensus seems to be that scenarios are "descriptions of how the future might unfold, rather than predictions of what the future will be. They reflect different assumptions about the evolution of current trends, the possible effects of critical uncertainties, and emerging influential factors" (UNEP 2002).

Participation in scenario processes means that societal actors beyond the core group of scenario developers are involved in the creation and assessment of alternative futures. Approaches for involving scenario users in the development process were originally developed in the business world (e.g. Wack 1985a; van der Heijden 1996), and increasingly find application in public policy. Recently, a number of publications reflected upon the potential roles and contributions of scenarios in addressing long-term policy issues, but so far it has not been explicitly reviewed how scenarios could contribute to long-term policy development and implementation. Furthermore, despite the increasing use of participatory scenario planning in long-term policy development, the level of effectiveness reached in actually influencing the relevant debates and political decision making often leaves room for improvement (Alcamo *et al.* 2006; Lebel *et al.* Chapter 13 in this volume).

This chapter attempts to provide an overview of the characteristics of participatory scenarios, to discuss the ways in which it can contribute to long-term policy making, and to investigate attributes of participatory scenarios which are influential in public discussions and decisions. The first section of the chapter proposes a typology for classifying participatory scenarios and synthesizes their potential contributions to policy making. It is based on a comprehensive review of relevant literature. The second section develops attributes of participatory scenarios that need to be fulfilled for yielding influence. A hypothesis on the attributes is developed by drawing on studies on the influence of science on policy, in particular the seminal Global Environmental Assessment Project (Mitchell *et al.* 2006b). A qualitative content analysis (Mayring 2000; Mayring 2008) of scenario publications is conducted to further qualify the hypothesis and to propose a conceptual framework of attributes of influential scenarios.

It is beyond the scope of this chapter to provide specific guidelines of how participatory scenario processes should be designed and which methods should be used. However, based on the analysis, the chapter will provide some preliminary recommendations for applying participatory scenario development in practice as well as issues for further research.

Participatory scenario types and potential contributions

Scenarios as a tool for planning and policy development have been used for more than five decades: Formal use of scenarios began at the end of World War II in the field of war game analysis (van der Heijden 1996; Shoemaker 1993). The civilian use of the scenario technique in a variety of planning purposes was pioneered by the work of Herman Kahn and others (Kahn and Wiener 1967) and further developed and applied in business planning (e.g. Gausemeier *et al.* 1995; Georgantzas and Acar 1995; Schwartz 1996; van der Heijden 1996; von Reibnitz 1987; Wack 1985b, 1985a). At least since the seminal "Limits of Growth" study by Meadows *et al.* (1972), scenarios have been applied to numerous long-term issues of public concern, ranging from studies at the global and regional (Raskin *et al.* 2002; Gallopin *et al.* 1997; Nakicenovic *et al.* 2000) to the local scale (e.g. Peterson *et al.* 2003; Walz *et al.* 2007; Albert *et al.* 2012; Bohnet and Smith 2007).

Facing the great number and diversity of studies in the field of scenario-based planning and assessment, recently various scholars aimed at better understanding and characterizing of scenario types. The studies have resulted in typologies with distinct differences. Examples include a study by Bradfield *et al.* (2005) that describes the evolution of three "schools" of scenario development. Börjeson *et al.* (2006) differentiate between predictive, explorative and normative scenarios with two sub-categories for each type. van Notten *et al.* (2003, 2005) present a typology of scenario approaches consisting of various parameters and spectrums of their respective characteristics.

While these typologies are valuable for classifying scenario studies, they necessarily remain broad in order to cover the range of scenario types available and do not focus on participatory scenario processes for long-term policy development and implementation. The much-cited typology by van Notten *et al.* (2003, 2005) is a very useful basis, but it also needs to be altered and amended since essential features of participatory scenario development are not included and relevant aspects of scenarios dealing with public governance issues cannot be usefully mapped into it (as exemplarily shown by Sondeijker *et al.* 2006).

All participatory scenario processes for supporting long-term policy development and implementation share some common characteristics: They focus on a long-term time horizon, describe both pathways of future change and the potential outcomes, and are participatory in involving decision makers, stakeholders, scientists, and/or lay citizens beyond the core team of scientists or consultants who facilitate the scenario exercise. Besides, participatory scenario development differs in the specific characteristics of nine important parameters (see Table 11.1).

1 *Function*: Participatory scenario studies place different emphases on the two key functions supporting long-term policy development. Product-focused scenario processes concentrate on the production of information. Process-oriented scenario studies aim more at facilitating discussions, developing mutual understanding and initiating social learning (cf. van Notten 2005).
2 *Subject*: The focus of participatory scenario studies can be a specific issue (e.g. the future of small scale agriculture), a geographic area, or a specific institution (cf. van Notten *et al.* 2003).
3 *Vantage point*: The vantage point can be either exploratory (forward-looking) or anticipatory (backcasting). Participation in exploratory studies allows participants to start from the present and explore how the future might evolve. Anticipatory scenarios assume a specific future situation and explore the range of actions or developments necessary to attain (or not attain) the projected condition.
4 *Inclusion of values*: Primarily descriptive scenarios explore consequences of plausible futures, while primarily normative ones assess the implications of probable, preferred, or undesired futures. Involvement of participants is possible in both variants, but it may be argued that stakeholder participation increases the normativity of a scenario. However, all scenarios are to some

Table 11.1 Parameters and characteristics of participatory scenarios

Parameters	Characteristics
1. Function	Process – Product
2. Subject	Area, Issue, and Institution
3. Vantage point	Exploratory – Anticipatory
4. Inclusion of values	Primarily Descriptive – Primarily Normative
5. Inputs in the scenario process	Qualitative – Quantitative
6. Level of involvement	Co-Decision, Co-Design, Co-Thinking, Consultation, Information
7. Frequency of involvement	Entire Process – Episodic
8. Meeting characteristic	Synchronously – Asynchronously
9. Resources availability	Extensive – Limited

Sources: Based on van Notten *et al.* (2003) and van Notten (2005), with amendments from Alcamo and Henrichs (2008), Pahl Wostl (2008), Swart *et al.* (2004), and Jäger *et al.* (2007).

extent normative since they always reflect the mindsets of the people creating them (cf. Swart *et al.* 2004).

5 *Inputs*: Qualitative scenarios use narrative outlines, texts, storylines, diagrams, pictures and/or collages to describe future developments with high levels of complexity and uncertainty. They may include non-quantifiable, normative aspects like values, mental maps and expectations of participants. Participation of non-scientific actors has a long tradition in qualitative scenario development. The participants can help developing a joint system under-standing, identify key driving forces and uncertainties, and develop the actual scenarios (cf. Kok *et al.* 2006a, 2006b). In contrast, quantitative scenarios apply numerical approaches and often use formal models. They offer structural consistency and scientific rigour through explicit assumptions. Non-scientific actors can contribute to the development of quantitative scenarios in providing judgment for making assumptions in scenarios. A disadvantage is that participation in quantitative scenario development decreases its usual transparency since the thought process of the participants in making the judgments cannot be made fully explicit (Alcamo and Henrichs 2008).

6 *Level of involvement*: By building on Arnstein's (1969) classical "Ladder of Citizen Participation", recent amendments from public participation research (e.g. Mostert 2006) and scenario literature (Pahl-Wostl 2008, Alcamo and Henrichs 2008), the following levels of participation in scenario development can be derived (cf. Volkery *et al.* 2008). At the lowest level, stakeholders and decision makers are only *informed* about the process and results of a scenario exercise. More intensive participation occurs when non-scientific actors are *consulted* during the exercise to provide input. *Co-thinking*, the third level, means that participants are actively involved in the development of the scenarios, but do not make decisions. At the *co-designing* stage, participants are furthermore engaged in the structuring of the scenario process and the joint definition of "game rules" for collaboration. Finally participants can *co-decide* and assume responsibility for the scenario process design, the analysis and the recommendations derived from them.

7 *Frequency of involvement*: Participants may be constantly involved in scenario development or take part only sporadically for certain phases of the process (cf. Pahl-Wostl 2008). Continuous involvement may foster mutual under-standing, developing trust and a feeling of ownership among participants. Episodic meetings may involve changing participants and can be more appropriate if large numbers of participants are to be included.

8 *Meeting characteristic*: One way to facilitate participatory scenario development is to hold workshops with the various participants. Another option is to organize an asynchronous process to which participants can contribute at different times and in different locations (for example via internet). While the first approach is strongly advisable for facilitating social learning, meeting asynchronaly may be more useful to obtain judgments and information from a large group of individuals (cf. Pahl-Wostl 2008). Special emphasis should be placed on providing all interested and affected actors a

chance to be involved, either directly or indirectly through representatives. Stakeholder analyses are advisable as a way to elaborate the range of participants to involve (Albert *et al.* 2012; Pahl-Wostl 2008).

9 *Resource availability*: Participatory scenario studies differ in the availability of temporal and financial resources as well as available manpower. For example, the urgency of issues or political time frames may force scenario developers to produce results very quickly. In other cases, longer time scales of several years can be invested. Involving participants is very complicated and time consuming – the higher the desired degree of involvement, the more resources are needed (cf. Alcamo and Henrichs 2008; van Notten *et al.* 2003).

A few studies explored the potential contributions of participatory scenario processes to the development and implementation of responses to complex, long-term and uncertainty-laden societal challenges. For example, Swart *et al.* (2004) explored how scenario analysis can serve as a key tool of sustainability sciences. Wiek *et al.* (2006) addressed the question of which functions scenarios can adopt in efforts for supporting sustainability transitions. Sondeijker *et al.* (2006) studied in greater detail the characteristics of so-called "transition scenarios" within the overall transition management concept (cf. Kemp *et al.* 2007; Rotmans *et al.* 2001). Others focused on scenarios in public policy (e.g. Ringland 2002), for addressing environmental issues (e.g. Xiang and Clarke 2003; Alcamo 2001; Alcamo *et al.* 2006; Pahl-Wostl 2008; Alcamo 2008b; Wollenberg *et al.* 2000), and as mechanisms to facilitate organizational or social learning (e.g. Robinson 2003; Chermack *et al.* 2006; Berkhout *et al.* 2002). From this array of publications, a range of potential benefits can be deducted that participatory scenario development may provide for long-term policy development and implementation.

First, participatory scenario development can contribute to the exploration of alternative future developments and their potential consequences. In this respect, involvement of societal actors is beneficial as it may enrich scenarios with local knowledge and creativity and ensure that relevant aspects are taken into account (Alcamo and Henrichs 2008; Pahl-Wostl 2008). The information created through participatory scenarios can take three main forms:

- Participatory scenario development may enhance understanding about the dynamics and evolution of complex and coupled human-environment systems beyond the control of the scenario users (Alcamo 2008b; Jäger *et al.* 2007). They can address complex issues and their interactions and integrate across different types of data, disciplines, institutions, as well as temporal and spatial scales and perspectives (cf. Swart *et al.* 2004; Alcamo 2008b). This exploration may include identifying "weak signals" of change and their potential cumulative impacts (Jäger *et al.* 2007; Kasemir *et al.* 2003), and the possibilities of inconsistencies, breaches-of-trends and surprises (van Notten 2005; Swart *et al.* 2004; Jäger *et al.* 2007; Wollenberg *et al.* 2000). As such, scenarios may raise awareness about future challenges (Alcamo 2008b;

Jäger *et al.* 2007), and thus serve as an important input for long-term policy development (Wiek *et al.* 2006; Jäger *et al.* 2007).

- Participatory scenario development may also provide information about the implications and robustness of alternative policy options. Such forward-looking scenarios assume different policy options and assess them concerning their consequences and the degree to which they might achieve specific objectives (cf. Alcamo 2008b; Jäger *et al.* 2007; Shoemaker and van der Heijden 1992; van der Heijden 1996).
- Participatory scenario development can link normative, long-term policy objectives with decisions necessary to attain them. Following this backcasting-approach, scenarios can serve as a guiding framework for interventions in the short- and medium-term (cf. Swart *et al.* 2004; Sondeijker *et al.* 2006; Pahl-Wostl 2008; Quist and Vergragt 2006; Robinson 2003).

Second, participatory scenario development may initiate and facilitate social learning through eliciting, critically discussing and challenging different perspectives and mental maps of system interdependencies, the future evolution of the issues at stake and the range and kinds of possible solutions (cf. Wollenberg *et al.* 2000; Jäger *et al.* 2007; Sondeijker *et al.* 2006; Robinson 2003; Swart *et al.* 2004; Berkhout *et al.* 2002; NRC 1999; Alcamo and Henrichs 2008). The key idea is that involving diverse societal actors may enhance legitimacy and mutual understanding, lead to the development of a feeling of ownership, and ease subsequent implementation (cf. Pahl-Wostl 2008; Alcamo and Henrichs 2008). In particular, participatory scenario development can fulfill the following functions:

- Participatory scenario development may ease and facilitate communication and discussions through providing a "language" that is understandable by diverse audiences (cf. Jäger *et al.* 2007; Swart *et al.* 2004), thus offering a way for stakeholders to take part in the creation and discussion of long-term policies (Alcamo 2008b).
- On the basis of this improved communication, participatory scenario development may facilitate discussions and conscious reflections on different perspectives and understandings (cf. Jäger *et al.* 2007; Swart *et al.* 2004; Alcamo 2008b). As a result, participants may adapt their mental models to new understandings. Through such "reperceiving" (Wack 1985a), scenarios have the potential to overcome various cognitive biases (for a review, see Wollenberg *et al.* 2000) and to serve as "heuristic tools that encourage social learning" (Berkhout *et al.* 2002).
- Finally, scenarios may initiate and structure short and medium-term collaborations towards a shared long-term objective (cf. Jäger *et al.* 2007; Wiek *et al.* 2006). Sondeijker *et al.* (2006) argue that scenarios – as a tool to bring together various perspectives – can initiate collaboration towards a common vision. Along these lines, Pahl-Wostl (2008) finds scenarios useful for supporting initiatives to put learning-based adaptive management approaches into practice.

Recent studies have stressed that the scenario process is at least as important as the results and the tools itself (Swart *et al.* 2004; Robinson 2003; Sondeijker *et al.* 2006). However, although scenario development is claimed to contribute to this diverse range of functions, its capacity to do so in practice is often limited. Furthermore, it is often impossible to fulfill multiple functions simultaneously.

Towards a hypothesis on influential participatory scenarios

Given the manifold potential contributions of participatory scenarios to the development and implementation of long-term policies, the question arises of which attributes determine the influence of scenarios in discussions and decision making. Before addressing this issue in detail, this section will review models for explaining the influence of science on policy and develop a hypothesis of attributes of effective scenario development. It is important to note that scenarios cannot be equated with science but rather blend design elements with scientific modelling and assessments. However, against the background of the little scholarship on the influence of scenario development on public policy, it is useful to draw on findings made in the science–policy field to develop a hypothesis for scenario influence.

Science–policy studies remain skeptical on the effectiveness of scientific input on policy making (Haas 2004, 2005). On the one hand, the influence of scientific information on decision making processes seems to be quite limited (cf. Funtowicz and Ravetz 2001). Decision makers cannot be assumed to solely base their decisions on objective scientific assessments on the issue at stake and on the various policy options to address it. Instead, they face substantial constraints on temporal resources and cognitive capacities when trying to make "good" decisions, especially on such complex issues as sustainable development. Consequently, decision makers usually act "boundedly rational" and tend to rely on personal experience and other heuristics that decrease the need to collect and process information (Kahnemann *et al.* 1982; Simon 1982, 1983).

On the other hand, many studies have shown that cognitive and normative uncertainties sometimes create contexts of so called "policy windows" or "fluid moments in history", in which innovative and creative ideas are considered and decision makers are receptive to and interested in new information (e.g. Kingdon 1984; Lee 1993). Baumheier (1993) notes that promoters of new policies need to react quickly since policy windows open up for only short time periods. Due to public debate and emerging political pressures, policy windows can have significant influence on decisions (Heiland 1999; Rucht 1994). Haas (2004, 2005) presents the notion of "usable knowledge" and discusses pathways through which such knowledge may be generated, disseminated and applied in policy.

The Global Environmental Assessment project (Mitchell *et al.* 2006b) asked how environmental assessments must be designed and conducted to be most likely to make use of opening "policy windows" and, in effect, influence decision making in public policy. On the basis of a number of empirical case studies from national and international environmental assessments (see Mitchell *et al.* 2006b), the authors concluded that environmental science is more likely to influence policy if the assessment process is perceived as not only scientifically credible but also salient to political concerns and legitimate by the assessment's audiences (Cash *et al.* 2003, Mitchell *et al.* 2006b; cf. NRC 2007). While other concepts for explaining the effectiveness of scientific assessments in policy making exist, this set of criteria has been identified as one of the most comprehensive (Mcknie 2007).

Scenario studies, however, can be perceived as a special kind of assessment that addresses not the current, but the future state of the environment (Alcamo 2001), resulting in dramatic increases of the degree of complexity and uncertainty involved. To reflect the need for innovative thinking about possibilities and surprises in scenario-based studies, Alcamo and colleagues (2006, 2008) proposed "creativity" as an additional criterion.

On the basis of these findings from the literature, the hypothesis becomes: scenarios tend to be influential in policy to the degree that they are perceived as simultaneously credible, salient, legitimate and creative by the scenario users.

Attributes of influential participatory scenario development

To further investigate the attributes of influential scenarios, a qualitative content analysis of scenario literature was conducted. The approach followed the inductive category development procedure as proposed by Mayring (2000, 2008). A criterion of definition was formulated as "characteristics of scenarios mentioned in the material as important for yielding influence". Published material was collected that considered the attributes of influential scenarios (see Table 11.2). Finally, the criterion of definition was applied in the analysis of the material and categories (in this case, sub-attributes) were deducted and iteratively revised. Figure 11.1 illustrates the resulting proposed framework of attributes for influential scenarios.

Table 11.2 Literature considered in the content analysis

Themes	*References*
Definitions of credibility, salience, legitimacy and creativity	Cash and Buizer (2005); Cash *et al.* (2003); Mitchell *et al.* (2006a); Alcamo *et al.* (2006); Alcamo and Henrichs (2008); NRC (1999); NRC (2007)
Scenarios in environmental studies	Alcamo (2001); Alcamo *et al.* (2006); Alcamo (2008a); Berkhout *et al.* (2001); Wollenberg *et al.* (2000)
Scenarios in public policy	Leney *et al.* (2004); Ringland (2002)
Scenarios in business	Götze (1991); Ringland (1998); Schwartz (1996); Shoemaker (1995); van der Heijden (1996); von Reibnitz (1987); Wack (1985b, 1985a)

Source: Compiled by the author.

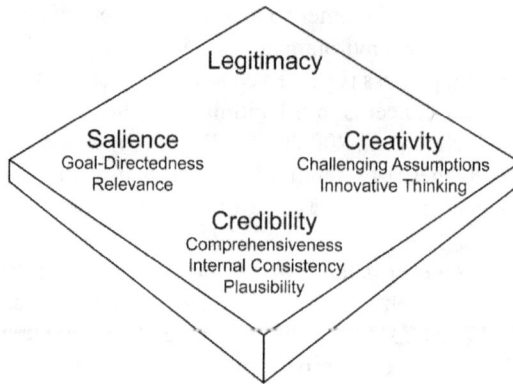

Figure 11.1 Proposed framework of attributes of influential scenarios.

Source: Own conceptualization based on Alcamo *et al.* (2006), Cash *et al.* (2003), Mitchell *et al.* (2006b), NRC (2007), and a content analysis of scenario literature.

Credibility

Credibility describes the degree to which the audiences consider the scenarios as correct and its arguments and conclusions as adequate (cf. Cash and Buizer 2005; Cash *et al.* 2003), or at least more correct than competing claims (cf. Mitchell *et al.* 2006a). It is an often cited attribute of effective scenarios that relates to four distinct qualities.

Most importantly, a scenario's credibility is determined by the degree to which its audiences perceive it as *plausible* (Alcamo *et al.* 2006; Götze 1991; Leney *et al.* 2004; van der Heijden 1996; von Reibnitz 1987; Schwartz 1996), or at least "not-implausible" (Alcamo 2001). Plausible scenarios are considered feasible and attainable within a given timeframe (Leney *et al.* 2004) and are based on a sound and empirically verified analysis of the existing conditions (Götze 1991; Wack 1985b). Only plausible scenarios are considered capable of serving as a basis from which the users can further develop knowledge and understanding (van der Heijden 1996) and failure in attaining plausibility thus risks easy dismissal by scenario users (Alcamo 2001).

Internal consistency both within each scenario (Alcamo 2001; Götze 1991; Leney *et al.* 2004; von Reibnitz 1987) and among the set of scenarios (Shoemaker 1995) is the second quality. It requires that the assumptions and causal relationships are consistent with existing information (Alcamo *et al.* 2006; Shoemaker 1995) and that the scenarios "grow logically (in a cause/effect way) from the past and the present" (van der Heijden 1996).

Another aspect of credibility is *comprehensiveness*, the degree to which the set of scenarios produced covers the range of available alternatives or possibilities (Götze 1991; van der Heijden 1996). Although there seems to be consensus that scenarios need to be comprehensive, it is not clear if the range of considered scenarios need to include all options (Wack 1985a), a wide range of possible or plausible options (Leney *et al.* 2004; Götze 1991; Shoemaker 1995) or at least the extremes of the assumed future alternatives (von Reibnitz 1987). Scenarios should highlight competing perspectives and describe generically different alternatives rather than variations on one theme (Shoemaker 1995). However, most authors propose sets of two to four scenarios as most effective to reflect the uncertainties and at the same time keep the number of scenarios at a manageable size (e.g. van der Heijden 1996).

Enhancing credibility requires a highly transparent and sufficiently documented scenario development process that is retraceable by the actors involved (Alcamo *et al.* 2006; Alcamo 2001; Schwartz 1996; Ringland 2002). Since sustainable development allows for multiple perspectives and mental models, the rationales for choosing a particular set of assumptions must be communicated (Alcamo *et al.* 2006; Götze 1991; Leney *et al.* 2004).

Salience

Salience is another crucial requirement that asks if a scenario is relevant to its audience and if the objectives are adequately addressed. The information must be provided in a way that is responsive to local conditions and issues of concern, must connect to aspects that the decision makers find relevant and that they can influence, and must be provided at an appropriate time period before relevant decisions are made (cf. Mitchell *et al.* 2006a). Salience has been interpreted as of uttermost importance for ensuring the effectiveness of scenarios and it should be sustained under all circumstances (van der Heijden 1996).

One aspect of salience, *goal directedness*, asks if the scenarios are explicitly attuned to address the issues at stake (Ringland 1998) and prove useful for acquiring the information necessary to make decisions among alternative options (Leney *et al.* 2004; Götze 1991).

Relevance, another aspect, includes that scenarios must be tailored to the existing knowledge, cognitive abilities, current concerns and mental maps of the potential scenario users (Shoemaker 1995; van der Heijden 1996). They should explicitly draw upon the audience's own language, history and context (Ringland 1998) and specifically address the "deepest concerns" of the users (Wack 1985b) so that they can easily assume ownership and consider the scenarios' implications in their activities (Schwartz 1996).

Scenario salience can be enhanced by designing and conducting the scenario development process explicitly according to the needs of the users, specifically adapted to the temporal and financial resources available (Berkhout *et al.* 2001) and with a constant focus on the decisions to be made (Alcamo 2001). Linking scenario exercises into current ongoing visioning, planning and implementation processes and facilitating constant exchanges and collaboration between scenario developers and users can heighten saliency through harmonization of the scenario agenda, its goals and expected results (Alcamo 2001; Wack 1985a; von Reibnitz 1987; van der Heijden 1996). However, such iterative reconciliations between scenario users and developers most often proved particularly difficult which led Wack (1985b) to identify the missing interface between developers and decision makers as one of the key problems of scenario planning.

Legitimacy

Legitimacy concerns the degree to which scenarios are perceived as unbiased in their conduct and respectful and procedurally fair to the divergent perspectives, interests, and beliefs of various stakeholders (cf. Alcamo *et al.* 2006; Cash *et al.* 2003). It includes considerations of the composition of the actors involved in the development of the scenarios, the evaluation of their consequences, as well as the decision-making and dissemination process (cf. Mitchell *et al.* 2006a). If the scenarios results shall be adopted as a basis for decisions, the process of producing them must be perceived as "fair and legitimate by those whose future they might affect" (NRC 1999).

The importance of legitimacy is noted mostly implicitly in publications on scenario methods by highlighting the need for joint scenario development (e.g. Ringland 2002). Very similar to the credibility criterion, the legitimacy of scenarios can be enhanced by making the process of information production, evaluation and dissemination open, transparent and observable (cf. Cash and Buizer 2005). Fostering interactions between users and producers of scenarios in a transdisciplinary setting and being explicit in the values and assumptions underlying the scenarios can be assumed to further improve the scenarios' scores on the legitimacy criterion (cf. NRC 1999). Participation should begin at an early stage of the process (Berkhout *et al.* 2001), include representatives with disparate sets of interests (Ringland 1998), and employ a simple framework for facilitating communication and collaboration across a wide range of divergent user groups (Ringland 2002).

Creativity

Creativity evaluates to what extent the process provokes unconventional and innovative thinking. It was found particularly important in scenarios and scenario development for imagining future surprises and non-linear trends that would not have been considered by following only "conventional" thinking. This notion is based on the finding that knowledge relevant for planning for the future can broadly be categorized into three classes: Things we know we know, things we know we do not know, and things we do not know we do not know (Shoemaker 1995). Conventional lines of thought often omit at least the latter category of future developments and thus leave many potential risks and opportunities not conceived.

The first quality of creativity is *innovative thinking*, the degree to which scenarios initiate and facilitate exploring the effects of nonlinear, interrupted, and unprecedented trends (Alcamo 2001). Scenarios are only worth pursuing if they shed light on a new perspective to the issues at stake (van der Heijden 1996) and engage their audiences to think outside of the conventional realm (Leney *et al.* 2004).

Challenging assumptions refer to the need to recognize, question, and alter their mental models of future developments, in case such modification is justified and necessary (Alcamo 2001; van der Heijden 1996; Wack 1985b). Scenarios must be surprising (Leney *et al.* 2004), have the capacity to break old stereotypes (Schwartz 1996), and broaden the understanding of the users (Alcamo 2001). One important aspect is to also consider scenarios that might be "low in probability but high in consequence" (cf. Alcamo 2001).

Interrelationships and relative importance of the attributes

The content analysis of scenario publications suggests that significant trade-offs exist between the attributes. This insight is consistent with the result of the Global Environmental Assessment Project that constituted a tight coupling of the criteria so that efforts to enhance one of them often undermine the others (Cash *et al.* 2003; Eckley *et al.* 2002; Mitchell *et al.* 2006a). For example, Haas (2004) argues that salience may be in conflict with credibility since developing credible knowledge often takes more time than available for deciding between given policy options. However, a low value or decrease of one of the attributes must not necessarily mean that the scenario influence in general diminishes. The attributes should rather be understood as basic requirements of which minimum levels have to be attained if a particular study shall influence policy making (William C. Clark, pers. comm.).

It can be assumed that the relative importance of the criteria differs among the phases of a participatory scenario process. While salience and creativity may be particularly important at the beginning of a scenario exercise in order to get people involved, questions of legitimacy and credibility gain in relative importance in designing and conducting scenario phases of actual scenario creation and assessment. Moreover, the relative importance of the attributes seems to vary across different participatory scenario purposes (cf. Alcamo and Henrichs 2008):

- Credibility is of particularly high importance if the prime goal of participatory scenarios is planning. If credibility cannot be attained, scenarios may not withstand criticism of implausibility and they may easily be disregarded. Enhancing credibility may result in a lowering of the creativity value: The more scenarios are credible in resonating with current mental models, the less they may be creative and surprising for challenging and influencing the users' thinking (van der Heijden 1996; Leney *et al.* 2004; Alcamo and Henrichs 2008; Wollenberg *et al.* 2000). Along these lines, Vygotsky (1986) coined the term "zone of proximal development" in referring to the interface at which the newly acquired knowledge of the scenario users come together with the logic of experienced reasoning. The learning capacity of the scenario users would ultimately be limited to this zone of proximal development.

- Salience is especially important in scenarios focusing on policy advice in order to be considered relevant to the decisions at stake. If salience cannot be achieved, the scenario outcomes are perceived as useless. An example of salience trade-offs is that by heightening its value, credibility may be lowered if the focal issue cannot be addressed with existing and rigorously validated models.
- Legitimacy is crucially important in scenarios for policy development and implementation. If the process of scenario development and assessment is perceived as unfair and disrespectful by some stakeholders, they may oppose any conclusions drawn from the studies and organize resistance to approaches to implementation. Higher values of legitimacy could be achieved through involving a greater diversity of participants (in particular democratically elected representatives) and the strengthening of qualitative methods that are more easily understood by the scenario audience. However, such approaches often occur at the cost of transparency and replicability, thus risking lower levels of credibility and salience.
- Creativity is especially relevant in scenarios with an education-objective in order to convey aspects of alternative future developments that had not been considered before. The degree of creativity that scenarios for policy development need to obtain can, however, be relatively low – the more scenarios are framed within a specific decision context, the smaller the possibility space of options becomes that can be considered (cf. Pahl-Wostl 2008). Enhancing creativity may result in lower degrees of perceived credibility and salience.

The difficult task of enhancing scenario attributes without lowering some of them below the necessary minimum level could most promisingly be performed through sensible *boundary management* (see Guston 1999) between divergent actors in the process of scenario co-production. For heightening credibility, salience, and legitimacy, three basic functions have been suggested (Cash *et al.* 2003; Mitchell *et al.* 2006b): *Active, iterative and inclusive communication* among the actors, *translation* to facilitate mutual understanding across disciplines and professions, and *mediation* to resolve situations in which strong conflicts persist among the actors which cannot be resolved with mere communication and translation. For enhancing creativity, the function of *inspiration* is required to reflect the need to involve imaginative people and to create an open and receptive climate in which unconventional ideas are embraced (cf. Ringland 1998). Integrating various stakeholder groups can result in a wide spectrum of perspectives on an issue that allows for innovative ideas and new considerations.

Conclusions and recommendations

This chapter shed light on participatory scenarios in long-term policy development and implementation. It summarized and categorized the contributions that participatory scenarios can provide, developed a typology of participatory scenarios, and discussed the context and attributes of scenario influence in policy making.

The typology showed that participatory scenarios share some commonalities, but also have several variants. The function, subject, vantage point, inclusion of values, inputs in the scenario process, level and frequency of involvement, meeting characteristic and resource availability were identified as important parameters of participatory scenarios. The synthesis of potential contributions of participatory scenarios to policy development and implementation illustrated several benefits both to the exploration of future changes and the facilitation of social learning processes. It was proposed that to be influential, participatory scenario processes and outcomes must be perceived by their audiences as simultaneously *credible*, *salient*, *legitimate* and *creative*. The qualitative content analysis of scenario literature lead to the proposition of sub-categories for these attributes. Finally, trade-offs between the attributes and their relative importance for different scenario purposes were discussed.

A few recommendations for the design and conduct of participatory scenario processes can be derived from this chapter's findings:

- The purpose of the exercise, the type of scenario to use and the range of participants to involve should be discussed and decided in the very beginning of a participatory scenario exercise. It must be made explicit how and to what degree participants will have influence on the design and outcome of the scenario process and common rules of collaboration should be adopted. Furthermore, it needs to be clarified how scenario results shall be used in subsequent discussions or decision making. It is important to remember that there are also limits to participation, since rising degrees of involvement require more time and resources. More and stronger participation does not always mean the best solution.

- The selection of participants in the process depends upon the specific objective of the exercise. For example, if decision support is the prime objective, it is crucial to actively involve policy and decision makers in the process. In other cases, if public education has been decided as the main focus, the involvement of "remarkable people" (Schwartz 1996) and "free thinkers" (cf. Kok *et al.* 2006a) like poets and artists who are used to think imaginatively is important to enhance the degree of creativity of the scenarios and thus engage people in new and innovative thinking.

- The design of the participatory process and the choice of scenario methods require a careful reflection of the desired levels of relative importance of the scenario attributes and the implicit trade-offs that come with enhancement efforts. Recognizing and accounting for stakeholders' motivation to participate (cf. Alcamo and Henrichs 2008) and making arrangements for implementing effective boundary management between actors in the design and implementation of the scenario process promises to be helpful.

- The core scenario team needs to be aware that heightening the level of participation in scenario processes has implications for its social role. The more participants are responsible for the creation of the scenarios, the more the task of the core team changes from actual scenario development to facilitation and support of a collaborative process.

Questions for further research include:

- Empirical verification of the proposed attributes of participatory scenario influence on policy making through comparative case study research
- Development of an overview of methods for facilitation of participatory scenario processes and experimental testing of their respective capacity to simultaneously enhance the attributes of scenario influence
- Development of framework guidelines for conducting participatory scenarios to be most influential in policy
- Development of guidelines for facilitators on how to best fulfill the role as mediator and boundary manager between scientists, decision makers and stakeholders in scenario processes.

Acknowledgements

This chapter profited from presentations and subsequent discussions at the Conference on the Human Dimensions of Global Environmental Change and the Integrated Assessment of Land Use Changes Conference that both took place in Berlin, Germany, 2008. I am particularly grateful to Sylvia Herrmann, Peter Mueller, Isabel Obendorf and Mark Rasmussen for their comments and ideas. Funding was provided by a dissertation research grant from the German National Academic Foundation (Studienstiftung des deutschen Volkes); it is gratefully acknowledged. The dissertation research project is endorsed by the Global Land Project, a joint research initiative by the International Geosphere-Biosphere Programme (IGBP) and the International Human Dimensions Programme on Global Environmental Change (IHDP).

References

Albert, C., Zimmermann, T., Knieling, J. and von Haaren, C. 2012. "Social Learning can Benefit Decision-making in Landscape Planning: Gartow case study on climate change adaptation, Elbe valley biosphere reserve". *Landscape and Urban Planning* 105: 347–360.

Alcamo, J. 2001. "Scenarios as Tools for International Environmental Assessments". *Environmental Issue Report*. Luxembourg: Office for Official Publications of the European Communities, European Environmental Agency.

Alcamo, J. (ed.) 2008a. *Environmental Futures: The Practice of Environmental Scenario Analysis*. Amsterdam, The Netherlands: Elsevier.

Alcamo, J. (2008b) "Introduction: the Case for Scenarios of the Environment". In Alcamo, J. (ed.) *Environmental Futures: The Practice of Environmental Scenario Analysis*. Amsterdam, The Netherlands: Elsevier.

Alcamo, J. and Henrichs, T. 2008. "Towards Guidelines for Environmental Scenario Analysis". In Alcamo, J. (ed.) *Environmental futures: The Practice of Environmental Scenario Anaylsis*. Amsterdam, The Netherlands: Elsevier.

Alcamo, J., Kok, K., Busch, G., Priess, J. A., Eickhout, B., Rounsevell, M., Rothman, D. S. and Heistermann, M. 2006. "Searching for the Future of Land: Scenarios from the Local to Global Scale". In Lambin, E. F. and Geist, H. (eds) *Land-Use and Land-Cover Change: Local Processes and Global Impacts.* Dordrecht, The Netherlands: Springer.

Arnstein, S. R. 1969. "A Ladder Of Citizen Participation". *Journal of the American Planning Association* 35: 216–24.

Baumheier, R. 1993. *Kommunale Umweltvorsorge: Chancen und Probleme präventiver Umweltpolitik auf der kommunalen Ebene am Beispiel der Energie-und der Verkehrspolitik.* Birkhäuser.

Berkhout, F., Hertin, J. and Jordan, A. 2001. "Socio-economic Futures in Climate Change Impact Assessment: Using Scenarios as 'Learning Machines'". *Working Paper.* Tyndall Centre for Climate Change Research.

Berkhout, F., Hertin, J. and Jordan, A. 2002. "Socio-economic Futures in Climate Change Impact Assessment: Using Scenarios as 'Learning Machines'". *Global Environmental Change* 12: 83–95.

Bohnet, I. and Smith, D. M. 2007. "Planning Future Landscapes in the Wet Tropics of Australia: A Social-ecological Framework". *Landscape and Urban Planning* 80: 137–52.

Börjeson, L., Höjer, M., Dreborg, K. H., Ekvall, T. and Finnveden, G. 2006. "Scenario Types and Techniques: Towards a User's Guide". *Futures* 38: 723–39.

Bradfield, R., Wright, G., Burt, G., Cairns, G. and Van der Heijden, K. 2005. "The Origins and Evolution of Scenario Techniques in Long Range Business Planning". *Futures* 37: 795–812.

Cash, D. W. and Buizer, J. 2005. *Knowledge-Action Systems for Seasonal to Interannual Climate Forecasting: Summary of a Workshop.* Washington, DC: The National Academies Press.

Cash, D. W., Clark, W. C., Alcock, F., Dickson, N. M., Eckley, N., Guston, D. H., Jäger, J. and Mitchell, R. B. 2003. "Knowledge Systems for Sustainable Development". *Proceedings of the National Academy of Sciences of the United States of America* 100: 8086–91.

Chermack, T. J., Lynham, S. A. and Van der Merwe, L. 2006. "Exploring the Relationship between Scenario Planning and Perceptions of Learning Organization Characteristics". *Futures* 38: 767–77.

Eckley, N., Clark, W. C., Farrell, A., Jäger, J. and Stanners, D. 2002. *Designing Effective Assessments.* Copenhagen, DK, Harvard: Global Environmental Assessment Project and European Environmental Agency.

Funtowicz, S. O. and Ravetz, J. R. 2001. "Global Risk, Uncertainty, and Ignorance". In Kasperson, J. X. and Kasperson, R. E. (eds) *Global Environmental Risk.* London: Earthscan.

Gallopin, G. C., Hammond, A., Raskin, P. and Swart, R. J. 1997. *Branch Points: Global Scenarios and Human Choice: A Resource Paper of the Global Scenarios Group.* Stockholm: Stockholm Environmental Institute.

Gausemeier, J., Fink, A. and Schlake, O. 1995. *Szenario-Management: Planen und Führen mit Szenarien.* München: Carl Hanser Verlag.

Georgantzas, N. C. and Acar, W. 1995. "Scenario-driven Planning: Learning to Manage Strategic Uncertainty". Westport, CT: Quorum Books.

Götze, U. 1991. "Szenario-Technik in der strategischen Unternehmensplanung". Wiesbaden: Deutscher Universitätsverlag.

Gunderson, L. H. and Holling, C. S. (eds) 2002. *Panarchy: Understanding Transformations in Human and Natural Systems.* Washington, DC, USA, Island.

Guston, D. H. 1999. "Stabilizing the Boundary between US Politics and Science: The Role of the Office of Technology Transfer as a Boundary Organization". *Social Studies of Science* 29: 87.

Haas, P. M. 2004. "When Does Power Listen to Truth? A Constructivist Approach to the Policy Process". *Journal of European Public Policy.* 11: 569–92.

Haas, P. M. 2005. "Science and International Environmental Governance". In Dauvergne, P. (ed.) *Handbook of Global Environmental Politics.* Cheltenham, UK: Edward Elgar.

Heiland, S. 1999. Voraussetzungen erfolgreichen Naturschutzes. ecomed-Verl.-Ges.

Jäger, J., Rothman, D., Anastasi, C., Kartha, S. and Van Notten, P. W. F. 2007. "Training Module 6, Scenario Development and Analysis". In Pintér, L., Swanson, D. and Chenje, J. (eds) *GEO Resource Book: A Training Manual on Integrated Environmental Assessment and Reporting.* Nairobi: UNEP and IISD.

Kahn, H. and Wiener, A. J. 1967. *The Year 2000.* New York: MacMillan.

Kahnemann, D., Slovic, P. and Tversky, A. 1982. *Judgement under Uncertainty: Heuristics and Biases.* New York, NY: Cambridge University Press.

Kasemir, B., Jäger, J., Jaeger, C. C. and Gardner, M. T. (eds) 2003. *Public Participation in Sustainability Science: A Handbook.* Cambridge, UK: Cambridge University Press.

Kates, R. W., Clark, W. C., Corell, R., Hall, J. M., Jaeger, C. C., Lowe, I., Mccarthy, J. J., Schellnhuber, H. J., Bolin, B., Dickson, N. M., Faucheux, S., Gallopin, G. C., Grübler, A., Huntley, B., Jäger, J., Jodha, N. S., Kasperson, R. E., Mabogunje, A., Matson, P., Mooney, H., Moore III, B., O'Riordan, T. and Svedin, U. 2001. "Sustainability Science". *Science* 292: 641–42.

Kemp, R., Loorbach, D. and Rotmans, J. 2007. "Transition Management as a Model for Managing Processes of Co-evolution Towards Sustainable Development". *International Journal of Sustainable Development and World Ecology* 14: 78–91.

Kingdon, J. W. 1984. *Agendas, Alternatives, and Public Policies,* Boston, MA: Little, Brown.

Kok, K., Patel, M., Rothman, D. S. and Quaranta, G. 2006a. "Multi-scale Narratives from an IA Perspective: Part II. Participatory Local Scenario Development". *Futures* 38: 285–311.

Kok, K., Rothman, D. S. and Patel, M. 2006b. "Multi-scale Narratives from an IA Perspective: Part I. European and Mediterranean Scenario Development". *Futures* 38: 261–84.

Lee, K. N. 1993. *Compass and Gyroscope: Integrating Science into Democracy,* Washington, DC: Island Press.

Leney, T., Coles, M., Grollman, P. and Vilu, R. 2004. *Scenarios Toolkit.* Office for Official Publications of the European Communities.

Mayring, P. 2000. "Qualitative Content Analysis". *Forum Qualitative Sozialforschung/ Forum: Qualitative Social Research* 1(2) 2000: Qualitative Methods in Various Disciplines I: Psychology.

Mayring, P. 2008. *Qualitative Inhaltsanalyse: Grundlagen und Techniken.* Weinheim: Beltz.

Mcknie, E. C. 2007. "Reconciling the Supply of Scientific Information with User Demands: An Analysis of the Problem and Review of the Literature". *Environmental Science and Policy* 10: 17–38.

Meadows, D. H., Meadows, D. L., Randers, J. and Behrens, W. W. 1972. *The Limits to Growth.* New York.

Mitchell, R. B., Clark, W. C. and Cash, D. W. 2006a. "Information and Influence". In: Mitchell, R. B., Clark, W. C., Cash, D. W. and Dickson, N. M. (eds) *Global Environmental Assessments: Information and Influence*. Cambridge, MA, USA: MIT Press.

Mitchell, R. B., Clark, W. C. Cash, D. W. and Dickson, N. M. 2006b. *Global Environmental Assessments: Information and Influence*. Cambridge, MA, USA: MIT Press.

Mostert, E. 2006. "Participation for Sustainable Water Management". In Guipponi, C., Jakeman, A., Karssenberg, D. and Hare, M. (eds) *Sustainable Management of Water Resources: An Integrated Approach*. Cheltenham, UK: Edward Elgar.

Nakicenovic, N., Alcamo, J., Davis, G., De Vries, B., Fenhann, J., Gaffin, S., Gregory, K., Grubler, A., Jung, T. Y., Kram, T., La Rovere, E. L., Michaelis, L., Mori, S., Morita, T., Pepper, W., Pitcher, H. M., Price, L., Riahi, K., Roehrl, A., Rogner, H.-H., Sankovski, A., Schlesinger, M., Shukla, P., Smith, S. J., Swart, R., Van Rooijen, S., Victor, N. and Dadi, Z. 2000. *Special Report on Emissions Scenarios: a special report of Working Group III of the Intergovernmental Panel on Climate Change*. New York, NY (US): Cambridge University Press.

NRC 1999. *Our Common Journey: a Transition toward Sustainability*. A Report of the Board on Sustainable Development of the National Research Council. Washington, DC: National Academy Press.

NRC 2007. *Analysis of Global Change Assessments: Lessons Learned*, Washington, DC: National Academies Press.

Pahl-Wostl, C. 2008. "Participation in Building Environmental Scenarios". In Alcamo, J. (ed.) *Environmental Futures: The Practice of Environmental Scenario Analysis*. Amsterdam, The Netherlands: Elsevier.

Peterson, G. D., Cumming, G. S. and Carpenter, S. R. 2003. "Scenario Planning: A Tool for Conservation in an Uncertain World". *Conservation Biology* 17: 358–66.

Quist, J. and Vergragt, P. 2006. "Past and Future of Backcasting: The Shift to Stakeholder Participation and a Proposal for a Methodological Framework". *Futures* 38: 1027–45.

Raskin, P., Banuri, T., Gallopin, G. C., Gutman, P., Hammond, A., Kates, R. W. and Swart, R. J. 2002. *Great Transition: The Promise and Lure of the Times Ahead*, Boston, MA: Stockholm Environmental Institute.

Ringland, G. 1998. *Scenario Planning: Managing for the Future*. Chichester: Wiley.

Ringland, G. 2002. *Scenarios in Public Policy*. Chichester: Wiley.

Robinson, J. 2003. "Future Subjunctive: Backcasting as Social Learning". *Futures* 35: 839–56.

Rotmans, J., Kemp, R. and Van Asselt, M. 2001. "More Evolution than Revolution". *Transition Management in Public Policy. Foresight*, 3: 15–31.

Rucht, D. 1994. *Modernisierung und neue soziale Bewegungen: Deutschland, Frankreich und USA im Vergleich*. Campus.

Schwartz, P. 1996. *The Art of the Long View*. New York, N Y, USA: Doubleday.

Shoemaker, P. J. H. 1993. "Multiple Scenario Development: Its Conceptual and Behavioral Foundation". *Strategic Management* 14: 193–213.

Shoemaker, P. J. H. 1995. "Scenario Planning: A Tool for Strategic Thinking". *Sloan Management Review*: 25–40.

Shoemaker, P. J. H. and Van der Heijden, K. A. J. M. 1992. "Integrating Scenarios into Strategic Planning at Royal Dutch/Shell". *Planning Review*. 20: 41–6.

Simon, H. A. 1982. *Models of Bounded Rationality*, Cambridge, MA: MIT Press.

Simon, H. A. 1983. *Reason in Human Affairs*. Stanford: Stanford University Press.

Sondeijker, S., Geurts, J., Rotmans, J. and Tukker, A. 2006. "Imagining Sustainability: The Added Value of Transition Scenarios in Transition Management". *Foresight* 8: 15–30.

Swart, R. J., Raskin, P. and Robinson, J. 2004. "The Problem of the Future: Sustainability Science and Scenario Analysis". *Global Environmental Change* 14: 137–46.

UNEP 2002. *Global Environmental Outlook-3: Past, Present and Future Perspectives*. London: Earthscan.

Van der Heijden, K. 1996. *Scenarios: The Art of Strategic Conversation*. Chichester: John Wiley and Sons.

Van Notten, P. 2005. *Writing on the Wall: Scenario Development in Times of Discontinuity*. Maastricht: Universiteit Maastricht.

Van Notten, P. W. F., Rotmans, J., Van Asselt, M. B. A. and Rothman, D. S. 2003. "An Updated Scenario Typology". *Futures* 35: 423–43.

Volkery, A., Ribeiro, T., Henrichs, T. and Hoogeveen, Y. 2008. "Your Vision or My Model? Lessons from Participatory Land Use Scenario Development on a European Scale". *Systemic Practice and Action Research* 21: 459–77.

Von Reibnitz, U. 1987. *Szenarien: Optionen für die Zukunft*, Hamburg: McGraw-Hill.

Vygotsky, L. S. 1986. *Thought and Language*. Cambridge, MA: MIT Press.

Wack, P. 1985a. "Scenarios: Shooting the Rapids". *Harvard Business Review* 63: 139–50.

Wack, P. 1985b. "Scenarios: Uncharted Waters Ahead". *Harvard Business Review* 63: 73–89.

Walz, A., Lardelli, C., Behrendt, H., Gret-Regamey, A., Lundstrom, C., Kytzia, S. and Bebi, P. 2007. "Participatory Scenario Analysis for Integrated Regional Modelling". *Landscape and Urban Planning* 81: 114–31.

Wiek, A., Binder, C. and Scholz, R. W. 2006. "Functions of Scenarios in Transition Processes". *Futures* 38: 740–66.

Wollenberg, E., Edmunds, D. and Buck, L. 2000. "Using Scenarios to make Decisions about the Future: Anticipatory Learning for the Adaptive Co-management of Community Forests". *Landscape and Urban Planning* 47: 65–77.

Xiang, W. N. and Clarke, K. C. 2003. "The Use of Scenarios in Land-use Planning". *Environment and Planning B: Planning and Design* 30: 885–909.

Part IV
Knowledge and learning

12 Coping with creeping catastrophes

National political systems and the challenge of slow-moving policy problems

Volker Schneider, Philip Leifeld and Thomas Malang

Introduction

Catastrophes are usually associated with phenomena like tsunamis, earthquakes or asteroid impacts – disasters that happen rapidly with immediately visible impacts. A different logic is involved when problems and challenges evolve incrementally, in slow-motion, and when they only become visible over long periods (Pierson 2004). Jared Diamond referred to such changes as "creeping normalcy" (Diamond 2005). Changes are perceived as normality if they happen in unnoticed increments. This concept was used to explain the varying adaptation capacities of human societies to long-term environmental changes.

A powerful metaphor illustrating the inherent dangers of such processes is the boiling-frog allegory. Al Gore used it in his movie "An Inconvenient Truth". If a frog is thrown into a pan of boiling water, it will immediately jump out, but if you put a frog in a jar of warm water and gradually heat it to boiling, the frog will stay until it boils to death. The frog's nervous system is apparently impervious to changes in temperature until their fatal consequence because it happens piecemeal-incrementally. Anthony Giddens was quick to baptize this temporal dilemma as the "Gidden's Paradox", stating that, "since the dangers posed by global warming aren't tangible, immediate or visible in the course of day-to-day-life, however awesome they appear, many will sit on their hands and do nothing of a concrete nature about them. Yet waiting until they become visible and acute before stirred to serious action will, by definition, be too late" (Giddens 2009: 2).

In the evolution of human societies, there are a number of processes that exhibit this pattern of "creepiness". The climate change is the most broadly discussed social and political problem of this kind. Other examples of creeping catastrophes are increasing social stress produced by aging societies, the slow accumulation of toxic chemicals in the environment and food chain, or global pandemics like SARS and AIDS combined with increasing antibiotics resistance. All these processes have in common that they evolve bit by bit, are cumulative, and possibly result in disastrous long-term consequences.

In this chapter, we are not interested in the material side of this process pattern, but rather in its political and social consequences. We try to determine if and how societies and their political systems differ in the capacity to detect such creeping problems early. We suppose that these differences are related to variations in their "nervous systems of governance", which control perception and adaptive behavior (Ashby 1956; Deutsch 1963). We are interested in how these social cybernetics are generated by internal differentiation and integration of societal mechanisms and how these "neural networks" perceive, communicate, and act. A key question is: Do democratic political systems, where political power is dispersed and shared among many, perform better regarding the perception of creeping challenges, or do we find examples of effective "eco-dictatorships"? Do decentralization and multilevel differentiation show adaptive advantages, as it is not only claimed by recent management tracts (Brafman and Beckstrom 2006), but also by collective action scholars such as Ostrom (2010)?

Based on a comparison of national policies related to global warming, the chapter will discuss and then develop some hypotheses detailing how, why, and under which conditions differently structured policy systems show varying performance. We will first outline an analytical framework of how political systems deal with this kind of long-term risk, and what adaptive advantages and disadvantages differently structured systems have. In the subsequent section, we will test some of these hypotheses related to the climate change topic empirically in a macro-quantitative model. We argue that internal structures and external factors both contribute to the varying pace and degree of governmental reaction. We will conclude with a list of weaknesses and limits these macro-quantitative models exhibit and propose some complementary research strategies.

Societal development and adaptation

The issue of political adaptation to environmental changes is a rediscovery within the last decade. During the 1960s, it was an important concept within the developmental theory of political systems (Almond 1965; Parsons 1964). In the last decade, it reentered the discussion with respect to the adaption of political systems to significant economic and political transformations (Grote *et al.* 2008), and it became a particularly powerful concept with respect to the impact ecological transformations have on political systems (Folke *et al.* 2005).

Traditional social theory strongly focused on the construction and maintenance of order. The question of how societies successfully overcome structural and behavioral changes in order to cope with critical problems was only raised in a few "grand theories". One of these theories is Marxism, which holds the optimistic belief of a teleological sequence of changes in economic systems and forces of production. These are ultimately driven by social conflict, where the whole process leads to an increasingly powerful mastery of nature and society. The other approach with a similar teleological content is systems theory. It emphasizes general adaptive capacities and openness of social and political systems, the latter of which are based on increasing structural and functional differentiation (Almond 1965; Deutsch 1963; Parsons 1964).

A serious problem with traditional systems theory is that systems and systemic processes, for the most part, remain "black boxes" in which actors, relations and mechanisms are opaque (Bunge 1996). In this respect, we use basic ideas of governance theory to identify varieties of actors with different functions and institutional structures enabling communication, integration and long-term adaptation (for an overview see Schneider and Bauer 2007).

A fundamental problem from this point of view is to understand under which conditions societies attain complete adaptive failures, i.e. "collapse". Historical analysis has demonstrated that there are many reasons for the collapse of past societies. External factors threatening the existence of a society are, for example: climate change, hostile neighbors, depletion of vital resources, natural catastrophes and a variety of economic factors (Diamond 2005; Tainter 1988). In addition to these environmental challenges, internal societal tensions such as class conflict and elite misbehavior may also lead to collapse. Since we are not interested in all reasons for failure but rather in socio-political ones, we concentrate on typical social processes that are related to *societies' perception and responses to critical problems.*

Complex societies develop differentiated political and cultural rule systems to cope with critical threats and problems. Why can a society fail in this respect? When we think of which essential parts of the problem-solving process can go wrong, we can separate the factors in a sequence of four phases (Diamond 2005). Some of these phases are well known in the "policy cycle" literature of political science (May and Wildavsky 1979).

First, a society can *anticipate* a problem. But anticipation can fail for several reasons: a society may have no prior experience of a given problem and cannot imagine the possibility of its occurrence. Another cause is reasoning by false analogy (Diamond 2005). While analogy is a well-known technique for solving ill-structured problems (Simon 1973), such constructions may be false and consequently suggest inappropriate strategies.

At the second stage, a society has to *perceive* a problem when it occurs. Once having anticipated a phenomenon, perception can still fail because the anticipated phenomenon is not recognized as a problem, or the dimensions of the problem are not fully understood. There are several reasons for a failure of perception. (1) The material origins of a problem can be imperceptible; (2) cultural and political factors can be responsible for an objective problem not being perceived subjectively as such; (3) a failure to perceive a problem may be implied in its temporal pattern: if it grows incrementally, bit by bit, and if these changes are concealed by continual fluctuations, even if there is an exponential growth during the first stages, societies may conceive this as "normalcy".

The third step is the *actual solving* process through collective action. Many societies fail at this stage, often due to conflicts of interest based on distributive effects of problem-solving, due to incompatible problem-solving philosophies, or due to coordination problems. Other possible reasons are described in models on social traps and dilemmas like the prisoners' dilemma or the logic of collective action. Finally, failure can also emerge from irrational behavior based on non-adaptive norms and values (Diamond 2005).

Even if a society has anticipated, perceived, and communicated the problem and controls the relevant resources, failure is still possible because the problem can be *beyond the solving capacities*. It could simply be too expensive to solve, efforts could be "too little, too late", or the solution could "disimprove" the situation.

Modern societies are differentiated and many heterogeneous agents and rule systems contribute to the problem solving process. Following the "Nerves of Government" analogy introduced by Deutsch, the various parts of a society are integrated in a central nervous system, communicating observations and perceptions between the components and controlling its collective behavior, which should contribute to problem-solving and adaptation (Deutsch 1963). But to avoid the functionalist blind alley of thinking of society as a super organism with a centralized brain, a more suitable concept is the "policy network" as outlined by Kenis and Schneider (1991: 24): "The core of this perspective is a decentralized concept of social organization and governance: society is no longer exclusively controlled by a central intelligence (e.g. the State); rather, controlling devices are dispersed and intelligence is distributed among a multiplicity of action (or "processing") units. The coordination of these action units is no longer the result of "central steering" [...] but emerges through the purposeful interactions of individual actors, who themselves are enabled for parallel action by exchanging information and other relevant resources" (for an overview see Lang and Leifeld 2007; Schneider *et al.* 2009).

Capacities of problem-solving: hypotheses and conjectures

Which roles and functions do the various societal agents – government, science, the media, and NGOs – have in the above-mentioned stages of problem-solving? Is it possible to relate the varying capacities to cope with creeping problems to their structural features (e.g. relational patterns and resource distributions)? In the following section, we apply the policy network perspective and derive some hypotheses associated to varying capacities of national political systems when coping with this specific type of policy problems.

Anticipation

There are only two ways of anticipating a problem which has not yet become manifest. The first is to rely on introspection or a kind of supra-natural "revelation knowledge". The other is predictive knowledge based on empirical evidence. Problems can frequently be anticipated through scientific forecasts, and science then works as an early warning system. In this instance, science as a cultural subsystem of society is considered to be a crucial part of the perceptual apparatus.

However, as we will argue, scientific anticipation alone is not a decisive factor for an effective start to a society's problem-solving process: it must be considered in conjunction with the importance a given society attributes to scientific knowledge. Even if we assume that science is able to predict the slowly emerging problem correctly, the early anticipation of a problem will fail to become socially relevant if a society does not consider science to be an authoritative and credible tool for at least approximately true "knowledge-making".

We can therefore conjecture that reputation and status of the national science systems depend on how advanced they are in scientific terms. Moreover, the higher the reputation and status of a national science system, the more likely it then is that problems get correctly anticipated because decision makers are more likely to hear their voice. The issue, however, is how to measure these differences in a macro-comparative perspective. While the measurement of reputation is difficult in all respects, two straight measures would be the share of researchers in a country and expenditures for research and development.

Perception

Perception is the core around which cybernetic metaphors such as nerves and neurons gravitate. Two crucial aspects are considered: First, we analyze conditions for the *scientific* perception of a given problem. Second, we emphasize *societal* perception of facts and analyze mechanisms through which they become socially relevant. The first one is primarily a scientific task whereas the second refers to how sensitively mass media, social movements and interest groups function as societal "neurotransmitters" that link a change in environmental conditions to a credible threat. Aside from the above-mentioned channels of interest intermediation transforming scientific findings into generalized knowledge, science may also be directly drawn into policy networks: science may be an influential agent by producing and communicating relevant knowledge (Leifeld and Schneider 2012). If the network operates effectively, relevant information may diffuse faster among political actors, and the politicization of a given problem should be easier than in tightly controlled autocratic or hierarchical systems. Assuming that this network argument is true, we expect a government to be more sensitive to climate change problems when there are more possibilities of getting access to the political agenda via decentralized policy networks.

This argument is also valid at the global level. In the contemporary "global society", science is part of the world polity in which information exchange cannot be restricted to national boundaries (Drori *et al.* 2003; Fisher 2003). Problem perception in one national science system quickly diffuses to other regions and countries, and this diffusion is particularly strong if countries are members of intergovernmental organizations such as the OECD, European Union, or specialized organizations such as the IPCC. These organizations not only facilitate but also sponsor exchange and cooperation in scientific knowledge-making and diffusion (Beck 2010; Haas 2005).

Various studies have shown that countries vary greatly in the way their scientists perceive the problem of climate change (Bray and Krück 2001; Grundmann 2007). However, these differences do not fully capture the national variations in perception. The latter has to be related to socio-political communication by intermediaries like social movements, interest groups, political parties and mass media, but also to the general cultural background in which a given problem such as climate change emerges (Verweij *et al.* 2006). Social movements are not just "problem communicators", they also help to frame and crystallize issues, making them socially relevant (Moser 2007). In the case of global warming, green NGOs are of particular importance (Carpenter 2001; Fisher 2003; Keohane 2002). Since major impacts of climate change will not occur in the near future, the topic is less tangible to the public and various stakeholders. Green NGOs therefore have to work for a sustained problem perception. Compared to single issue campaigning generally associated with the approaches of NGOs to environmental and public risks, climate change "ushers in a new era of engagement" (Gough and Shackley 2001).

It is not surprising that green social movements are closely linked with green parties. Since environmental problems and, in particular, global warming imply long-lasting and high-risk problems, the emergence of green parties from social movements can be understood as a consolidation of this issue area. In line with our neural model, we assume that the more numerous and politically integrated social movements and green parties are in a given society, the better and more stable the societal perception of global warming will be.

Another risk transmitter is the media. It has a crucial function as a source of information and opinion about scientific findings for citizens (Carvalho 2007; Weingart *et al.* 2000). Public perception of this domain is significantly influenced by the representation of scientific knowledge transmitted through various means of mass communication (Corbett and Durfee 2004; Krosnick *et al.* 2000). In this respect mass media are also important for the understanding of perceived risks, and it is obvious that only individuals who understand the complex relation between causes and effects are willing to take action to impede the risk (Stamm *et al.* 2000).

The ways in which people think about environmental problems are not necessarily accurate or complete. Nevertheless, these cognitive processes are likely to influence both the willingness and ability of societal agents to participate in problem-solving. We consequently assume that uncensored media coverage has two effects on problem perception: It transforms scientific perception of a problem into a general societal perception, and it also contributes to the understanding of the nature of the problem and thereby motivates collective action. The relation between these factors can be expressed in the following hypothesis: The better the understanding of the issue of global warming, the more likely it is that a society will take action to prevent the problem, and without a free press, the step from scientific perception to social perception is less likely to be realized. Therefore we believe that the greater the freedom of press in a society is, the more likely the societal perception of a creeping problem will be.

Agenda setting

The intermediate step between societal perception and a policy solution is the shift from the social to the political realm in problem-processing. A first stage in this process is the transformation of the issue to a topic on the priority list of a political system. Communication science and policy research call this process "agenda-setting" (Kingdon 2003). A jump on the political agenda may be triggered through communication by non-governmental actors and mass media. But agenda-setting may also originate from the inside of politics – the bureaucratic or parliamentary arena. Another powerful trigger is the environment of a political system, as it is emphasized in the literature on policy transfer, diffusion, and convergence (Holzinger and Knill 2005).

There are several dimensions where political systems can differ with respect to the openness and permeability of their policy-agendas. One important factor is the access of social movements and NGOs to participation in policy networks. Political systems vary widely in terms of the degree to which they integrate new and rather weak interests (Kriesi 1995). In this respect, it seems reasonable to assume that inclusion-prone or consensus-oriented political systems incorporating all actors concerned in policy processes are likely to perform better with the political perception of societal problems (Dryzek 2009; Jost and Jacob 2004; Scruggs 2003). While this "openness" is difficult to measure in a quantitative perspective, a proxy measure could be Lijphart's index on consensus democracy (Lijphart 1999).

Problem-solving

Once a problem is on the political agenda, the struggle for a policy solution is often a process which is driven by conflicting interests and the quest for power. Accordingly, it seems to be appropriate to take the institutional structures of governmental systems (in the narrow sense) into account. A classical political question is if the dispersion and sharing of political power enhances or reduces the capacity for collective action (Norris 2008). In the political science literature, there are two contrasting hypotheses: (1) Tsebelis' veto player model states that an increasing number of veto players in a political system reduces its capacity to change the status quo by collective action (Tsebelis 2002). (2) Lijphart's studies on democratic systems point to performance advantages of decentralized political systems where power is shared among many actors and different levels (Lijphart 1999; Wälti 2004). Power dispersion sums up the arrangement of executive power, party systems and electoral regimes, interest group structures, but also the vertical division of power in federal systems. From this perspective, there are two major streams of argumentation: on the one hand, it is conceivable that "majoritarian systems" with only one real center of power are able to produce policy solutions faster and more radical than consensus models. On the other hand, governments in more consensus-oriented democracies, which have to look at several different actor positions when designing a policy in a deliberative way, could be affiliated with more encompassing, mature and long-term policy solutions. In such arrangements, electoral cycles and pressures have less impact than in majoritarian democracies, which are more short-term oriented. For instance, a minority party like the Greens in Germany can be considered more influential in consensus systems because they, at the very least, must be integrated in policy making, whereas in majority systems environmental problems could be ignored.

The case of climate change: applying macro-quantitative analysis

The previous sections sketched a theoretical framework for system analysis. We argued that different political and social systems structures contribute to both the varying pace and degree of governmental reaction in coping with long-term risks. To illustrate our point, we will now discuss the case of climate change and show some analytical results. After presenting our findings and discussing weaknesses of this approach, we conclude with a proposal for complementary research strategies.

The issue of anthropogenic global warming was first hypothesized by the Swedish physicist and chemist Svante Arrhenius about 100 years ago. But only during the last two or three decades, climate change has been perceived as a pressing global risk to be tackled both at the national and the global level of world society. However, various countries react rather differently to this common challenge. We will try to test whether this variation is caused by political characteristics of these countries.

Hypotheses and operationalizations

Successful coping – our explanandum – is measured by two dependent variables: The first is the duration between the agreement on the Kyoto protocol, initially adopted on 11 December 1997, and the date of ratification, acceptance, accession or approval of the protocol by countries measured in days. The second is the countries' ratification time span of the "Montreal Protocol on Substances That Deplete the Ozone Layer" which was opened for signature on 16 September 1987. These time spans show which countries are early adopters and which countries are laggards.

Our assumption is that governments are willing and able to control the level of CO_2 emissions only if they assign a high priority to this risk. Following our theoretical framework, we identify four different ways in which the national level of risk awareness is affected. These four hypothesized connections and their respective operationalizations are outlined in the following.

The first dimension which should have an influence on the urgency national governments assign to the climate change question is the *level of risk-exposure* of each country. Risk exposure can be measured by dividing the length of the coast lines of a country by the country's area. Countries with a high coast/area ratio are often directly threatened by extreme weather conditions and especially by rising sea levels.

The second aspect captures the effect of research and education on the national capacity of *problem anticipation*. On a very basic level, our indicators of Research

& Development (R&D) expenditures and the number of researchers working in the R&D sector simply measure the quantitative importance of the scientific sector in a country, e.g., how much money and manpower is put into research. This leads to the hypothesis that the bigger the R&D share in a country, the higher the possibility that a creeping problem is anticipated. However, since science and research is very much a *globalized* undertaking, the crucial role of national researchers is in fact the transformation of scientific inference into public knowledge: it is not about which national scientific system has first discovered that there is a phenomenon like climate change and which problems this could spur for mankind. It is rather the question which national scientific system is credible in forecasting global development. Hence, R&D expenditures and the number of researchers also capture the qualitative credibility a society attributes to science in delivering expertise, and the institutionalized position science has in a national political system. We assume that the higher the shares of these indicators, the more scientific inference is considered as a basis for societal and political action, hence the faster a country will anticipate the dangers of global warming.

The possibility of obtaining and publishing diverse information and opinion is the third aspect which is hypothesized to make governments consider global warming as a pressing problem. The possibility of communicating societal problems is a necessary condition for public discourse, which we assume to increase the chances of perceiving climate change as a threat. We operationalize this by the number of newspapers in a country, the percentage of internet users and the Freedom House Index, which measures the political rights in a country, such as freedom of speech and freedom of assembly.

Our last dimension departs from the discourse argument but additionally considers the possibilities of *organized collective action* in a country. It is hypothesized that the better the legal and factual possibilities for organizing political claims, the more likely the emergence of organized interests concerning the mitigation of climate change. We use readily available measures of good governance (Kaufmann *et al.* 1999), electoral participation (Vanhanen 2000), and the Polity III Index as indicators of the nation states' capacity to serve as the arena of extensive public discourse and the possibility of public claims to be transformed into political programs. We expect democratic countries to actively engage in climate protection policy while authoritarian countries rather shy away from becoming very active.

Analysis and results

Why are countries early adopters or laggards? The pace of government activity can be assessed by looking at the Kyoto Protocol and Montreal Protocol survival data. More specifically, we analyze the ratification dates as a function of our indicators presented above. Survival analysis, which is also known as event history analysis, is an econometric method which allows the analysis of durations as a function of time by fitting parametric distributions (e.g., the exponential or the Weibull distribution), or as a function of covariates (such as risk exposure). In the case of the Kyoto Protocol, there is obviously no distribution that could reasonably well be fitted to the ratification durations because the hazard rate is bimodal. A survival model which is capable of estimating the effect of country-level variables on the time to ratification is the Cox Proportional Hazard Model. The assumption of this model, however, is that the hazard ratios are constant, i.e., the survival curves in Figures 12.1 and 12.2 should not cross each other. As this is clearly not the case, the proportional hazard assumption is violated. In such a case, Tableman and Kim (2004: 136) propose to use a non-parametric survival model. Moreover, the data is right-censored because not all countries have ratified the protocol. We therefore use the non-parametric Kaplan-Meier approach for each covariate separately and report the survival curves in Figures 12.1 and 12.2 (see Efron 1988 for further references to survival analysis).

What factors – beside diffusion – are responsible for early versus late adoption? We include several of the above-mentioned covariates (Table 12.1) in our model and estimate their effect one by one. The black survival rate represents the value 0 of a dummy variable, while the gray line is the value 1 of the same dichotomous variable. If an explanatory variable is continuous, we dichotomize the values at the median value.

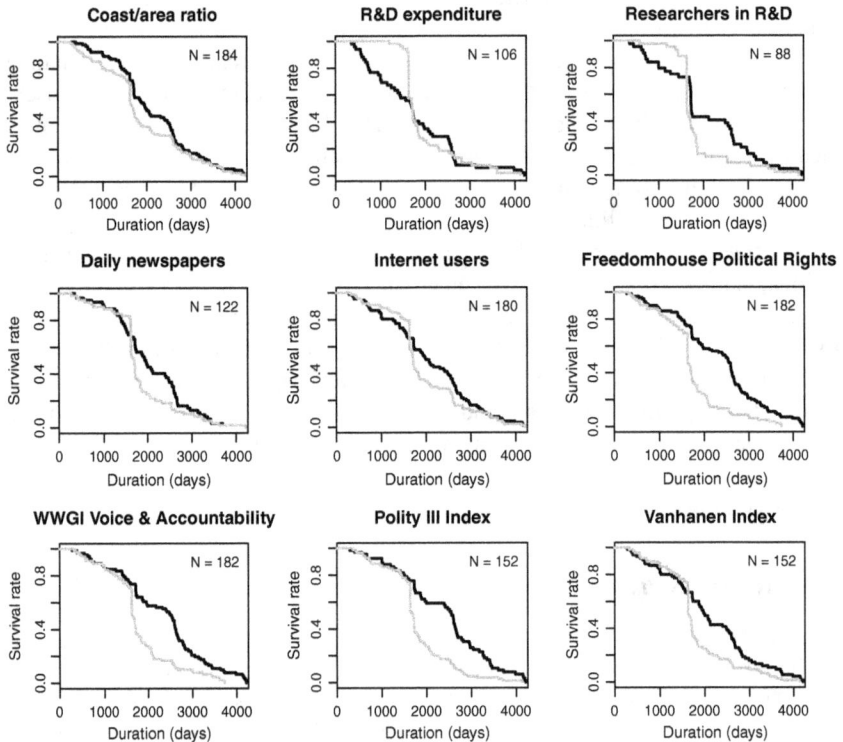

Figure 12.1 The ratification of the Kyoto Protocol.
Source: compiled by authors.

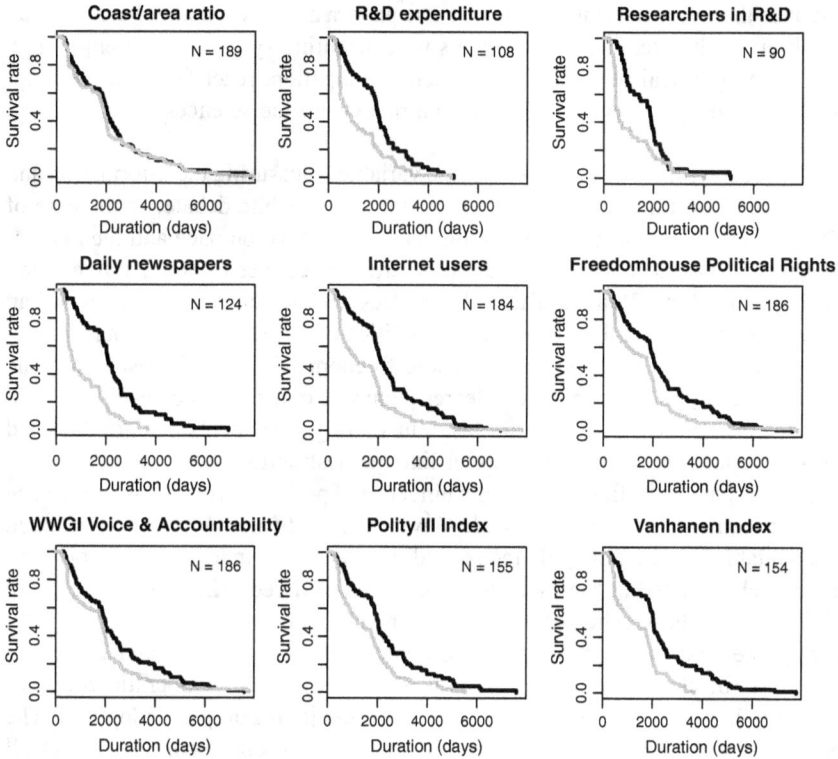

Figure 12.2 The ratification of the Montreal Protocol.
Source: Compiled by authors.

In the first plot, the level of risk-exposure is analyzed. The cost/area ratio is dichotomized at the median value of the distribution in order to partition countries into a group of strongly exposed (value 1) and less exposed countries (value 0). There is a clear difference in the survival rates of the two groups: After the first few ratifications of the Kyoto protocol, exposed countries ratify the protocols faster than less exposed countries. However, in this respect the Montreal data show a much the weaker effect on the pace of ratification. The gray and the black line are almost identical, but more risk-exposed countries are still consistently faster at reacting.

Social and political explanatory factors are more interesting in the context of our theory. In the following graphs, we test the effect of the scientific system on ratification speed. In the case of the Montreal Protocol, it is evident that nations with higher R&D expenditures and more research staff are faster in adopting the protocol at any time. For the Kyoto Protocol, we find the same pattern as for the risk exposure analysis. Since almost all countries of the EU exhibit high values on the two measurement items, up to the date of the collective European ratification, countries with lower importance of the scientific system adopt the protocol faster, but once the European states sign, the same pattern as in the Montreal analysis can be observed. Hence, countries with a strong scientific system, which enjoy high public and political reputation in problem anticipation, react faster to the long-term threat of global warming than countries where the sciences have a weaker position.

The second line of our plots shows the variables measuring the information and communication infrastructures necessary for a free public debate. In the case of Kyoto, there is obviously a correlation between ratification pace and the number of newspapers in a country, the share of internet access per 1,000 inhabitants, and the Freedom House Political Rights Index. Besides the delay due to the European coordination, nations that have the possibilities of a free public discourse adopt the protocols faster than countries where freedom of speech is restricted. The Montreal analysis draws an even clearer picture: Countries which enable a vivid and diverse political discourse are faster in signing agreements that are designed to correct dangerous societal behavior like the destruction of the ozone layer.

The last part of the figure shows the influence of political institutions on the pace of treaty ratification. The Worldwide Governance Indicator (WWGI) "Voice and Accountability", the Polity III index, and the Vanhanen index of democracy, all again dichotomized at the median value, are considered. These indices capture different aspects of whether a country is democratic or autocratic. For Kyoto, during the first third of the process, democratic (grey curve) and autocratic countries (black curve) perform identically, but then the democratic countries appear to have reached a certain critical mass (the joint European adoption). The process is then slowed down again. This pattern is strongly consistent over all democracy measures we have tested. The finding generally suggests that the more stable, participatory and effective a political system is, the more likely it is that the Kyoto protocol is ratified rapidly, particularly after the initial spin-off after about 1,550 days. The Montreal analysis confirms the Kyoto result. Here, democracies are faster in signing the protocol throughout the whole period. Apparently, not only the free communication of political views is of significance for the perception of a long-term problem; it also takes free democratic systems for the transformation of political views into political programs and political action. Our analysis shows that democracies perform better – which means faster in our case – in responding with political claims to newly perceived incremental problems (for this observation, see also Bättig and Bernauer 2009). The possibility of political mobilization supports for the translation of perceived societal problems into political outputs.

The analysis has provided some clues of how political systems cope with long-term risks. Important factors promoting governmental activity seem to be a high extent of the problem for the country at risk, an important role of the scientific system for the credible anticipation of the problem, free and diverse channels of information distribution and communication for perceiving the problem and debating in the public, as well as a democratic and open political system that allows collective action on emerging societal problems. Note, however, that these findings are merely correlations, and we do not know how far each effect is persistent if all other proposed variables are held constant.

Limits and drawbacks

A general problem in this analysis, however, is that the independent variables not only explain the dependent variables, but also explain each other (i.e. *multicollinearity*). In this respect it is difficult to differentiate between democracy and economy. Supporting the famous Lipset hypothesis (Lipset 1959), recent studies have shown that democracy and economic development are closely related (Norris 2008; Przeworski 2000). In the cross-sectional analysis above, a separate model was therefore estimated for every indicator, showing that a democratic and economic effect is indeed at work.

A further limitation is associated with the *independence of cases* problem. In inferential statistics, observations are assumed to be independent from each other. Not only in the context of globalization, such *independence* between political systems is highly doubtable. Great powers have the ability to create and enforce international norms. Globalization and Europeanization make this even more problematic, since inter- and supranational organizations can harmonize policies by collective decision mechanisms. In this context, developed countries offer other countries development assistance and expect their compliance in the international arena (e.g., the "adaptation fund" initiated at the Bali summit or the "forest carbon partnership" offered by the German government and the World Bank). Russia's ratification of the Kyoto protocol in November 2004 was tied to the issue of Russian WTO accession as a package deal. Once such incentives are offered to less wealthy and less democratic countries, the variance between countries cannot be reliably explained anymore on the grounds of democratic and economic mechanisms in a simple cross-sectional design. It might be possible to solve this problem of autocorrelation, which is also known as Galton's problem, by identifying and incorporating the underlying mechanisms of diffusion (Jahn 2006).

Another type of problem is related to the operationalization of some variables: even when we are able to measure outputs or reaction speed as a form of "policy commitment", the varying effectiveness of policy instruments (e.g., emission trading) is not taken into account. As for the independent variables, we cannot ascertain whether GDP per capita, for instance, has an effect on voters' values, i.e., post-materialism, and on the possibility of asserting these values in a participatory political system (since democracy and wealth are correlated), or whether it is just a proxy for development, i.e., fewer competing societal risks promote a higher priority of climate change in governmental policy making. This leads to the multicollinearity issue again, which in the last instance is a theoretical rather than a methodological problem.

A final difficulty is that countries are exposed to a variety of simultaneous challenges. Some of these have a global scope like environmental issues, and some do not or hardly exceed state boundaries, e.g., civil wars, economic decline, or demographic change. The role of these *competing risks* in causing governments to act has largely been neglected. Governments face trade-offs when anticipating and fighting risks, i.e., they will only see the most pressing problems and neglect

234 Volker Schneider et al.

others (Jones and Baumgartner 2005). If a government has to suppress upcoming ethnic tensions, for instance, it will assign a very low priority to climate change, given the time, staff and budget constraint. Climate change is only one of these risks. If one tries to infer more abstract mechanisms from this single case, one might face an extreme small-n problem. In other words, we cannot be sure that our theory and our findings equally apply to other creeping catastrophes.

Conclusions

Better data and more advanced methods undoubtedly lead to advancements in the social sciences to explain why some institutional structures produce better results or why some policy instruments have a better effect. Macro-quantitative analysis in our context supposes that we are able to find "quasi laws" in societies of the kind "an increment of x in democracy leads to an decrement of y in reaction time". The problem is, first, that this macro-relationship is intermediated by so many additional variables inside the black box of national political systems. From a pure macro perspective, one can only guess some internal mechanisms, such as: wealthy voters have post-materialist attitudes and promote green policy, or wealthy countries usually have fewer competing societal risks and can prioritize less urgent matters like climate change, etc. The second problem is that countries at the same democracy level might have quite different party systems, interest group structures, and various ways of integrating science and social movements in policy formulation. With respect to the assumption that countries are homogeneous, there might actually be big differences between policy sectors. This was emphasized already in the debate on meso-corporatism in the late 1980s. A recent study shows that findings in one sector can be very different from findings in another sector (Grote et al. 2008).

In this respect it might be hasty to transfer macro-quantitative findings on general environmental policy to the climate change policy domain (cf. Dryzek 2009), since the issue at stake, actor constellations and communication structures between major components of the political system are quite diverse. For this reason, we argue that qualitative or quantitative country case studies can provide more accurate insights into domestic processes and lead to a better qualitative foundation of the mechanisms. Macro-quantitative studies should be triangulated with meso-level studies using "nested analysis" (Lieberman 2005): after conducting a preliminary large-n analysis, one should go down to the level of "on- and off-the-line" individual cases, refine the model, develop implications and then test them again on the macro level in a large-n analysis.

Such case studies may concentrate on some of the following aspects, which cannot be included in a pure macro-comparative analysis. (1) What role does policy coordination between the countries play from the perspective of national states? (2) What is the role of specific institutions like the parliament, the executive government, direct participation of the electorate, or the integration of scientific consulting, social movements, interest groups and the media in agenda-setting and policy-making? (3) How does the public discourse about risk evolve,

Table 12.1 Description of Data and Sources (URLs accessed in May 2010)

Variable	Description	Unit and value range	Source
Dependent variables			
Montreal Protocol ratification dates		days; from 16 September 1987 to 01 May 2010	http://ozone.unep.org/Ratification_status/
Kyoto Protocol ratification dates		days; from 11 December 1997 to 01 May 2010	http://unfccc.int/kyoto_protocol/status_of_ratification/items/2613.php
Independent variables			
Coast/area ratio	Total length of the boundary between the land area (including islands) and the sea in km, divided by the sum of all land and water areas delimited by international boundaries and/or coastlines in square km	0.00 to +8.71	https://www.cia.gov/library/publications/the-world-factbook/fields/2060.html https://www.cia.gov/library/publications/the-world-factbook/fields/2147.html
R&D expenditure	World Development Indicators : R&D expenditure (% GDP)	+0.02 to +4.00	http://data.worldbank.org/data-catalog
Researchers in R&D	World Development Indicators : number of researchers in R&D per million inhabitants	+8.03 to +6892.88	http://data.worldbank.org/data-catalog
Daily newspapers	World Development Indicators : number of daily newspapers per 1,000 people	+0.09 to +563.34	http://data.worldbank.org/data-catalog
Internet users	World Development Indicators : Number of internet users per 100 inhabitants	mean value 1996-2005; 0.00 to 54.53	http://data.worldbank.org/data-catalog
Freedom House Political Rights Index	Freedom House Index of Political Rights and Civil Liberties; sub-index of Political Rights; version of 2007	+1 to +7	http://www.freedomhouse.org/
Polity III Index	Polity III Index; always the latest polity ending in 1994 the Vanhanen Index of Democracy 1997	−88 to +10	http://www.systemicpeace.org/polity/
Vanhanen Index		+0.19 to +42.75	http://www.prio.no/CSCW/Datasets/Governance/Vanhanens-index-of-democracy/
World Wide Governance Indicators: Voice & Accountability	World Bank: World Wide Governance Indicators 2007; voice and accountability in 2006	−2.19 to +1.72	http://info.worldbank.org/governance/wgi/

Source: compiled by authors.

and what organizations have an interest in promoting a given position? Can this be aggregated to a cross-country pattern? (4) What different interest or discourse configurations can we identify in the countries? Policy network analysis might be a valuable tool for the investigation of this question. Do certain configurations or the intensity of cleavage lines affect the policy outcome if compared on a macro scale?

Many of these questions can be answered by analyzing the actor constellations and networks in the formulation and implementation of these policies (Schneider *et al.* 2009). Although this method is increasingly used in policy analysis, its analytical power is still not fully tapped.

References

Almond, G. A. 1965. "A Developmental Approach to Political Systems". *World Politics* 17: 183–214.

Ashby, W. R. 1956. *An Introduction to Cybernetics*. London: Chapman & Hall.

Bättig, M. and Bernauer, T. 2009. "National Institutions and Global Public Goods: Are Democracies More Cooperative in Climate Change Policy?" *International Organization*, 63: 281–308.

Beck, S. 2010. "Klimawandel zwischen Wissenschaft und Politik: Trügerisches Hoffen auf 'Win-Win-Lösungen'". In Schüttemeyer S. (ed.). *Verhandlungen des 24. wissenschaftlichen DVPW-Kongress*, Baden-Baden: Nomos.

Brafman, O. and Beckstrom, R. A. 2006. *The Starfish and the Spider: The Unstoppable Power of Leaderless Organizations*. New York: Portfolio.

Bray, D. and Krück, C. 2001. "Some Patterns of Interaction Between Science and Policy: Germany and Climate Change". *Climate Research*, 19: 69–90.

Bunge, M. 1996. *Finding Philosophy in Social Science*. New Haven: Yale University Press.

Carpenter, C. 2001. "Businesses, Green Groups and the Media: The Role of Non-Governmental Organizations in the Climate Change Debate". *International Affairs*, 77: 313–28.

Carvalho, A. 2007. "Ideological Cultures and Media Discourses on Scientific Knowledge: Re-reading News on Climate Change". *Public Understanding of Science*, 16: 223.

Corbett, J. B. and Durfee, J. L. 2004. "Testing Public (Un)Certainty of Science: Media Representations of Global Warming". *Science Communication*, 26: 129.

Deutsch, K. W. 1963. *Nerves of Government*. New York: Free Press.

Diamond, J. M. 2005. *Collapse: How Societies Choose to Fail or Succeed*. London: Allen Lane.

Drori, G., Meyer, J., Ramirez, F. and Schofer, E. 2003. *Science in the Modern World Polity*. Stanford: Stanford University Press.

Dryzek, J. S. 2009. *Democracy and Earth System Governance*. Paper presented at the Amsterdam Conference on the Human Dimensions of Global Environmental Change "Earth System Governance: People, Places and the Planet", 2–4 December 2009.

Efron, B. 1988. "Logistic Regression, Survival Analysis, and the Kaplan-Meier Curve". *Journal of the American Statistical Association*, 83: 414–25.

Fisher, D. R. 2003. "Global and Domestic Actors within the Global Climate Change Regime: Toward a Theory of the Global Environmental System". *International Journal of Sociology and Social Policy*, 23: 5–30.

Folke, C., Hahn, T., Olsson, P. and Norberg, J. 2005. "Adaptive Governance of Social-ecological Systems". *Annual Review of Environment and Resources*, 30: 441–73.

Giddens, A. 2009. *The Politics of Climate Change*. Cambridge: Polity Press.

Gough, C. and Shackley, S. 2001. "The Respectable Politics of Climate Change: The Epistemic Communities and NGOs". *International Affairs*, 77: 329–46.

Grote, J. R., Lang, A. and Schneider, V. (eds) 2008. *Organized Business Interests in Changing Environments: The Complexity of Adaptation*. New York: Palgrave Macmillan.

Grundmann, R. 2007. "Climate Change and Knowledge Politics". *Environmental Politics*, 16: 414–32.

Haas, P. M. 2005. "International Institutions and Social Learning in the Management of Global Environmental Risks". *Policy Studies Journal*, 28: 558–75.

Holzinger, K. and Knill, C. 2005. "Causes and Conditions of Cross-national Policy Convergence". *Journal of European Public Policy*, 12: 775–96.

Jahn, D. 2006. "Globalization as 'Galton's Problem': The Missing Link in the Analysis of Diffusion Patterns in Welfare State Development". *International Organization*, 60: 401–31.

Jones, B. and Baumgartner, F. 2005. "A Model of Choice for Public Policy". *Journal of Public Administration Research and Theory*, 15: 325.

Jost, G.F. and Jacob, K. 2004. "The Climate Change Policy Network in Germany". *European Environment*, 14: 1–15.

Kaufmann, D., Kraay, A. Zoido-Lobatón, P., World Bank Development Research Group, M. Growth, *et al.* 1999. *Aggregating Governance Indicators*. World Bank, Development Research Group, Macroeconomics and Growth, and World Bank Institute, Governance, Regulation, and Finance.

Kenis, P. and Schneider, V. 1991. "Policy Networks and Policy Analysis: Scrutinizing a New Analytical Toolbox". In Marin, B. and Mayntz, R. (eds) *Policy Networks. Empirical Evidence and Theoretical Considerations*, Frankfurt/Main: Campus, 25–59.

Keohane, R. O. 2002. "Climate for Change: Non-state Actors and the Global Politics of the Greenhouse". *Journal of Politics*, 64: 328–30.

Kingdon, J. W. 2003. *Agendas, Alternatives, and Public Policies*. New York: Longman.

Kriesi, H. 1995. *New Social Movements in Western Europe: A Comparative Analysis*. London: Routledge.

Krosnick, J. A., Holbrook, A. L. and Visser, P. S. 2000. "The Impact of the Fall 1997 Debate about Global Warming on American Public Opinion". *Public Understanding of Science*, 9: 239–60.

Lang, A. and Leifeld, P. 2007. "Die Netzwerkanalyse in der Policy-Forschung: Eine theoretische und methodische Bestandsaufnahme". In Janning, F. Töns, K. (eds) *Die Zukunft der Policy-Forschung, Wiesbaden*: VS-Verlag, 223–41.

Leifeld, P. and Schneider, V. 2012. "Information Exchange in Policy Networks". *American Journal of Political Science*, 53(3): 731–744.

Lieberman, E. S. 2005. "Nested Analysis as a Mixed-Method Strategy for Comparative Research". *American Political Science Review*, 99: 435–52.

Lijphart, A. 1999. *Patterns of Democracy: Government Forms and Performance in Thirty-Six Countries*. Yale: Yale University Press.

Lipset, S. 1959. "Some Social Requisites of Democracy: Economic Development and Political Legitimacy". *American Political Science Review*, 53: 69–105.

May, J. V. and Wildavsky, A. B. 1979. *The Policy Cycle*. London: Sage.

Moser, S. C. 2007. "In the Long Shadows of Inaction: The Quiet Building of a Climate Protection Movement in the United States". *Global Environmental Politics* 7.

Norris, P. 2008. *Driving Democracy: Do Power-sharing Regimes Work?* New York/ Cambridge: Cambridge University Press.

Ostrom, E. 2010. "Polycentric Approach for Coping with Climate Change". Background Paper to the 2010 World Development Report. Policy Research Working Paper 5095. www.iadb.org/intal/intalcdi/PE/2009/04268.pdf.

Parsons, T. 1964. "Evolutionary Universals in Society". *American Sociological Review*, 29: 339–57.

Pierson, P. 2004. *Politics in Time: History, Institutions, and Social Analysis*. Princeton: Princeton University Press.

Przeworski, A. 2000. *Democracy and Development: Political Institutions and Well-being in the World, 1950–1990*. Cambridge, MA: Cambridge University Press.

Schneider, V. and Bauer, J. 2007. "Governance: Prospects of Complexity Theory in Revisiting System Theory". Presented at the annual meeting of the Midwest Political Science Association. Panel 33.26 Political Theory and Theories of Political Science. Chicago, Illinois, 14 April 2007 www.uni-konstanz.de/FuF/Verwiss/Schneider/ePapers/ MPSA2007Paper_vs_jmb.pdf.

Schneider, V., Janning, F., Leifeld, P. and Malang, T. 2009. *Politiknetzwerke. Modelle, Anwendungen und Visualisierungen*. Wiesbaden: VS-Verlag.

Scruggs, L. 2003. *Sustaining Abundance: Environmental Performance in Industrial Democracies*. Cambridge, MA: Cambridge University Press.

Simon, H. A. 1973. "The Structure of Ill Structured Problems". *Artificial Intelligence*, 4: 181–201.

Stamm, K. R., Clark, F. and Eblacas, P. R. 2000. "Mass Communication and Public Understanding of Environmental Problems: The Case of Global Warming". *Public Understanding of Science*, 9: 219–37.

Tableman, M. and Kim, J. S. 2004. *Survival Analysis Using S: Analysis of Time-to-event Data*. Boca Raton: Chapman & Hall/CRC.

Tainter, J. A. 1988. *The Collapse of Complex Societies*. Cambridge, MA: Cambridge University Press.

Tsebelis, G. 2002. *Veto Players: How Political Institutions Work*. Princeton: Princeton University Press.

Vanhanen, T. 2000. "A New Dataset for Measuring Democracy, 1810–1998". *Journal of Peace Research*, 37: 251.

Verweij, M., Douglas, M., Ellis, R., Engel, C., Hendriks, F., *et al.* 2006. "Clumsy Solutions for a Complex World: The Case of Climate Change". *Public Administration*, 84: 817–43.

Wälti, S. 2004. "How Multilevel Structures Affect Environmental Policy in Industrialized Countries". *European Journal of Political Research*, 43: 599–634.

Weingart, P., Engels, A. and Pansegrau, P. 2000. "Risks of Communication: Discourses on Climate Change in Science, Politics, and the Mass Media". *Public Understanding of Science*, 9: 261–834.

13 Scenarios as boundary objects in the allocation of water resources and services in the Mekong region

Louis Lebel

Introduction

Scenarios are internally coherent stories of the future. As such they are an important tool for long-term planning and policy. They can be qualitative or quantitative, look forwards or backwards and be constructed at different scales (van Notten *et al.* 2003). Scenarios have been widely used in business and the military to plan in situations of high uncertainty with respect to opportunities and threats (Masini and Vasquez 2000; Neumann and Overland 2004). More recently scenarios have been used in studies of environmental change, natural resources management and development to understand dynamic vulnerabilities and explore alternative, long-term, policy responses (Gallopin *et al.* 1997; Wollenberg *et al.* 2000; Peterson *et al.* 2003; Swart *et al.* 2004; Millennium Ecosystem Assessment 2005).

Scenarios can be understood as learning processes or products (Hulme and Dessai 2008; O'Neill *et al.* 2008). Emission scenarios in the IPCC process have been a crucial foundation for understanding and communicating possible future changes to climate (IPCC 2007). In the Millennium Ecosystem Assessment process scenarios were seen as helping with education, communication, and decision making (Millennium Ecosystem Assessment 2003). Strong engagement of stakeholders in construction and interpretation of scenarios in the sub-global assessments enhanced mutual learning about interests, capabilities and beliefs (Lebel *et al.* 2006; Lebel and Bennett 2008).

Scenarios and associated mathematical models – including, the graphs, maps, images and figures used to summarize their outputs – may function as boundary objects. A boundary object is an artifact which serves as interface among different communities of practice or social worlds (Star and Griesemer 1989; Guston 2001; Lamont and Molnar 2002). In climate science, for instance, the parameterizations of new model components are boundary objects structuring the relationships between modelers and observers of climate change (Sundberg 2007).

In scenario planning, constructing storylines requires people with different viewpoints and knowledge to work together. Quantifying parts of a scenario using models again demands that scenarios do boundary work between more holistic qualitative experts and modelers. Scenarios as products may also be objects around which experts, policy makers and other stakeholders discuss implications (Garb *et al.* 2008). The IPCC's emission scenarios, for example, are a result of both science and negotiation. They are boundary objects around which scientists and policy makers have come together constructing and refining individual scenario storylines and sets (Girod *et al.* 2009).

Boundary objects, as devices supporting research-action arenas (van Kerkhoff and Lebel 2006) and assessments (Cash and Moser 2000), can help bring different forms of knowledge together and lead to co-production of new knowledge. Scenarios used iteratively are potentially important tools for long-term, adaptive and reflexive policy-making (Voss *et al.* 2009), especially where they are seen as objects to support deliberation rather than substitutes for politics or for overriding differences in world views (de Vries and Petersen 2009; Meadowcroft 2009).

This paper is a review of how scenarios have been used to address allocation of water resources and services in the Mekong Region. We focus on regional applications with a significant international component contrasting the use of scenarios by the Mekong River Commission (MRC) with possibilities suggested by other studies (Table 13.1). The scenario studies considered in this chapter varied in several important dimensions. Most had a strong emphasis on quantitative models and only a few on developing full, qualitative, story lines. Most were built by experts, sometimes with consultation with a relatively narrow group of peers, and only a few with a broader range of stakeholders. The various MRC studies often used similar or subsets of the same scenarios in different combinations.

The main body of this chapter analyses these experiences with scenarios in the Mekong region. Our arguments are organized into three parts. First, how scenario exercises start. Second, how scenarios are made and used. And, third, how scenarios influence learning and decisions. The chapter ends with a discussion of the political significance of scenario exercises in the Mekong Region focusing on the social work that scenarios do as boundary objects.

Initiation

Scenarios are made for different reasons and in varied circumstances. During the last decade in the Mekong Region most exercises have been, one way or the other, concerned with the opportunities and risks from investments in large-scale infrastructure, including dams, diversions, inter-basin transfers, flood embankments, irrigation schemes, transmission lines and road networks.

The Mekong River Commission initially constructed a set of "development scenarios" after the completion of the Decision Support Framework (DSF) in March 2004 as part of work carried out under the Water Utilization Program (WUP). The original seven scenarios (WUP-DSF, Table 13.1) were constructed primarily to evaluate and test the DSF. Several scenarios addressed indicators relevant to articles in the 1995 Mekong Agreement, in particular, minimum dry season flows (Article 6A), reverse flow in Tonle Sap in wet season (Article 6B)

Table 13.1 Main scenario studies explored in this chapter

Scenario study	Convener	Number of scenarios	Participation in construction	Quantitative models	Qualitative story lines
OPTIM – Water Allocation Scenarios (Ringler 2001; Ringler and Cai 2006)	IFPRI & Bonn University	4	No	Yes	Basic
WUP - DSF evaluation scenarios (MRCS 2008)	MRC	7	No	Yes	None
BDP1 – Development scenarios Phase I (MRC 2005)	MRC	5	Narrow	Yes	Basic
WUP-EP-IBFM – Flow scenarios (MRCS 2008)	MRC	4	No	Yes	Basic
MWRAS – Mekong Water Resources Assistance Strategy Scenarios (World Bank 2004; World Bank and Asian Development Bank 2006)	World Bank & ADB	6	Narrow	Yes	Basic
BDP2 – Development scenarios Phase II (MRCS 2008)	MRC	9	Narrow	Yes	Basic
HYDRO – Hydropower dams (MRC 2008b)	MRC	6	Narrow	Yes	Basic
WUP-FIN – Policy Scenarios (MRC and WUP-FIN 2006, 2008)	Finnish Research Consortium for MRC	4	Narrow	Yes	Basic

(continued)

Table 13.1 – continued

Scenario study	Convener	Number of scenarios	Participation in construction	Quantitative models	Qualitative story lines
IWRM-BDS – Basin Development Strategy (MRC 2010a)	MRC	13	Narrow	Yes	Basic
UPLAND – Upland development alternatives in Montane Mainland Southeast Asia (Lebel 2006; Thomas et al. 2008)	Chiang Mai University	4 (4)	No	No	Elaborate
NSEC – North-south economic corridor project scenario (Foran and Lebel 2007)	M-POWER network & Chiang Mai University	4 (8)	Broad	No	Elaborate
CSIRO – Impacts of climate change on Mekong River Basin water resource (Eastham et al. 2008)	CSIRO	2	No	Yes	None
TKK – Climate change assessment (TKK, and SEA-START RC 2009; Keskinen et al. 2010)	Helsinki University of Technology & Chulalongkorn University	3 (3)	No	Yes	None
FISH – Hydrological scenarios and fisheries (Baran et al. 2007)	WorldFish	4	No	Yes	Basic

Source: Compiled by author.

and average daily peak flows in the flood season (Article 6C). Subsequently the set was revised to meet different, but often closely related objectives.

A World Bank (2004) study released in November 2004 evaluating and using the DSF models aimed to "demonstrate the likely impacts of a credible variety of single- and multi-sectoral development scenarios" (MWRAS, Table 13.1). The report is clear that the aim was not to evaluate individual projects or merits of a specific development scenario. The key conclusion from this study was that "there is scope for significant levels of co-ordinated development with associated benefits to all basin countries".

Phase I of the Basin Development Plan (BDP) focused on investigating hydrological and environmental impacts of a range of development alternatives (MRC 2005). Scenarios were released in May 2005 to assist with strategic planning (BDP1, Table 13.1). The focus was on hydropower and irrigation as two sectors expected to have significant effects on mainstream flow. Lack of sufficient consultation with member countries created some difficulties in understanding the purpose of scenarios as well as the relationship between basin-wide and sub-area activities (MRC 2006a). Scenario planning was not a conventional practice in the respective national bureaucracies. Moreover, key actors in National Mekong Committees, working consultants and MRC staff were keen to filter and control the issues explored; thus, from the very beginning, scenario-building activities at MRC were tightly constrained.

According to Dr. Vu Van Tuan, team leader of the MRC's Basin Development Programme at the MRC Secretariat, scenarios were being used in the development plan to:

> investigate the likely development space within which the Lower Mekong Basin will operate over the next 20 years, based on national policies and plans, demographic trends and market demands, as well as external factors such as the impact of development in the Upper Mekong.
>
> (Tuan 2007)

This reflection is fairly similar to the declared purpose of the World Bank (2004) study which pre-empted the BDP scenarios (Table 13.1). From the start the narrow focus on flows arising from the limitations of the DSF tools chosen would hinder more integrated assessment of impacts.

In phase II of the BDP the basin-wide scenario exercise continues to focus on existing, planned and potential significant, large scale, water resources development projects over the next 20 years (MRC 2006b). The emphasis remains on projects which have transboundary impacts or benefits.

Over time the MRC has made more explicit references to the boundary functions of scenarios. A plan for a scenario-based impact assessment report presented in the October 2009 meeting stated the main aims were to:

> facilitate basin wide stakeholder discussions, government consultations and the detailed evaluations that each country must undertake to define the range

of "acceptable trade-offs", and ultimately assist in the preparation of the Basin Development Strategy, in particular the definition of the "development space" and the strategic guidance for the integrated development and management of the various water-related sectors.

(MRCS 2009)

Apart from the MRC several other groups in the region have undertaken scenario-based analysis (Table 13.1). These have been less driven by treaty obligations or immediate policy or investment demands and as a result are a much more diverse group.

Several studies were explicitly designed to look at effects of climate change on water resources and agriculture (TKK and CSIRO, Table 13.1). Two larger ones are highlighted here. The study by Helsinki University of Technology and START Regional Center at Chulalongkorn University "aims to contribute to the discussion about the climate change-related impacts and adaptation strategies" (TKK and SEA-START RC 2009). Another study by CSIRO "investigates how the climate is likely to change in the Mekong Basin by 2030, and quantifies the uncertainty around future climate projections" (Eastham *et al.* 2008). Both studies refer to but do not attempt to directly incorporate interactions with the MRC's development scenarios.

Several other studies listed in Table 13.1 arose, at least in part, out of concerns about impacts on fisheries (OPTIM, FISH, WUP-FIN). Two other scenario exercises (UPLAND, NSEC) were triggered by concerns about livelihoods and ecological conditions in upper tributary watersheds in the Mekong region – areas largely ignored in other basin-wide scenarios and impact assessments except as drivers in changes in flood risk in downstream areas.

All scenario studies included an element of demonstration about them from the outset – they were not thought of as definitive exercises. This was a particularly prominent rationale of the initial MRC models (WUP-DSF), economic scenario study (OPTIM) and upland multi-level analysis (UPLAND). Another commonly shared element across many scenario studies was a stated concern with issues of poverty alleviation and regional development. These two common features enhance the potential of scenarios to perform boundary work among different social groups both in construction and exploration.

Construction

How scenarios are made varies. Important dimensions include the emphasis placed on storylines and model quantification, who is involved and their level of participation. When participation is extensive the distinction between making (construction) and using (exploration and communication) of scenarios is less useful. Most scenario processes have an iterative history and this can also lessen the separation between making and using. The vast majority of scenarios in the Mekong Region have been constructed primarily by experts, including consultants, but under the guidance of officials.

Basin development plans

In the MRCs' work scenarios have been seen essentially as alternative hydrological model runs with particular sets of existing or possible future infrastructure. Adding, dropping and adjusting individual scenarios from the set is straightforward and has happened regularly as different interests have stepped up to shape the boundaries of assessment and analysis. The initial set of development scenarios arising from the WUP program, for example, consisted of seven scenarios (WUP-DSF), the World Bank mission study (MWRAS) a related but different six, and the BDP settled on five (BDP1, Table 13.2). The third phase of the Integrated Basin Flow Management adopted a subset of four from the BDP1 set, renaming some to more neutral terms (IBFM3, Table 13.2). A consultation process with the hydropower program used yet another set (HYDRO, Table 13.2). At a regional consultation workshop in October 2009 a total of nine scenarios were listed and references made to additional work on climate change yet to be included (MRCS 2009). The Basin Development Strategy released in September 2010 had 13 scenarios (IWRM-BDS, Table 13.2). The plethora of scenarios used within MRC activities creates an additional layer of complexity.

Control of how scenarios are constructed has a technical as well as rhetorical significance. Consider the labelling of scenarios and sets in the MRC series. The prefix "definite future" and "likely future" are used to label particular sets of scenarios (BDP2, Table 13.2). In some applications it is "Chinese dams"; in others it is "Upper dams". Different numbers of dams are called "low development" or "high development" (MWRAS, BDP1, Table 13.2). Moreover, irrigation and flood protection issues are labelled distinctly from considerations focused on hydropower energy "development".

There has been substantial controversy over the content of the scenarios; for instance, how operating rules are set for these dams is likely to be crucial to their flow effects, but information about those assumptions has not been made public. Another debate is what should constitute "baseline". Scenario-builders and users who wish to downplay effects of infrastructure overall have tried, for example, to shift the baseline to include already constructed mainstream dams in China.

The sequence with which infrastructure is built is also very important for impacts on flows and thus ecosystems sensitive to changes in seasonal flood regimes. Somewhat extraordinarily much of the scenario and modeling analyses carried out in the MRC series gloss over the dynamic time dimension of impacts of cumulative additions of infrastructure. Indeed consideration of these is often eliminated by comparing scenarios which are run for different lengths of time. The lack of supporting storylines for modelling work makes it hard to gauge plausibility of sequence of events, to explore assumptions and alternatives, and consider responses of people affected by infrastructure development. The scenarios, in short, are not plausible stories of the future, but little more than alternative model runs. Explicit storylines would help guide modelling

Table 13.2 A selection of storylines from scenario exercises

Scenario study	Scenarios in brief
OPTIM	Basin optimization Parity in water allocation Inter-basin transfer Upstream hydropower development
WUP	Baseline Climate change Catchment change High irrigation China dams LMB dams Flood embankments
BDP1	Baseline Upper dams Low development Irrigation High development
IBFM3	Baseline Flow Regime 1 (BDP1-Low) Flow regime 2 (BDP1-Irrigation) Flow regime 3 (BDP1-High)
MWRAS	**Baseline** – conditions existing in year 2000 **China dams** – including all proposed Chinese dams **Low development** – based on population and water demand growth to 2020 with dams in Lao PDR and China **Embankments** – as for low development scenario but including 130,000 ha isolated from Cambodian floodplain **Agriculture** including substantial growth in water use for irrigation with dams in lower basins, inter-basin transfers, and hydropower similar to low development **High development** – similar to agriculture but including substantially more hydropower growth, including many proposed dams in Laos, Vietnam and Cambodia
BDP2	Baseline Upper Mekong Dam Definite Future LMB 20-year plan with 6 m/s (upper) LMB 20-year plan with 9 m/s Mekong delta flood management

	Forseeable future situation	Long term future
IWRM-BDS	LMB 20 year plan LMB 20 year plan without mainstream dams	LMB long-term development LMB very high development
	Baseline Definite future (to 2015) 2 variants	Forseeable future (to 2030) 7 variants Long term future (to 2060) 3 variants
HYDRO	Baseline Upper Mekong Dam Definite future	LMB Mainstream Dam LMB Tributary Dam LMB 20-year plan
WUP-FIN	Economic growth Poverty reduction	Environmental sustainability Integrated-compromise
UPLAND	Rural first Food bowl	Glocalization Services Park
NSEC	Business as usual Green modernity	Economic colony Back to the village
CSIRO	Baseline	Future climate
TKK	Change basin hydrology Sea-level rise	Change basin+sea-level
FISH	Baseline Intensive basin development	Extreme basin development Limited development for tonle sap watershed

Source: Compiled by author.

developments in the basin more explicitly and help reveal assumptions about interactions between infrastructure that now remain hidden.

Another important constraint in the MRC scenario exercises is the "requirement" that some aspects of the scenario work be approved by member countries – for instance the hydrological model set in DSF has been formally approved but not some of the tools critical for socio-economic assessment or models used in geographically more restricted analyses. As a consequence work done by the secretariat is not done with the best available methods. Nevertheless, some amount of exploration appears to proceed regardless of "formal" approval suggesting that scenarios potentially could play an important preparation role ahead of formal negotiations among states.

Despite these limitations the persistence of scenarios in basin development discussions illustrates their utility to key actors. Scenarios are flexible and ambiguous enough that they can meet a certain range of objectives easily; in short, they do some boundary work useful to those engaged in the process. The problem is that not enough have been engaged. It was not until the second phase of BDP that wider stakeholder consultation on the development scenarios became more extensive and even here there has been little evidence that critical feedback is taken into consideration in subsequent iterations of the scenarios (Lebel *et al.* 2010).

The draft Basin Development Strategy released in September 2010 (IWRM-BDS) again focuses on the value of different levels of hydropower development over the next 5, 20 and 50 years (MRC 2010a). It considers a total of 13 scenarios that confound time and set "baselines" and "definite futures" which already include substantial impacts (IWRM-BDS, Table 13.2). Although the Strategy aims to foster integrated water resources management, and makes claims about national-level benefits from increased irrigation, capacities to mitigate or compensate for adverse impacts on fisheries and livelihoods are hardly dealt with. In defense of the assessment modelling specialist at the MRC, Thanapon Piman argued that the focus on hydrology and flows is an outcome of the 1995 Mekong Agreement but that this can be built on in the future to address other issues such as food security and fisheries:

> if we don't have a framework to start our work together, we may not move to other stages [...] and if we don't have a framework, they will build a dam anyway, once one dam can be built, others will follow, without much planning.
>
> (Wongruang 2010)

Uncertainties and scale

Scenario exercises that are independent of treaty procedures, while still expert-driven, have explored a wider range of approaches to constructing scenarios and a broader set of development and water management issues than infrastructure impacts on water flows. In this section we consider treatment of uncertainties in climate and regional development as well as issues of scale.

Scenario studies about the impacts of climate change focus their efforts on comparing projected future climate with a historical baseline. Uncertainties are handled in different ways. For example the study by CSIRO (Eastham *et al.* 2008) used 11 GCM models all driven with the same IPCC A1B emission scenario to create 11 variants of historical climate (1952–2002) and future climate (target year, 2030). Medians were used to characterize most likely climate and variation among models "uncertainty". The use of multiple models by the CSIRO study is in sharp contrast to the MRC process where only the approved DSF model is used, thus essentially eliminating an important source of uncertainty from consideration. Climate projection scenarios do boundary work between researchers more interested in climate and those concerned with impacts and adaptation. They can also help with communication to a wider audience, for example, in explaining why business-as-usual strategies may not work.

Other studies use more or fewer models and one or more emission scenarios (IWMI and World Fish 2009: 25). In all cases the focus is on future precipitation and temperature. Other models or trend analyses are then used to assess impacts, for example, with respect to water availability, agricultural production and changing population distributions (Chinvanno *et al.* 2008; Eastham *et al.* 2008, TKK and SEA-START RC 2009). One recent study took examples of wettest, driest and average hydrological decades to construct alternative floodplain scenarios (Keskinen *et al.* 2010). Typically, other sources of uncertainty are not considered as part of the scenarios or immediate analyses but may be referred to in interpretation of findings as cautionary notes. For example, land-use is often assumed to remain as present apart from specific assumptions about water withdrawals for irrigation.

More holistic scenario exercises need ways to identify and systematically explore major uncertainties. One simple way sets of scenarios are constructed is to focus on a small number of key uncertainties and take extreme combinations of sets of assumptions about these uncertainties (Figure 13.1). In a study about upper tributary watersheds scenarios were constructed at the wider regional level based on different combinations of uncertainties in market (horizontal axis) and sectoral (vertical axis) development (Lebel 2006). The Food Bowl scenario, for example, is strongly export agri-business oriented. Under this regional scenario the expansion and intensification of agriculture in lowland and wider valleys means much greater pressure on water resources and thus controls on water and land uses in upstream upper tributary watershed areas (Lebel 2006). Developing more elaborate storylines with explicit time sequences, key drivers and triggering events requires making assumptions explicit. Here opportunities for storylines to do boundary work among disciplines and among participants with different perspectives and beliefs is high – allowing constructive interaction to continue even when understandings are not exactly the same, preferences differ, and fits between complex pieces of evidence are imperfect but improving.

What should now be clear is that insights do not only come from the articulation of individual story-lines, but also the contrasts between scenarios and the overall space of possibilities which they span. Comparisons among scenarios

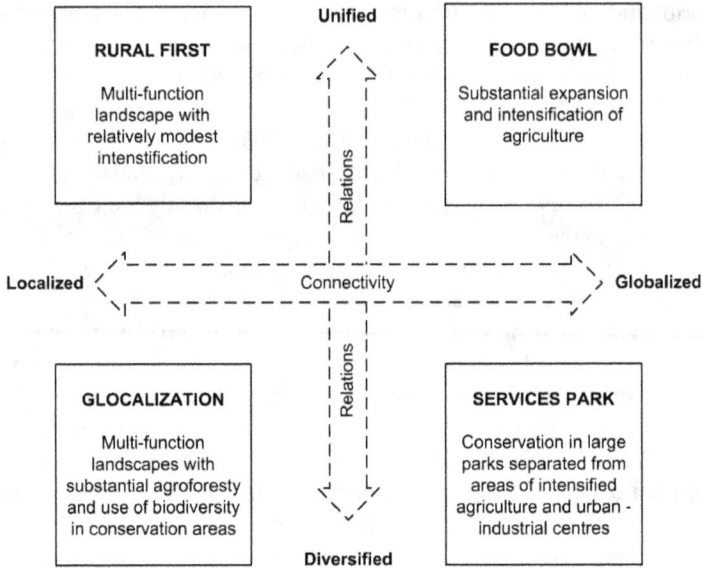

Figure 13.1 Four scenarios of regional uncertainties.
Source: Lebel 2006.

are more likely to be interesting if each is plausible and some participants think it is likely. If each scenario has some positive and negative elements for most stakeholders then the kinds of discussion encouraged can move away from the "picking winners" type to exploring alternative assumptions and understandings. In some situations the scenarios may be designed to evolve towards divergent preferences, for example, following common policy narratives.

Scale issues are often subsumed under assumptions about external conditions. The MRC has put a strong emphasis on transboundary impacts in its scenario analyses. Small tributary projects are simple nodes in the model and assumed to have little or no impact at the basin level that cannot be dealt with by local mitigation actions. Multiple local effects are rendered invisible to this type of scenario and modelling work.

The scenario study of impacts of built-structure on fisheries analysis explicitly dealt with impacts from interventions at three geographical scales – the Mekong Basin, Tonle Sap Watershed and Tonle Sap Floodplains – on the hydrology, ecology and fisheries of Tonle Sap Lake (Baran *et al.* 2007). Although the four scenarios were not nested (FISH, Table 13.1) the first three include assumptions about development at the basin scale while a fourth focused on changes within the Tonle Sap watershed.

One way to handle scale issues is to explicitly build scenarios at more than one level and analyse them jointly (Zurek and Henrichs 2007). The Millennium Ecosystem Assessment (MA) was explicitly multi-scale with sub-global regional assessments sometimes contrasting their own local scenarios with the over-arching set of global scenarios (Millennium Ecosystem Assessment 2005; Lebel *et al.* 2006). Lebel (2006) nested scenarios at two spatial levels to explore key uncertainties that would impact livelihoods and landscapes in upper tributary watersheds of montane mainland Southeast Asia. The two scenarios are summarized in Figure 13.2. At the regional level the scenarios highlight the implications of different forms of market and political integration. At the upper tributary level the scenarios highlight changing dependencies on local natural resources and the extent of empowerment of local stakeholders in their management.

The explicit consideration of scale in scenarios opens up more possibilities for level-dependent interests and uses of water to be explicitly considered. In the Mekong region this is vital as otherwise myriads of local interests are over-looked in low resolution, large scale, assessment processes (Lebel *et al.* 2005).

Building scenarios together

In a few instances scenarios are constructed together with a wider group of stakeholders. Building scenarios together serves two functions (Lebel *et al.* 2006, Lebel and Bennett 2008). First it can help stakeholders get a better understanding of what each, in the longer term, thinks is desirable or not. Second, because scenarios are plausible stories about the future, they require articulation and discussion about people's beliefs about cause-and-effect in development. A better, mutual, understanding of assumptions that stakeholders have about water resources, climate change, technology, international relations and many other factors that shape development can help guide additional assessment where uncertainties are large and capacity building where key technical information is simply not understood or understandable.

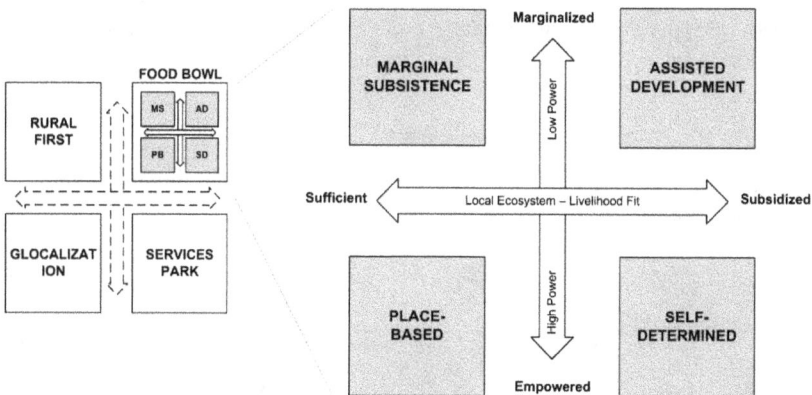

Figure 13.2 Multi-level scenarios for analysis of alternative futures of upper tributary watersheds in mainland Southeast Asia Upland scenarios.

Source: Modified after Lebel 2006.

In October 2006 USER and M-POWER organized a workshop in Chiang Mai, Thailand, to specifically follow-up discussions at the Mekong Water Futures Dialogue (IUCN *et al.* 2007a) on the ADB-facilitated North-South Economic Corridor (Foran and Lebel 2007). At the event participants explored development assumptions by building scenarios at local, regional and global scales (Figure 13.3). A substantial effort was put into training neutral facilitators to guide a process in which all participants were given opportunities for meaningful input and encouraged to explain their reasoning and explore differences in views. Participation in scenario-building exercises may help understanding because it encourages examination of assumptions held by others.

In the MRC process, consultation with other member states, and in some cases approval of specific elements by the Joint Committee, is seen in some ways as "participation". Clearly this is a much lighter and narrower notion of "engagement" in the construction of scenarios than was explored by some other. Nevertheless, from the Secretariat's perspective scenarios are boundary objects that help them deal with other Commission bodies, like the Joint Committee and Council.

Building scenarios together can help improve legitimacy of analysis. This is one of the key reasons why participation and deliberation can be valuable. Legitimacy comes from both who gets involved and the quality of reasoning and debate. Wider participation in scenario-building itself is not yet a common practice in the Mekong Region.

Exploration

Once constructed, scenarios can be used in several ways. One of the key functions of boundary objects is to improve communication. Scenarios have been used for both supporting dialogue as well as more one-way marketing of desired projects and futures. Another is to take the scenarios as input into further analyses, for example, as part of an assessment of environmental or social impacts. The distinction between "the scenario" and "its analysis" is not always sharp.

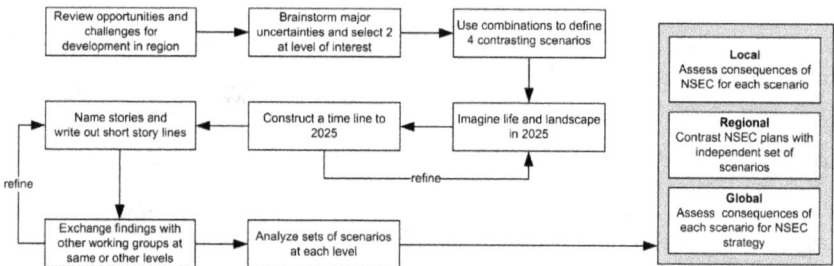

Figure 13.3 The scenario-building process used to engage participants in a dialogue to explore the Asian Development Bank's North-South Economic Corridor plans and reasoning.

Source: After Foran and Lebel 2007.

Communication and deliberation

Scenarios are sometimes made primarily as a tool to communicate ideas. In this mode the boundary object has translation or mediation functions. How scenarios are received may not match the intentions of those communicating. The outcome may be acceptance, refinement or rejection.

In June 2006 the Asian Development Bank released a working paper co-authored with the World Bank on an assistance strategy for water resources development in the Mekong Region (World Bank and Asian Development Bank 2006). The report aggressively re-confirmed the World Bank's (2004) initial analysis which drew on the hydrological models in the MRC's Decision Support Framework:

> The bottom line message of this Mekong Water Resources Assistance Strategy is that the analytical work on development scenarios has, for the first time, provided evidence that there remains considerable potential for development of the Mekong water resources. The Mekong basin has flexibility and tolerance, which suggests that sustainable, integrated management and development can lead to wide-spread benefits. This may contrast with the more precautionary approach of the past decade that tended to avoid any risk associated with development, at the expense of stifling investments.
>
> (World Bank and Asian Development Bank 2006: 4)

Critiques of the ADB and World Bank's Mekong Water Resources Assistance Strategy followed. The absence of important ecological details from the models or assessment reduced the credibility of the findings. Other research in the region, including work done with and at the Mekong River Commission Secretariat, for example, has highlighted the importance of sediments, nutrient transport and even modest changes in flood pulse behaviour for ecosystem dynamics (Lamberts 2006; Kummu *et al.* 2008; MRC and WUP-FIN 2008). Others were concerned with the process of consultation. There is need, for example, to make available all relevant documents sufficiently in advance of consultations. Some actors, like the International Rivers Network, had criticized the MWRAS as just a tool to create investments (IRN 2006). Others have pointed out to the limited civil society engagement and incorporation of inputs in the lead-up process (Cuomo and Frewer 2007).

In Vientiane, Lao PDR, in July 2006 the World Conservation Union (IUCN), the Thailand Environment Institute (TEI), the International Water Management Institute (IWMI) and the Mekong Program on Water Environment and Resilience (M-POWER) convened the "Mekong Region Waters Dialogue: exploring water futures together" (IUCN *et al.* 2007a, 2007b). The regional multi-stakeholder platform was meant as a contribution to "improving water governance in the Mekong Region". A key part of the meeting was to evaluate the Mekong Water Resources Assistance Strategy. The Banks had gone through their own consultation process but with little civil society participation. The need for greater transparency and stakeholder participation was a key message from the event. Another was a better understanding of the limitations of models (Adamson 2007) and the framings that scenarios had created eliminating consideration of alternative types of development. The dialogue event was followed up by exchange of correspondence between conveners and these agencies (IUCN *et al.* 2007a).

Follow-up meetings included a participatory scenario building exercise focussed on exploring the Asian Development Banks' plans for the north-south economic corridor (Foran and Lebel 2007). The scenario-building event offered a different way of exploring uncertainties and alternative visions of development. Apart from deliberation about assumptions and beliefs inherent in constructing scenarios together there were also sessions designed specifically for explaining and exploring scenarios with members of other groups (Figure 13.3). Presenting preliminary scenario analyses to others working at the same or a different level helped some groups further refine their own scenario sets (Foran and Lebel 2007). In this condensed exercise scenarios played an important direct boundary function among participants from different countries and backgrounds.

In the early history of international cooperation on the Mekong a key and early notion was that scenarios were options amongst which the member states ultimately had to agree. The 1987 revision of the earlier 1970 Indicative Basin Plan was prepared by consultants and staff of the Mekong Committee secretariat and published as "Perspectives for Mekong Development" (Le-Huu *et al.* 2003). Short and longer-term development scenarios were supposed to be developed and a single one elaborated as the development plan. The consultants at the time said given the political context "establishment of a rigid blueprint for the basin's development [was] an exercise with little practical meaning" (Le-Huu *et al.* 2003: p. 40).

Scenario planning in BDP2 appears to be returning to this earlier logic of "identifying the appropriate scenario" (MRCS 2008) as opposed to broader notions of exploring the space for development as espoused in the early World Bank (2004) study. BDP2 experts recognize that the actual choice is one for the member states and Joint Committee but expect iteratively refined scenarios to be useful in negotiations. The boundary work of the scenario, if it unfolds as the BDP anticipates, would continue to help stabilize the policy and research agenda.

In more recent years the MRC has increasingly held consultations on its analyses and plans including development scenarios. At the regional multi-stakeholder consultation on MRC's hydropower programme held in September 2008 in Vientiane, results of modelled flow changes from various water resources development scenarios were presented by the MRC (2008a). The six scenarios were discussed in terms of hydropower assumptions (HYDRO, Table 13.2). According to the presenter the scenarios and indicators were discussed by National Mekong Committees, line agencies and other regional organizations. The presenter also noted that "results will be discussed in various forums". In an interesting use of framing rhetoric the last three scenarios are treated as "Future

Plans" in contrast to the "Definite Future" which includes both existing and yet to be built but "on-going" projects.

At the first stakeholder consultation on BDP2 held in Vientiane, 12–13 March 2008, participants argued that "the analyzed results of scenarios should be open for peer review" and "include public stakeholder consultation process before decision-making takes place". The exact steps in how the scenarios would be used in relation to Joint Committee, Council and stakeholder consultations were debated in meetings of the Regional Technical Working Group and the process was adjusted again. In short which boundaries a scenario object is supposed to help manage is subject to contest with different actors pushing and pulling to be included or exclude others.

Another limiting feature is the lack of attention given to uncertainties, exactly the type of analysis for which scenario planning is most suited. Key assumptions are buried within the DSF and are not open for full scrutiny. Risks and surprises have been reduced and eliminated rather than expanded and explored; as a consequence, very little can be said about the robustness or resilience of the "development scenarios" as strategies for regional development. Some of these limitations can be understood as arising from too strong a focus on quantification of the mainstream hydrograph and insufficient engagement with multiple stakeholders whose interests in water-related resource development and management go well beyond these narrow considerations. These in turn are explainable in part by the political context in which scenarios are seen by key actors as boundary objects in negotiations among member states.

Assessing impacts

Among several findings presented at the hydropower program consultation (HYDRO, Table 13.2) it was noted that average dry season flows would increase by 30–50 per cent in northern parts of Thailand and Laos (MRC 2008a). Impacts on the flood pulse in the downstream part of the Lower Mekong Basin (LMB), including flow reversals for Tonle Sap, were argued to be small fraction of historical year-to-year variability. It was asserted that the LMB Mainstream dam scenario would have no additional impacts because these projects would be run-of-river. The conclusions drawn by the presenter at that event using scenario analysis were particularly positive about low impacts of LMB developments:

> the flow changes caused by possible water resource developments in the LMB will result in small mostly positive changes in salinity intrusion in the Vietnam Delta and relatively small changes in flooding patterns around the Tonle Sap compared to the natural year-to-year variability. The LMB mainstream dams would not cause flow changes beyond a daily timeframe.
> (MRC 2008a)

Hydrological models are the foundations of the MRC DSF but not always the most appropriate tools for specific applications. The MRC/IBFM program using

DSF predicted changes in water levels in the lower basin of 0.15m whereas other studies have suggested effects as high as 0.30m and 0.60m. The scheme used to assess hydropower dam impacts in the DSF is a simple add-on to software originally adapted from the Murray Darling Basin; it has been criticized as less than ideal for this application and should be improved (Adamson 2007; MRC and WUP-FIN 2008). The CEO of the MRC at the time attempted to prevent presentation of these critical comments at a public forum, but these went ahead anyway (IUCN *et al.* 2007b).

There are other problems related to transparency as well. Scenarios cannot work as boundary objects for communication if they are opaque. Some important work using models to assess impacts of flows has been done but not shared. The results of a scenario study for MRC's BDP by Beecham and Cross were not released. Work in the IBFM program assessed impacts of a "high development" scenario but IBFM Report 8 was not released for public distribution and discussion (MRC and WUP-FIN 2008) until very recently.

Despite these concerns and criticisms the MRC continues to work closely with the model-supplier and consulting firm Halcrow, especially within the Information and Knowledge Management Programme (IKMP) process. Competition for contracts among different consulting and research groups is to be expected and normal, but underlines the need for a high level of transparency in modelling activities or risk loss of credibility. The final report from the WUP-FIN project noted that "the MRC would benefit greatly from continuing validation and scientific review of the model system, which is necessary for its transparency and credibility, not least in transboundary context" (MRC and WUP-FIN 2008: 18).

More independent development and application of basin wide models is needed to study impacts of new infrastructure, climate and other variables. Progress would ensue from model inter-comparison exercises, using standardized inputs and scenarios. Models like VIC and VMod would be examples of suitable instruments to compare against components present in the current DSF.

The narrow hydrological focus of the "development" scenarios convened by the MRC illustrates how scenarios as boundary objects can also be used to narrow debate. Hydropower is justified by reference to the low impact of development on the hydrograph according to their own hydrological models. Scientific studies suggest much more care is needed about drawing inferences about ecosystem impacts (Kummu and Sarkkula 2008; Friend and Blake 2009). A study using largely the same development scenarios of the MRC draws attention to possible adverse impacts of structures on fisheries in Tonle Sap (Baran *et al.* 2007). Dry season flows are particularly important in this context because they affect fish migration patterns and habitats.

Ecosystem and social impacts

The MRC's use of scenarios in IBFM work under the BDP focuses on effects on flows. The initial World Bank (2004) study acknowledged that the output of the models "is quite narrowly hydrological". For some structures in some locations this may not be the most important impact. Consideration is also needed for impacts on sediment transport, local impacts in specific sub-basins near structures, and ecosystems. Different kinds of impacts have very different levels of difficulty associated with them. Estimating impacts on changing water levels and water quality as in sediment capture is relatively straightforward, whereas estimating effects on ecosystem productivity and interaction among structures, or cumulative impacts, is much harder to estimate.

Scenarios could benefit from more explicit consideration of ecological impacts and their uncertainties. Scenarios and mathematical models can be used together to simulate and interpret biophysical or social processes and interactions that would otherwise be hard to describe and thus explore. The level of quantitative detail required in technical simulation and analysis of hydrological, ecological and social processes depends very much on the purpose for which scenarios are being built and their technical plausibility and capacities. The many different models made of the Mekong basin or parts thereof, like the delta, were built to serve different purposes (Sarkkula *et al.* 2007).

The WUP-FIN project developed a number of models that could more explicitly examine ecosystem processes, especially in the Tonle Sap Lake, river and floodplain. The models allow exploration of different scenarios of, for example, tributary inflows, flow speed and direction, flooding characteristics, dissolved oxygen concentrations, sedimentation, larvae and juvenile fish drift (Sarkkula *et al.* 2004; Kummu *et al.* 2006; Sarkkula *et al.* 2007; Kummu *et al.* 2008). Kummu *et al.* (2005), for instance, used the DSF scenarios to drive the hydrodynamic and water quality model they had developed for Tonle Sap Lake. In an initial study they compared the baseline to high development scenario and found significant impacts on floods and water quality characteristics in Tonle Sap Lake and floodplain (Kummu *et al.* 2005).

Costa-Cabral and colleagues (2007a) used the Variable Infiltration Capacity (VIC) model to study interactions between soil land-use and cover, soil moisture, and precipitation and how they affect run-off at large spatial scales in the Mekong River basin. They found that spatial variation in soil moisture of deeper soil layers, a variable strongly affected by presence of deep roots as in forests, results in various delays in run-off relative to patterns of precipitation. Another important finding was that irrigation works in various parts of the basin, such as the Korat Plateau and Mekong Delta or around Tonle Sap Lake, by storing water in ponds increase re-infiltration and evapo-transpiration with the result that net run-off is further reduced. As expected snow melt is important for base flows in the dry season of the Mekong River (Costa-Cabral *et al.* 2007a). In a follow-up study the researchers explored several scenarios to study impacts of changes in land-use and -cover and climate on run-off generation (Costa-Cabral *et al.* 2007b).

The work of Costa-Cabral and colleagues (2007b) underlines the importance of considering all major factors affecting flows together. Changes in climate, land use and regulation of streamflow by dams interact with each other in complex ways. In their study they combined the VIC hydrologic model with another model of reservoir operations to explore effects of dams. Scenarios for climate came from general circulation model outputs whereas those for land-use from historical remote sensing studies.

In both the VIC and WUP-FIN modelling applications scenarios were implemented as sets of parameter settings in a complex model which was then run to simulate a set of variables of interest. The scenarios are very modestly developed: no broader vision about how such parameter settings could come about and with what sequence over time is provided. One consequence of this common approach is that there is no larger, coherent world, in which to interpret modeling finds, as would be the case if such investigations were combined with qualitative story lines (Figure 13.4).

Many of the sub-global and global activities in the Millennium Ecosystem Assessment, for example, tried to explicitly incorporate ecological processes into scenarios (Bennett *et al.* 2003). Ecosystems were not just impacted by changes in economic and social development, but changes in them could also feedback on development processes, for example, through changes in provision of goods and services (Millennium Ecosystem Assessment 2005; Lebel *et al.* 2006).

The limitations of current scenario exercises concerned with water allocation and impacts of alternative water resources developments with respect to social processes are even greater than for ecological ones. At its simplest level there is the notion of linear analysis in which outputs from hydrological and ecological studies are carried over into social impacts at aggregate levels. One example is Ringler (2001) who used a coupled, aggregated, economic-hydrological model to study water allocation and use under alternative policy scenarios. She considered five main water uses: irrigation, hydropower generation, urban-industrial water uses, fisheries, and wetlands. Trade-offs and complementarities between sectors and countries were explored. The Resource Allocation Model developed by BDP1 has some similar features. At this very broad-brush level impacts on livelihoods cannot be assessed in much detail. More detailed models still need to be developed. In more sophisticated versions the over-arching scenarios which guide the modelling work should themselves incorporate a contrasting but coherent set of assumptions about key social and institutional factors in development (see Figure 13.4). In the 2006–2010 strategic plan the MRC claimed it "can develop a wide range of scenarios, extending the analysis from analyzing

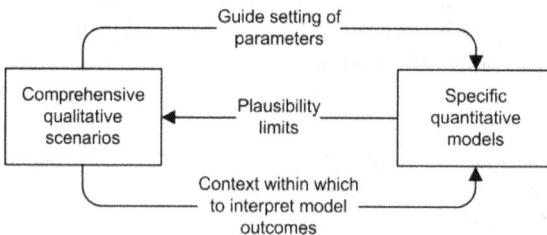

Figure 13.4 Ideal iterations between scenarios and models.
Source: Compiled by author.

the initial hydrological implications to addressing the full economic, social and environmental impact" (MRC 2006b: 16). Better models and scenarios alone, however, will not make much difference to negotiations and decision making unless the constructive influence of scenarios as boundary objects can be improved.

Influence

The influence of scenarios is difficult to assess with precision (Hulme and Dessai 2008). Most scenario building activities are poorly documented making it hard to assess learning unless the analyst was closely involved in the process. Scenario products are typically part of a wider assessment process and just one element of a wider set of factors supporting (or resisting) policy change making it challenging to attribute impact. Nevertheless a few tentative observations can be made from some of the studies discussed.

Building scenarios together provides the best opportunities for learning. Initial involvement in construction provides real opportunities to discuss assumptions and differences in beliefs (NSEC, Table 2). Here scenarios can perform many of the desired boundary functions simultaneously – helping communication and translation of ideas and understanding among disparate groups of people who although they work together may still have different interests, expectations and hopes for the future.

Where such close interaction is not feasible allowing wider input into "scenarios" that are treated as drafts to be refined is another approach. Channels for meaningful input and iteration, in short, may also foster learning between scenario developers and a wider group of stakeholders. Where the organizational interests of the conveners in some outcomes are high, independent facilitation may improve the quality of consultation feedback. Otherwise actors may rightly perceive consultations as a marketing exercise and reject a process and thus product as lacking legitimacy.

The history of MRC scenario sets suggests a tendency towards gaining broader public acceptance of narrowly circumscribed expert-driven scenario products. The feedback from consultations, however, has not fundamentally altered the scope, the types of scenarios being explored or the hydrological flow focus (Table 13.2). The constraints on "learning" include some which arise from control of the research and policy agendas by member states as well as filtering done within the secretariat itself.

In the Mekong region scenarios are still a "modest" part of the "discursive landscape". Most scenario exercises have yet had little impact on allocation of water resources. The MRC scenario stream, however, has undoubtedly had some influence, in particular, after the World Bank analyses and launching of the Mekong Water Resources Assessment Strategy. The investment push encouraged by the multilateral banks was supported by some government actors in the region.

At the same time the content and use of scenarios was challenged by other, especially non-state, actors. Scenarios here had a boundary function but not the one intended by their developers: a launching pad for wider criticisms of roles and strategies of multilateral organizations in water governance more broadly (IUCN *et al.* 2007a, 2007b). Scenarios exercises, like other knowledge-intensive activities, are never completely separable from politics in the Mekong where claims are highly contested and stakes for different interests are high (Käkönen and Hirsch 2009). It is exactly these tensions cutting across issues of power and knowledge which suggest that scenarios could do important boundary work.

The history of construction and reaction to the MRC scenarios underlines several cautionary notes about policy impact. First, the most influential scenarios are not necessarily the ones produced by the best process. Alignment with powerful interests is crucial. Second, while good quality products matter these are no guarantee of constructive policy impact. Scenario products also need to be well-tailored to specific policy-making targets or their saliency will be lost. Third, the perceived legitimacy of scenario exercises is critical to their fate, and state actors are no longer seen as having an automatic monopoly; legitimacy can also be achieved through deliberative channels.

Discussion

In the Mekong Region scenarios have been used as tools to assess and explore water resource allocation. Most applications have been little more than alternative model runs; a few have developed more elaborate storylines; none have successfully combined simulation modelling with qualitative storyline approaches (Table 13.1). Participation in scenario-building construction has been very constrained, rarely going beyond the immediate peer or client group. In short, the full potential of scenario-building exercises as boundary objects to support deliberative processes has not been realized.

Scenarios reflect the social context in which they were developed. The MRC scenarios view development through the lens of dams and diversions – the hydropower they might generate, hectares of fields which might be irrigated – and not the many other ecological and social changes that would accompany major infrastructure development. Other alternatives for achieving livelihood and well-being objectives are not considered because they do not fit this hydrological lens. Storylines are under-developed because all that is needed to run the models are assumptions about which dams and diversions are in place and how they are operated. Scenarios as products and boundary objects record the social work that was put into them. The narrower framing of successive sets of DSF-derived scenarios reflects this pre-occupation with transboundary impacts on flow to the exclusion of much else that matters. Scenarios were not intended as tools for deliberation but as techniques of legitimization of a single development storyline.

Most effort to improve scenario exercises remains in technical dimensions – better input datasets, higher quality models. Much less attention has been given to storylines or the assumptions made about development, for example, which set of dams and diversions are being built, and what their ecological and social consequences will be. The technical style of presentation of many current scenario products – as tables of model outputs and graphs of water levels with scenarios tagged with simple labels like "high development" – limits their eligibility for exploration to a much more exclusive group in ways that a storyline does not.

Wider, more deliberative, use of scenarios in the Mekong Region could improve the accountability of major private and state actors involved in water resources development and management in several ways. First, by encouraging actors to be more explicit about the key assumptions they make regarding causal connections, benefits and risks. Deliberative opportunities need to be created for this to happen, whether in discussion around a table, or through periods where reports and findings are open for scrutiny and comment. Second, by strengthening the capacity of stakeholders to think strategically about the future, side-effects and unforeseen consequences are more likely to be identified. Scenario exercises force actors to explore time frames beyond typical planning horizons, and to consider alternatives beyond familiar, comfort zones. This can help generate creative solutions; and maybe explains why such approaches are avoided by actors wishing to pursue narrow individual interests.

There are also important constraints. In the Mekong Region lack of appropriate data and knowledge – about different kinds of hydrological, social and ecological processes and possible impacts of stream flow regulation, land and water uses, or climate – remains an important constraint on making and using scenarios. For some issues quantification or detailed assessment may simply be impossible (Sarkkula *et al.* 2007). One recent promising exception was the social impact monitoring and vulnerability assessment study undertaken in 2008–09 by the MRCS that looked at the livelihoods of more than 1,300 households along the floodplains of the mainstream (MRC 2010b). Further work of this type is needed. For scenarios to be helpful for some allocation problems credible models are also needed. If models are not open for scrutiny and comparisons their results are harder to trust. These constraints on model-based tool development have been noted in Europe where much effort has been put into tools to support water management in large rivers under the Water Framework Directive (Petts *et al.* 2006; Borowski and Hare 2007).

The constraints are also political. The ease and effectiveness with which scenarios can be used as boundary objects is affected by the broader political and scientific context in which they are undertaken. In an international river basin the primacy of governments in cooperative frameworks is often taken for granted. In the MRC's work the focus has been on supporting negotiations among lower Mekong member states. It is only as a result of pressures from civil society that some expansion of the notion of participation beyond state officials has begun to penetrate the logic of international cooperation. Opportunities for non-state actors to directly influence scenario development – to shape the boundary object – however remain small as the primary clients continue to constrain its evolution. Alternative storylines have simply been suppressed. Modellers and scientists working within the politically accepted decision-making tool box, may be more successful. Slowly they have been improving, extending and integrating modelling tools – literally converting a politically validated model into a more scientifically-validated one. If these could be combined with more comprehensive and genuine alternative scenarios then they could do much more useful social work.

The notion of boundary objects provides a useful starting point for examining scenario processes, products and influence. As boundary objects, scenarios may do a substantial amount of social work (Garb *et al.* 2008). They help bring different types of expertise – scientific, managerial and political – together in all stages, from initial conception through to construction and use. The ambiguity and flexibility can allow different parties to continue a conversation and negotiation without having identical understandings or objectives. Moreover, if well-constructed, a set of scenarios spans a meaningful space in which a substantial range of pathways and perspectives can be captured, beyond the individual scenarios articulated in detail.

Scenarios are not automatically deliberative or inclusive. Scenarios as simplifications are also useful for marketing and persuasion, not just as entry points for debate and exploration. Scenarios and modeling mark-off an issue as scientific and technical allowing scientists to maintain some autonomy from other authorities (Lamont and Molnar 2002). Such boundary work, however, also helps legitimize the claims of actors who wield scenarios as authoritative tools. Even where deliberative, the extent to which space is given to vulnerable and politically marginalized voices depends greatly on how scenario exercises are convened and led and the channels opened for input in the process.

The circumstances under which scenarios emerge, the process by which they are constructed and used, the understandings they produce, and their influence on negotiations, decisions and actions need further evaluation. Expanding on our initial questions for this study we suggest it will be useful for future work to systematically consider scenario development from initiation through to use in terms of process, product and influence dimensions (Table 13.3). Scenario exercises are a process that creates products and both dimensions can be important to boundary work. Putting scenarios into the wider negotiation, deliberation and decision contexts is necessary to understand their influence. Ethnographical studies of scenario making and use are likely to be particularly helpful in understanding the social work they do and how they relate more broadly to framing, assessment and decision-making processes. This should include exploring how consideration of alternative scenarios is suppressed.

Scenario-building exercises could strengthen the quality of deliberations around water allocation problems in the Mekong Region. Scenarios could be important boundary objects through which researchers, policy-makers, water managers, users and affected people could interact to explore and generate alternative solutions. But so far, scenarios in the Mekong – with a few exceptions – have been used primarily to help experts work together on models and then communicate findings from those modelling exercises to a narrow set of clients concerned with just gross changes in flows. This is such a narrow interpretation of

Table 13.3 Simple analytical framework for assessing and comparing scenario exercises used in this chapter

	Process	Product	Influence
Initiation	What triggered? Who convened?	How was product framed?	What were the sources of legitimacy? What was the purpose?
Construction	How were scenarios constructed? Who participated? Which boundaries did scenarios span?	Which trends, uncertainties, and scales were considered? Which resource uses and users were considered? How were models and storylines used?	Did participants learn from each other? How was credibility and saliency sought?
Exploration	How were scenarios communicated and received? Who facilitated? Who was consulted?	How was deliberation enhanced (constrained)? What features of product enabled (limited) exploration? Did the product fit social context in which it was explored?	Did scenarios influence negotiations or decisions? Were scenarios perceived as credible and salient? What did stakeholders learn?

Source: Compiled by author.

what scenarios are that it restricts the boundary functions they could play in improving water governance in the Mekong Region.

Acknowledgements

Funding for this work came from the European Commission via the Challenge Program on Water and Food grant for project PN67. This chapter is a contribution to the M-POWER program (www.mpowernetwork.org). Thanks to Tira Foran, Juha Sarkkula, Robert Arthur, David Hall, Diana Suhardiman, Edsel Sajor, Francois Molle and John Dore for constructive feedback on earlier drafts.

References

Adamson, P. 2007. "Hydrological and Water Resources Modelling in the Mekong Region: A Brief Overview". In *Exploring Water Futures Together*. Mekong Region Waters Dialogue, Resource papers from regional Dialogue, Vientiane, Lao PDR, 6-7 July 2006. The World Conservation Union (IUCN), Thailand Environment Institute (TEI), International Water Management Institute (IWMI) and Mekong Program on Water Environment and Resilience (M-POWER), 69–74.

Baran, E., Starr, P. and Kura, Y. 2007. *Influence of Built Structures on Tonle Sap Fisheries*. Cambodian National Mekong Committee and the WorldFish Center. Phnom Penh. Cambodia.

Bennett, E. M., Carpenter, S. R., Peterson, G. D., Cumming, G. S., Zurek, M. and Pingali, P. L. 2003. "Why Global Scenarios Need Ecology". *Frontiers in Ecology and Environment*, 1: 322–9.

Borowski, I. and Hare, M. 2007. "Exploring the Gap between Water Managers and Researchers: Difficulties of Model-based Tools to Support Practical Water Management". *Water Resources Management*, 21: 1049–74.

Cash, D. W. and Moser, S. C. 2000. "Linking Global and Local Scales: Designing Dynamic Assessment and Management Processes". *Global Environmental Change*, 10: 109–20.

Chinvanno, S., Souvannalath, S., Lersupavithnapa, B., Kerdsuk, V. and Thuan, N. T. H. 2008. "Climate Risks and Rice Farming in the Lower Mekong River Countries". In Leary, N., Adejuwon, J., Barros, V., Burton, I., Kulkarni, J. and Lasco, R. (eds) *Climate Change and Vulnerability*. London: Earthscan, 333–50.

Costa-Cabral, M., Richey, J., Goteti, G., Lettenmaier, D., Feldkotter, C. and Snidvongs, A. 2007a. "Landscape Structure and Use, Climate, and Water Movement in the Mekong River Basin". *Hydrological Processes*, 22: 1731–46.

Costa-Cabral, M., Richey, J. E., Lettenmaier, D. and Beyene, T. 2007b. *Synergies between Changes in Climate, Land Use, and Streamflow Regulation in the Mekong River Basin*. Pages Poster H341 G-0747. In AGU Fall 2007.

Cuomo, M. and Frewer, T. 2007. *Unpacking the Mekong Water Resources Assistance Strategy*. Sydney: Australian Mekong Resource Centre.

de Vries, B. J. M. and Petersen A. C. 2009. "Conceptualizing Sustainable Development: An Assessment Methodology Connecting Values, Knowledge, Worldviews and Scenarios". *Ecological Economics*, 68: 1006–19.

Eastham, J., Mpelaskoka, F., Mainuddin, M., Ticehurst, C., Dyce, P., Hodgson, G., Ali, R. and Kirby, M. 2008. *Mekong River Basin Water Resources Assessment: Impacts of*

Climate Change. Canberra: CSIRO: Water for a Healthy Country National Research Flagship.

Foran, T., and Lebel, L. 2007. "Informed and Fair? Water and Trade Futures in the Border Regions of Mainland Southeast Asia". *USER Working Paper WP-2007-02*. Unit for Social and Environmental Research, Chiang Mai University, Chiang Mai, available at: www.sea-user.org/download_pubdoc.php?doc3730.

Friend, R. M. and Blake, D. J. H. 2009. "Negotiating Trade-offs in Water Resources Development in the Mekong Basin: Implications for Fisheries and Fishery-based Livelihoods". *Water Policy*, 11: 13–30.

Gallopin, G., Hammond, A., Raskin, P. and Swart, R. 1997. "Branch Points: Global Scenarios and Human Choice". PoleStar Series Report No. 7. Global Scenarios Group, Stockholm. Stockholm Environment Institute.

Garb, Y., Pulver, S. and VanDeveer, S. D. 2008. "Scenarios in Society, Society in Scenarios: Toward a Social Scientific Analysis of Storyline-driven Environmental Modeling". *Environ. Res. Lett.* 3.

Girod, B., Wiek, A., Mieg, H. and Hulme, M. 2009. "The Evolution of the IPCCC's Emissions Scenarios". *Environmental Science and Policy*, 12: 103–18.

Guston, D. H. 2001. "Boundary Organizations in Environmental Policy and Science: An Introduction". *Science, Technology and Human Values*, 26: 399–408.

Hulme, M. and Dessai, S. 2008. "Predicting, Deciding, Learning: Can One Evaluate the 'Success' of National Climate Scenarios?". *Environ. Res. Lett.* 3: 7.

IPCC 2007. *Climate Change 2007: Impacts, Adaptation and Vulnerability*. Contribution of Working Group II to the Fourth Assessment Report of the IPCC. Cambridge, UK: Cambridge University Press.

IRN. 2006. Mekong Under Threat. New Strategy Promotes Dams and Diversions. Berkely: International Rivers Network.

IUCN, TEI, IWMI, and M-POWER 2007a. *Exploring Water Futures Together: Mekong Region Waters Dialogue*. Report from regional Dialogue, Vientiane, Lao PDR. World Conservation Union, Thailand Environment Institute, International Water Management Institute, Mekong Program on Water, Environment and Resilience. Available at www. mpowernetwork.org/Knowledge_Bank/Key_Reports/PDF/Dialogue_Reports/Mekong_Region_Waters_Dialogue_July_2006.pdf.

IUCN, TEI, IWMI, and M-POWER 2007b. *Exploring Water Futures Together: Mekong Region Waters Dialogue*. Resource papers from regional Dialogue, Vientiane, Lao PDR. World Conservation Union, Thailand Environment Institute, International Water Management Institute, Mekong Program on Water, Environment and Resilience, available at www.mpowernetwork.org/Knowledge_Bank/Key_Reports/PDF/Dialogue_Reports/Mekong_Region_Waters_Dialogue_Resource_Papers.pdf.

IWMI, and World Fish. 2009. *Scoping Study on Natural Resources and Climate Change in Southeast Asia with a Focus on Agriculture*. Final Report to Swedish International Development Cooperation Agency. Vientiane, International Water Management Institute.

Käkönen, M., and Hirsch, P. 2009. "The Antipolitics of Mekong Knowledge Production". In Molle, F., Foran, T. and Käkönen, M. (eds) *Contested Waterscapes in the Mekong Region: Hydropower, Livelihoods and Governance*. London: Earthscan, 333–6.

Keskinen, M., Chinvanno, S., Kummu, M., Nuorteva, P., Snidvongs, A., Varis, O. and Västilä, K. 2010. "Climate Change and Water Resources in the Lower Mekong River Basin: Putting Adaptation into Context". *Journal of Water and Climate Change*, 1: 103–17.

Kummu, M., Koponen, J. and Sarkkula, J. 2005. "Assessing Impacts of the Mekong Development in the Tonle Sap Lake". In *Role of Water Sciences in Transboundary River Basin Management, Bangkok*. 89–98.

Kummu, M., Penny, D., Sarkkula, J. and Koponen, J. 2008. "Sediment: Curse or Blessing for Tonle Sap Lake?" *Ambio*, 37: 158–63.

Kummu, M., and Sarkkula J. 2008. "Impact of the Mekong River Flow Alteration on the Tonle Sap Flood Pulse". *Ambio*, 37: 185–92.

Kummu, M., Sarkkula, J., Koponen, J. and Nikula J. 2006. "Ecosystem Management of the Tonle Sap Lake: An Integrated Modelling Approach". *Water Resources Development* 22: 497–519.

Lamberts, D. 2006. "The Tonle Sap Lake as a Productive Ecosystem". *Water Resources Development* 22: 481–95.

Lamont, M. and Molnar, V. 2002. "The Study of Boundaries in the Social Sciences". *Annu. Rev. Sociol.* 28: 167–95.

Lebel, L. 2006. "Multi-level Scenarios for Exploring Alternative Futures for Upper Tributary Watersheds in Mainland". *Southeast Asia Mountain Research and Development*, 26: 263–73.

Lebel, L. and Bennett, E. 2008. "Participation in Building Scenarios of Regional Development". In Norberg, J. and Cumming, G. S. (eds) *Complexity Theory for a Sustainable Future*. New York: Columbia University Press, 207–22.

Lebel, L., Garden, P. and Imamura, M. 2005. "Politics of Scale, Position and Place in the Governance of Water Resources in the Mekong Region". *Ecology and Society*, 10: 18.

Lebel, L., Thongbai, P., Kok, K., *et al.* 2006. "Sub-global Scenarios". In Millennium Ecosystem Assessment, Ecosystems and Human Well-being: Multiscale Assessment. New York: Findings of the Sub-global Assessments Working Group, 229–59, Island Press.

Lebel, L., Grothmann, T. and Siebenhüner, B. 2010. "The Role of Social Learning in Adaptiveness: Insights from Water Management". *International Environmental Agreements*, 10: 333–53.

Le-Huu, T., Nguyen-Duc, L., Anukularmphai, A., Phan, D. H., Phonekeo, K., Sokhem, P. and Hai-Lun, Z. 2003. "Mekong Case Study". Technical Documents in Hydrology. PCCP series No. 10. Paris: UNESCO-IHP.

Masini, E. B., and Vasquez, J. M. 2000. "Scenarios as seen from a Human and Social Perspective". *Technological Forecasting and Social Change*, 65: 49–66.

Meadowcroft, J. 2009. "What about the Politics? 'Sustainable Development, Transition Management, and Long Term Energy Transitions'". *Policy Sciences*, 42: 323–40.

Millennium Ecosystem Assessment. 2003. *Ecosystems and Human Well-being: A Framework for Assessment*. Washington DC: Island Press.

Millennium Ecosystem Assessment. 2005. *Ecosystems and Human Well-being: Synthesis*. Washington DC: Island Press.

MRC. 2005. *BDP Library*. March 2005. Revised November 2005, Vol 4 Mekong River Commission.

MRC. 2006a. *Basin Development Plan*. Programme Phase 2. 2006–2010. 15 Final version. August 2006, Mekong River Commission.

MRC. 2006b. *Strategic Plan 2006–2010: Meeting the Needs, Keeping the Balance*. Mekong River Commission Vientiane.

MRC. 2008a. "Modelling of flow changes in the Mekong Mainstream for a range of water resources development scenarios: Preliminary Results". In: *Regional Multi-stakeholder*

Consultation on the MRC's Hydropower Programme, 25–27 September 2008, Vientiane, Lao PDR.

MRC. 2008b. *Regional Multi-stakeholder Consultation on the MRC Hydropower Programme*. Consultation Proceedings. Mekong River Commission, Vientiane, Lao PDR.

MRC. 2010a. *IWRM-based Basin Development Strategy for the Lower Mekong Basin.* First complete draft for discussion. 15 September 2010 Mekong River Commission, Vientiane.

MRC. 2010b. *Social Impact Monitoring and Vulnerability Assessment (SIMVA)*. Regional report and database (draft report). Mekong River Commission, Vientiane.

MRC, and WUP-FIN. 2006. *Mekong Delta Socio-Economic Analysis: Interconnections between Water and Livelihoods in the Mekong Delta of Vietnam.* WUP-FIN Phase II - Hydrological, Environmental and Socio-Economic Modelling Tools for the Lower Mekong Basin Impact Assessment. Mekong River Commission and Finnish Environment Institute Consultancy Consortium, Vientiane, Lao PDR.

MRC, and WUP-FIN. 2008. *Hydrological, Environmental and Socio-economic Modelling Tools for the Lower Mekong Basin Impact Assessment.* Water Utilization Programme. WUP-FIN Phase 2. Impact Assessment Report. February 2008. Mekong River Commission, Finnish Environment Institute, EIA Centre of Finland Ltd., Helsinki University of Technology, Vientiane, Helsinki.

MRCS. 2008. "Approach and Process to Formulate and Assess Basin-wide Development Scenarios". *BDP2 Discussion Paper Number 1. Draft 4 July 2008*. Vientiane: Mekong River Commission Secretariat.

MRCS. 2009. "Development Scenarios for Basin Development Planning". Presentation by Dr. Phoumin Han, BDP Programme at 2nd Regional Stakeholder Forum on Basin Development Plan, 15–16 October 2009, Chiang Rai, Thailand. Mekong River Commission Secretariat, Vientiane, Lao PDR.

Neumann, I. B. and Overland, E. F. 2004. "International Relations and Policy Planning: The Method of Perspectivist Scenario Building". *International Studies Perspectives*, 5: 258–77.

O'Neill, B., Pulver, S., VanDeveer, S. D. and Garb, Y. 2008. "Where Next with Global Environmental Scenarios?". *Environ. Res. Lett.* 3.

Peterson, G. D., Cumming, G. S. and Carpenter, S. R. 2003. "Scenario Planning: A Tool for Conservation in an Uncertain World". *Conservation Biology*, 17: 358–66.

Petts, G., Nestler, J. and Kennedy, R. 2006. "Advancing Science for Water Resources Management". *Hydrobiologia*, 565: 277–88.

Ringler, C. 2001. "Optimal Water Allocation in the Mekong River Basin". ZEF - Discussion Papers on Development Policy No. 38. Bonn: Centre for Development Research.

Ringler, C. and Cai, X. 2006. "Valuing Fisheries and Wetlands using Integrated Economic-hydrologic Modeling: Mekong River Basin". *Journal of Water Resources Planning and Management*, 132: 480–7.

Sarkkula, J., Baran, E., Chheng, P., Keskinen, M., Koponen, J. and Kummu, M. 2004. *Tonle Sap Pulsing System and Fisheries Productivity*. In *SIL XXIX* International Congress of Limnology, Lahti, Finland.

Sarkkula, J., Keskinen, M., Koponen, J., Kummu, M., Nikula, J., Varis, O. and Virtanen, M. 2007. "Mathematical Modeling in Integrated Management of Water Resources: Magical Tool, Mathematical Toy or Something in between?". In Lebel, L., Dore, J.,

Daniel, R. and Koma, Y. S. (eds) *Democratizing Water Governance in the Mekong Region*. Chiang Mai: Mekong Press, 127–56.

Star, S. L. and Griesemer, J. R. 1989. "Institutional Ecology, "Translations" and Boundary Objects: Amateurs and Professionals in Berkeley's Museum of Vertebrate Zoology". *Social Studies of Science*, 19: 387–420.

Sundberg, M. 2007. "Parameterizations as Boundary Objects in the Climate Arena". *Social Studies of Science*, 37: 473–88.

Swart, R., Raskin, P. and Robinson, J. 2004. "The Problem of the Future: Sustainability Science and Scenario Analysis". *Global Environmental Change*, 14: 137–46.

Thomas, D. E., Ekhasing, B., Ekhasing, M., Lebel, L., Ha, H. M., Ediger, L., Thongmanivong, Jianchu. S. X., Saengchayosawat, C. and Nyberg, Y. 2008. *Comparative Assessment of Resource and Market Access of the Poor in Upland Zones of the Greater Mekong Region. Report submitted to the Rockefeller Foundation under Grant No. 2004 SE 024*. Chiang Mai: World Agroforestry Centre.

TKK, and SEA-START RC. 2009. *Water and Climate Change in the Lower Mekong Basin*: Water and Development Research Group, Helsinki University of Technology (TKK) and Southeast Asia START Regional Center (SEA-START RC). Chulalongkorn University.

Tuan, V. V. 2007. "Lower Mekong River Basin Development Plan Programme (2001–2006): An Introduction". In 7th World General Assembly of the International Network of Basin Organizations, 7–9 June 2007, Debrecen, Hungary.

van Kerkhoff, L. and Lebel, L. 2006. "Linking Knowledge and Action for Sustainable Development". *Annual Review of Environment and Resources*, 31: 445–77.

van Notten, P. W. F., Rotmans, J., van Asselt, M. B. A. and Rothman, D. S. 2003. "An Updated Scenario Typology". *Futures*, 35: 423–43.

Voss, J.-P., Smith, A. and Grin, J. 2009. "Designing Long-term Policy: Rethinking Transition Management". *Policy Sciences*, 42: 275–302.

Wollenberg, E., Edmunds, D. and Buck, L. 2000. "Using Scenarios to make Decisions about the Future: Anticipatory Learning for the Adaptive Co-management of Community Forests". *Landscape and Urban Planning*, 47: 65–77.

Wongruang, P. 2010. "Reshaping the Mekong". *23 August 2010*. In Bangkok Post, Bangkok.

World Bank. 2004. *Mekong Regional Water Resources Assistance Strategy: Modelled Observations on Development Scenarios in the Lower Mekong Basin*. World Bank.

World Bank, and Asian Development Bank. 2006. "WB/ADB Joint Working Paper on Future Directions for Water Resources Management in the Mekong River Basin: Mekong Water Resources Assistance Strategy (MWRAS). June 2006". The World Bank and Asian Development Bank.

Zurek, M. B. and Henrichs, T. 2007. "Linking Scenarios across Geographical Scales in International Environmental Assessments". *Technological Forecasting and Social Change*, 74: 1282–95.

14 Stakeholder integration and social learning in integrated sustainability assessment

Lisa Bohunovsky and Jill Jäger

Introduction

Sustainable development is a policy objective of the European Union. However, the concept of sustainable development is contested, both scientifically and socially, so by definition it is subjective and ambiguous. This makes it difficult to operationalize the concept. Universal implementation is impossible. Sustainability is context-bound and needs to be interpreted and implemented by a range of stakeholders within that specific context. Developing long-term strategies to achieve sustainability goals requires processes that can deal with the context-dependence, ambiguities and uncertainties of these problems. This has been discussed widely in the growing literature on sustainability science (see, for example, Jäger 2011) and transition management (see, for example, Grin *et al.* 2010).

This chapter considers a new form of assessment designed explicitly to address the persistent problems of unsustainability, for which the current policy-making regime has found no solutions. Assessment is fundamentally a communication process, not simply a report (Farrell *et al.* 2005) and it provides a bridge between the realms of knowledge and action. Currently, most practical applications of sustainability assessment fulfill a pragmatic role in screening already tabled sectoral policy proposals that have no sustainability orientation per se (Hertin *et al.* 2007). In this chapter we consider an assessment process that is not designed to screen policy proposals but instead aims to support the development and implementation of long-term strategies for sustainability. Two aspects of this process are treated in detail: the integration of stakeholders and the processes of learning.

Stakeholder integration and social learning

Stakeholder integration and social learning are two closely related concepts that are often discussed in the context of sustainability. *Stakeholder integration* mobilizes expertise of the participants, it improves awareness and support for policy measures, it can enhance the legitimacy of decisions or it may help to build new networks and coalitions (see Chapter 1 in this volume; Tuinstra *et al.* 2008; Van De Kerkhof 2006). Bouwen *et al.* (2006) mention deliberative approaches as a relevant strategy for dealing with multiple knowledge frames, i.e. multiple or conflicting views about how to understand the system. Participation can also help to reduce incomplete knowledge (Brugnach *et al.* 2008). Thus, it is argued that stakeholder integration is necessary for dealing with several aspects of sustainability (see Chapter 1 in this volume): uncertainty, complexity, ambiguity and the subjectivity of persistent problems. In terms of post-normal science, which is, for example, more problem-oriented and interdisciplinary than interest-driven and disciplinary science, participation is an integral part of approaches taken (Funtowicz and Ravetz 1991).

This chapter concentrates on the contribution that participatory approaches can make to *social learning*. Social learning refers to individual learning from each other about new issues, but also learning about other's perceptions on these issues, thus new perspectives – and can thus lead to changes in behaviour (see Chapter 1 in this volume). Social learning includes sharing different points of view and types of knowledge and can be induced by promoting (public) participation (Tàbara and Pahl-Wostl 2007). Moreover, it provides an opportunity for mutual understanding and mutual influence and might enable participants to initiate fundamental changes within regard to conditions and contexts (Tuinstra *et al.* 2008). Learning in general can exhibit different forms. According to Argyris and Schön (1978, 1995) single-loop learning includes the adoption of new knowledge without changing the underlying mental model, thus allowing for the correction of errors. Double loop-learning includes resetting the framework of learning, thus also changing values, norms and beliefs. A further type, named deutero-learning, includes learning to learn. Learning processes within assessment processes often include single-loop learning, or – in some cases – also double loop-learning. Deutero-learning is rather rare (Tuinstra *et al.* 2008). Participation promotes double-loop learning, as the interaction with other people, their beliefs and norms, makes people reflect on underlying structures.

In addition to social learning, *sustainability learning* adds the normative aspect of sustainability to learning. Thus, it stresses learning contents that support a sustainable development and the capacity of agents to cope with diverse (negative) impacts of development on both – the individual and the societal level (Tàbara and Pahl-Wostl 2007). According to Weaver, Haxeltine *et al.* (2006) sustainability learning enables people to frame and reframe (double-loop learning) the issue at stake in a way that allows for a development of socio-ecologically robust strategies. It thus includes the integration of innovative potentials and creative solutions, the acknowledgment of different world-views and the creation of social capacities to deal with the problems at hand. As argued in Chapter 1 of this volume (Siebenhüner *et al.*), learning based on uncertain knowledge about long-term developments cannot be right or wrong. But, in order to come back to the argument made before, sustainability learning includes learning about and learning how to deal with the uncertainty, complexity, ambiguity as well as subjectivity of persistent problems. As others have emphasized, managing a transition to sustainability *requires* improved learning and the ability to adapt to changing conditions (Pahl-Wostl *et al.* 2009). Siebenhüner (2004) discusses various examples of social learning within a sustainability context and refers to the empowerment and education, the increase of legitimacy of scientific research, as well as the generation of knowledge and the promotion of its practical implementation through the integration of institutional stakeholders and decision makers.

In summary, development of long-term strategies to achieve transitions to sustainability will require processes that support social learning and sustainability learning. The integration of stakeholders in these processes is essential, so that learning can support both the development and implementation of the strategies. The following sections describe a process that meets these aims.

The MATISSE project

As a response to the pressing governance and management challenges of sustainable development, the MATISSE ("Methods and Tools for Integrated Sustainability Assessment") project aimed at achieving a step-wise advance in the science and application of Integrated Sustainability Assessment (ISA) of EU policies. ISA is an innovative new mode of knowledge development, where the objective is to help develop long-term, cross-sectoral policies expressly designed to contribute to sustainable development. MATISSE aimed to contribute to sustainability-oriented governance by providing innovative methods, tools and process-architecture for conducting Integrated Sustainability Assessments (ISA).

The MATISSE project started in April 2005 and ended in March 2008 and included 21 partners from institutions all over Europe. The project addressed the use of sustainability assessment in the European context, but the innovative methods, tools and insights it was developing are relevant generally to questions concerning the role that sustainability assessment might play in supporting sustainability-oriented governance and in the analysis of potential sustainability "transitions". The approach taken to learning within the project may also hold wider implications for other projects in the emerging field of science in support of sustainable development.

Fundamentally, MATISSE was a project with a mandate to be innovative methodologically; it sought to begin work on a new generation of approaches and tools for integrated sustainability assessment that will be capable of exploring transition pathways. This was a long-haul and ambitious endeavour that is continuing beyond the duration of the MATISSE project, but MATISSE marked an important beginning and was challenged with setting out the overall "concept" and developing some of the key elements that guide subsequent work.

The main activities within MATISSE were:

- the development of a common conceptual framework for ISA
- the delivery of a future tool portfolio for ISA
- the application and test of improved and new ISA tools in four case studies
- capacity-building and outreach tasks and stakeholder engagement.

Further information on the project can be found at www.matisse-project.net/

Integrated Sustainability Assessment (ISA)

ISA is intended as a pro-active, strategic and potentially transformative process to give an explicit sustainability orientation to policy-making and other undertakings concerned with the development of social–ecological systems. Such undertakings would be expressly intended to address persistent complex problems of unsustainable development and to take up opportunities for more sustainable development.

The objectives of an ISA are to develop a shared interpretation among stakeholders of the dimensions of sustainability for a particular social–ecological system (scoping), transform these into a shared vision on a sustainable future (envisioning), and explore various solution directions for a transition towards sustainability through a range of innovative experiments (experimenting), as a basis for learning about key relationships and ways of reframing problems and solutions (learning/evaluating). The formal definition of ISA reflects these means and ends:

> ISA is a cyclical, participatory process of scoping, envisioning, experimenting, and learning through which a shared interpretation of sustainability for a specific context is developed and applied in an integrated manner in order to explore solutions to persistent problems of unsustainable development.
>
> (Weaver and Rotmans 2006)

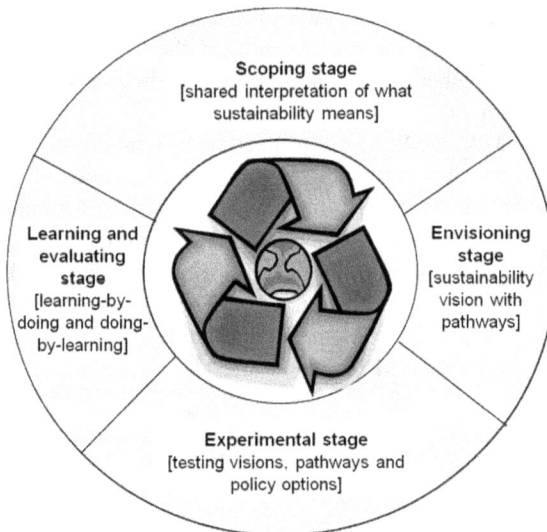

Figure 14.1 The ISA-cycle.

Source: Compiled by author.

The essential design requirements for ISA stem directly from its intended role as a process for exploring and supporting reframing and reorientation (regime change) and transition. ISA represents a new mode of knowledge production that responds to the governance and management challenges of sustainable development. It offers a forum for:

- defining "socially- and ecologically-robust" targets and thresholds;
- integrating these as elements of operational, context-specific sustainability interpretations; and
- exploring alternative pathways of transition.

ISA therefore has both a process dimension and an analytical dimension. It brings together an integrated systems analysis and a participatory process involving a selection of relevant stakeholders and actors. The integration of stakeholders selected to represent different perspectives and interests is a basic requirement of ISA in order to develop a rich and robust interpretation of sustainability for a specific context (Weaver and Rotmans 2006).

ISA can be used to support the development of policy proposals and other undertakings that have a special sustainability orientation. Such undertakings would be expressly intended to address problems of unsustainable development, take up possibilities for more sustainable development and maximize synergies among policy objectives. ISA is based on the principles of: addressing inter-generational equity, the integration of the economic, ecological and socio-cultural domains and the interaction of scales.

> The underlying set of ISA-principles deals with trade-offs between values, between longer and shorter term horizons, between social-cultural, economic and ecological domains, between places and parties, and between different scale levels that need to be taken into account. The principal methods to deal with this set of ISA principles are a combination of an analytical approach in the form of an integrated systems analysis, and a process approach in the form of a participatory process involving relevant stakeholders.
>
> (Weaver and Rotmans 2006)

Therefore, ISA is a fundamentally participatory approach to sustainability assessment. As discussed above, stakeholder integration is a must if science wants to address persistent problems of unsustainability. There is no complete knowledge about these issues, computer models describing the system have clear limitations and there are many uncertainties especially when it comes to future issues. Therefore, the knowledge of stakeholders provides valuable input. Moreover, value conflicts have to be taken into account in order to come up with socially robust knowledge (Van De Kerkhof *et al.* 2002).

Through the engagement of stakeholders, experts and decision makers ISA becomes a social learning process. Stakeholder integration helps to ensure that an ISA asks salient questions and provides relevant answers, and enables the researchers to clarify and integrate different values of the community into their work. Moreover, through participation of stakeholders throughout an ISA the attempt is made to embed the integrated sustainability assessment in the policy process and to promote the formulation of sustainability policy proposals, i.e. linking "knowledge" to "action". At all stages of the assessment it is of great importance to make explicit to the stakeholders to what extent and how their knowledge and expertise is used in assessing the policy proposals and experiments.

According to the above considerations, stakeholders are integrated within all four stages of ISA:

Scoping stage

The scoping stage of the ISA-process involves a thorough definition of the persistent problem in question. This requires an integrated systems analysis, where "thought-tools", such as the sustainability framework, can be used to perform a cross-cutting analysis. A stakeholder analysis is conducted in order to identify all persons or groups with interests in the project or programme, those affected by the (results of) the project (negatively or positively), potential winners, losers, and those involved in, influential on or excluded from decision making. It is also important to identify their interests in the relation to the persistent unsustainability problem being addressed. Moreover an appropriate participatory method is selected and stakeholder input is used to refine understanding of the persistent problem in question, the policy context and the conceptual model. Thus, the unsustainability "problematique" can be looked at from multiple perspectives, and the extent to which it is possible to draw a common picture of the issue at stake can be explored. Major differences between the norms, values and perceptions of the project team and the stakeholders can also be examined. Models and other tools can be useful in the scoping stage to support the development of a common ground regarding the problem perception among a diverse group of actors, in particular when the problem is largely ill-defined (although this does not imply consensus building) (Tàbara and Pahl-Wostl 2007).

Envisioning stage

During the envisioning phase a context-specific interpretation of sustainability that is acceptable to a wide range of stakeholders needs to be developed, wherein different perspectives on this unsustainability problem among different actors and stakeholders are made explicit. Moreover, visions and scenarios are developed with the stakeholders – a process which also provides a great mobilizing capacity for the stakeholders involved. Stakeholder input can also be used to formulate explicit and implicit policy options in the scenarios, and to make a narrative assessment of the impacts of these proposals.

Experimenting stage

The experimenting stage uses ISA-tools and methods to test the sustainability visions and policy proposals in terms of consistency, adequacy, robustness and feasibility. Transition pathways (scenarios) from drivers to sustainability goals, the sustainability impact of policy proposals and trade-offs are tested and explored. At this stage the knowledge of stakeholders can help to choose the appropriate set of ISA tools and to ensure that the assessment is salient (i.e. capable of answering questions that stakeholders think are important). Moreover, stakeholders can provide valuable input for the analysis of the results, e.g. the assessment of policy proposals and of ISA experiments.

Participatory approaches to ISA modelling can help to provide a better representation of social agents' behaviour and a social–ecologically robust depiction of the system of reference under consideration (Tàbara *et al.* 2007a).

Learning, evaluating and monitoring stage

In the learning, evaluating and monitoring stage, learning experiences and lessons during the ISA-process need to be made explicit. Besides internal evaluation through the researchers themselves, the views of the stakeholders on the ISA-process and – tools and – results are elicited and the social and individual learning processes in the ISA are evaluated. In order to enable those engaged in the process to understand each other's language and frames, as well as to develop methods and approaches that provide an effective process it is important to explicitly organize the process of reflection, evaluation and learning (Tuinstra *et al.* 2008). This stage also forms the basis and input for a next ISA-cycle, eventually leading to a possible reframing of the shared problem perception, an adjustment of the sustainability vision and related pathways, and reformulation of the experiments to be conducted. Regarding stakeholder integration, evaluation regarding the composition of the stakeholder group (include new ones, leave some out) and the methods of engagement (interviews, workshops, etc.) has to take place.

Stakeholder integration in MATISSE

Within the MATISSE project stakeholders were integrated to:

- construct "visions" of, and "pathways" to, sustainable futures – that reflect the experiences, views and concerns of different stakeholders;
- look at the different options (including options for transformation of and collaboration between stakeholders) and trade-offs between options that different pathways entail;
- increase the mutual understanding of the science and policy and to improve the representation of the policy arena in the models that were developed;

- test and improve participatory methods for policy assessment and social learning; and
- disseminate our research and raise the profile of institutions involved in MATISSE.

Stakeholders were formally engaged through workshops, in-depth interviews and questionnaires. In addition we had informal contact (via email, phone and face-to-face meetings) with several relevant groups (academics, government agencies, and industry representatives) who also acted as advisors and data providers. Furthermore, a high-level advisory group, comprising senior academics, politicians and industry representatives, has given feedback on the project as a whole and advised on how findings could be applied to real-world sustainability challenges. In order to disseminate the project's results and work to the stakeholders and decision makers who might be interested in implementing an ISA within their sphere of influence, a project summary for policymakers and stakeholders was issued as a brochure at the end of the project. It gives an overview of the work done and the elaborated process in an adequate language and a reasonable length (see matisse-project.net).

The integration of stakeholders within MATISSE can be seen on two levels: (1) it was important to include stakeholders' knowledge during the theoretical elaboration of the ISA process. This was done in order to analyse the practice of policy assessment in Europe (Hertin *et al.* 2007). Besides this, (2) stakeholders were integrated in the work of the case studies in order to examine possible methods to be used in order to ensure the participatory character of the ISA-approach. The following discussion builds mainly on the latter, in order to enhance the benefits of stakeholder integration in future ISA-processes.

Four case studies provided the real-world context for testing and developing the ISA methodology and its tools within the MATISSE-project. The case studies were designed to cover the broad spectrum of domains and contexts of ISA in the EU. The themes were

1   agriculture, forestry and land-use (AFLU);
2   resource use, waste and dematerialisation (with two sub-cases following different approaches);
3   water (using the example of Ebro Delta, Spain);
4   sustainable environmental technology development (again with two sub-cases, one on hydrogen/sustainable mobility (European wide) and one on Ecological Tax Reform (concentrating on the Czech Republic)

Table 14.1 gives an overview of the stakeholder events within MATISSE:

Most of the workshops were addressing experts in the respective fields, whereas four workshops were explicitly citizens' workshops. The aims of the citizens' workshops were to elicit citizens' perspectives on transport and housing, and to use this information to inform Integrated Sustainability Assessments (ISA) of mobility and housing/communities. The workshops also aimed to test and

Table 14.1 Stakeholder workshops in the MATISSE project

Topic	Activities & Contents
Dematerialisation	'Science-Policy-Dialogue on Sustainable Resource Management and Impact Assessment' in October 2005 in order to present the project and discuss sustainability challenges for sustainable resource management with representatives of the European Commission. Further workshops were held within the framework of the EU-funded FORESCENE project and also delivered valuable input for the scoping and envisioning phases of the ISA (long-term sustainability goals, core elements for policy, pathways towards sustainability). The sub-cases on dematerialisation provided important input into the stakeholder workshop on Ecological Tax Reform in the Czech Republic (see below).
Water	Four stakeholder meetings between November 2005, and February 2008 in the area of the case study (Zaragoza and Tortosa). 5–9 citizens took part in each of the meetings. This case-study followed a participatory modelling approach, which included a gaming tool in order to facilitate a structured dialogue among stakeholders to support reflexive learning in the domain of water. The game can also be used as an empowering tool, to illustrate differences in the agents' policy competence and in the fairness of power distribution. The game forms part of the ISA experimenting stage, in which the insights obtained during the scoping and visioning stages were tested and refined (Pahl-Wostl *et al.* 2008; Tàbara *et al.* 2007a; Tàbara and Pahl-Wostl 2007; Tàbara *et al.* 2007b)
Agriculture, Forestry and Land Use	Workshop with stakeholders from the EU Commission and other relevant organizations in October 2006 at the premises of DG Research in Brussels. In total 18 individuals attended the meeting representing the policy and academic communities, non-governmental organizations and partners in the case study. The meeting aimed to elicit stakeholder input on sustainable development objectives and policy instruments to be considered in the assessment. Stakeholder perspectives on the sustainability problems in the AFLU sector were also discussed alongside their views on the future in the AFLU sector (for more information see Briefing Sheet of WP4, based on 18 months report [www.matisse-project.net/projectcomm/uploads/tx_article/WP04_BS18months_final2_01.pdf]).
Hydrogen/ Sustainable Mobility	Two workshops were held in Frankfurt (February 2006, June 2007). MATISSE researchers moderated focus groups, and distributed self-completion questionnaires. The workshops were organized as clustering workshops with other projects working in the field, therefore there was a strong bias towards experts in sustainable transport and hydrogen transport technology. In total, 46 and 30 participants from research, automotive industry, energy industry, and policy in February 2006 and June 2007, respectively took part in the workshops). The stakeholders' inputs were used in order to (re)frame the case study and get feedback on the modelling results. The questionnaire also included questions on the learning of the

(continued)

Table 14.1 – continued

Topic	Activities & Contents
	stakeholders (Whitmarsh *et al.* 2007a for June 2007 workshop; Whitmarsh *et al.* 2007b for Febrary 2006 workshop). Furthermore, two $2\frac{1}{2}$–3 hours deliberative workshops were held in Norwich, UK, between September 2006 and March 2007 in order to elicit citizens' perspectives on transport and to test and improve participatory methods for policy assessment and social learning. About 15 citizens took part in each of the workshops which were organized as part of events to engage the public in science or environmental issues: the BA Festival of Science in September 2006, and the Norwich Forum Trust's Earth Event in March 2007 (Whitmarsh 2007).
Environmental Technology/ Ecological Tax Reform – the Czech Republic	Two workshops were held in Prague in 2006 (April and September) in order to elaborate a sustainability vision on the Czech republic. A third workshop was held in November 2007 together with colleagues from the case study on dematerialisation, with a clear focus on Environmental Tax Reform (ETR). Approx 10 stakeholders (policy makers on the upper executive level from ministries, the statistical office and CSOs) took part in each workshop; The aim of the workshop was to get feedback on the modelling of the consequences of the introduction of different forms of ETR. Moreover, the stakeholders were asked to evaluate elements of the elaborated sustainability vision according to how important they are and how challenging they are to achieve. Modelling assumptions were also cross-checked, and learning of the stakeholders was explicitly evaluated (Barker *et al.* 2008)
Sustainable housing and communities	Two *citizens' workshops* focussed on sustainable housing and communities (Whitmarsh 2007). Like the citizen workshops on transport (see above) they took place in the UK and involved about 15 citizens each.

Source: Compiled by authors.

improve participatory methods for policy assessment and social learning; and to stimulate a social learning process among participants taking part in the workshops (Whitmarsh 2007).

Learning

Evaluation and learning are an explicit step in the ISA-cycle. All sustainability assessment processes seek to generate and integrate information. But in contrast to other forms of sustainability assessment, which aim to develop evidence for immediate instrumental purposes, ISA aims to develop insights able to promote conceptual learning, reframing and other transformative outcomes (Tuinstra *et al.* 2008). The participatory process of ISA is designed in order to allow participants to gain insights into the nature of context-specific problems of sustainable development and how these are embedded in the broader social–ecological system. In addition, it focuses on different perspectives on these problems, including how issues (and solution possibilities) are framed presently. As Tuinstra *et al.* (2008) have elaborated, whereas other sustainability assessment processes focus on projecting the impacts of proposed undertakings, ISA is more concerned with improving understanding among all those engaged in the assessment process about:

- key relationships in the social–ecological system and how they relate to sustainability (sustainability learning);
- how issues are framed by different stakeholders and how these framings relate to the possibilities to resolve persistent problems of unsustainable development (social learning);
- possible pathways toward more sustainable futures (transition learning).

Of critical importance is that "sustainability learning" takes place through a participatory process of social learning so that it includes learning about (and reflection on) one's own understanding, perspectives on and framing of the issues as well as others" understandings, perspectives and framings. This is needed in order to establish shared visions of desirable futures and to provoke a process of social capital building around the exploration of pathways toward these, which is needed for "transition learning".

However, there is another reason why learning and evaluation are essential in ISA. Perhaps one of the most important insights about ISA is that any specific ISA application will need to be tailored to its context of application. Both in the development of the general elements of the ISA approach and in customizing ISA to the specifics of a particular application, ISA calls for a process of co-development of methods and tools involving mutual learning among those developing methods and tools and those using them. By implication the development of ISA methods and tools will have to be achieved through an adaptive "learning-by-doing" approach involving interplay between tool developers and users supported by evaluation. Evaluation will necessarily involve the stakeholders, since it is their experiences as users of the methods and tools and their insights into their "fitness-for-purpose" that are needed to support adjustment and corrective action.

In the following "learning in MATISSE" is discussed on three different levels:

1 Stakeholders get new inputs when participating in workshops; they can change their opinion due to discussions with other stakeholders or after hearing about the scientific findings of the project. This is referred to as "Learning in ISA – by stakeholders".
2 MATISSE project partners learn due to stakeholder participation. New topics are raised, new quantitative or qualitative input can lead to a changing interpretation of results, etc. This is referred to as "Learning in ISA – by research".
3 Finally, the MATISSE project aimed at developing a new process. Stakeholder participation is an important part of this process – the MATISSE project

helped to understand how this could be best organized, what can be expected and what are potential fields of improvement for stakeholder participation in ISA. This is referred to as "Learning to do ISA".

The following description of cases concentrates on two case studies, namely the hydrogen/sustainable mobility case study and the ETR-case study. Both of these case studies used the ISA-approach and the authors of this chapter were actively involved in them. Experiences from other case studies draw on personal communications from the respective case study leaders or on respective publications.

Learning in ISA – by stakeholders

Questionnaires administered in several of the MATISSE stakeholder workshops provided an opportunity to explore whether the stakeholder engagement methods had fostered learning amongst stakeholders.

For example, in the Hydrogen case study, when asked what they (the stakeholders) had learned from the break-out discussions, most felt they had learnt something. Responses often referred to learning about other participants" points of view, as well as technological aspects, etc. Table 14.2 reflects the stakeholder responses in the second workshop in detail (Whitmarsh, Bohunovsky *et al.* 2007a).

At the workshop on ETR in the Czech Republic, the views of the stakeholders on the sustainability vision, which was elaborated according to inputs from former workshops, and the key challenges in achieving it were gathered through questionnaires at the beginning of the workshop, before any presentations or

Table 14.2 Categorisation of answers to the open question 'What, if anything, do you feel you have learned from the break-out discussion?'

Divergent opinions (despite sharing same analysis)	2
Consensus between discussants	2
Complexity and contingency	2
Information about hydrogen	1
Problems of introducing hydrogen cars	1
Multiple solutions needed for H_2 and biofuels introduction	1
Discussion too focused on supply, not individuals' acceptance	1
Different technologies are necessary	1
Global view is necessary	1
Renewable energies will become competitive due to rising oil prices	1
Transport modes and modal split for different distances	1
Wind energy considered for H2 production	1
Various	1
Learning during whole workshop	1
Experts are relatively clueless	1
No answer	9

Source: Whitmarsh, Bohunovsky *et al.* 2007a.

discussions. For this exercise, the sustainability vision was split up into seven elements – each of which had to be ranked according to (a) how important it seems to the stakeholders and (b) how challenging the stakeholders thought it would be to achieve. At the end of the workshop the stakeholders were asked if their opinion had changed due to the presentations/discussions. Although no clear trend in the direction of changes can be seen from the results, the answers clearly show that people changed their view concerning a sustainability vision for their country, and thus learned from the presentations and discussions at the workshop. Table 14.3 shows the detailed results (Barker *et al.* 2008).

In the water case study Tàbara, Roca and Madrid (2007b) observed that the participants developed a very strong perception about the key role of the institutional dimension during stakeholder workshops on the sustainability of the Ebro Delta.

Moreover, the experiences from MATISSE show that the stakeholders learned about the process itself and made recommendations for improvements or elements that should receive more attention.

Learning in ISA – by research

There was also considerable learning within the project as a result of the stakeholder activities. The results of our stakeholder engagement work considerably influenced the work of the hydrogen case study, the ETR case study, and also provided input to the AFLU-case study and the case study about the water management of the Ebro River Delta.

Within the hydrogen case study, the assessment was broadened to encompass a range of technical and behavioural options for addressing "unsustainable mobility" (rather than restricting the assessment to hydrogen-based transport as originally intended) due to stakeholder input in the first workshop.

The same is true for the ETR-case study in the Czech Republic: Initial work and discussions within the environmental technology case study in the Czech Republic aimed at providing stakeholders with information on underlying trends and indicative impacts that technology might be able to achieve in relation to

Table 14.3 Change of opinion regarding importance/challenge of elements of the Czech sustainability vision

	More important	*Less important*	*More challenging*	*Less challenging*
1: economic growth	1	2	0	2
2: standard of living	1	3	1	2
3: workforce	2	0	1	0
4: good jobs	1	1	0	1
5: cultural heritage	1	1	0	1
6: burden shifting	1	1	2	1
7: material use	1	1	3	0

Source: Compiled by authors.

sustainable development. For the second iteration of the ISA, stakeholders suggested that a scenario exploring the effects of an ecological tax reform (ETR) would be of interest, in order to provide more focus on potential drivers of change.

Besides this very fundamental influence of stakeholders, participants of the workshops within the MATISSE offered valuable feedback on the modelling work, they pointed out risks and requirements, and identified or emphasized different sustainability criteria (e.g. Whitmarsh, Jäger *et al.* 2007b). Moreover, they highlighted areas where further work may be needed to modify the visions and assumptions underpinning the models or raised concerns about possible unsustainability of proposed scenarios and pathways (e.g. Whitmarsh, Bohunovsky 2007).

In her work Whitmarsh (2007) also highlights the different perspectives of citizens and experts: The views of the experts highlighted, for example, a need for both technological and non-technological measures to tackle rising transport demand. Citizen stakeholders supported the view of experts that transport in its current form and ongoing trends in the sector are unsustainable and that a "business-as-usual" approach should be rejected. Citizens and experts identified similar environmental, social and economic criteria for sustainable transport and located responsibility for fostering sustainable transport primarily with governments. In contrast to experts, citizens tended to place more emphasis on behavioural change policies than on transport technologies. Moreover, citizens considered amenity aspects of transport to be most important, while experts stressed the technological issues.

Learning to do ISA

In addition to reporting on learning within the case studies, it is important to report on findings about learning on how to do an ISA. MATISSE aimed at developing the ISA-process, thus ISA is in its infancy and the project is, first and foremost, a methodology development and testing project, which responds to a gap in sustainability assessment practice. ISA is intended to fill this gap and the project tested ways to implement the ISA process architecture and analytical dimensions. ISA is challenging, since it calls for capacities and features that are unconventional. Hence the most urgent task at this stage is to build awareness among scientists of these challenges and requirements.

The degree and nature of stakeholder involvement varied in the case studies (see above). For those case studies that were more open towards the participation of stakeholders and external experts, it broadened the scope of the case studies and was an enriching experience. At the same time it was a major challenge for the case studies to engage stakeholders in the process and to keep them involved. An important lesson was that a lot of time and resources and professional skills are required to manage stakeholder processes. Also it has been a major challenge to include stakeholder input in the assessments in a consistent way.

The four steps of the ISA cycle were in principle useful in structuring the complex process of doing sustainability assessments. The scoping stage was an important step for all case studies to broaden the perspective of the issue and to put the case study into context. An important lesson seems to be that although the concept of ISA seems to be simple, logical and straightforward, it is not at all easy to apply to real life complex problems with multiple levels.

Since the project was limited both in length (three years) and financial resources, it was only possible to carry out a small number of case studies and not all of those engaged with stakeholders. Certainly on the basis of the small number of case studies carried out with stakeholder involvement, it is not possible to make any robust generalizations about effective design of processes. This points, however, to a major barrier to "learning to do ISA". While it is increasingly recognized that linking knowledge to action for sustainable development requires iterative, participatory processes of the kind illustrated by ISA, funding is still geared to time- and resource-limited projects (Jäger *et al.* 2008). "Learning to do ISA" will require projects that can perform multiple iterations of an assessment process with stakeholder involvement in all stages. Project evaluation will also have to change, so that credit is given for single-loop learning. That is, learning from mistakes and correcting them in the next iteration has to be evaluated positively and those guiding the project should not be forced to hide the mistakes because they fear that subsequent funding would suffer, if an admission is made that something did not work.

Conclusions

Experience gained within in the MATISSE project show the value of stakeholder input in ISA. Short, half-day workshops or even one hour break-out groups within a broader setting can bring significant input to an ISA.

ISA is intended to be a process to explore and support reframing, reorientation (regime change) and transition. The input of stakeholders provided the basis for such reframing in several case studies (e.g. change of hydrogen focus to sustainable mobility or from environmental technologies to ETR). In both cases, the research started from a much narrower framework. Due to stakeholders" input the case studies could meet the ISA-requirement of taking a broader system view and of being potentially transformative. Moreover, these two cases have shown that being explorative (goal-searching), instead of trying to follow a given goal, opens the possibility to be innovative and to explore new ways of system-management.

Feedback from involved stakeholders also documented their learning within the project. Thus it can be argued that deliberative workshops provide valuable fora to co-construct knowledge and elicit informed views of citizens and experts. They can also empower these groups to participate in important social issues related to sustainability. This probably is especially true for citizens" workshops, as their opinion often rather represents "niches" due to lack of voice in the broader debate.

Learning also took place with regard to the organization of the participatory process, which showed that combining a deliberative workshop with questionnaires that were filled in individually helped to assess the learning processes and to get additional and more concrete feedback on particular issues.

The experiences from the MATISSE project have shown that daring to embark on the adventure of opening the process to the input of stakeholders and following together with them a goal-searching approach offers new opportunities not only for science, but – as ISA is intended to initiate policy changes – for societal development. ISA can only come up to its promises of being potentially transformative, if stakeholders are integrated in a comprehensive and open way. This is a new and challenging mode of knowledge production for science. At the same time, it is also clear that current funding mechanisms do not support the development of ISA-like processes, which need a much longer-term process of engagement, iteration and learning.

Acknowledgments

This chapter builds on several case studies and (working) papers of the MATISSE project, which was coordinated by Jan Rotmans (DRIFT, Netherlands). The project was supported by the 6th Framework Programme of the European Union (Contract number: 004059 (GOCE) – MATISSE). We are very grateful to all of the MATISSE partners, who integrated participatory elements in their ISA-case studies, most of all Lorraine Whitmarsh, Martin Wietschel, Anthony Barker and David Tàbara. We also gratefully acknowledge Willemijn Tuinstra and Paul Weaver, who extensively investigated the learning-related issues. Many thanks also to the workshop participants for their time and contributions to making the participatory work a success.

References

Argyris, C. and Schön, D. 1978. *Organizational Learning. A Theory of Action Perspective.* Reading, MA: Addison-Wesley.

Argyris, C. and Schön, D. 1995. *Organizational Learning II: Theory, Method and Practice.* Reading, MA: Addison-Wesley.

Barker, A., Bohunovsky, L., Jäger, J., Kovanda, J. and Van de Sand, I. 2008. "Using Environmental Tax Reform to Support Sustainable Development in Transition Economies: the case for the Czech Republic". *MATISSE Working Paper 19.*

Bouwen, R., Dewulf, A. and Craps, M. 2006. "Participatory Development of Technology Innovation Projects: Collaborative Learning among Different Communities of Practice". Anales de la Universidad de Cuenca, 127–42.

Brugnach, M., Dewulf, A., Pahl-Wostl, C. and Taillieu, T. 2008. "Toward a Relational Concept of Uncertainty: About Knowing too Little, Knowing too Differently, and Accepting not to Know". *Ecology and Society* 13: 30.

Farrell, A. E., Jäger, J. and VanDeveer, S. 2005. "Overview: Understanding Design Choices". In Farrell, A. and Jäger, J. (eds). *Assessments of Regional and Global Environmental Risks* Washington DC: Resources for the Future.

Funtowicz, S. and Ravetz, J. 1991. "A New Scientific Methodology for Global Environmental Issues". In Constanza, R. (ed.) *Ecological Economics: The Science and Management of Sustainability,* 137–52, New York: Columbia University Press.

Grin, J., Rotmans, J., and Schot, J. 2010. *Transitions to Sustainable Development: New Directions in the Study of Long-term Transformative Change.* Routledge, New York.

Hertin, J., Jordan, A., Nilsson, M., Nykvist, B., Russel, D. and Turnpenny, J. 2007. "The Practice of Policy Assessment in Europe: An Institutional and Political Analysis". *MATISSE Working Paper 6.*

Jäger, J. 2009. "Sustainability Science in Europe". Paper prepared for DG Research. Brussels: European Commission. Available at http://ec.europa.eu/research/sd/pdf/workshop-2009/background_paper_sust_science_workshop_october_2009.pdf#view=fitandpagemode=none.

Jäger, J. 2011. "Risks and Opportunities for Sustainability Science in Europe". In Jäger, C. C., Tabara, J. D. and Jäger, J. (eds). *European Research on Sustainable Development. Volume 1. Transformative Science Approaches for Sustainability* Berlin Heidelberg: Springer-Verlag.

Jäger, J., Bohunovsky, L. and Binder, J. 2008. *Methods and Tools for Integrated Sustainability Assessment.* Project Summary Vienna: Sustainable Europe Research Institute.

Pahl-Wostl, C., Mostert, E. and Tàbara, D. 2008. "The Growing Importance of Social Learning in Water Resources Management and Sustainability Science". *Ecology and Society* 13: 24.

Pahl-Wostl, C., Sendzimir, J. and Jeffrey, P. 2009. "Resources Management in Transition". *Ecology and Society* 14.

Siebenhüner, B. 2004. "Social Learning and Sustainability Science: Which Role can Stakeholder Participation Play?" *International Journal of Sustainable Development* 7: 146–63.

Tàbara, J. D. and Pahl-Wostl, C. 2007. "Sustainability Learning in Natural Resource Use and Management". *Ecology and Society* 12: 3.

Tàbara, J. D., Elmqvist, B., Ilhan, A., Madrid, C., Olson, L., Schilperoord, M., Valkering, P., Wallman, P. and Weaver, P. 2007a. "Participatory Modelling for the Integrated Sustainability Assessment of Water: the World Cellular Model and the MATISSE Project". *MATISSE Working Paper 9.*

Tàbara, J. D., Roca, E. and Madrid, C. 2007b. "Developing New Methods and Tools for the Integrated Sustainability Assessment of Water". The MATISSE project and the Ebro River Basin. *MATISSE Working Paper 8.*

Tuinstra, W., Jäger, J. and Weaver, P. M. 2008. "Learning and Evaluation in Integrated Sustainability Assessment". *International Journal of Innovation and Sustainable Development* 3: 128–52.

Van De Kerkhof, M. 2006. "Making a Difference: On the Constraints of Consensus Building and the Relevance of Deliberation in Stakeholder Dialogues". *Policy Sciences*, 39: 279–99.

Van De Kerkhof, M. F., Tuinstra, W., Spanjersberg, M., Hisschemöller, M. and Mol, A. P. J. 2002. "Conclusions and Lessons for Participatory Integrated Assessment". In Hirschemöller, M. and Mol, A. P. J. (eds) *Evaluating the COOL Dialogues. Climate Options for the Long Term. Final Report* 93–102. Bilthoven: Programme Office NRP.

Weaver, P. M. and Rotmans, J. 2006. "Integrated Sustainability Assessment: What Is It, Why Do It, and How?" *International Journal of Innovation and Sustainable Development* 1: 284–303.

Weaver, P. M., Haxeltine, A., Van De Kerkhof, M. and Tabara, J. 2006. "Mainstreaming Action on Climate Change through Participatory Appraisal". *International Journal of Innovation and Sustainable Development* 1: 238–59.

Whitmarsh, L. 2007. "Citizens" Workshops on Sustainable Futures: Report on Findings". *MATISSE Working Paper 14.*

Whitmarsh, L., Bohunovsky, L., Jäger, J. and Nykvist, B. 2007a. "Stakeholder Feedback on MATISSE Sustainable Hydrogen Visions and Pathways: Findings from the June 2007 Hydrogen Stakeholder Workshop". *MATISSE Working Paper 18.*

Whitmarsh, L., Jäger, J., Nykvist, B., Schade, W., Seydel, P., Strasser, S., Weaver, P. M. and Wietschel, M. 2007b. "Stakeholder Feedback on MATISSE Sustainable Hydrogen Scope and Visions: Findings from the February 2006 Hydrogen Stakeholder Workshop". *MATISSE Working Paper 17.*

Index

For Product Safety Concerns and Information please contact our EU
representative GPSR@taylorandfrancis.com
Taylor & Francis Verlag GmbH, Kaufingerstraße 24, 80331 München, Germany

www.ingramcontent.com/pod-product-compliance
Lightning Source LLC
Chambersburg PA
CBHW070717280326
41926CB00087B/2398